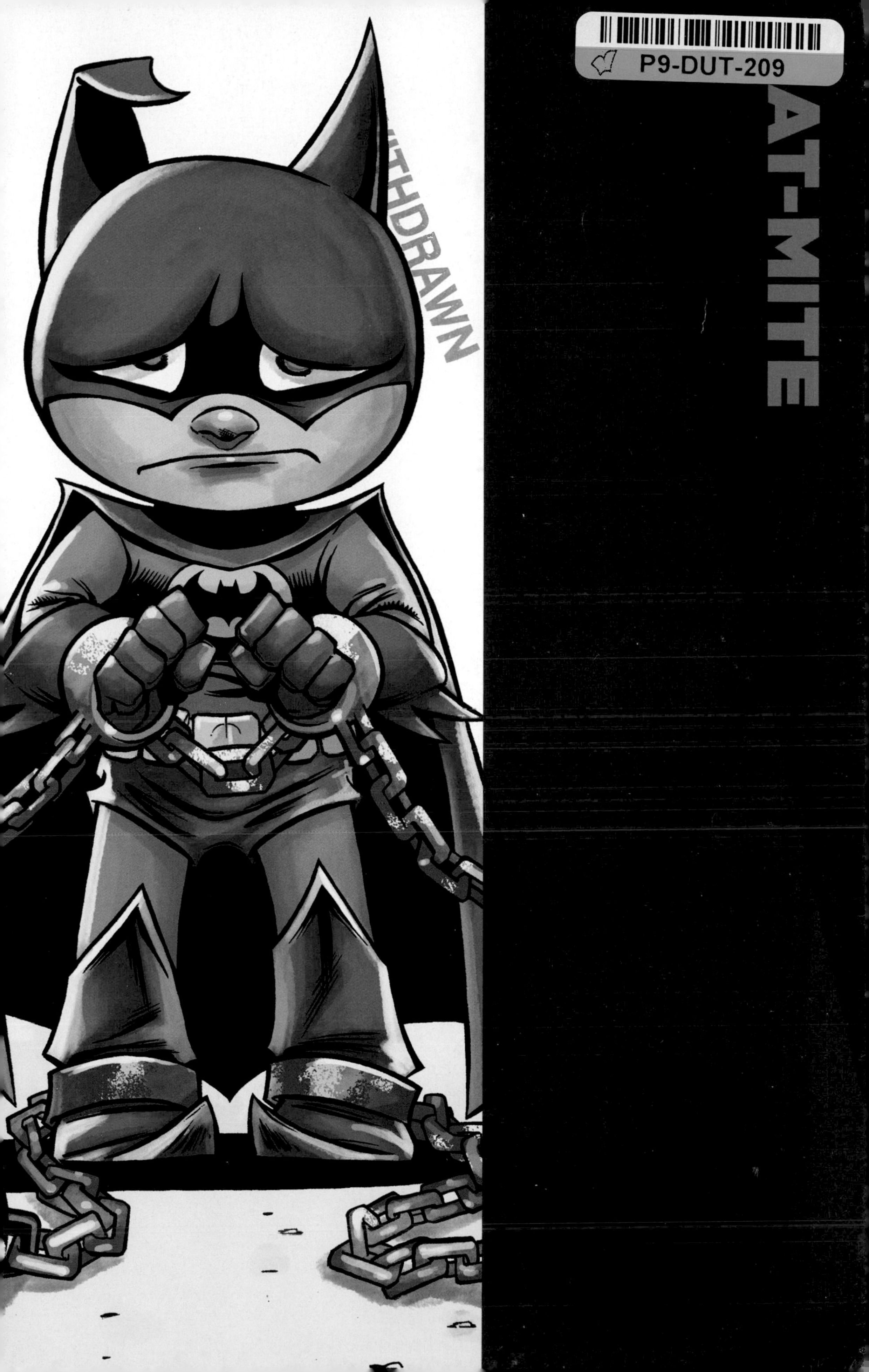

AT-MITE

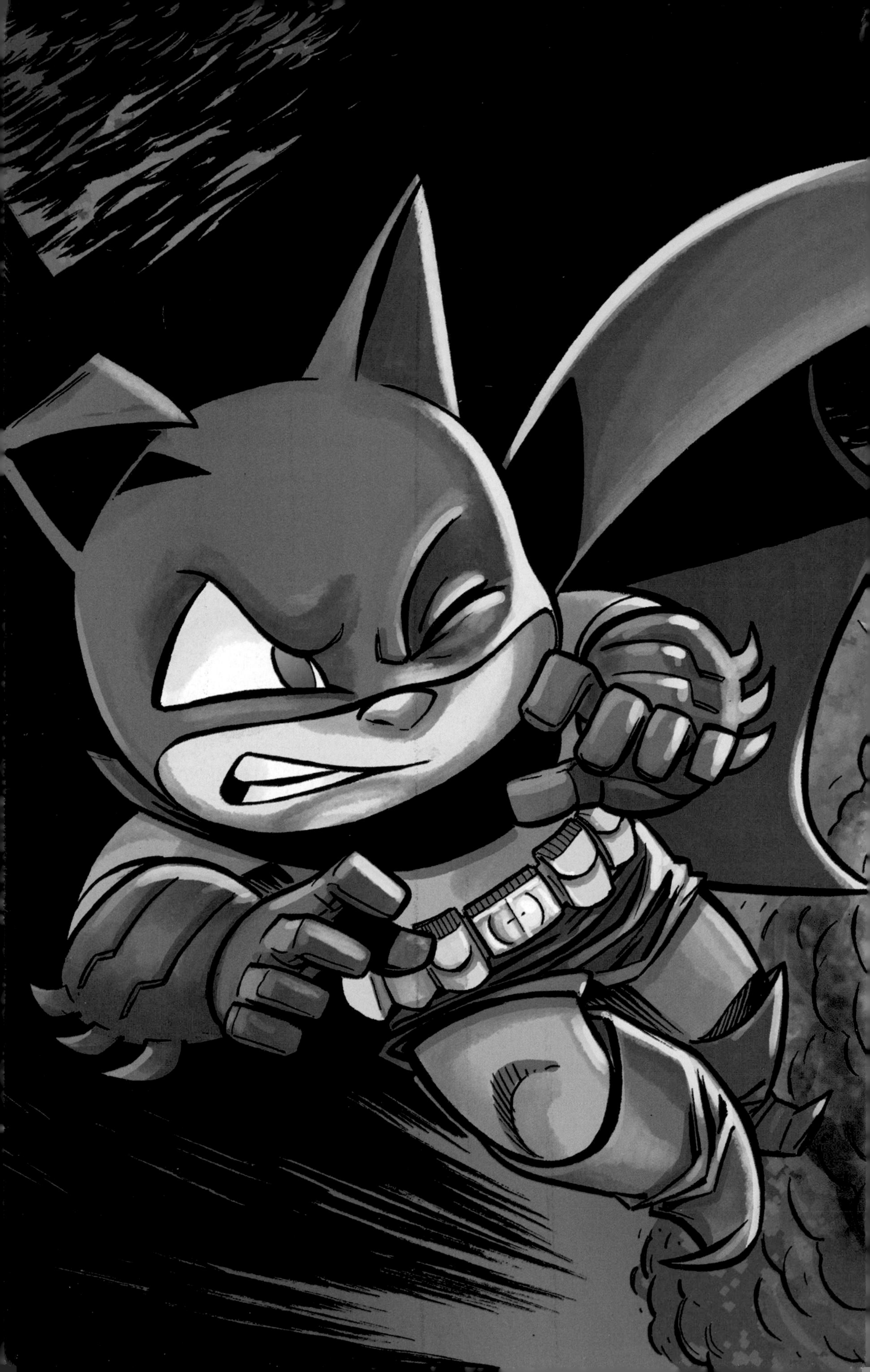

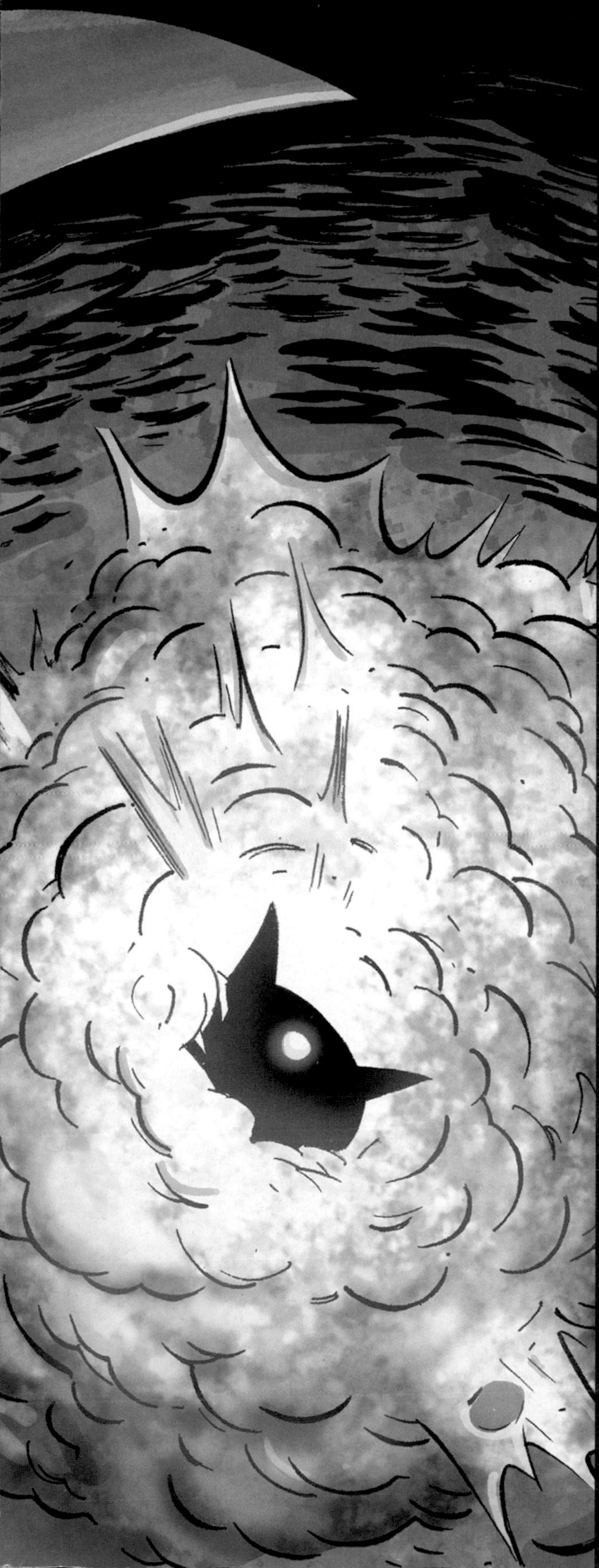

BAT-MITE

WRITTEN BY
DAN JURGENS

ART BY
CORIN HOWELL
ANDRES PONCE

COLOR BY
MIKE ATIYEH

LETTERS BY
TOM NAPOLITANO

COLLECTION COVER ART BY
CORIN HOWELL
WITH MIKE ATIYEH

BOOSTER GOLD CREATED BY
DAN JURGENS

SUPERMAN CREATED BY
JERRY SIEGEL &
JOE SHUSTER
BY SPECIAL ARRANGEMENT
WITH THE JERRY SIEGEL FAMILY

JIM CHADWICK JOEY CAVALIERI Editors – Original Series
DAVID PIÑA Assistant Editor – Original Series
JEB WOODARD Group Editor – Collected Editions
LIZ ERICKSON Editor – Collected Editions
STEVE COOK Design Director – Books
DAMIAN RYLAND Publication Design

BOB HARRAS Senior VP – Editor-In-Chief, DC Comics

DIANE NELSON President
DAN DIDIO and JIM LEE Co-Publishers
GEOFF JOHNS Chief Creative Officer
AMIT DESAI Senior VP – Marketing & Global Franchise Management
NAIRI GARDINER Senior VP – Finance
SAM ADES VP – Digital Marketing
BOBBIE CHASE VP – Talent Development
MARK CHIARELLO Senior VP – Art, Design & Collected Editions
JOHN CUNNINGHAM VP – Content Strategy
ANNE DEPIES VP – Strategy Planning & Reporting
DON FALLETTI VP – Manufacturing Operations
LAWRENCE GANEM VP – Editorial Administration & Talent Relations
ALISON GILL Senior VP – Manufacturing & Operations
HANK KANALZ Senior VP – Editorial Strategy & Administration
JAY KOGAN VP – Legal Affairs
DEREK MADDALENA Senior VP – Sales & Business Development
JACK MAHAN VP – Business Affairs
DAN MIRON VP – Sales Planning & Trade Development
NICK NAPOLITANO VP – Manufacturing Administration
CAROL ROEDER VP – Marketing
EDDIE SCANNELL VP – Mass Account & Digital Sales
COURTNEY SIMMONS Senior VP – Publicity & Communications
JIM (SKI) SOKOLOWSKI VP – Comic Book Specialty & Newsstand Sales
SANDY YI Senior VP – Global Franchise Management

BAT-MITE

DC Comics, 2900 West Alameda Ave., Burbank, CA 91505
Printed by RR Donnelley, Salem, VA, USA. 1/15/16. First Printing.
ISBN: 978-1-4012-6100-9

Library of Congress Cataloging-in-Publication Data is Available.

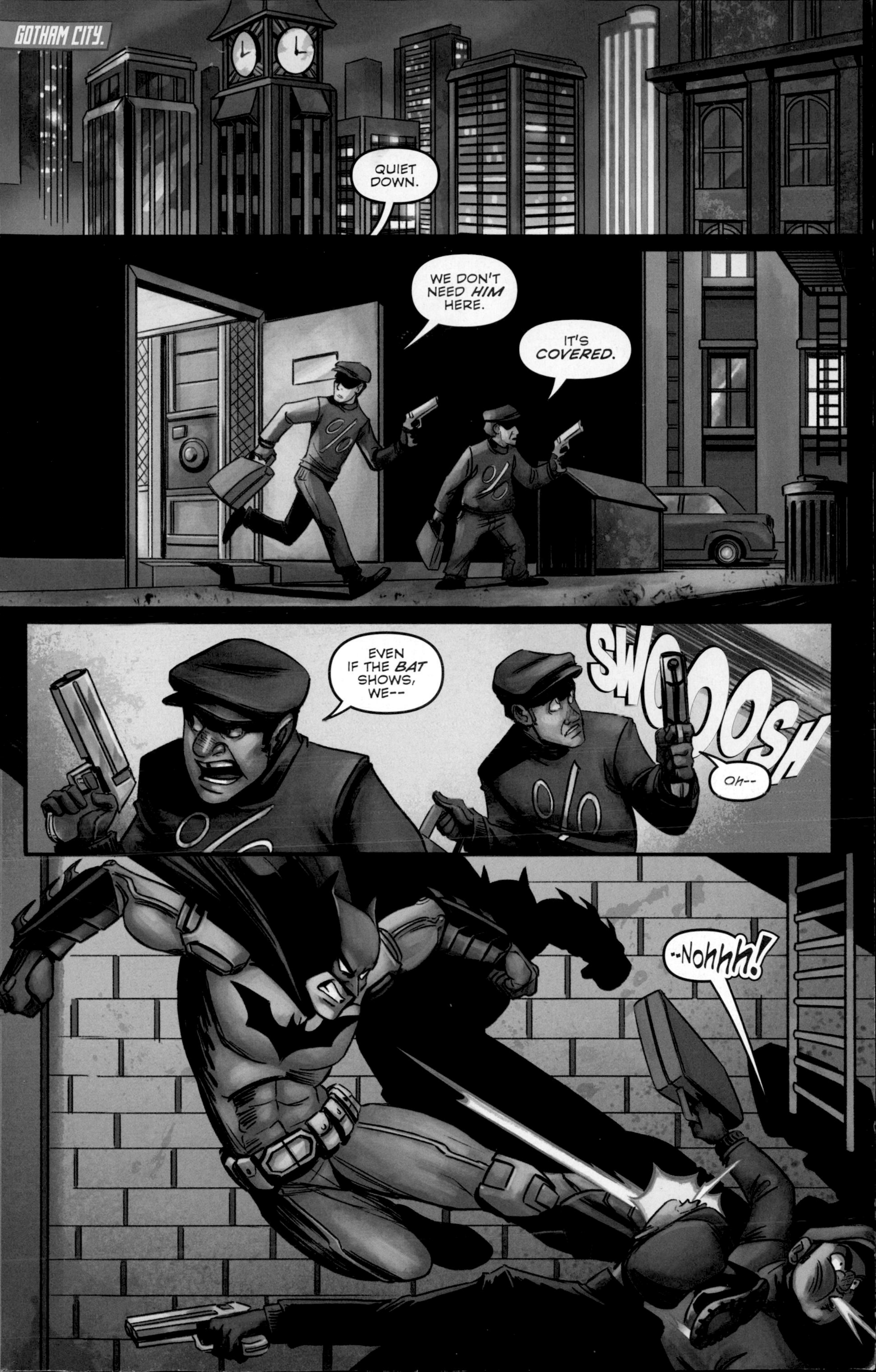
GOTHAM CITY.
QUIET DOWN.
WE DON'T NEED *HIM* HERE.
IT'S *COVERED.*
EVEN IF THE *BAT* SHOWS, WE--
SWOOOSH
Oh--
--Nohhh!

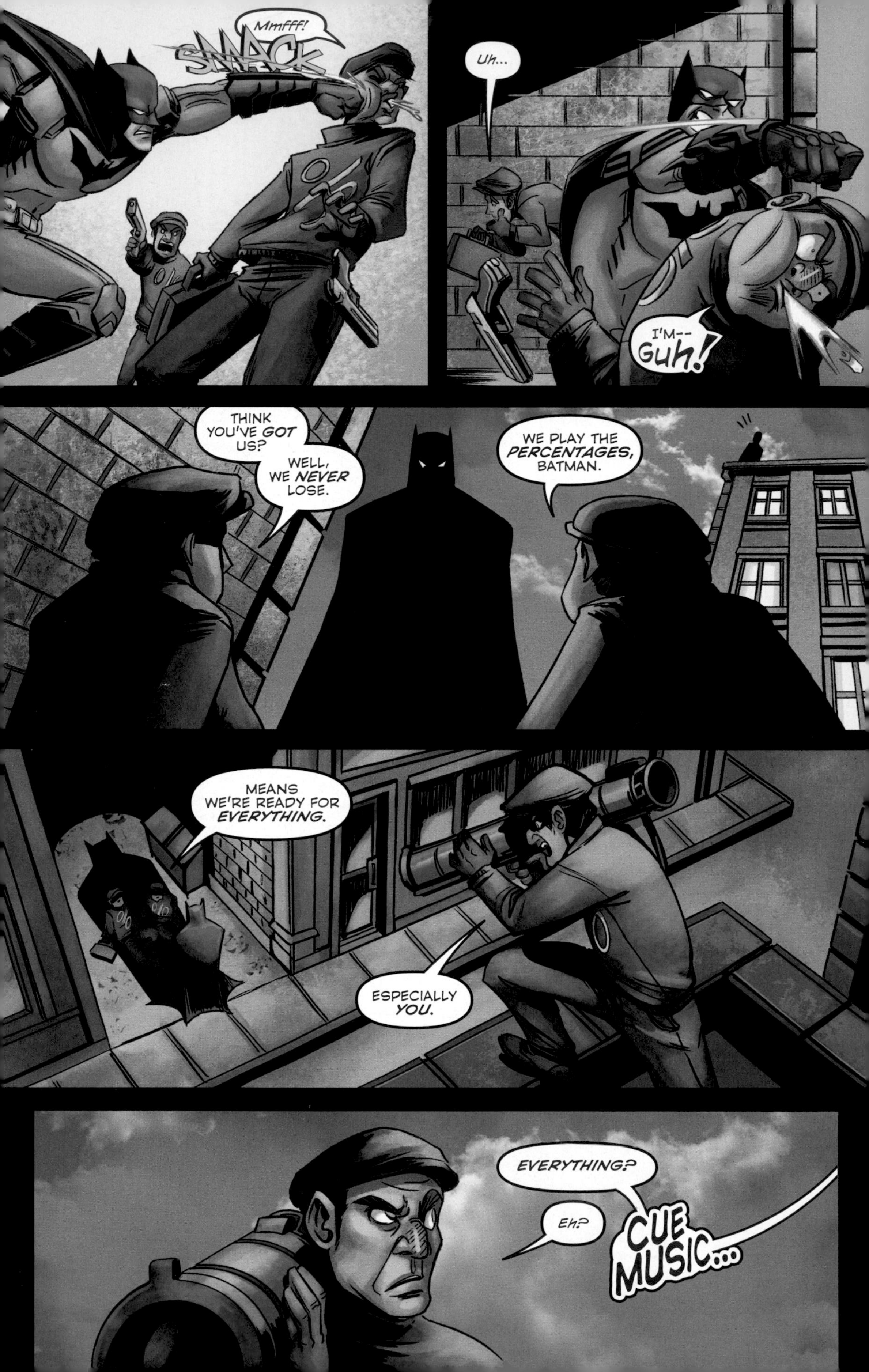

Mmfff!
SMACK
Uh...
I'M--
Guh!
THINK YOU'VE *GOT* US?
WELL, WE *NEVER* LOSE.
WE PLAY THE *PERCENTAGES*, BATMAN.
MEANS WE'RE READY FOR *EVERYTHING*.
ESPECIALLY *YOU*.
EVERYTHING?
Eh?
CUE MUSIC...

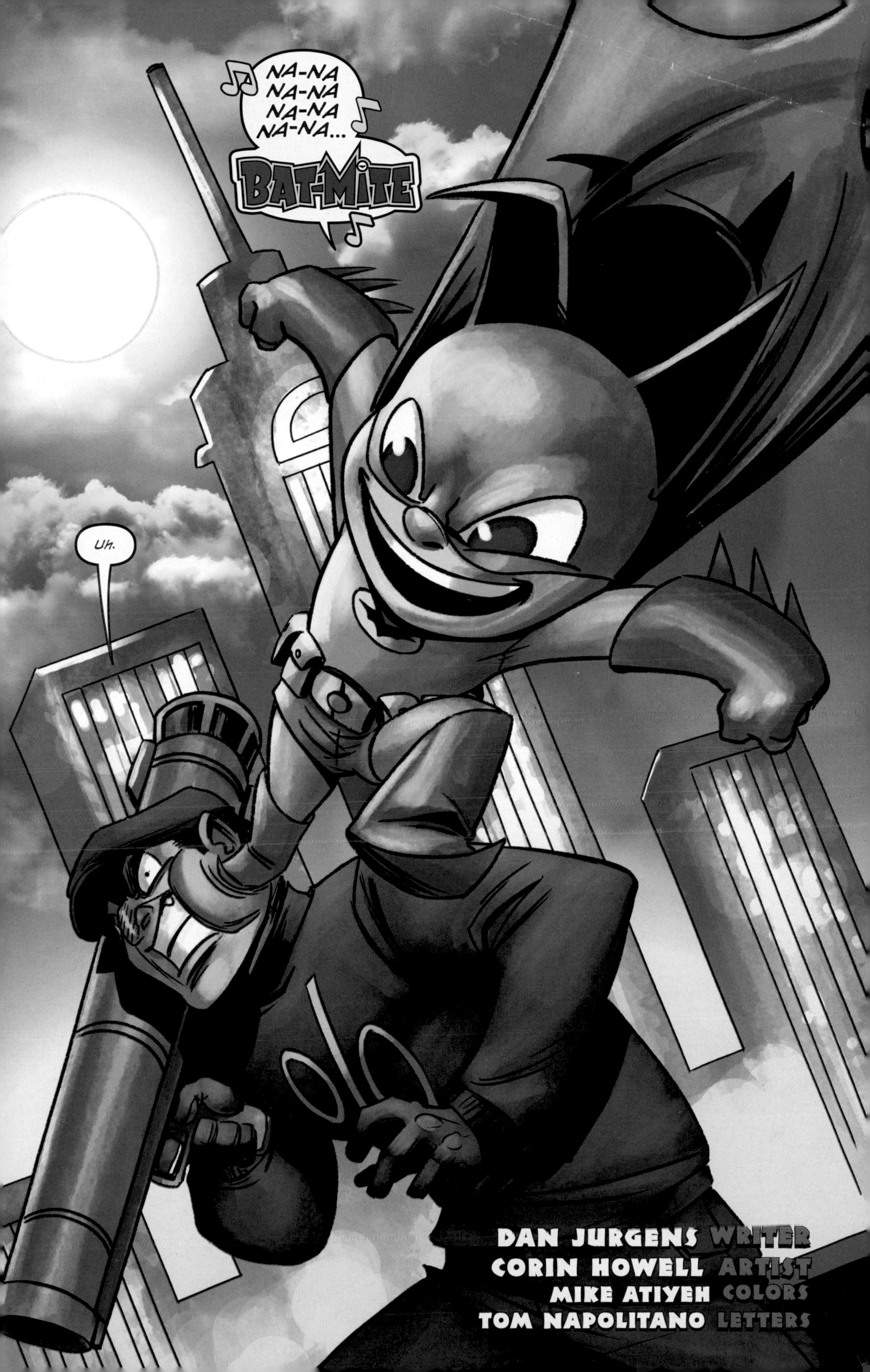
NA-NA NA-NA NA-NA NA-NA...
BAT-MITE
Uh.
DAN JURGENS WRITER
CORIN HOWELL ARTIST
MIKE ATIYEH COLORS
TOM NAPOLITANO LETTERS

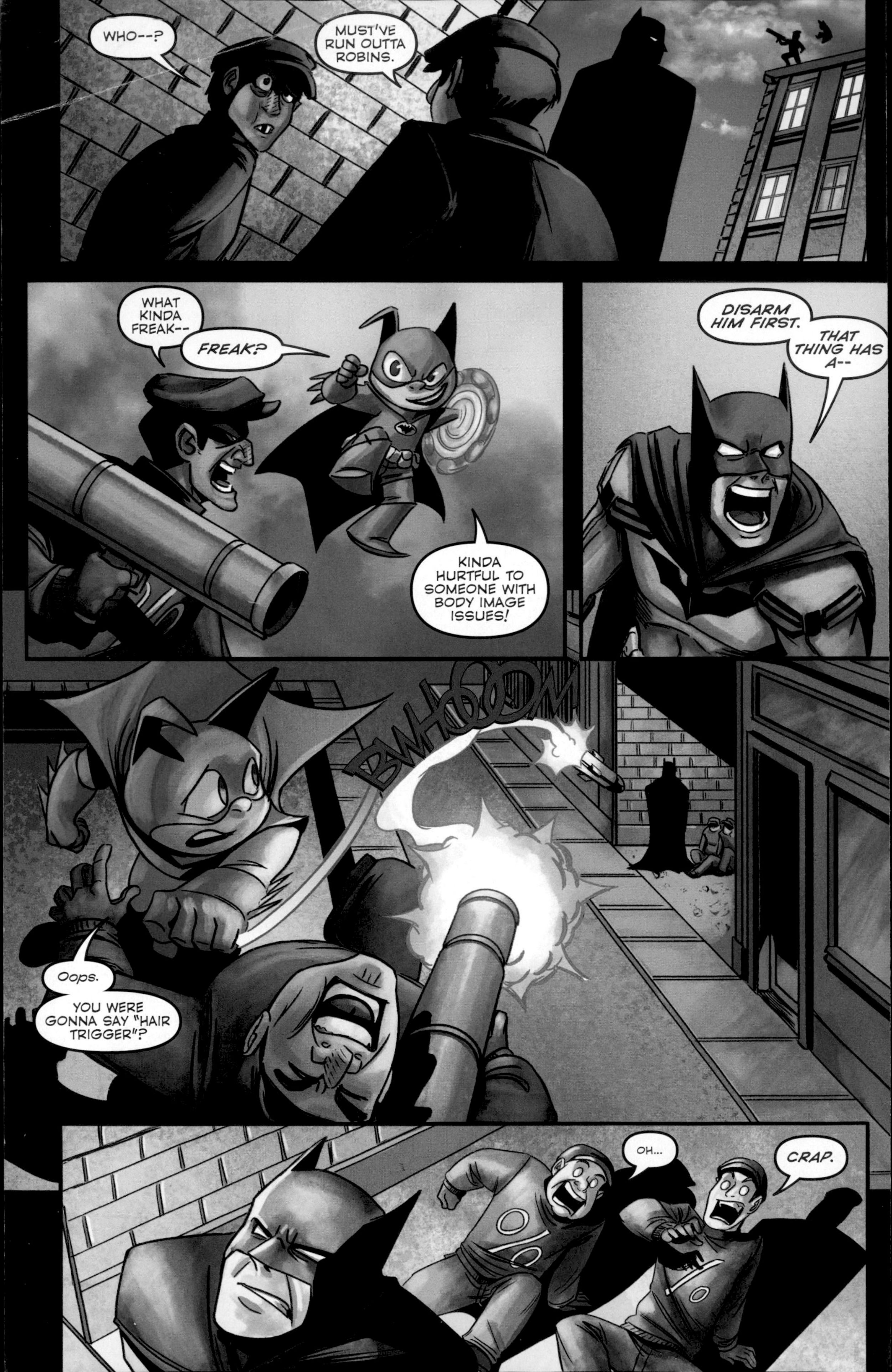
WHO--?
MUST'VE RUN OUTTA ROBINS.
WHAT KINDA FREAK--
FREAK?
KINDA HURTFUL TO SOMEONE WITH BODY IMAGE ISSUES!
DISARM HIM FIRST.
THAT THING HAS A--
BWHOOOOM
Oops.
YOU WERE GONNA SAY "HAIR TRIGGER"?
OH...
CRAP.

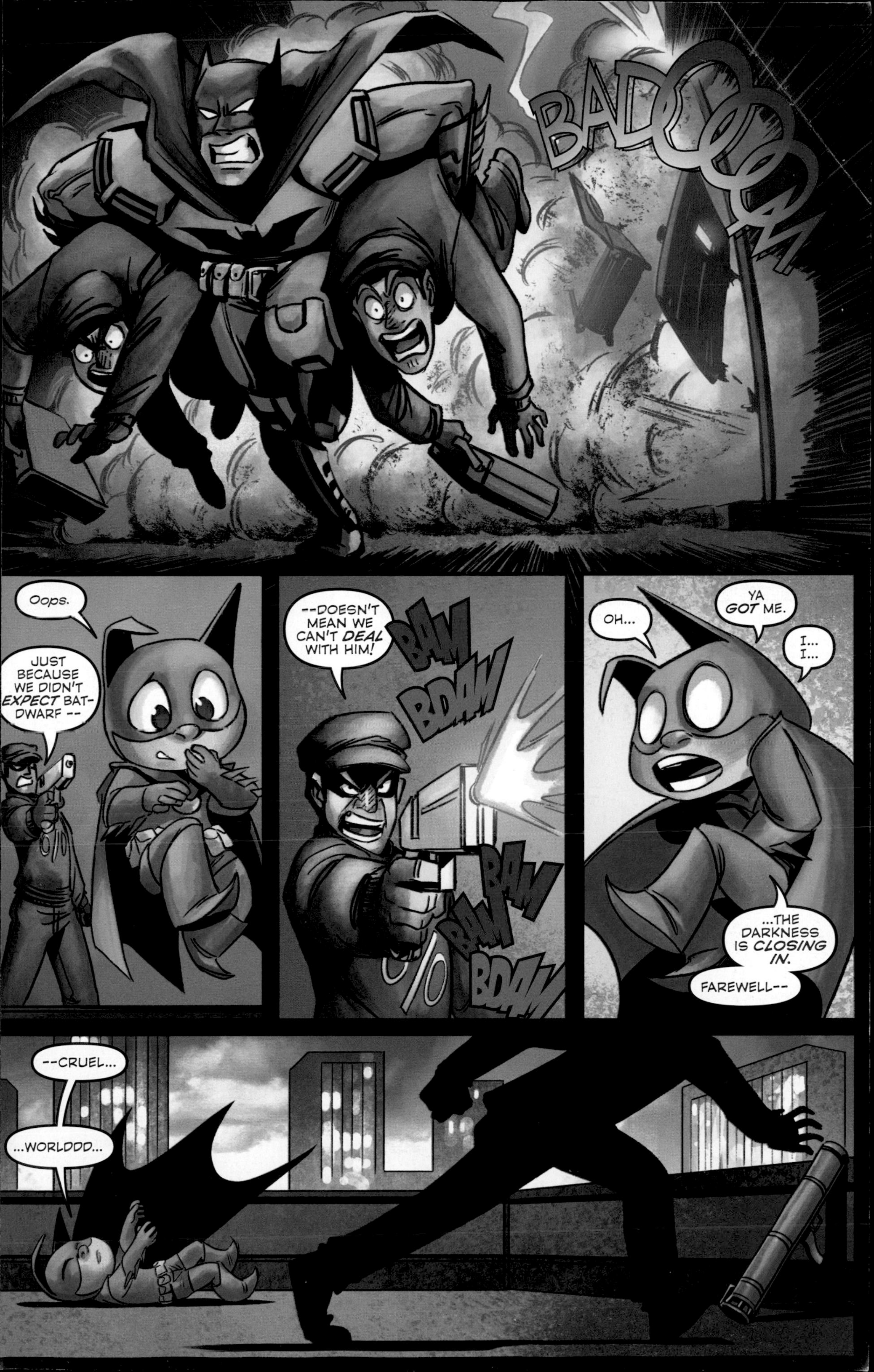
BADOOOOM
Oops.
JUST BECAUSE WE DIDN'T EXPECT BAT-DWARF --
--DOESN'T MEAN WE CAN'T DEAL WITH HIM!
BAM
BDAM
BAM
BAM
BDAM
OH...
YA GOT ME.
I... I...
...THE DARKNESS IS CLOSING IN.
FAREWELL--
--CRUEL...
...WORLDDD...

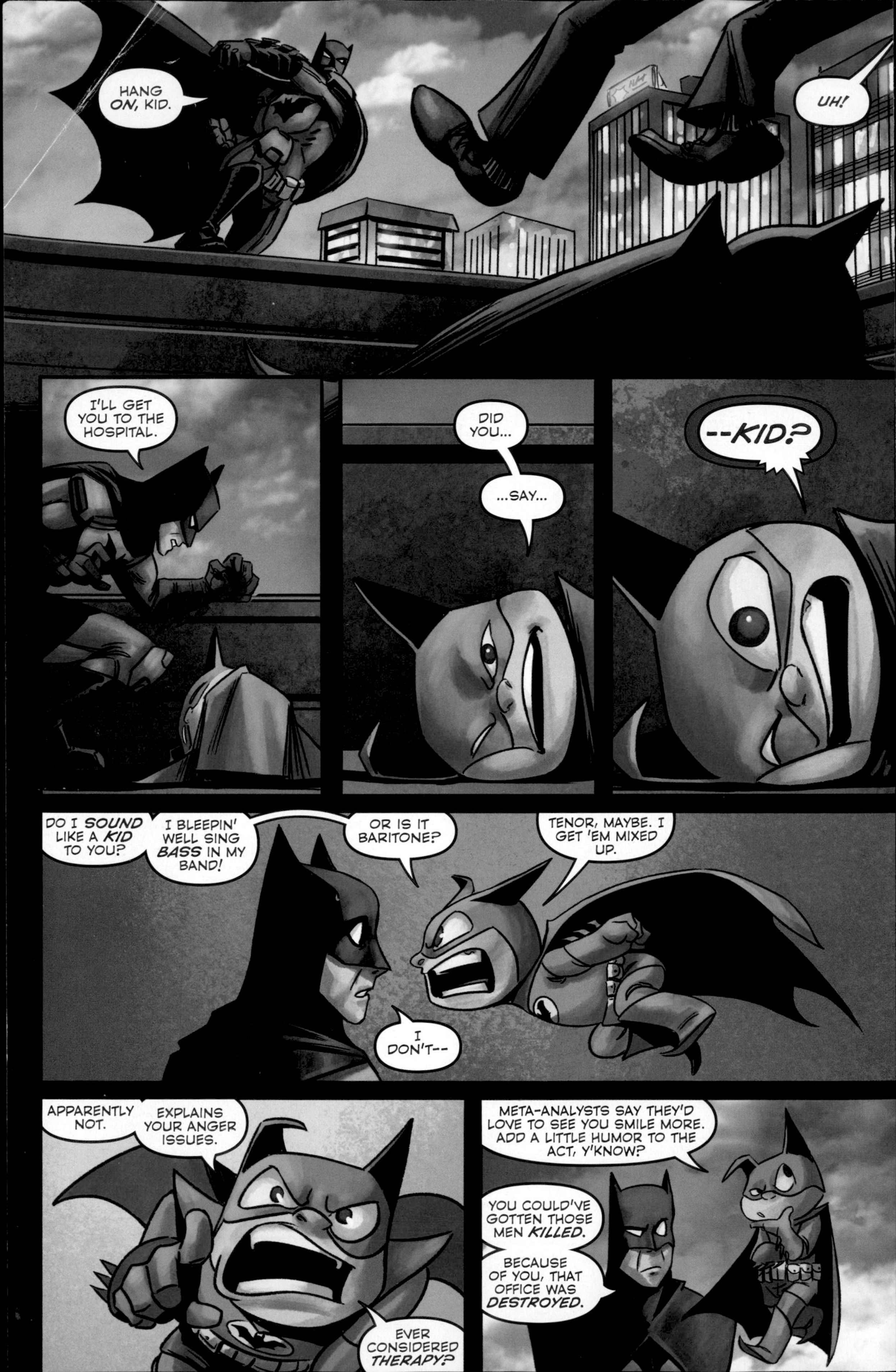
HANG ON, KID.
UH!
I'LL GET YOU TO THE HOSPITAL.
DID YOU...
...SAY...
--KID?
DO I SOUND LIKE A KID TO YOU?
I BLEEPIN' WELL SING BASS IN MY BAND!
OR IS IT BARITONE?
TENOR, MAYBE. I GET 'EM MIXED UP.
I DON'T--
APPARENTLY NOT.
EXPLAINS YOUR ANGER ISSUES.
EVER CONSIDERED THERAPY?
META-ANALYSTS SAY THEY'D LOVE TO SEE YOU SMILE MORE. ADD A LITTLE HUMOR TO THE ACT, Y'KNOW?
YOU COULD'VE GOTTEN THOSE MEN KILLED.
BECAUSE OF YOU, THAT OFFICE WAS DESTROYED.

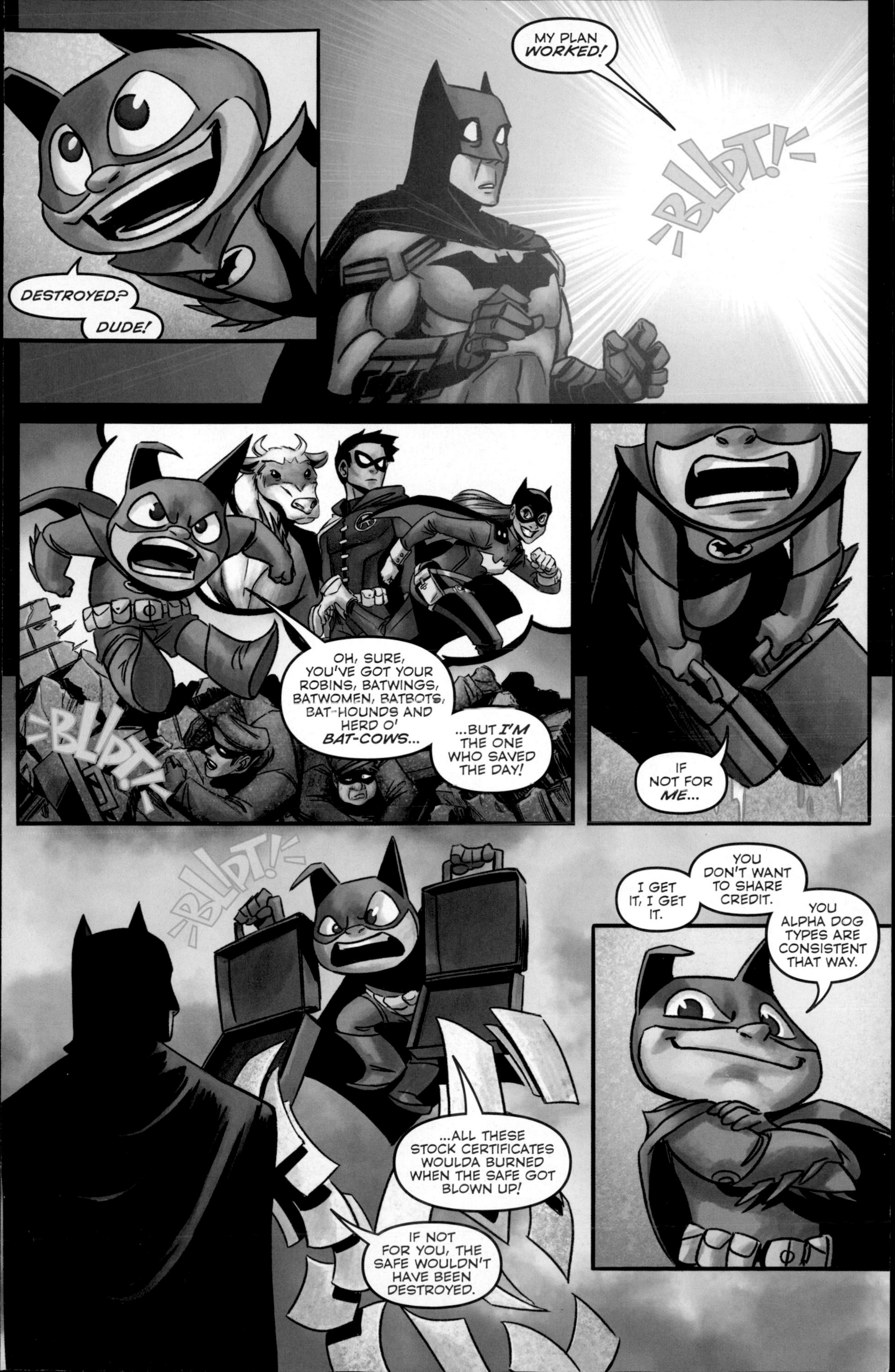
DESTROYED?
DUDE!
MY PLAN WORKED!
BLIPT!
OH, SURE, YOU'VE GOT YOUR ROBINS, BATWINGS, BATWOMEN, BATBOTS, BAT-HOUNDS AND HERD O' BAT-COWS...
...BUT I'M THE ONE WHO SAVED THE DAY!
BLIPT!
IF NOT FOR ME...
BLIPT!
...ALL THESE STOCK CERTIFICATES WOULDA BURNED WHEN THE SAFE GOT BLOWN UP!
IF NOT FOR YOU, THE SAFE WOULDN'T HAVE BEEN DESTROYED.
I GET IT, I GET IT.
YOU DON'T WANT TO SHARE CREDIT.
YOU ALPHA DOG TYPES ARE CONSISTENT THAT WAY.

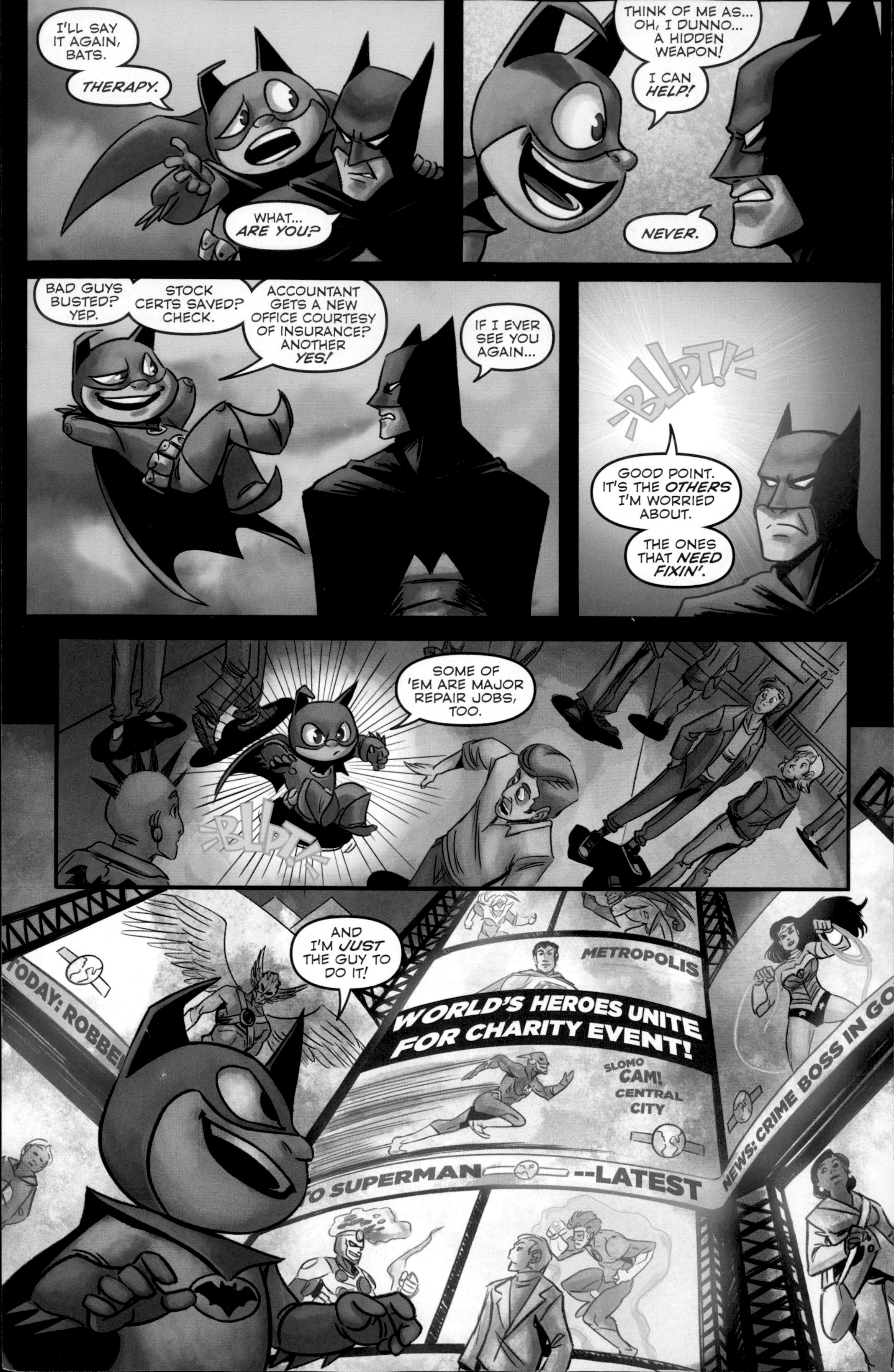
I'LL SAY IT AGAIN, BATS.
THERAPY.
WHAT... ARE YOU?
THINK OF ME AS... OH, I DUNNO... A HIDDEN WEAPON!
I CAN HELP!
NEVER.
BAD GUYS BUSTED? YEP.
STOCK CERTS SAVED? CHECK.
ACCOUNTANT GETS A NEW OFFICE COURTESY OF INSURANCE? ANOTHER YES!
IF I EVER SEE YOU AGAIN...
BLIPT!
GOOD POINT. IT'S THE OTHERS I'M WORRIED ABOUT.
THE ONES THAT NEED FIXIN'.
SOME OF 'EM ARE MAJOR REPAIR JOBS, TOO.
BLIPT!
AND I'M JUST THE GUY TO DO IT!
TODAY: ROBBE
METROPOLIS
WORLD'S HEROES UNITE FOR CHARITY EVENT!
SLOMO CAM! CENTRAL CITY
TO SUPERMAN --LATEST
NEWS: CRIME BOSS IN GO

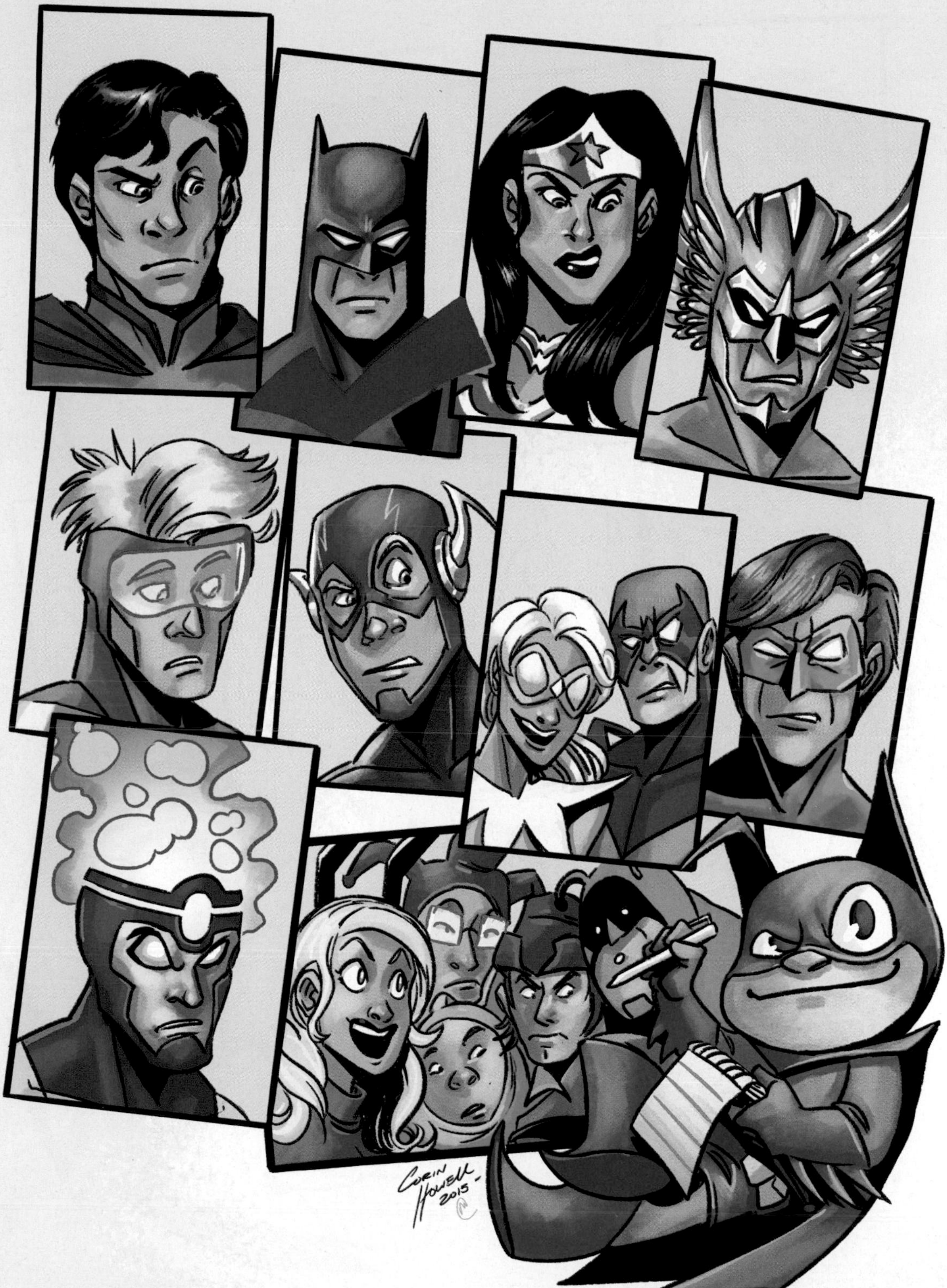
CORIN HOWELL 2015

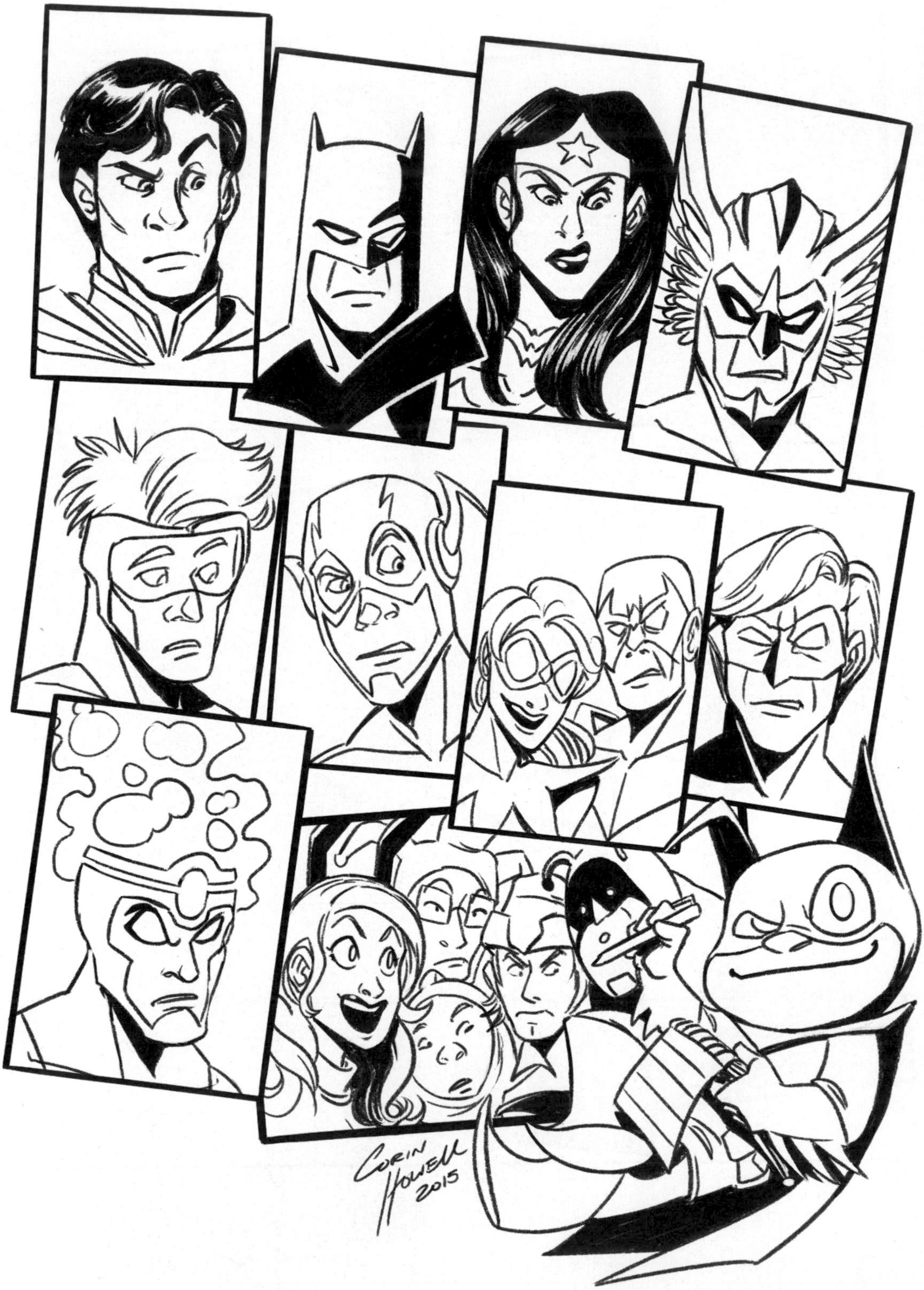
CORIN HOWELL 2015

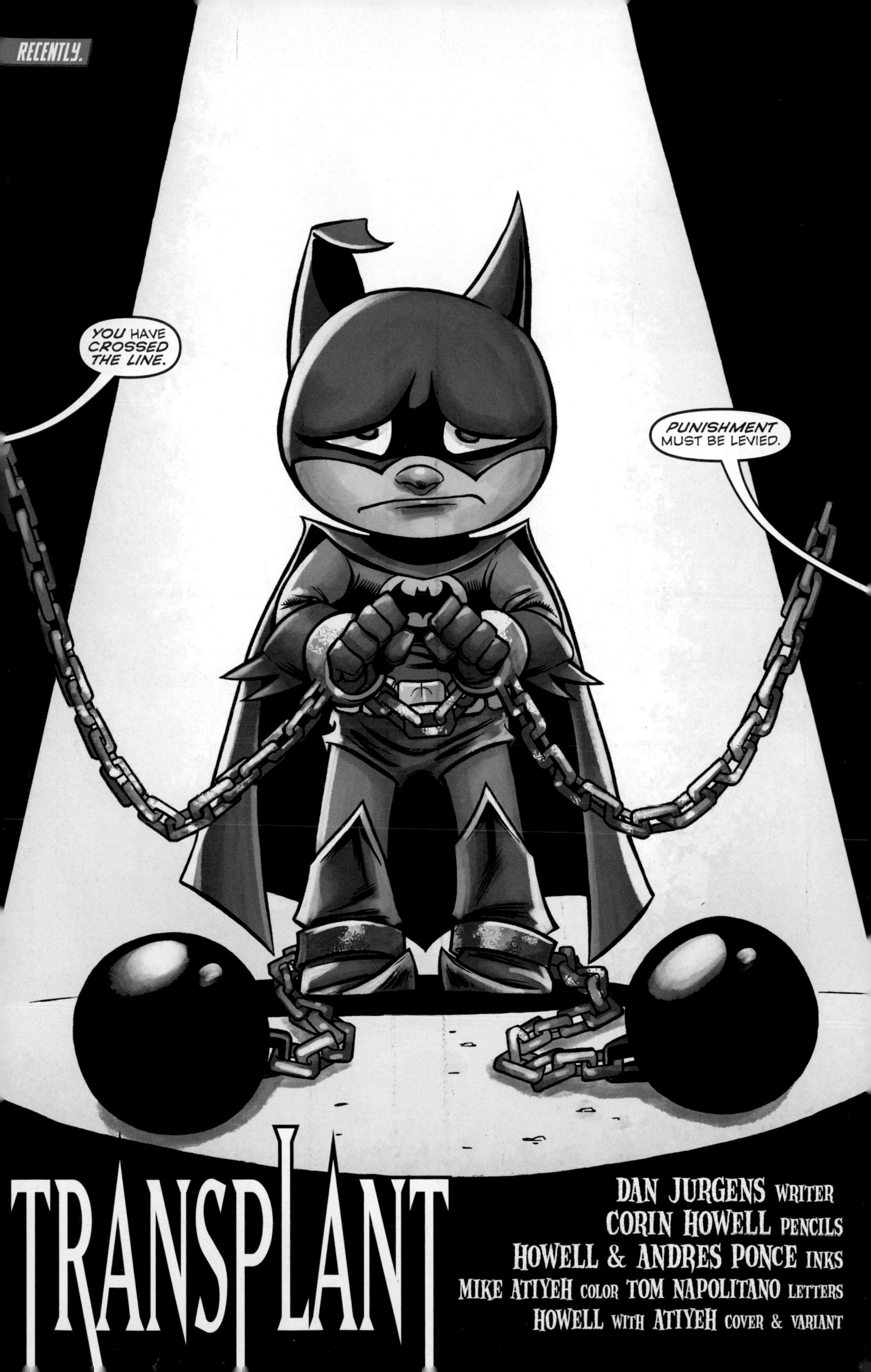
RECENTLY.
YOU HAVE CROSSED THE LINE.
PUNISHMENT MUST BE LEVIED.
TRANSPLANT
DAN JURGENS WRITER
CORIN HOWELL PENCILS
HOWELL & ANDRES PONCE INKS
MIKE ATIYEH COLOR TOM NAPOLITANO LETTERS
HOWELL WITH ATIYEH COVER & VARIANT

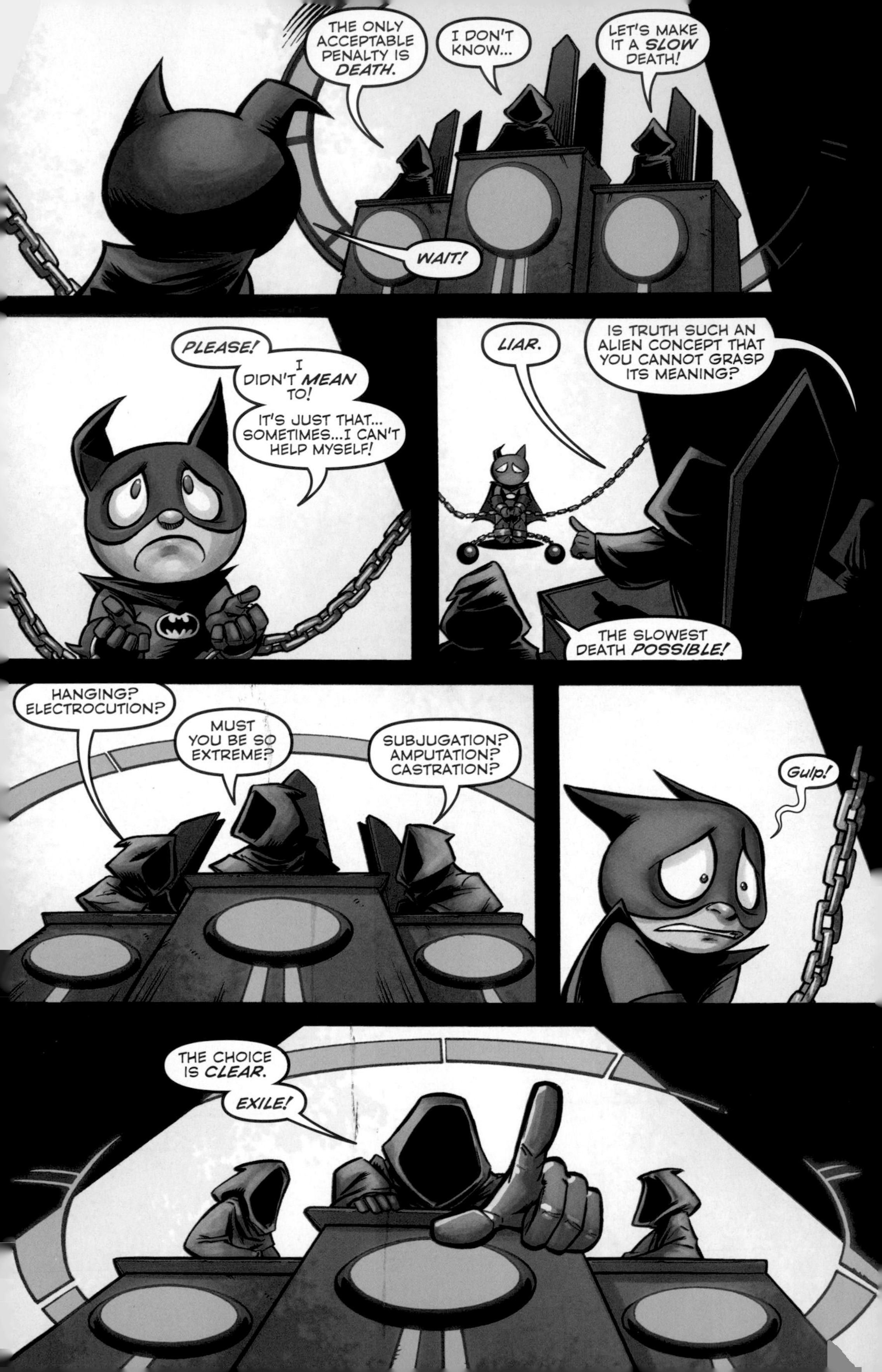
THE ONLY ACCEPTABLE PENALTY IS DEATH.
I DON'T KNOW...
LET'S MAKE IT A SLOW DEATH!
WAIT!
PLEASE!
I DIDN'T MEAN TO!
IT'S JUST THAT... SOMETIMES...I CAN'T HELP MYSELF!
LIAR.
IS TRUTH SUCH AN ALIEN CONCEPT THAT YOU CANNOT GRASP ITS MEANING?
THE SLOWEST DEATH POSSIBLE!
HANGING? ELECTROCUTION?
MUST YOU BE SO EXTREME?
SUBJUGATION? AMPUTATION? CASTRATION?
Gulp!
THE CHOICE IS CLEAR.
EXILE!

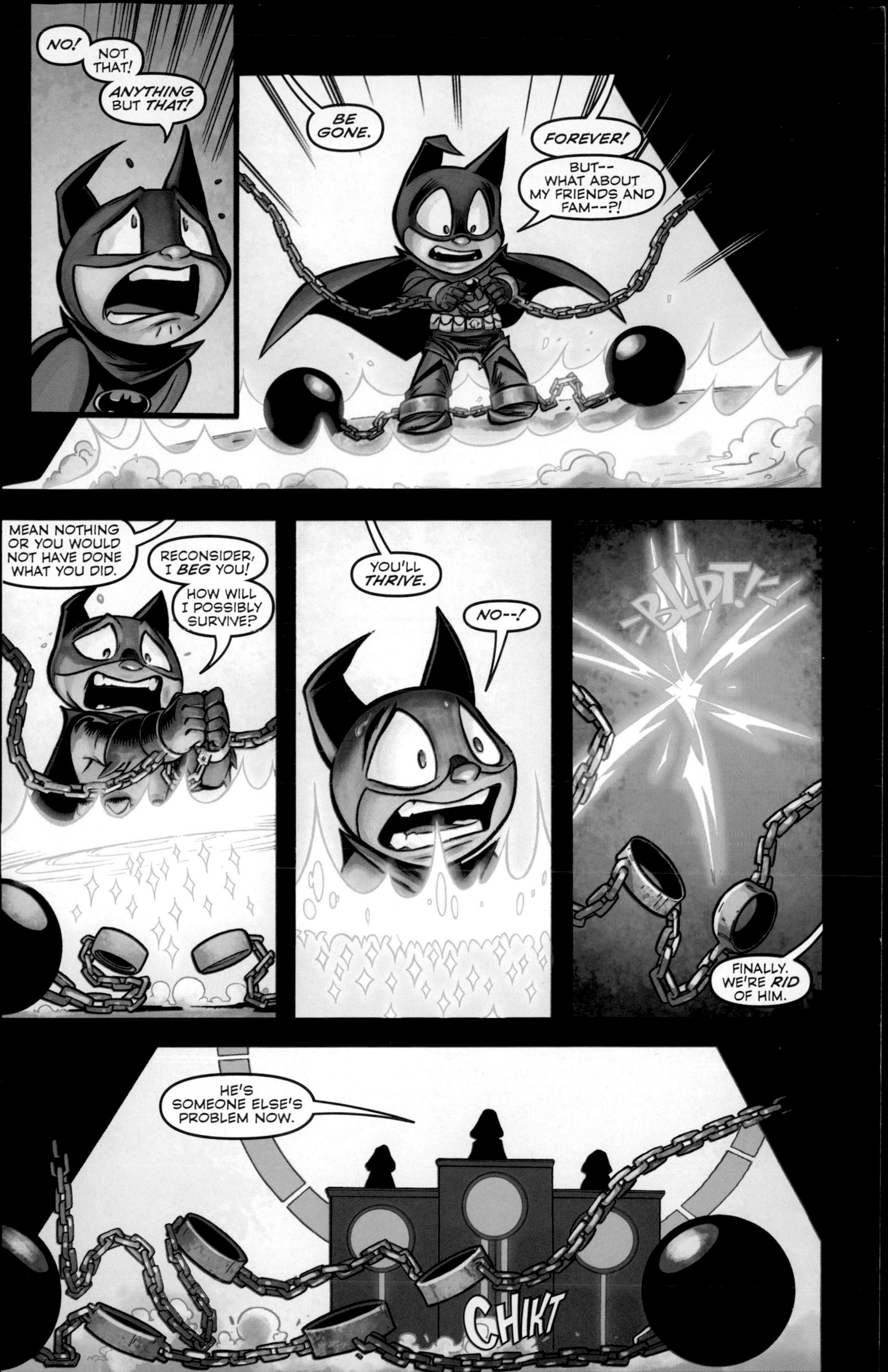
NO!
NOT THAT!
ANYTHING BUT THAT!
BE GONE.
FOREVER!
BUT-- WHAT ABOUT MY FRIENDS AND FAM--?!
MEAN NOTHING OR YOU WOULD NOT HAVE DONE WHAT YOU DID.
RECONSIDER, I BEG YOU!
HOW WILL I POSSIBLY SURVIVE?
YOU'LL THRIVE.
NO--!
BLIPT!
FINALLY. WE'RE RID OF HIM.
HE'S SOMEONE ELSE'S PROBLEM NOW.
CHIKT

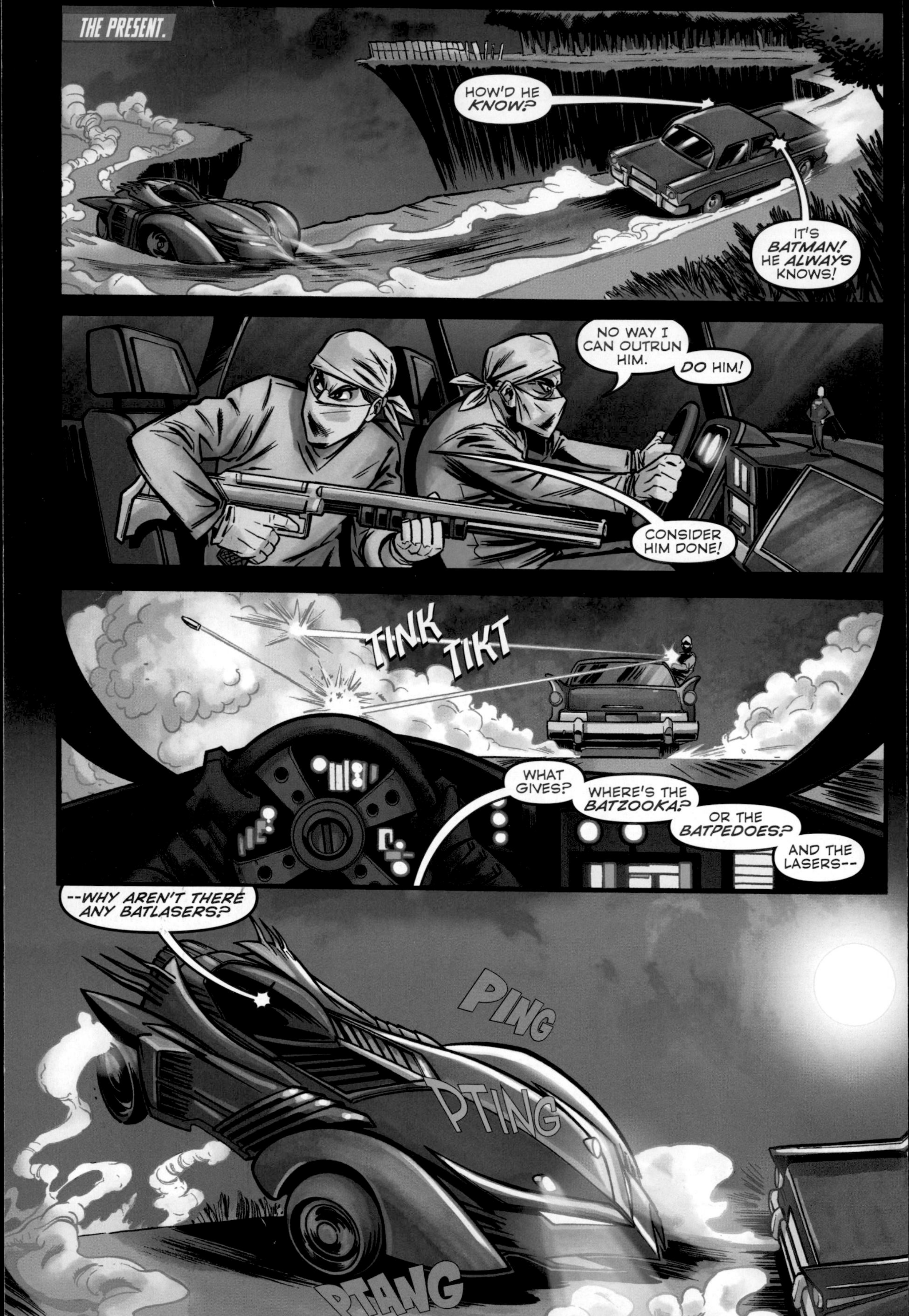
THE PRESENT.
HOW'D HE KNOW?
IT'S BATMAN! HE ALWAYS KNOWS!
NO WAY I CAN OUTRUN HIM.
DO HIM!
CONSIDER HIM DONE!
TINK
TIKT
WHAT GIVES?
WHERE'S THE BATZOOKA?
OR THE BATPEDOES?
AND THE LASERS--
--WHY AREN'T THERE ANY BATLASERS?
PING
PTING
PTANG

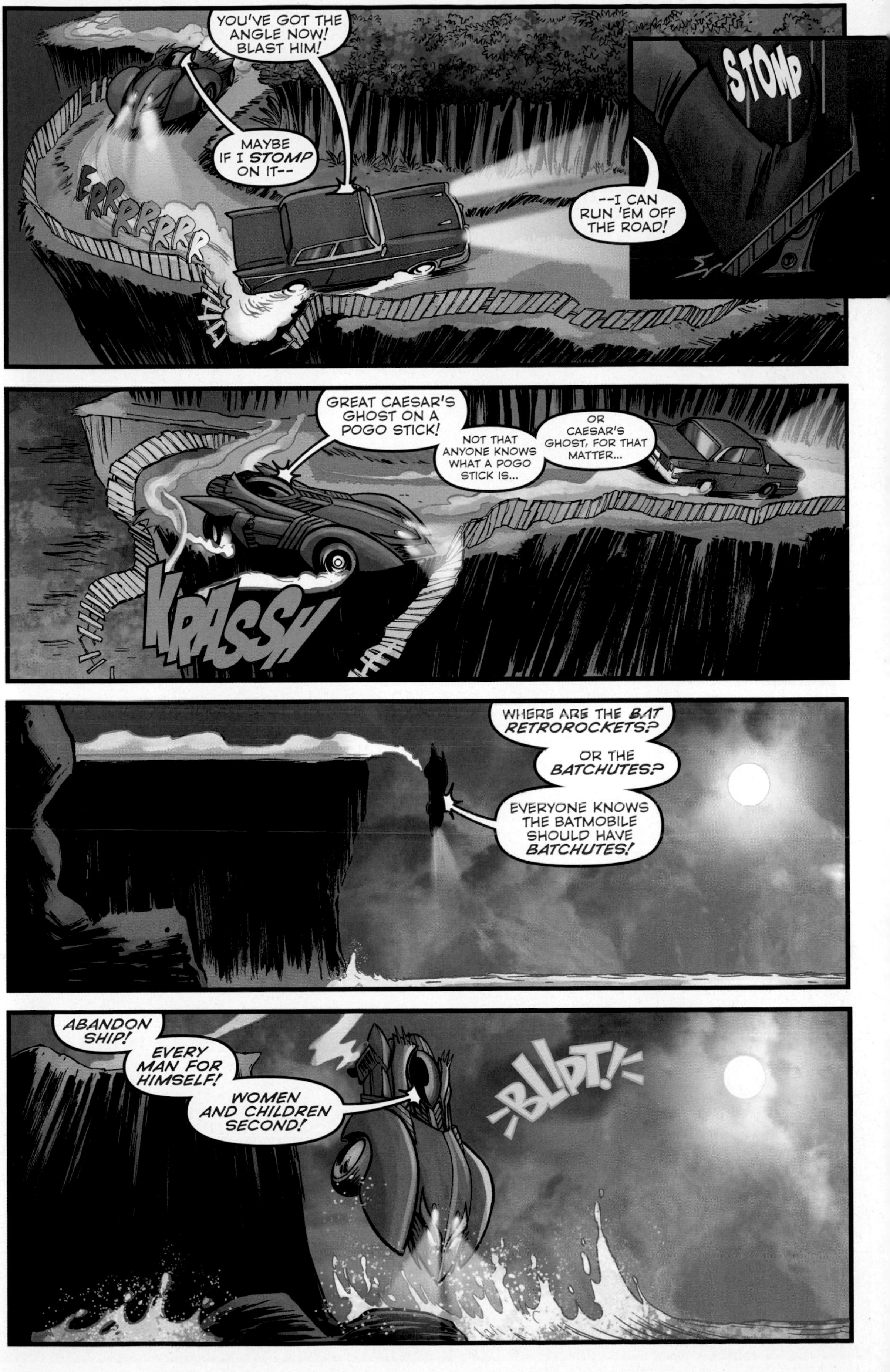
YOU'VE GOT THE ANGLE NOW! BLAST HIM!
MAYBE IF I STOMP ON IT--
ERRRRRRRR
--I CAN RUN 'EM OFF THE ROAD!
STOMP
GREAT CAESAR'S GHOST ON A POGO STICK!
NOT THAT ANYONE KNOWS WHAT A POGO STICK IS...
OR CAESAR'S GHOST, FOR THAT MATTER...
KRASSH
WHERE ARE THE BAT RETROROCKETS?
OR THE BATCHUTES?
EVERYONE KNOWS THE BATMOBILE SHOULD HAVE BATCHUTES!
ABANDON SHIP!
EVERY MAN FOR HIMSELF!
WOMEN AND CHILDREN SECOND!
BLIPT!

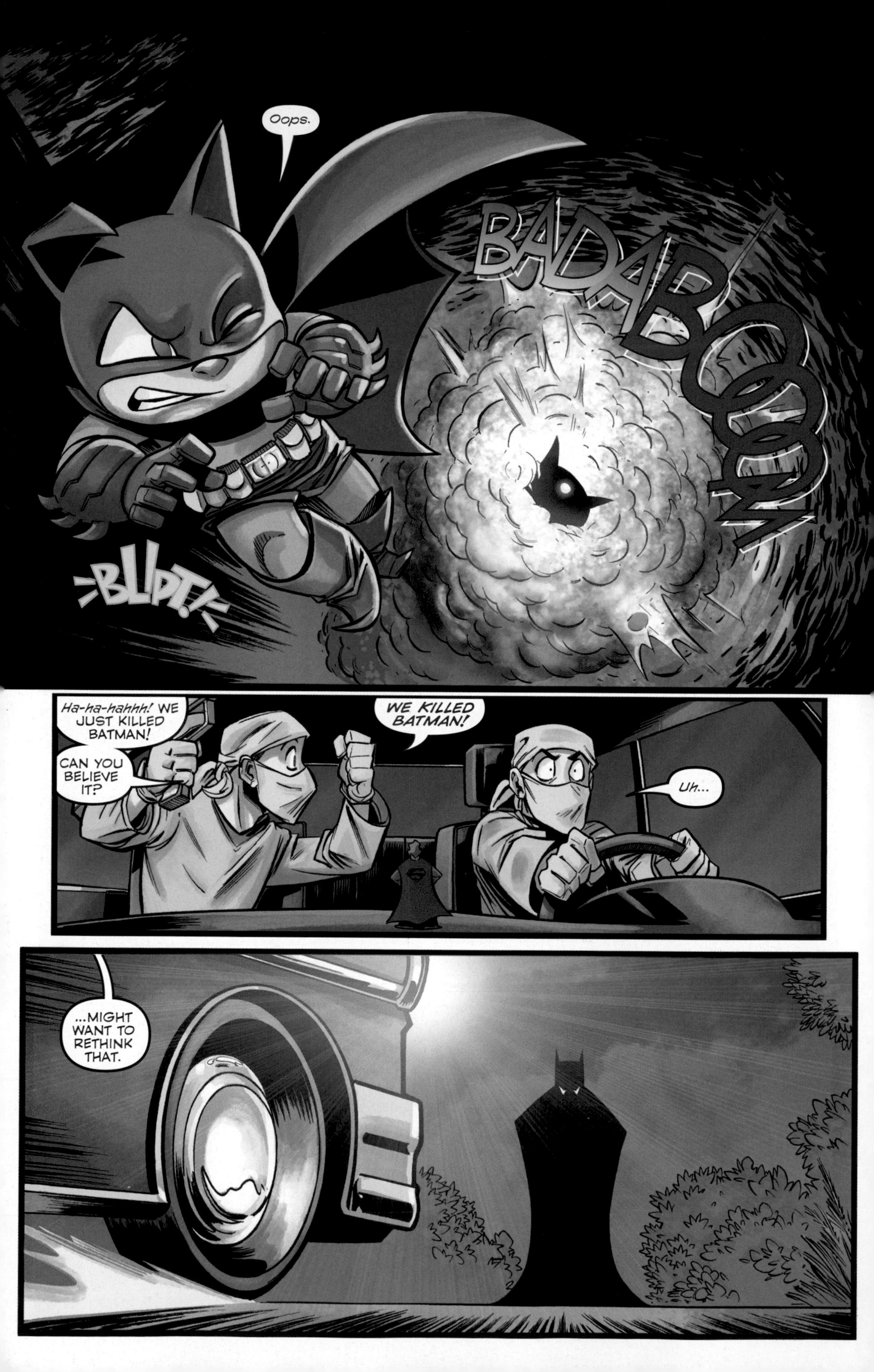
Oops.
BADABOOOM
BLIPT!
Ha-ha-hahhh! WE JUST KILLED BATMAN!
CAN YOU BELIEVE IT?
WE KILLED BATMAN!
Uh...
...MIGHT WANT TO RETHINK THAT.

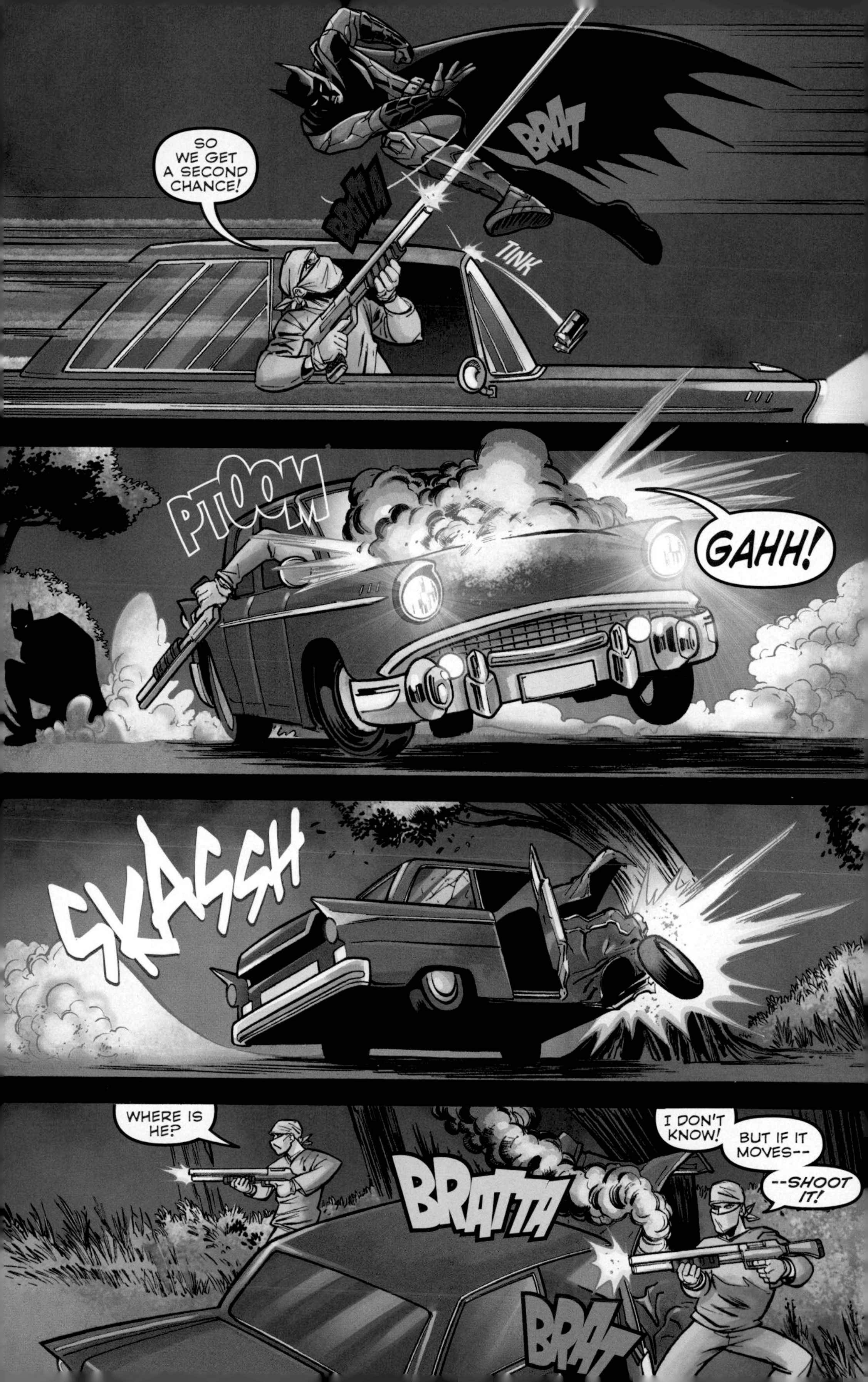
SO WE GET A SECOND CHANCE!
BRAT
BRATTA
TINK
PTOOM
GAHH!
SKASSH
WHERE IS HE?
I DON'T KNOW!
BUT IF IT MOVES--
--SHOOT IT!
BRATTA
BRAT

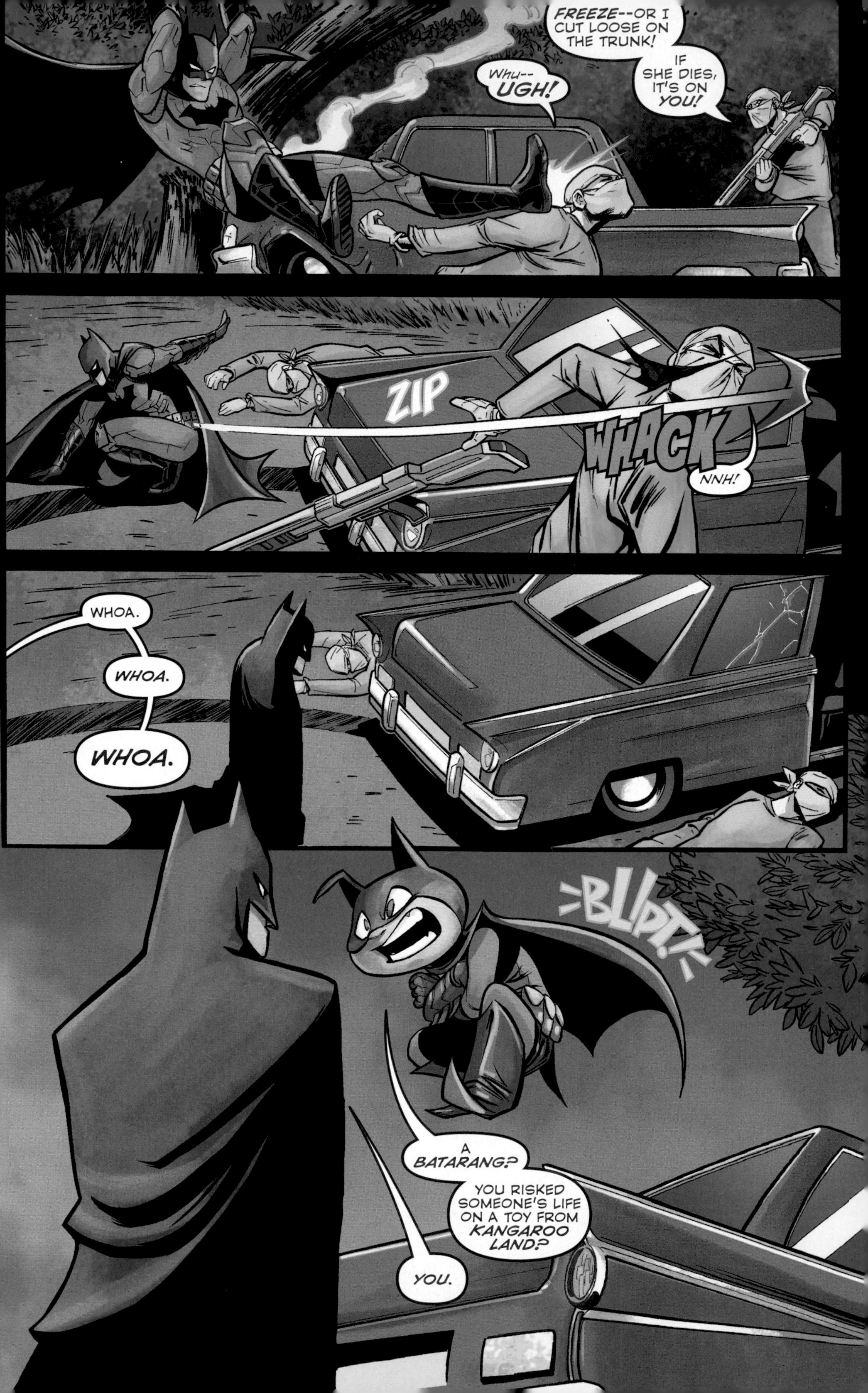
FREEZE--OR I CUT LOOSE ON THE TRUNK!
Whu-- UGH!
IF SHE DIES, IT'S ON YOU!
ZIP
WHACK
NNH!
WHOA.
WHOA.
WHOA.
BLIPT!
A BATARANG?
YOU RISKED SOMEONE'S LIFE ON A TOY FROM KANGAROO LAND?
YOU.

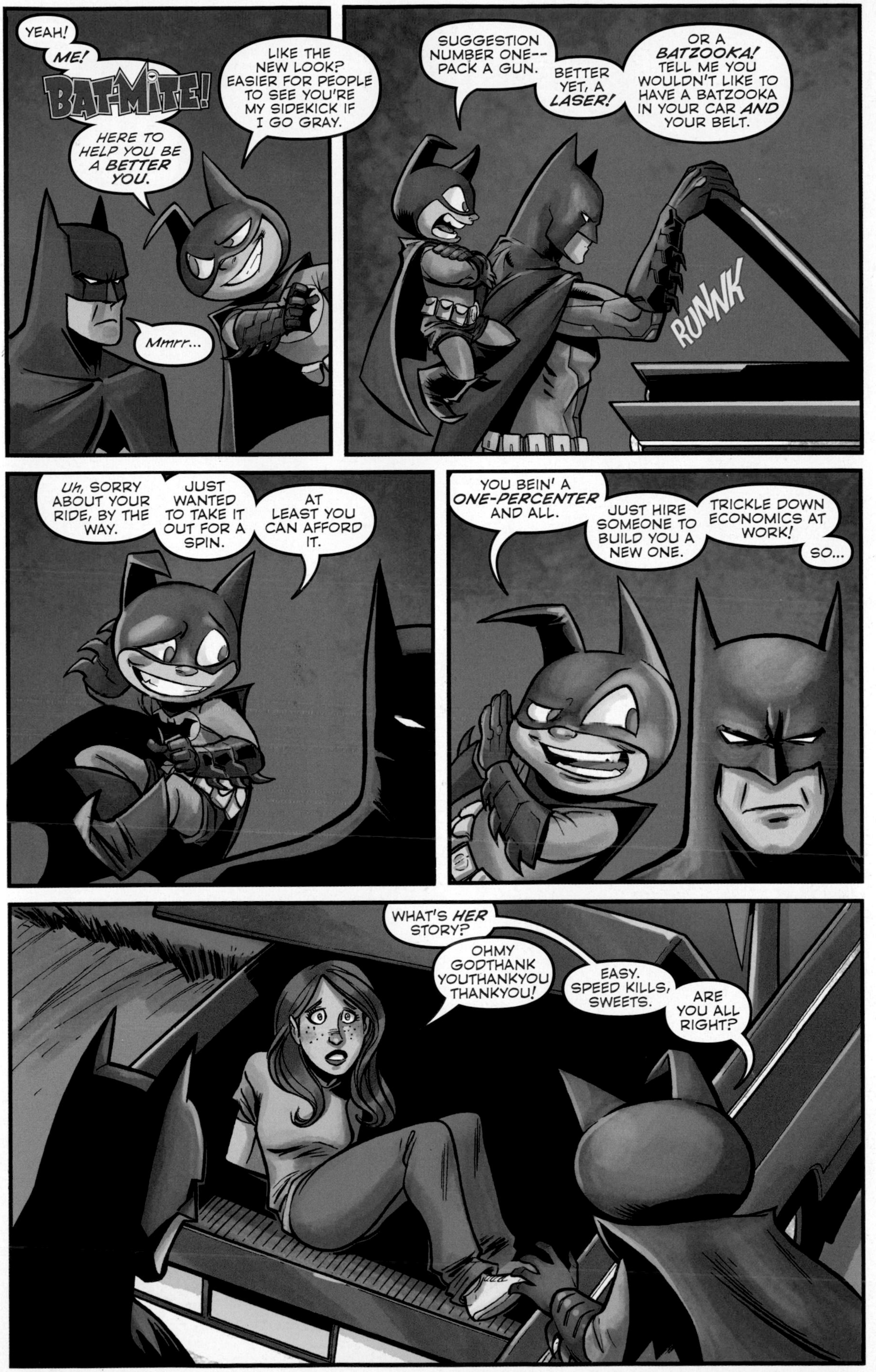
YEAH!
ME!
BAT-MITE!
HERE TO HELP YOU BE A BETTER YOU.
LIKE THE NEW LOOK? EASIER FOR PEOPLE TO SEE YOU'RE MY SIDEKICK IF I GO GRAY.
Mmrr...
SUGGESTION NUMBER ONE-- PACK A GUN.
BETTER YET, A LASER!
OR A BATZOOKA! TELL ME YOU WOULDN'T LIKE TO HAVE A BATZOOKA IN YOUR CAR AND YOUR BELT.
RUNNK
Uh, SORRY ABOUT YOUR RIDE, BY THE WAY.
JUST WANTED TO TAKE IT OUT FOR A SPIN.
AT LEAST YOU CAN AFFORD IT.
YOU BEIN' A ONE-PERCENTER AND ALL.
JUST HIRE SOMEONE TO BUILD YOU A NEW ONE.
TRICKLE DOWN ECONOMICS AT WORK!
SO...
WHAT'S HER STORY?
OHMY GODTHANK YOUTHANKYOU THANKYOU!
EASY. SPEED KILLS, SWEETS.
ARE YOU ALL RIGHT?

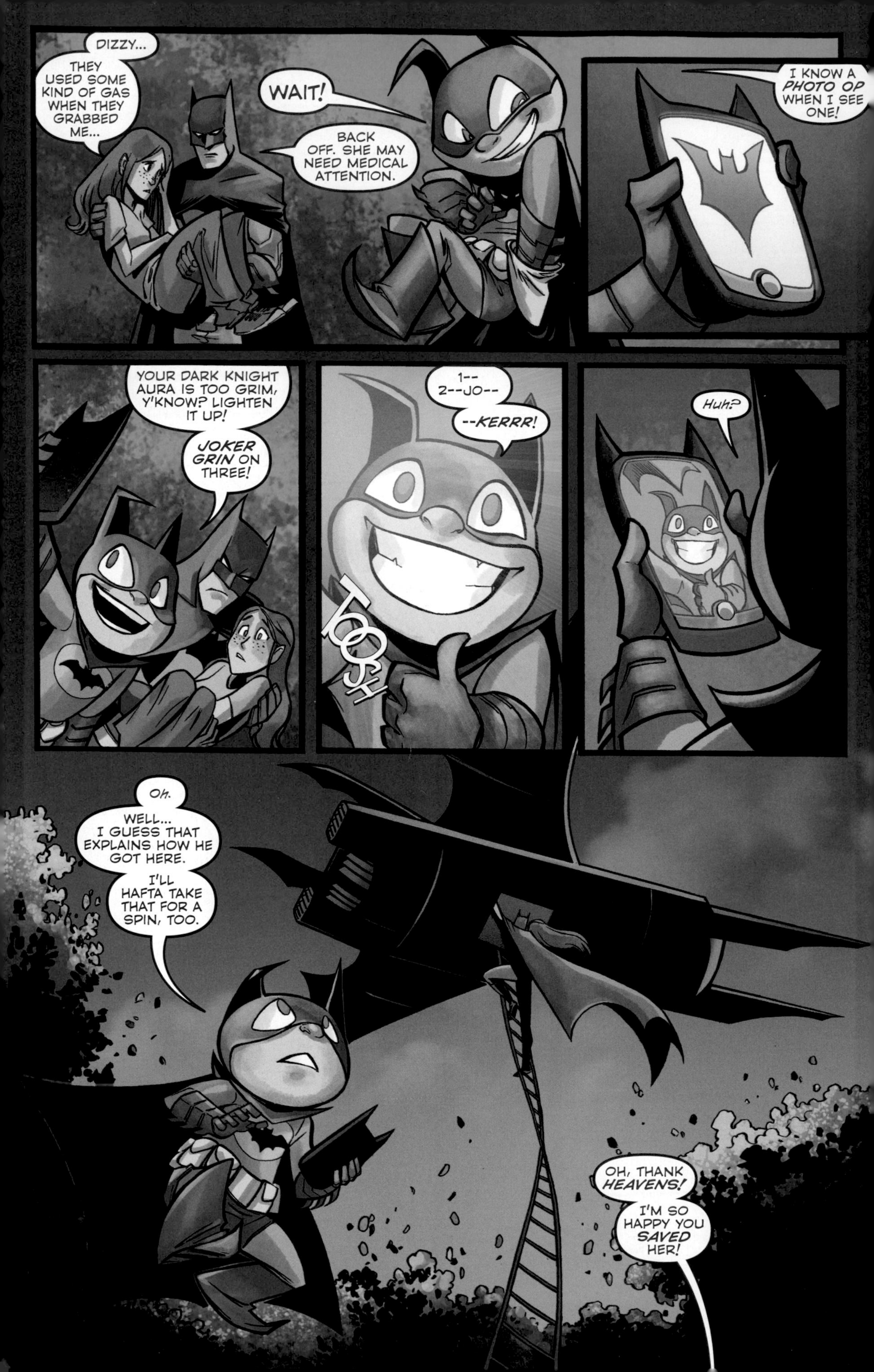
DIZZY...
THEY USED SOME KIND OF GAS WHEN THEY GRABBED ME...
WAIT!
BACK OFF. SHE MAY NEED MEDICAL ATTENTION.
I KNOW A *PHOTO OP* WHEN I SEE ONE!
YOUR DARK KNIGHT AURA IS TOO GRIM, Y'KNOW? LIGHTEN IT UP!
JOKER GRIN ON THREE!
1--
2--JO--
--*KERRR!*
TOOSH
Huh?
Oh.
WELL... I GUESS THAT EXPLAINS HOW HE GOT HERE.
I'LL HAFTA TAKE THAT FOR A SPIN, TOO.
OH, THANK *HEAVENS!*
I'M SO HAPPY YOU *SAVED* HER!

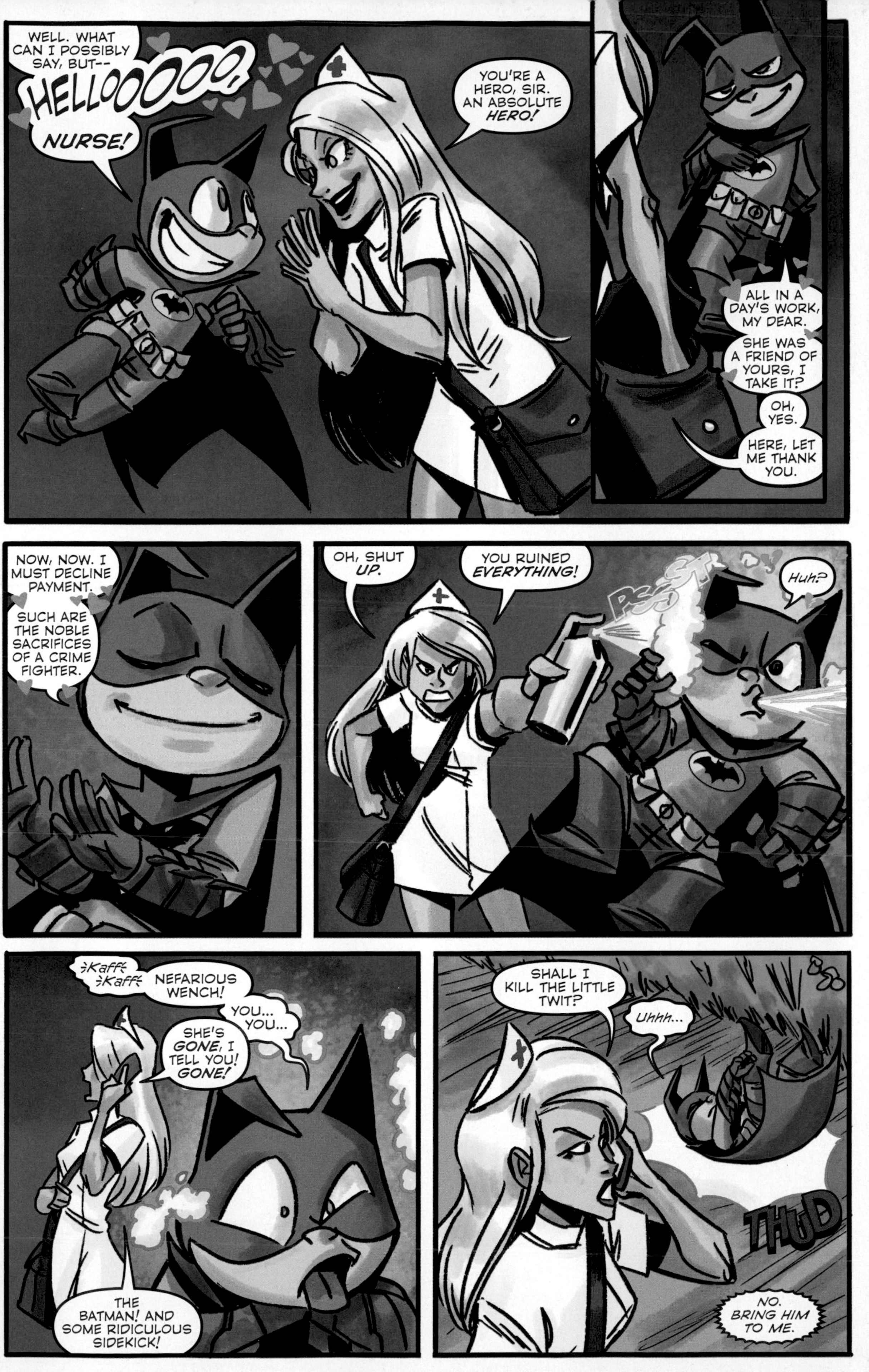
WELL. WHAT CAN I POSSIBLY SAY, BUT--
HELLOOOOO,
NURSE!
YOU'RE A HERO, SIR. AN ABSOLUTE HERO!
ALL IN A DAY'S WORK, MY DEAR.
SHE WAS A FRIEND OF YOURS, I TAKE IT?
OH, YES.
HERE, LET ME THANK YOU.
NOW, NOW. I MUST DECLINE PAYMENT.
SUCH ARE THE NOBLE SACRIFICES OF A CRIME FIGHTER.
OH, SHUT UP.
YOU RUINED EVERYTHING!
PSSSST
Huh?
Kaff
Kaff
NEFARIOUS WENCH!
YOU... YOU...
SHE'S GONE, I TELL YOU! GONE!
THE BATMAN! AND SOME RIDICULOUS SIDEKICK!
SHALL I KILL THE LITTLE TWIT?
Uhhh...
THUD
NO. BRING HIM TO ME.

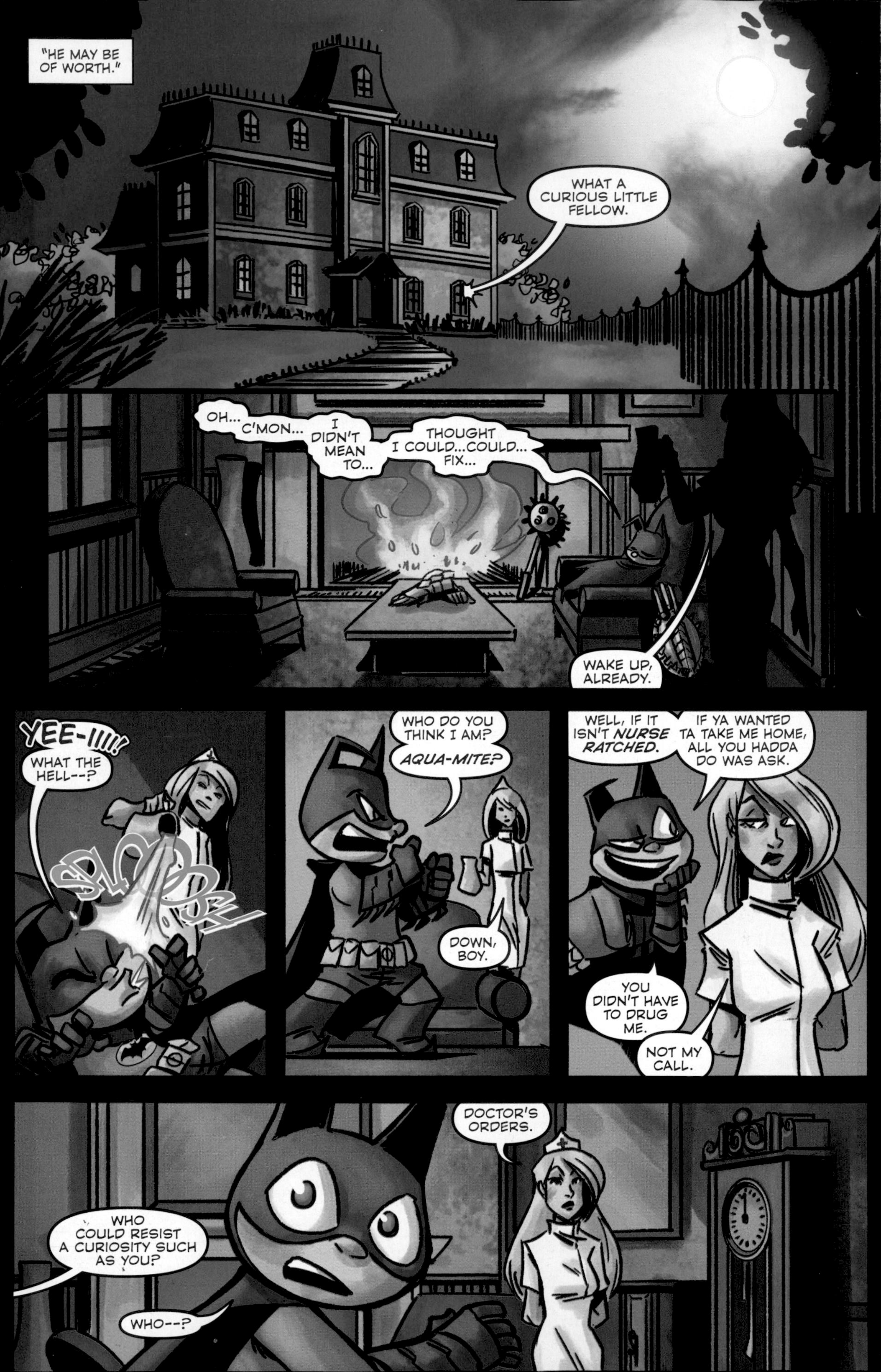
"HE MAY BE OF WORTH."
WHAT A CURIOUS LITTLE FELLOW.
OH...
C'MON...
I DIDN'T MEAN TO...
THOUGHT I COULD...COULD... FIX...
WAKE UP, ALREADY.
YEE-IIII!
WHAT THE HELL--?
SPLOOSH
WHO DO YOU THINK I AM? AQUA-MITE?
DOWN, BOY.
WELL, IF IT ISN'T NURSE RATCHED.
IF YA WANTED TA TAKE ME HOME, ALL YOU HADDA DO WAS ASK.
YOU DIDN'T HAVE TO DRUG ME.
NOT MY CALL.
DOCTOR'S ORDERS.
WHO COULD RESIST A CURIOSITY SUCH AS YOU?
WHO--?

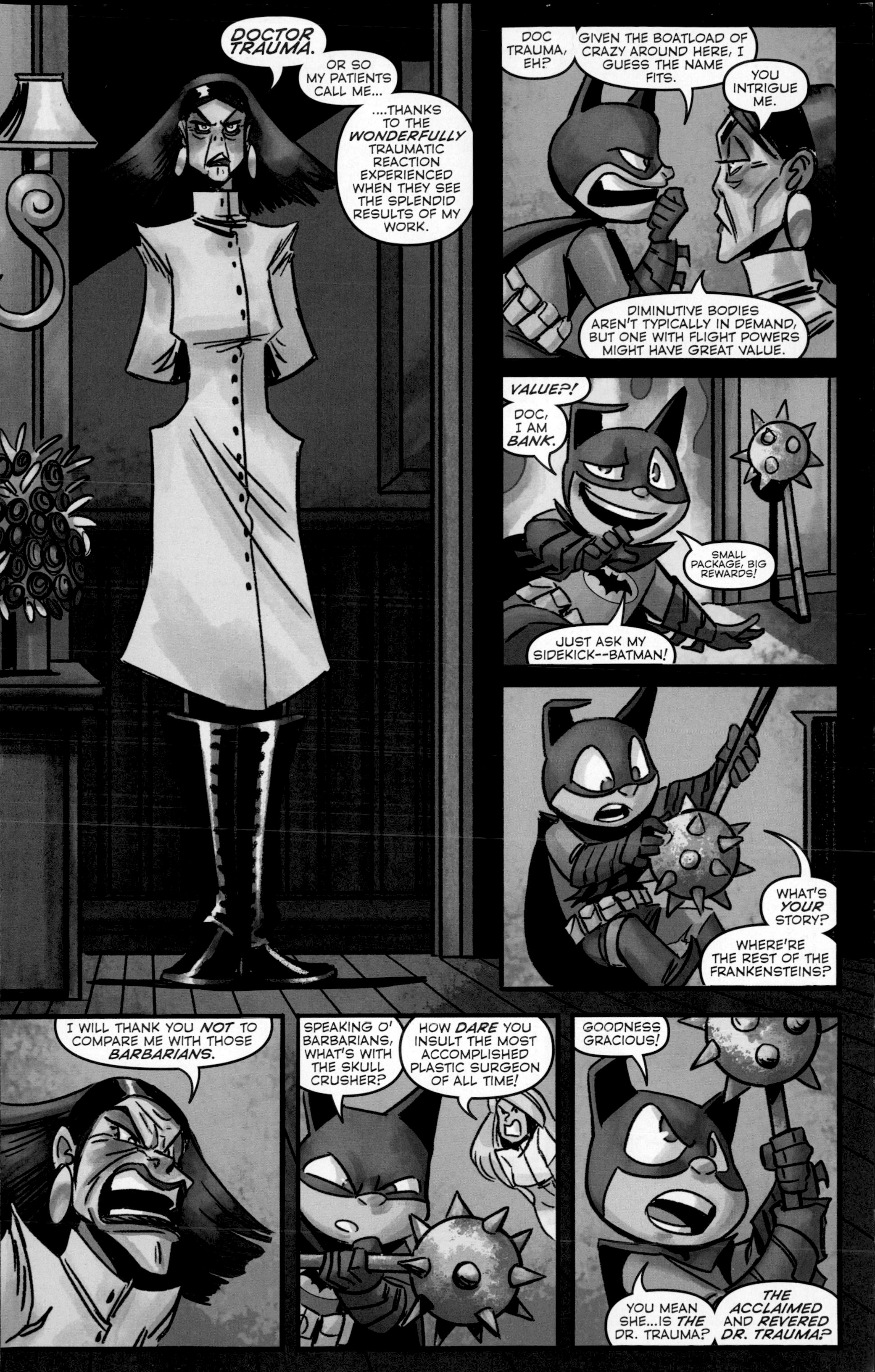
DOCTOR TRAUMA.
OR SO MY PATIENTS CALL ME...
....THANKS TO THE WONDERFULLY TRAUMATIC REACTION EXPERIENCED WHEN THEY SEE THE SPLENDID RESULTS OF MY WORK.
DOC TRAUMA, EH?
GIVEN THE BOATLOAD OF CRAZY AROUND HERE, I GUESS THE NAME FITS.
YOU INTRIGUE ME.
DIMINUTIVE BODIES AREN'T TYPICALLY IN DEMAND, BUT ONE WITH FLIGHT POWERS MIGHT HAVE GREAT VALUE.
VALUE?!
DOC, I AM BANK.
SMALL PACKAGE, BIG REWARDS!
JUST ASK MY SIDEKICK--BATMAN!
WHAT'S YOUR STORY?
WHERE'RE THE REST OF THE FRANKENSTEINS?
I WILL THANK YOU NOT TO COMPARE ME WITH THOSE BARBARIANS.
SPEAKING O' BARBARIANS, WHAT'S WITH THE SKULL CRUSHER?
HOW DARE YOU INSULT THE MOST ACCOMPLISHED PLASTIC SURGEON OF ALL TIME!
GOODNESS GRACIOUS!
YOU MEAN SHE...IS THE DR. TRAUMA?
THE ACCLAIMED AND REVERED DR. TRAUMA?

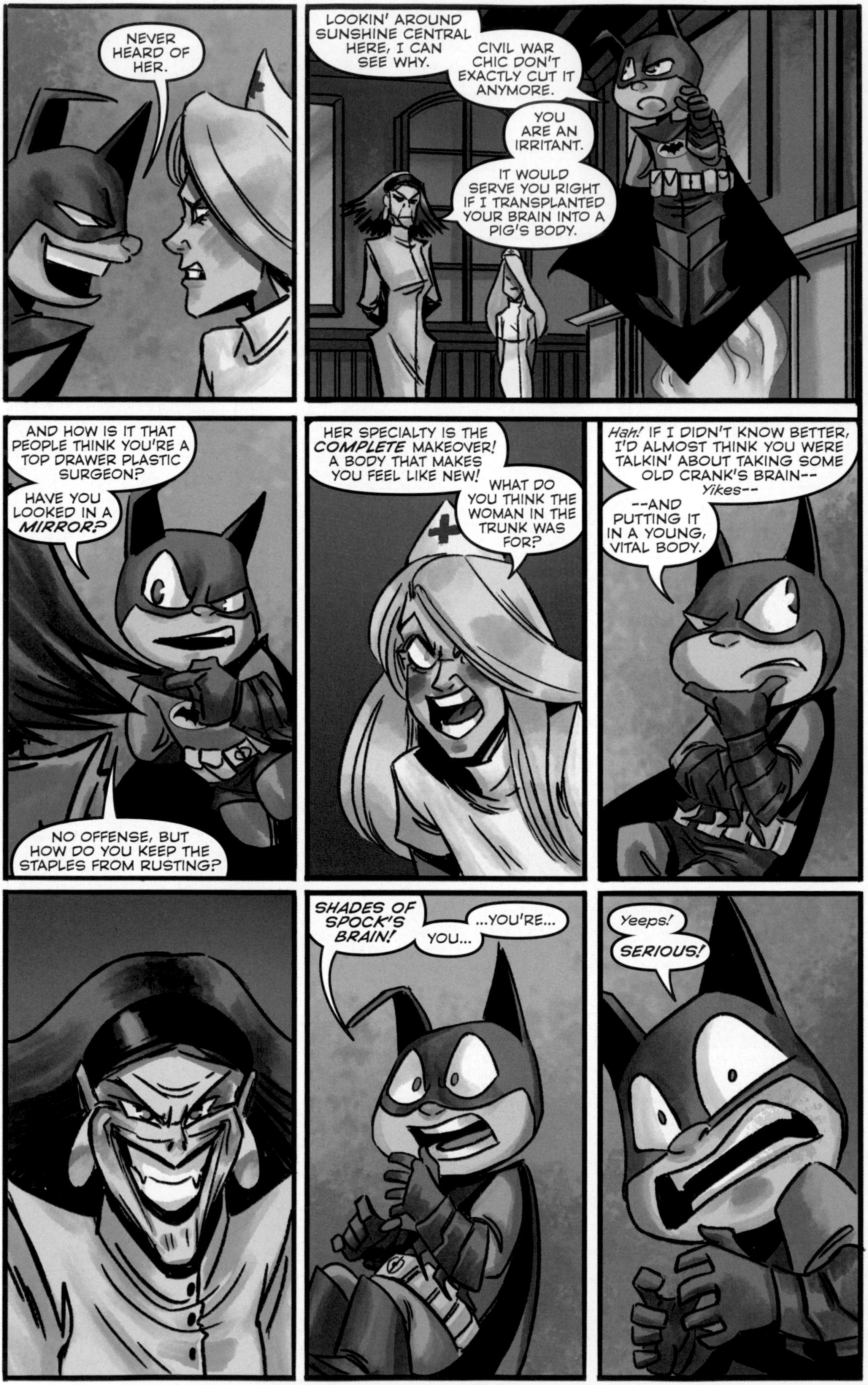
NEVER HEARD OF HER.
LOOKIN' AROUND SUNSHINE CENTRAL HERE, I CAN SEE WHY.
CIVIL WAR CHIC DON'T EXACTLY CUT IT ANYMORE.
YOU ARE AN IRRITANT.
IT WOULD SERVE YOU RIGHT IF I TRANSPLANTED YOUR BRAIN INTO A PIG'S BODY.
AND HOW IS IT THAT PEOPLE THINK YOU'RE A TOP DRAWER PLASTIC SURGEON?
HAVE YOU LOOKED IN A MIRROR?
NO OFFENSE, BUT HOW DO YOU KEEP THE STAPLES FROM RUSTING?
HER SPECIALTY IS THE COMPLETE MAKEOVER! A BODY THAT MAKES YOU FEEL LIKE NEW!
WHAT DO YOU THINK THE WOMAN IN THE TRUNK WAS FOR?
Hah! IF I DIDN'T KNOW BETTER, I'D ALMOST THINK YOU WERE TALKIN' ABOUT TAKING SOME OLD CRANK'S BRAIN-- Yikes--
--AND PUTTING IT IN A YOUNG, VITAL BODY.
SHADES OF SPOCK'S BRAIN!
YOU...
...YOU'RE...
Yeeps!
SERIOUS!

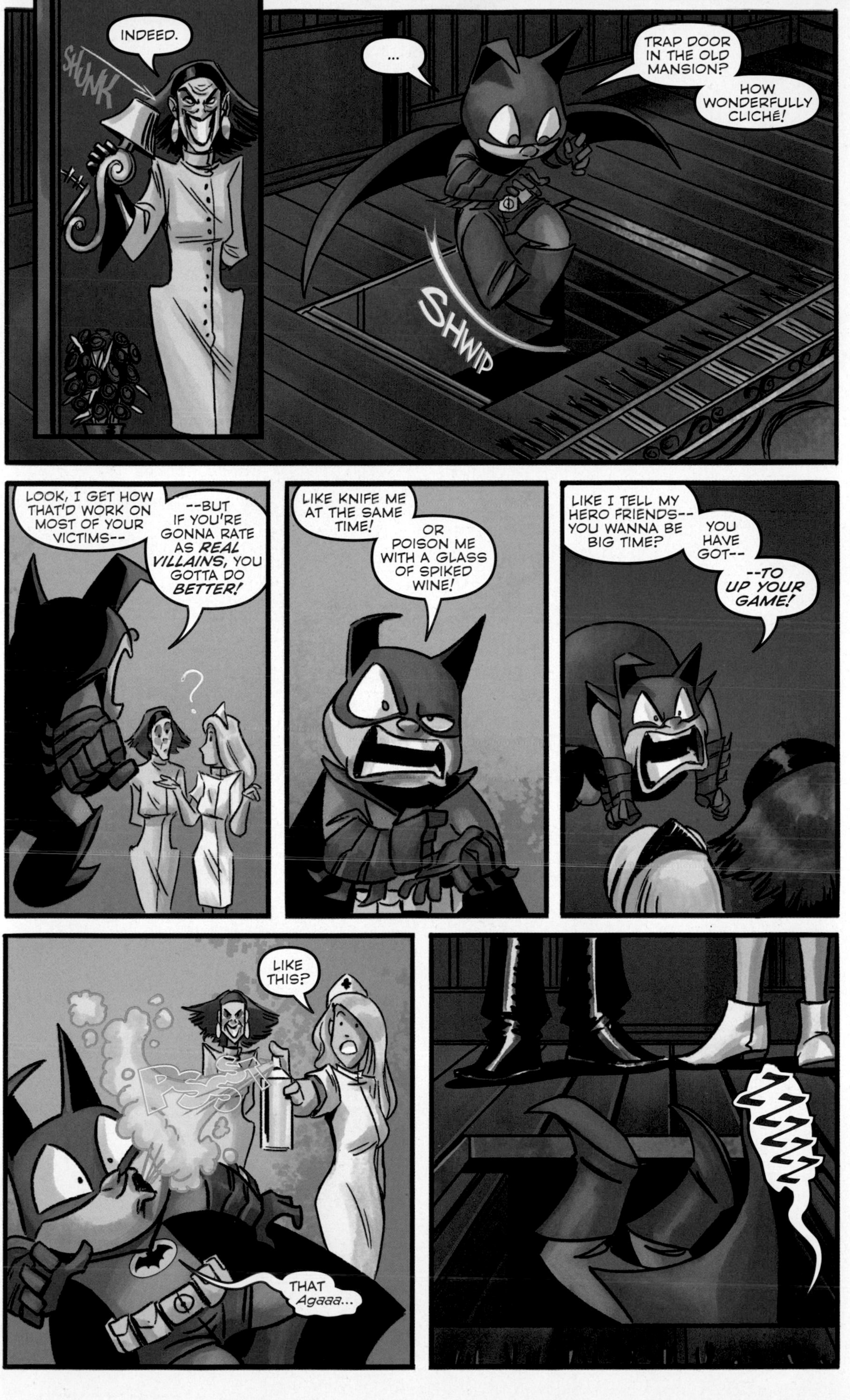
INDEED.
SHUNK
...
TRAP DOOR IN THE OLD MANSION?
HOW WONDERFULLY CLICHÉ!
SHWIP
LOOK, I GET HOW THAT'D WORK ON MOST OF YOUR VICTIMS--
--BUT IF YOU'RE GONNA RATE AS *REAL VILLAINS*, YOU GOTTA DO *BETTER!*
?
LIKE KNIFE ME AT THE SAME TIME!
OR POISON ME WITH A GLASS OF SPIKED WINE!
LIKE I TELL MY HERO FRIENDS-- YOU WANNA BE BIG TIME?
YOU HAVE GOT--
--TO *UP YOUR GAME!*
LIKE THIS?
PSSST
THAT *Agaaa...*
ZZZZZ

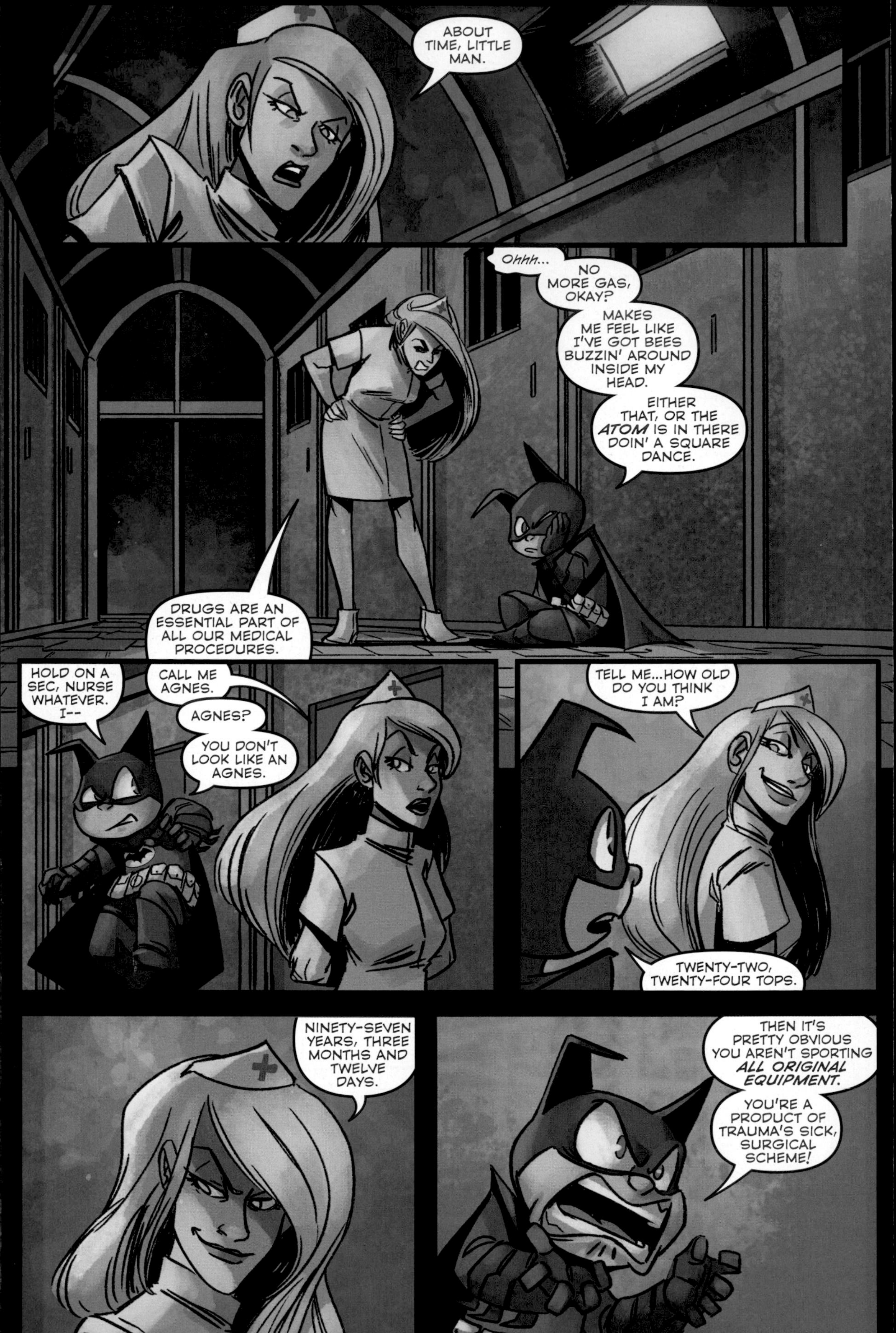
ABOUT TIME, LITTLE MAN.
Ohhh...
NO MORE GAS, OKAY?
MAKES ME FEEL LIKE I'VE GOT BEES BUZZIN' AROUND INSIDE MY HEAD.
EITHER THAT, OR THE ATOM IS IN THERE DOIN' A SQUARE DANCE.
DRUGS ARE AN ESSENTIAL PART OF ALL OUR MEDICAL PROCEDURES.
HOLD ON A SEC, NURSE WHATEVER. I--
CALL ME AGNES.
AGNES?
YOU DON'T LOOK LIKE AN AGNES.
TELL ME...HOW OLD DO YOU THINK I AM?
TWENTY-TWO, TWENTY-FOUR TOPS.
NINETY-SEVEN YEARS, THREE MONTHS AND TWELVE DAYS.
THEN IT'S PRETTY OBVIOUS YOU AREN'T SPORTING ALL ORIGINAL EQUIPMENT.
YOU'RE A PRODUCT OF TRAUMA'S SICK, SURGICAL SCHEME!

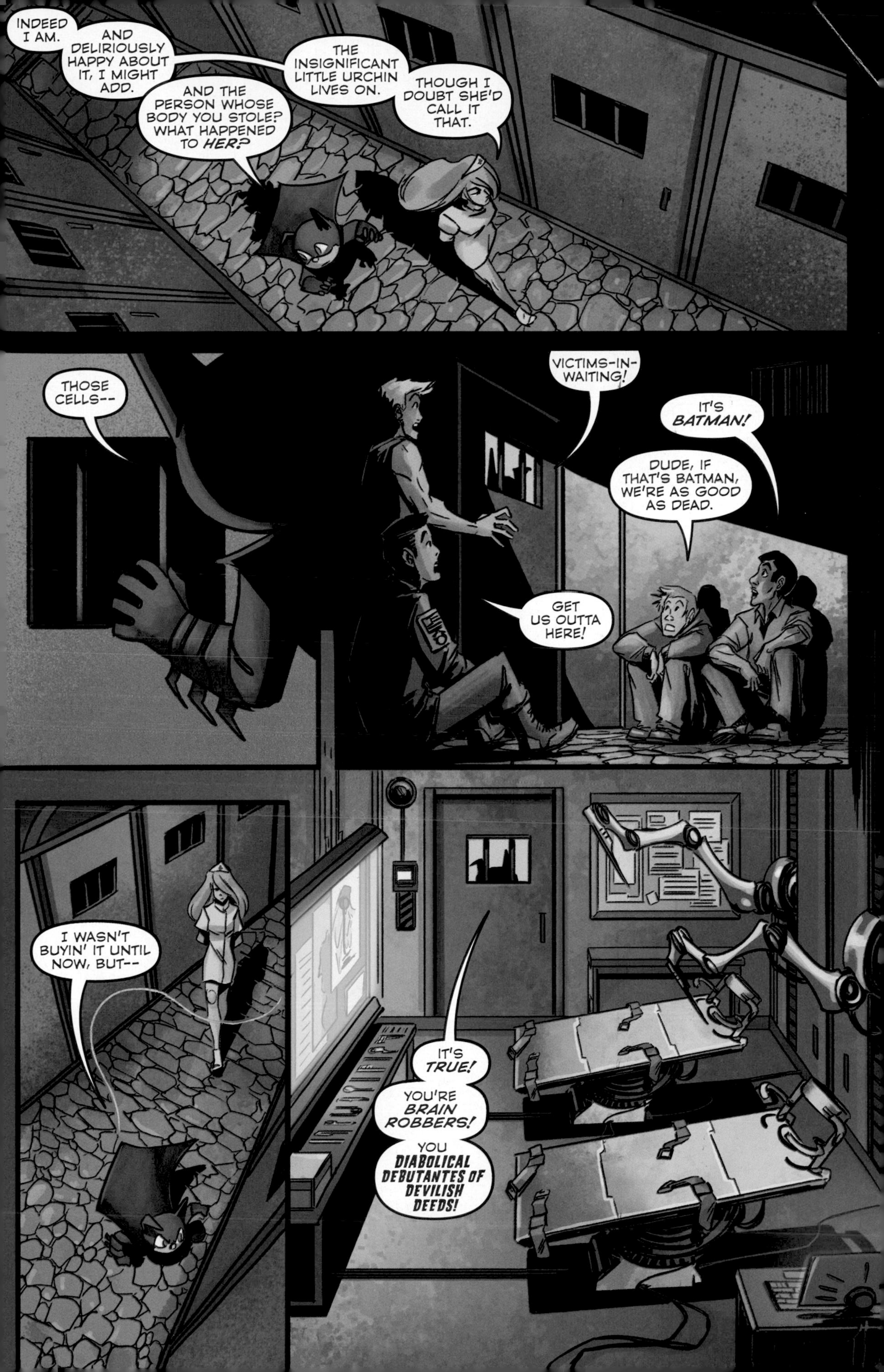
INDEED I AM.
AND DELIRIOUSLY HAPPY ABOUT IT, I MIGHT ADD.
THE INSIGNIFICANT LITTLE URCHIN LIVES ON.
THOUGH I DOUBT SHE'D CALL IT THAT.
AND THE PERSON WHOSE BODY YOU STOLE? WHAT HAPPENED TO HER?
THOSE CELLS--
VICTIMS-IN-WAITING!
IT'S BATMAN!
DUDE, IF THAT'S BATMAN, WE'RE AS GOOD AS DEAD.
GET US OUTTA HERE!
I WASN'T BUYIN' IT UNTIL NOW, BUT--
IT'S TRUE!
YOU'RE BRAIN ROBBERS!
YOU DIABOLICAL DEBUTANTES OF DEVILISH DEEDS!

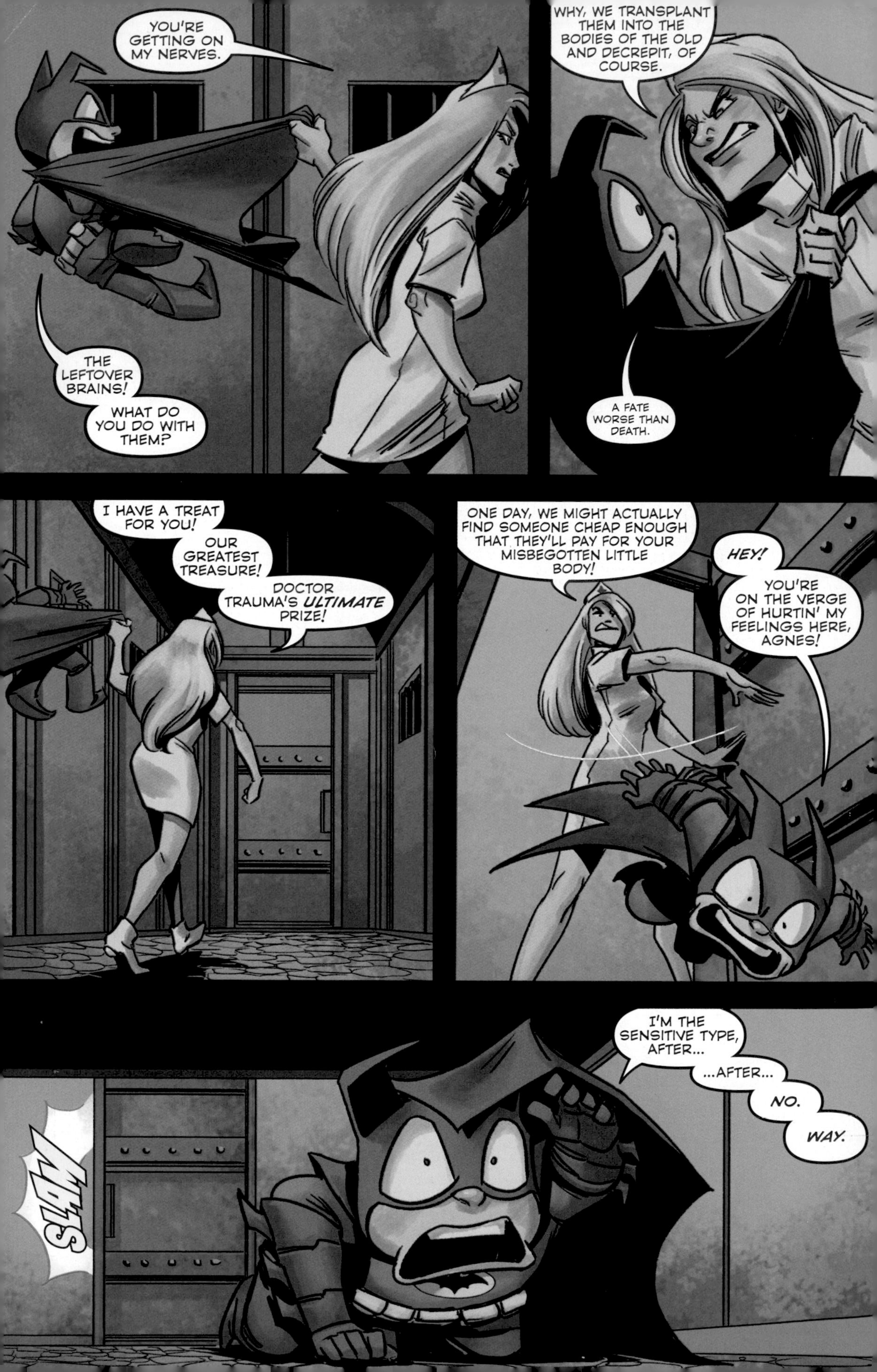

YOU'RE GETTING ON MY NERVES.
THE LEFTOVER BRAINS!
WHAT DO YOU DO WITH THEM?
WHY, WE TRANSPLANT THEM INTO THE BODIES OF THE OLD AND DECREPIT, OF COURSE.
A FATE WORSE THAN DEATH.
I HAVE A TREAT FOR YOU!
OUR GREATEST TREASURE!
DOCTOR TRAUMA'S *ULTIMATE* PRIZE!
ONE DAY, WE MIGHT ACTUALLY FIND SOMEONE CHEAP ENOUGH THAT THEY'LL PAY FOR YOUR MISBEGOTTEN LITTLE BODY!
HEY!
YOU'RE ON THE VERGE OF HURTIN' MY FEELINGS HERE, AGNES!
SLAM
I'M THE SENSITIVE TYPE, AFTER...
...AFTER...
NO.
WAY.

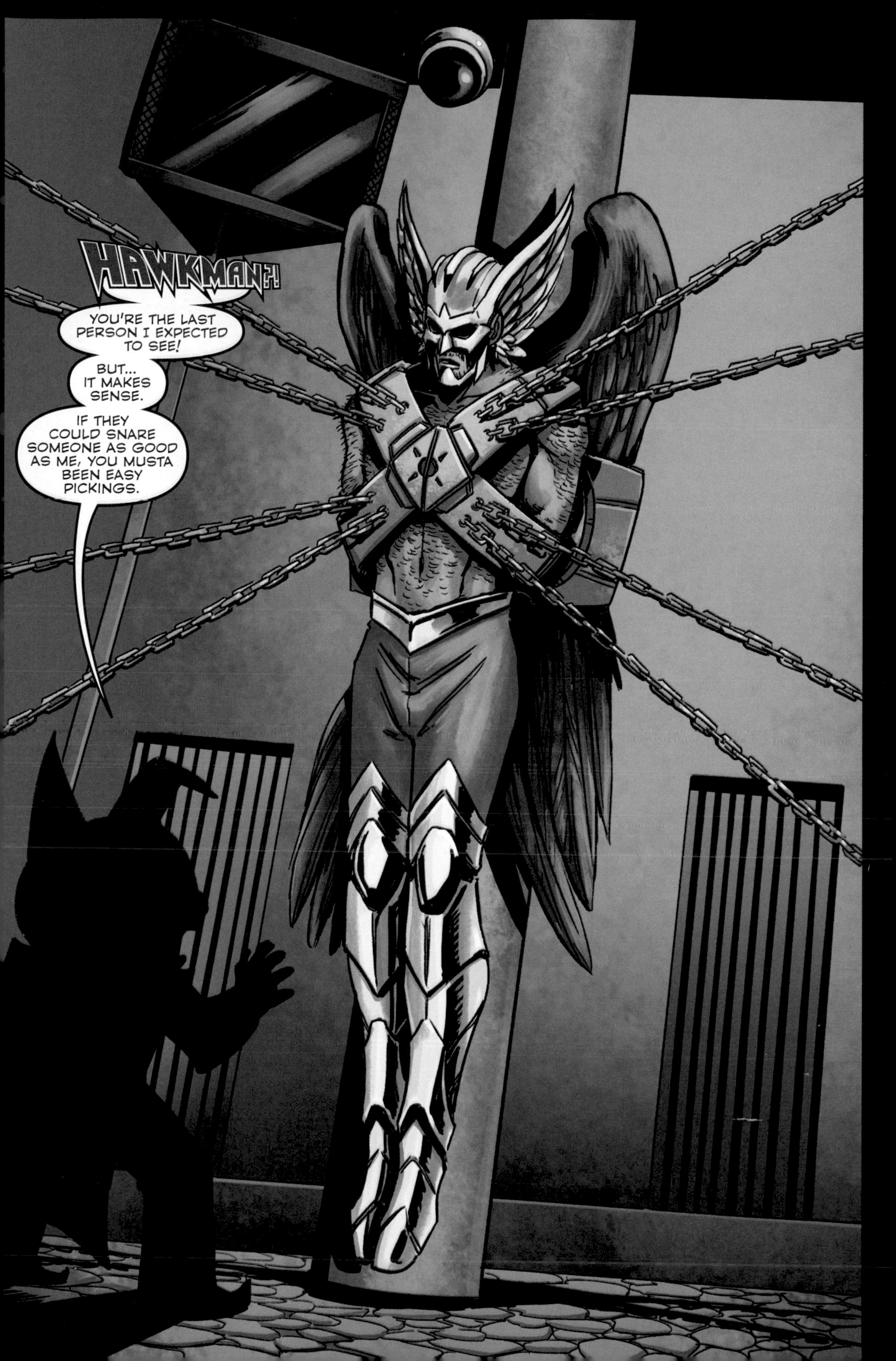
HAWKMAN?!
YOU'RE THE LAST PERSON I EXPECTED TO SEE!
BUT... IT MAKES SENSE.
IF THEY COULD SNARE SOMEONE AS GOOD AS ME, YOU MUSTA BEEN EASY PICKINGS.

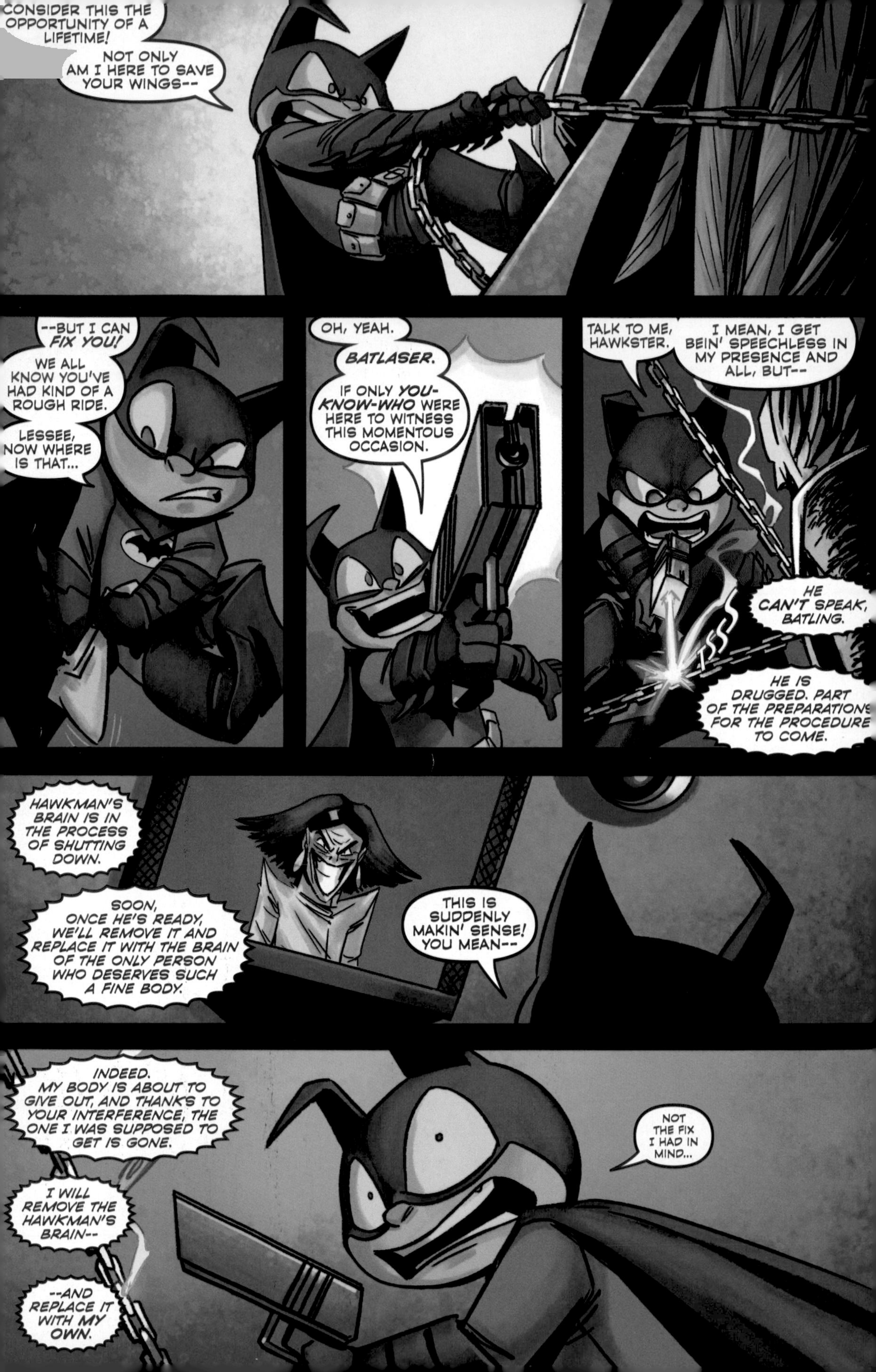
CONSIDER THIS THE OPPORTUNITY OF A LIFETIME!
NOT ONLY AM I HERE TO SAVE YOUR WINGS--
--BUT I CAN FIX YOU!
WE ALL KNOW YOU'VE HAD KIND OF A ROUGH RIDE.
LESSEE, NOW WHERE IS THAT...
OH, YEAH.
BATLASER.
IF ONLY YOU-KNOW-WHO WERE HERE TO WITNESS THIS MOMENTOUS OCCASION.
TALK TO ME, HAWKSTER.
I MEAN, I GET BEIN' SPEECHLESS IN MY PRESENCE AND ALL, BUT--
TSSS
HE CAN'T SPEAK, BATLING.
HE IS DRUGGED. PART OF THE PREPARATIONS FOR THE PROCEDURE TO COME.
HAWKMAN'S BRAIN IS IN THE PROCESS OF SHUTTING DOWN.
SOON, ONCE HE'S READY, WE'LL REMOVE IT AND REPLACE IT WITH THE BRAIN OF THE ONLY PERSON WHO DESERVES SUCH A FINE BODY.
THIS IS SUDDENLY MAKIN' SENSE! YOU MEAN--
INDEED. MY BODY IS ABOUT TO GIVE OUT, AND THANKS TO YOUR INTERFERENCE, THE ONE I WAS SUPPOSED TO GET IS GONE.
NOT THE FIX I HAD IN MIND...
I WILL REMOVE THE HAWKMAN'S BRAIN--
--AND REPLACE IT WITH MY OWN.

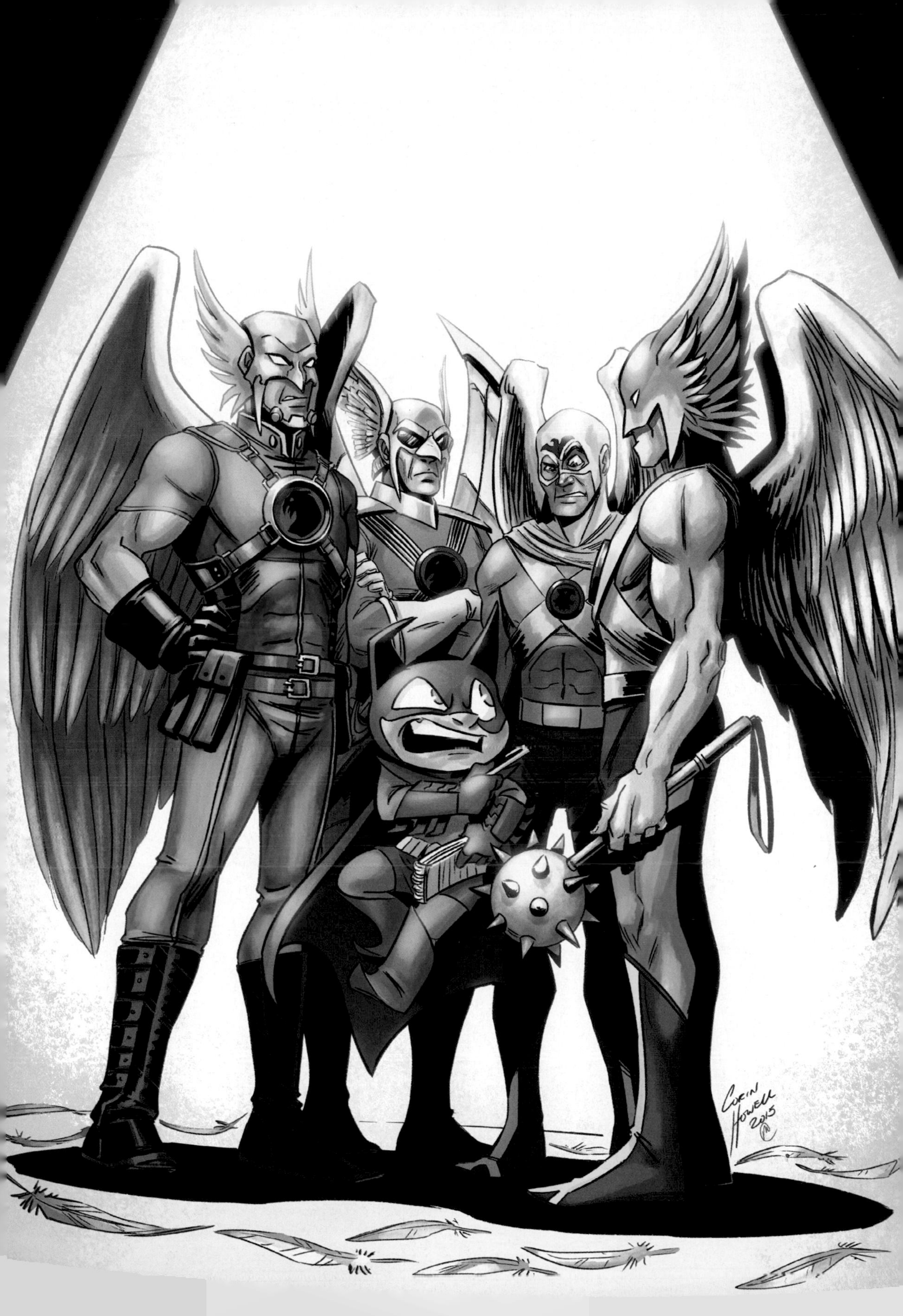
CORIN
HOWELL
2015

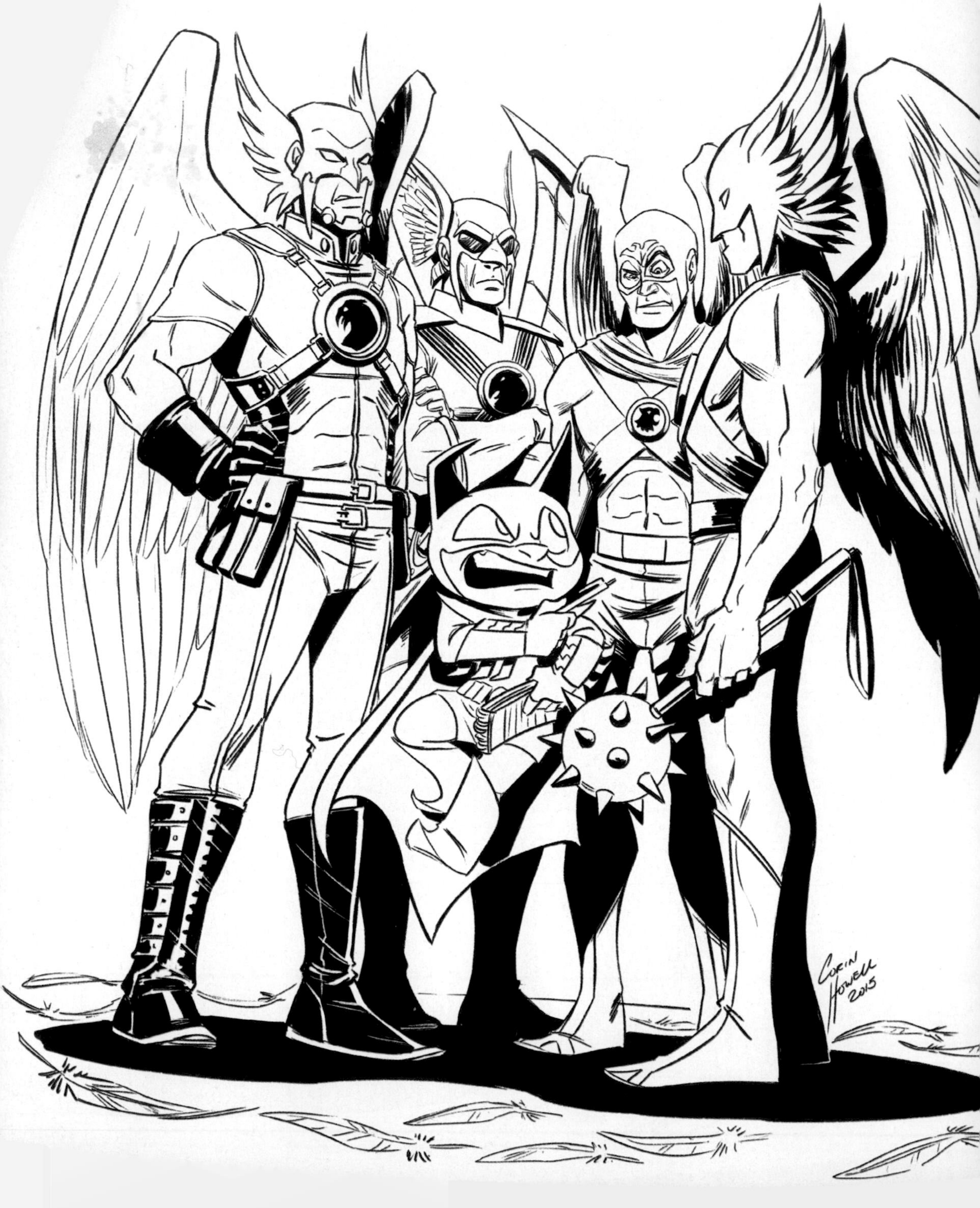
CORIN HOWELL 2015

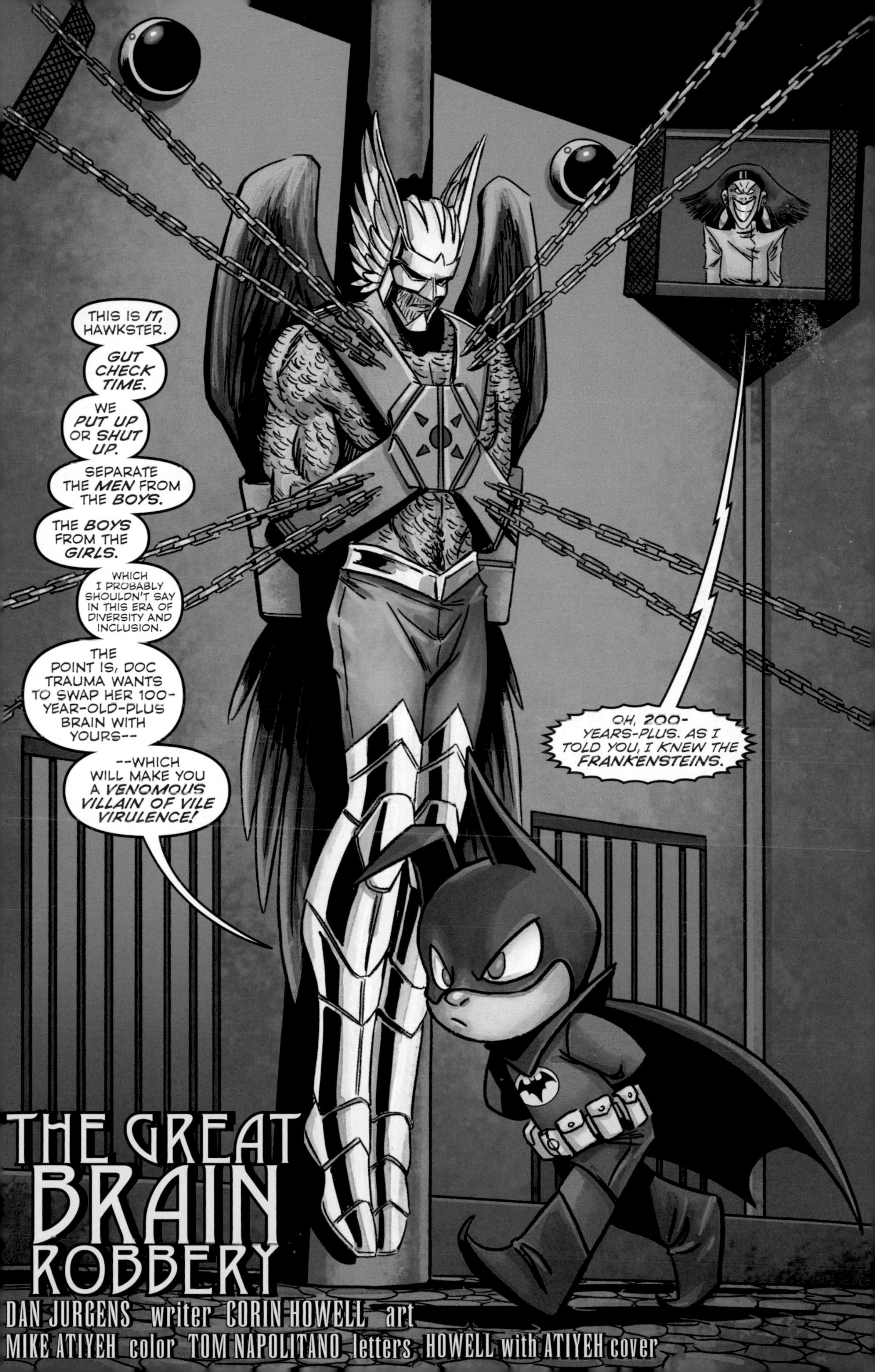
THIS IS IT, HAWKSTER.
GUT CHECK TIME.
WE PUT UP OR SHUT UP.
SEPARATE THE MEN FROM THE BOYS.
THE BOYS FROM THE GIRLS.
WHICH I PROBABLY SHOULDN'T SAY IN THIS ERA OF DIVERSITY AND INCLUSION.
THE POINT IS, DOC TRAUMA WANTS TO SWAP HER 100-YEAR-OLD-PLUS BRAIN WITH YOURS--
--WHICH WILL MAKE YOU A VENOMOUS VILLAIN OF VILE VIRULENCE!
OH, 200-YEARS-PLUS. AS I TOLD YOU, I KNEW THE FRANKENSTEINS.
THE GREAT BRAIN ROBBERY
DAN JURGENS writer CORIN HOWELL art
MIKE ATIYEH color TOM NAPOLITANO letters HOWELL with ATIYEH cover

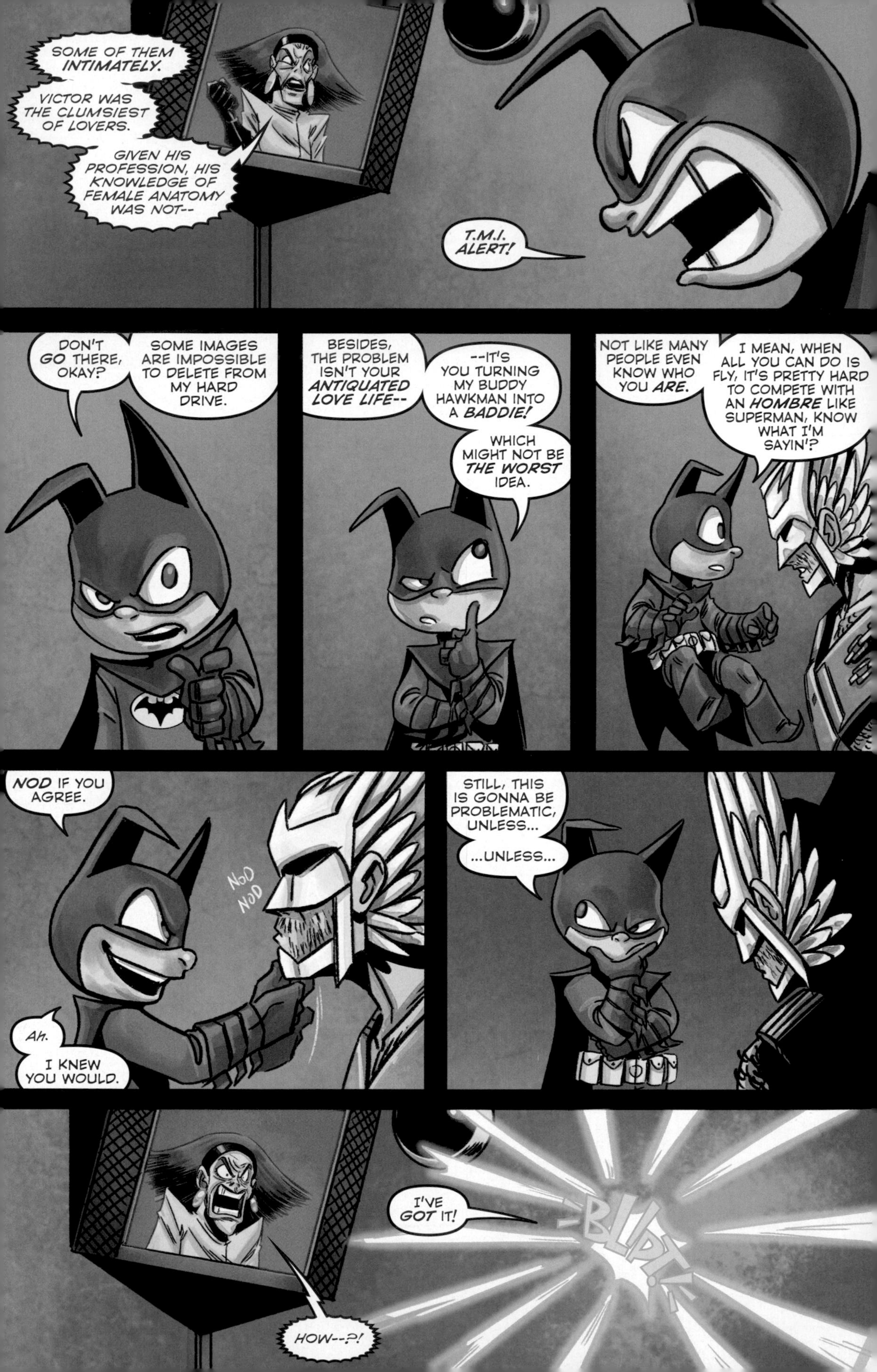

SOME OF THEM INTIMATELY.
VICTOR WAS THE CLUMSIEST OF LOVERS.
GIVEN HIS PROFESSION, HIS KNOWLEDGE OF FEMALE ANATOMY WAS NOT--
T.M.I. ALERT!
DON'T GO THERE, OKAY?
SOME IMAGES ARE IMPOSSIBLE TO DELETE FROM MY HARD DRIVE.
BESIDES, THE PROBLEM ISN'T YOUR ANTIQUATED LOVE LIFE--
--IT'S YOU TURNING MY BUDDY HAWKMAN INTO A BADDIE!
WHICH MIGHT NOT BE THE WORST IDEA.
NOT LIKE MANY PEOPLE EVEN KNOW WHO YOU ARE.
I MEAN, WHEN ALL YOU CAN DO IS FLY, IT'S PRETTY HARD TO COMPETE WITH AN HOMBRE LIKE SUPERMAN, KNOW WHAT I'M SAYIN'?
NOD IF YOU AGREE.
NOD NOD
Ah.
I KNEW YOU WOULD.
STILL, THIS IS GONNA BE PROBLEMATIC, UNLESS...
...UNLESS...
I'VE GOT IT!
BLIDT!
HOW--?!

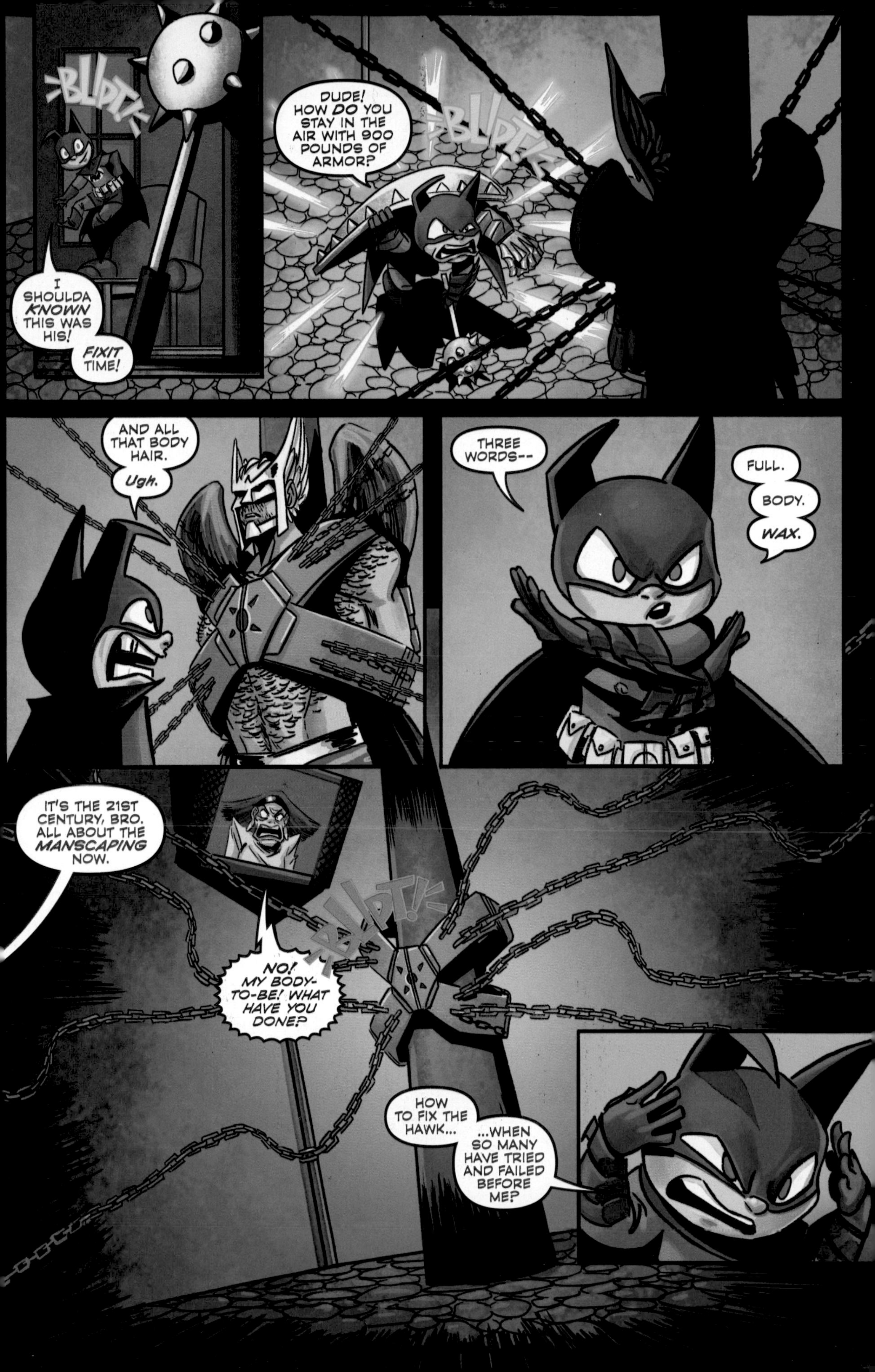
BLIDT!K
I SHOULDA KNOWN THIS WAS HIS!
FIXIT TIME!
DUDE! HOW DO YOU STAY IN THE AIR WITH 900 POUNDS OF ARMOR?
BLIDT!K
AND ALL THAT BODY HAIR.
Ugh.
THREE WORDS--
FULL.
BODY.
WAX.
IT'S THE 21ST CENTURY, BRO. ALL ABOUT THE MANSCAPING NOW.
BLIDT!K
NO! MY BODY-TO-BE! WHAT HAVE YOU DONE?
HOW TO FIX THE HAWK...
...WHEN SO MANY HAVE TRIED AND FAILED BEFORE ME?

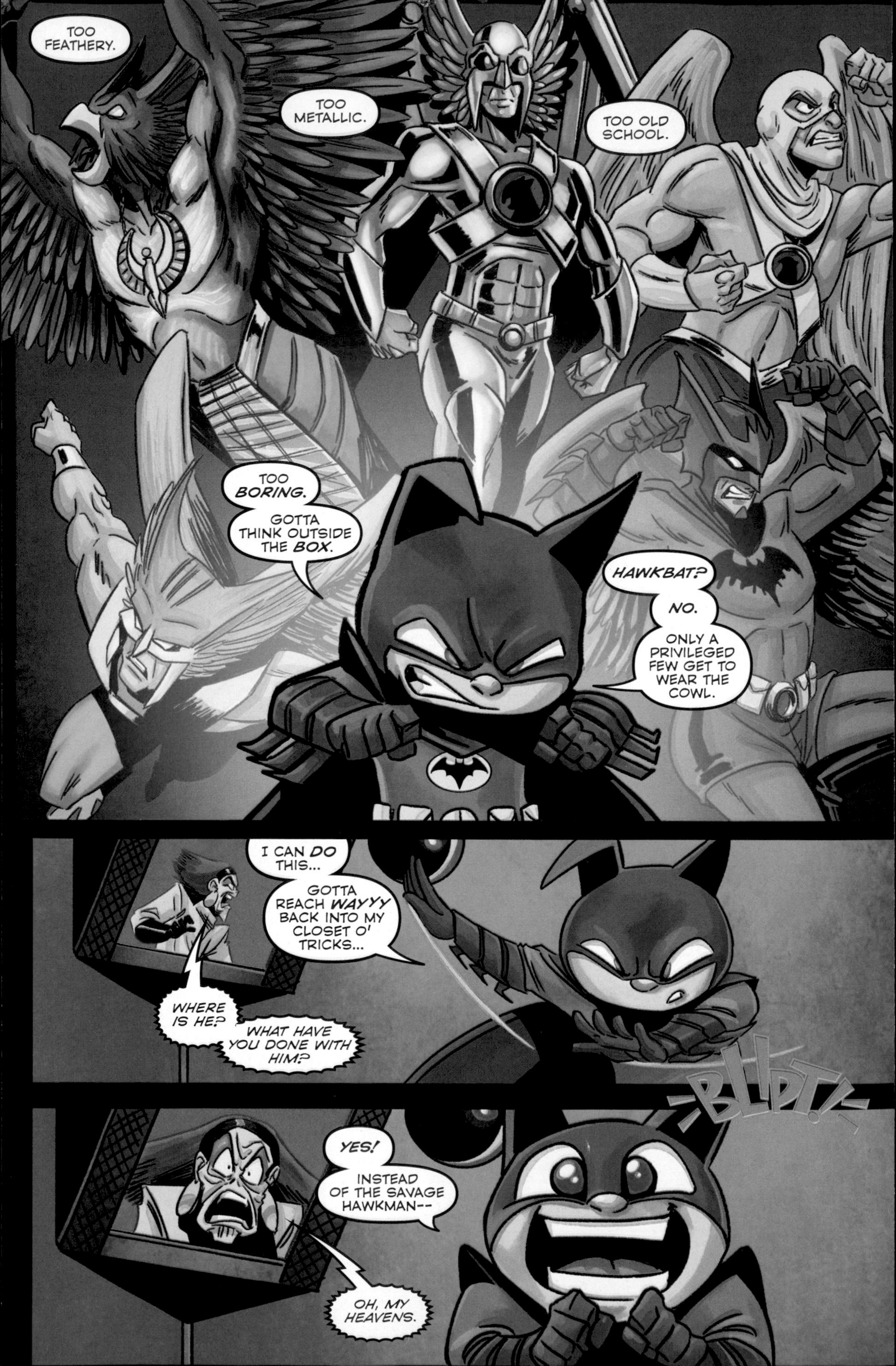
TOO FEATHERY.
TOO METALLIC.
TOO OLD SCHOOL.
TOO BORING.
GOTTA THINK OUTSIDE THE BOX.
HAWKBAT?
NO.
ONLY A PRIVILEGED FEW GET TO WEAR THE COWL.
I CAN DO THIS...
GOTTA REACH WAYYY BACK INTO MY CLOSET O' TRICKS...
WHERE IS HE?
WHAT HAVE YOU DONE WITH HIM?
BLIPT!
YES!
INSTEAD OF THE SAVAGE HAWKMAN--
OH, MY HEAVENS.

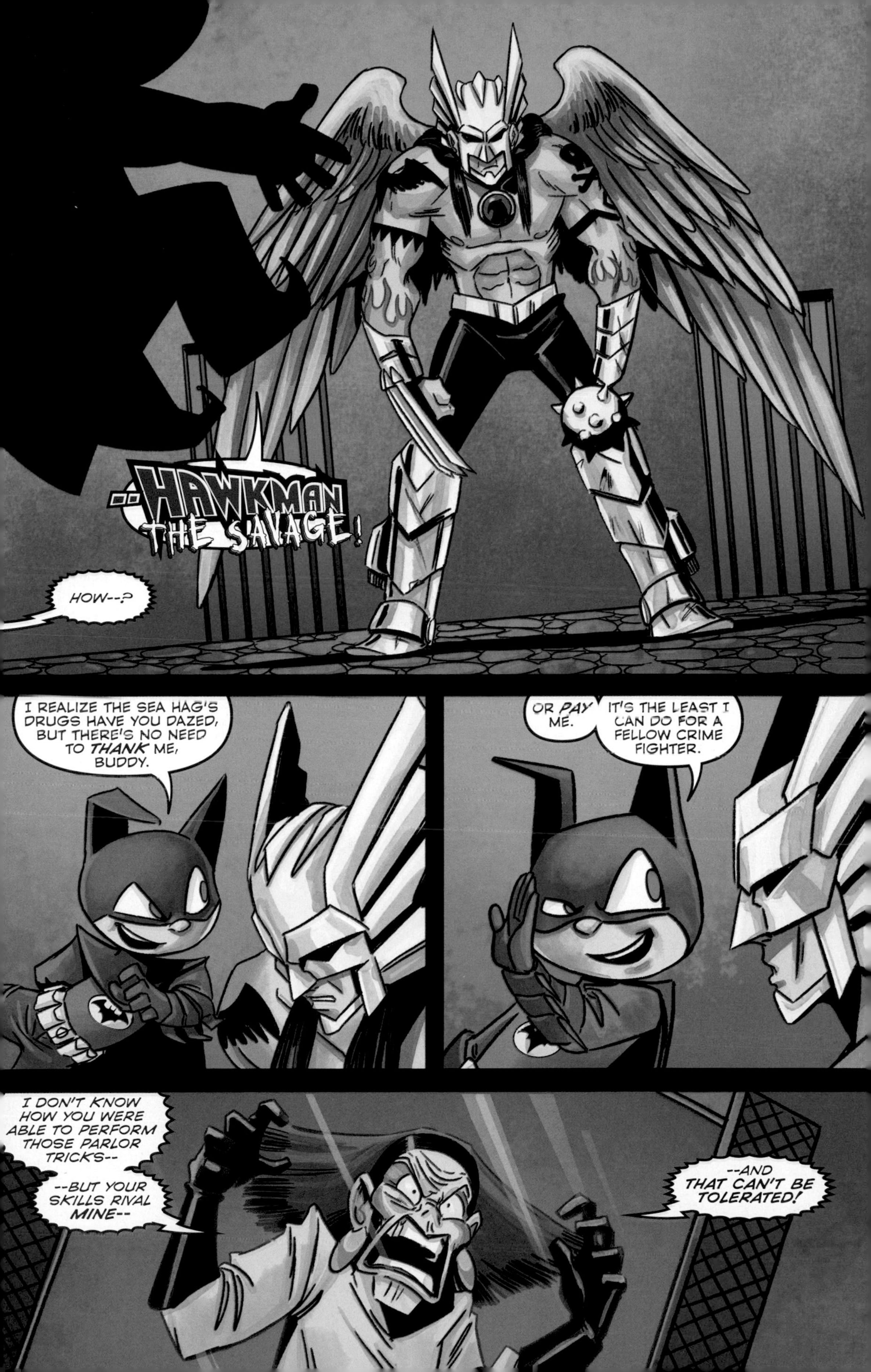

...HAWKMAN THE SAVAGE!
HOW--?
I REALIZE THE SEA HAG'S DRUGS HAVE YOU DAZED, BUT THERE'S NO NEED TO THANK ME, BUDDY.
OR PAY ME.
IT'S THE LEAST I CAN DO FOR A FELLOW CRIME FIGHTER.
I DON'T KNOW HOW YOU WERE ABLE TO PERFORM THOSE PARLOR TRICKS--
--BUT YOUR SKILLS RIVAL MINE--
--AND THAT CAN'T BE TOLERATED!

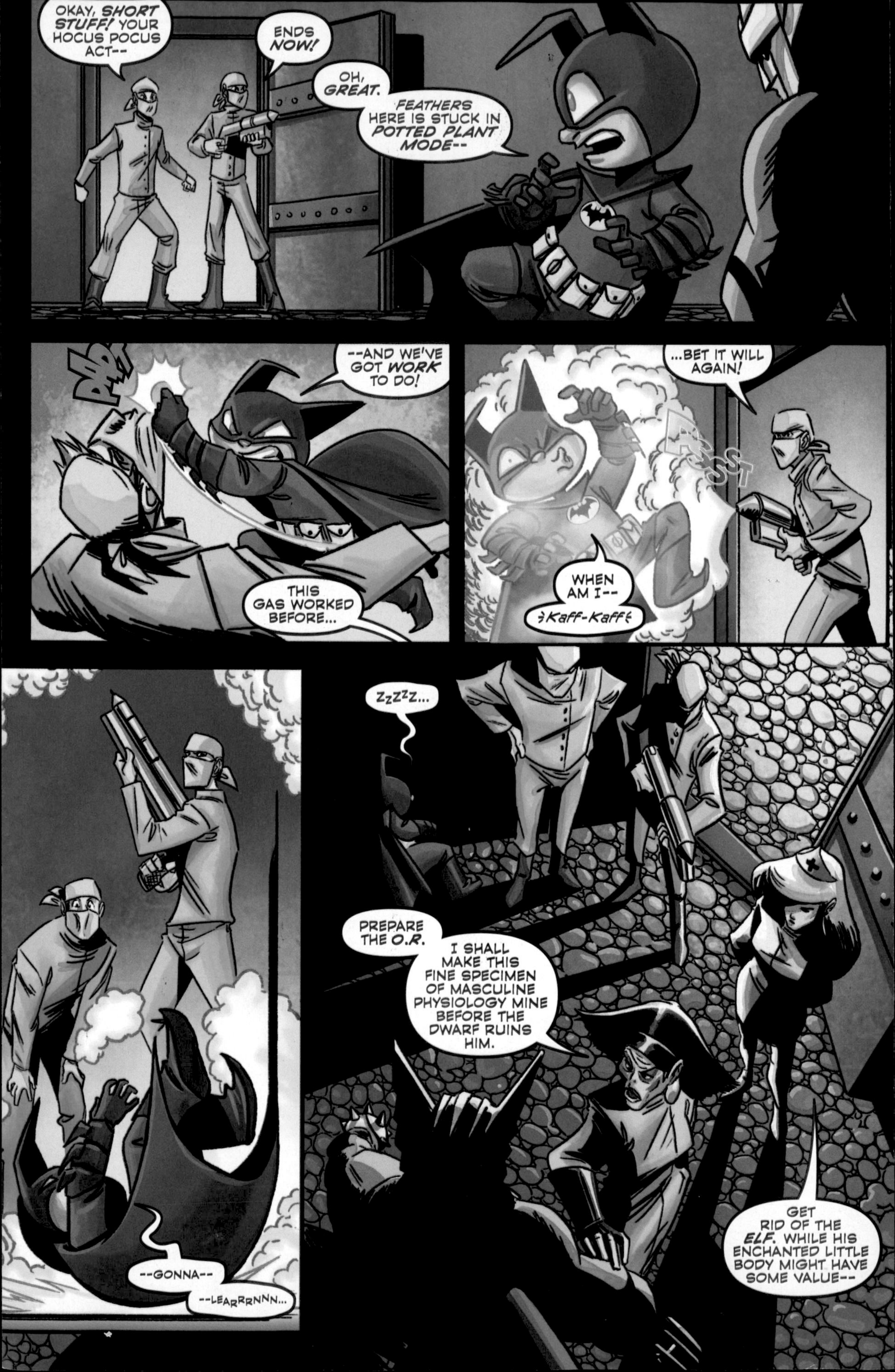
OKAY, SHORT STUFF! YOUR HOCUS POCUS ACT--
ENDS NOW!
OH, GREAT.
FEATHERS HERE IS STUCK IN POTTED PLANT MODE--
--AND WE'VE GOT WORK TO DO!
THIS GAS WORKED BEFORE...
...BET IT WILL AGAIN!
WHEN AM I--
Kaff-Kaff
--GONNA--
--LEARRRNNN...
ZzZzZ...
PREPARE THE O.R.
I SHALL MAKE THIS FINE SPECIMEN OF MASCULINE PHYSIOLOGY MINE BEFORE THE DWARF RUINS HIM.
GET RID OF THE ELF, WHILE HIS ENCHANTED LITTLE BODY MIGHT HAVE SOME VALUE--

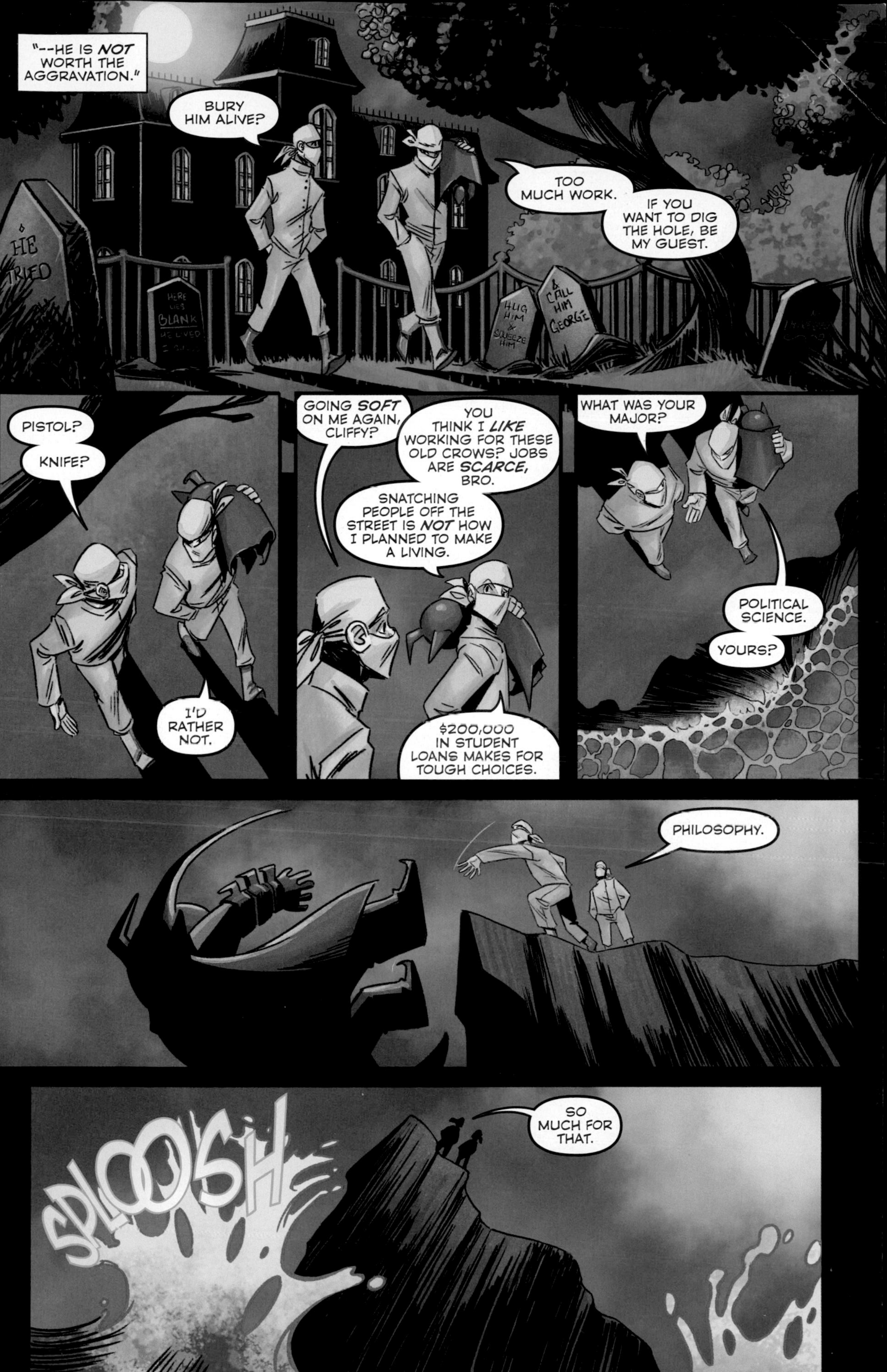
"--HE IS *NOT* WORTH THE AGGRAVATION."
BURY HIM ALIVE?
HE TRIED
HERE LIES BLANK HE LIVED
HUG HIM & SQUEEZE HIM
& CALL HIM GEORGE
TOO MUCH WORK.
IF YOU WANT TO DIG THE HOLE, BE MY GUEST.
PISTOL?
KNIFE?
I'D RATHER NOT.
GOING *SOFT* ON ME AGAIN, CLIFFY?
YOU THINK I *LIKE* WORKING FOR THESE OLD CROWS? JOBS ARE *SCARCE,* BRO.
SNATCHING PEOPLE OFF THE STREET IS *NOT* HOW I PLANNED TO MAKE A LIVING.
$200,000 IN STUDENT LOANS MAKES FOR TOUGH CHOICES.
WHAT WAS YOUR MAJOR?
POLITICAL SCIENCE.
YOURS?
PHILOSOPHY.
SPLOOSH
SO MUCH FOR THAT.

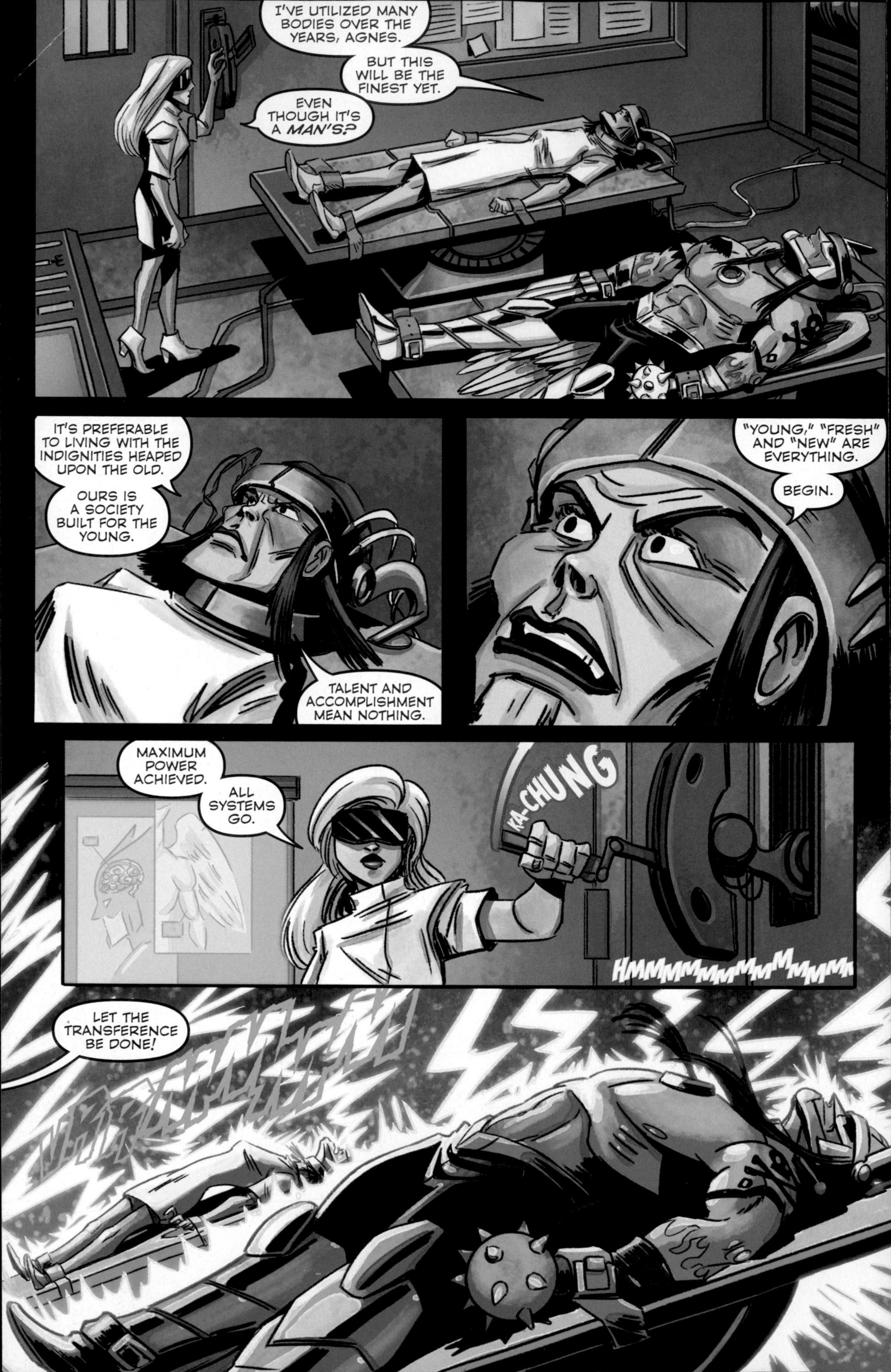
I'VE UTILIZED MANY BODIES OVER THE YEARS, AGNES.
BUT THIS WILL BE THE FINEST YET.
EVEN THOUGH IT'S A *MAN'S?*
IT'S PREFERABLE TO LIVING WITH THE INDIGNITIES HEAPED UPON THE OLD.
OURS IS A SOCIETY BUILT FOR THE YOUNG.
TALENT AND ACCOMPLISHMENT MEAN NOTHING.
"YOUNG," "FRESH" AND "NEW" ARE EVERYTHING.
BEGIN.
MAXIMUM POWER ACHIEVED.
ALL SYSTEMS GO.
KA-CHUNG
HMMMMMMMMMMMMMM
LET THE TRANSFERENCE BE DONE!

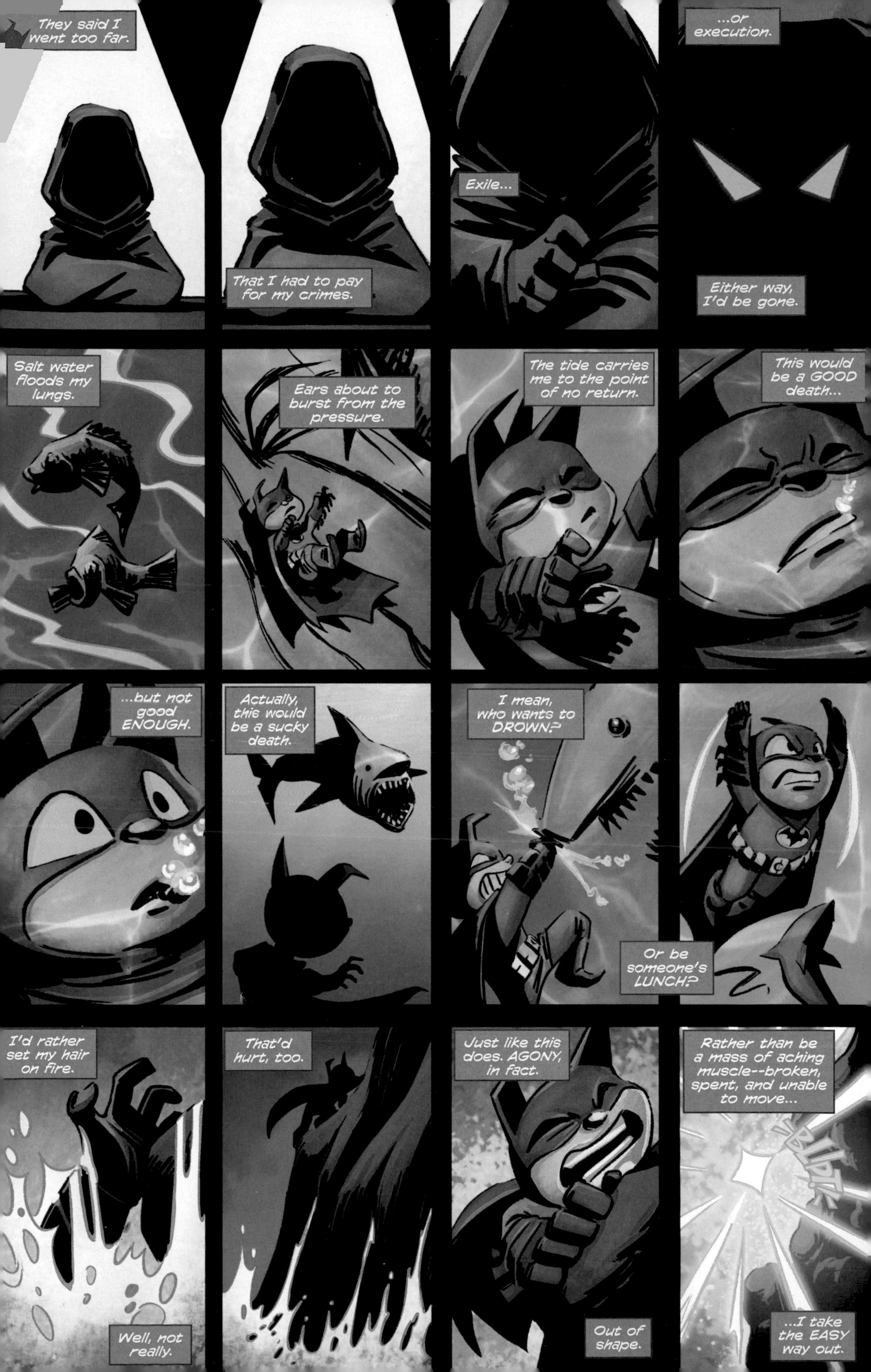
They said I went too far.
That I had to pay for my crimes.
Exile...
...or execution.
Either way, I'd be gone.
Salt water floods my lungs.
Ears about to burst from the pressure.
The tide carries me to the point of no return.
This would be a GOOD death...
...but not good ENOUGH.
Actually, this would be a sucky death.
I mean, who wants to DROWN?
Or be someone's LUNCH?
I'd rather set my hair on fire.
Well, not really.
That'd hurt, too.
Just like this does. AGONY, in fact.
Out of shape.
Rather than be a mass of aching muscle--broken, spent, and unable to move...
...I take the EASY way out.

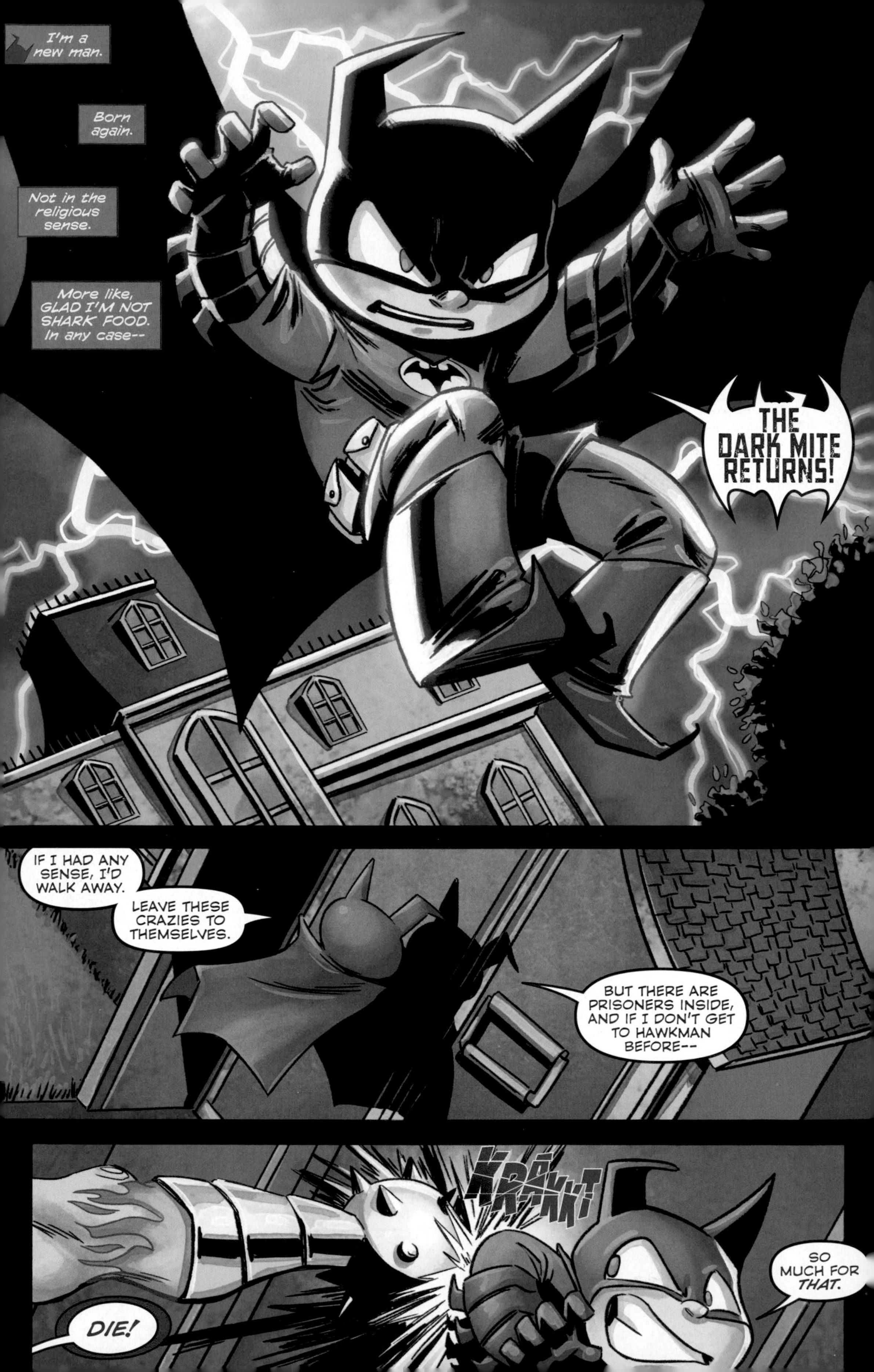
I'm a new man.
Born again.
Not in the religious sense.
More like, GLAD I'M NOT SHARK FOOD. In any case--
THE DARK MITE RETURNS!
IF I HAD ANY SENSE, I'D WALK AWAY.
LEAVE THESE CRAZIES TO THEMSELVES.
BUT THERE ARE PRISONERS INSIDE, AND IF I DON'T GET TO HAWKMAN BEFORE--
KRAKKT
DIE!
SO MUCH FOR THAT.

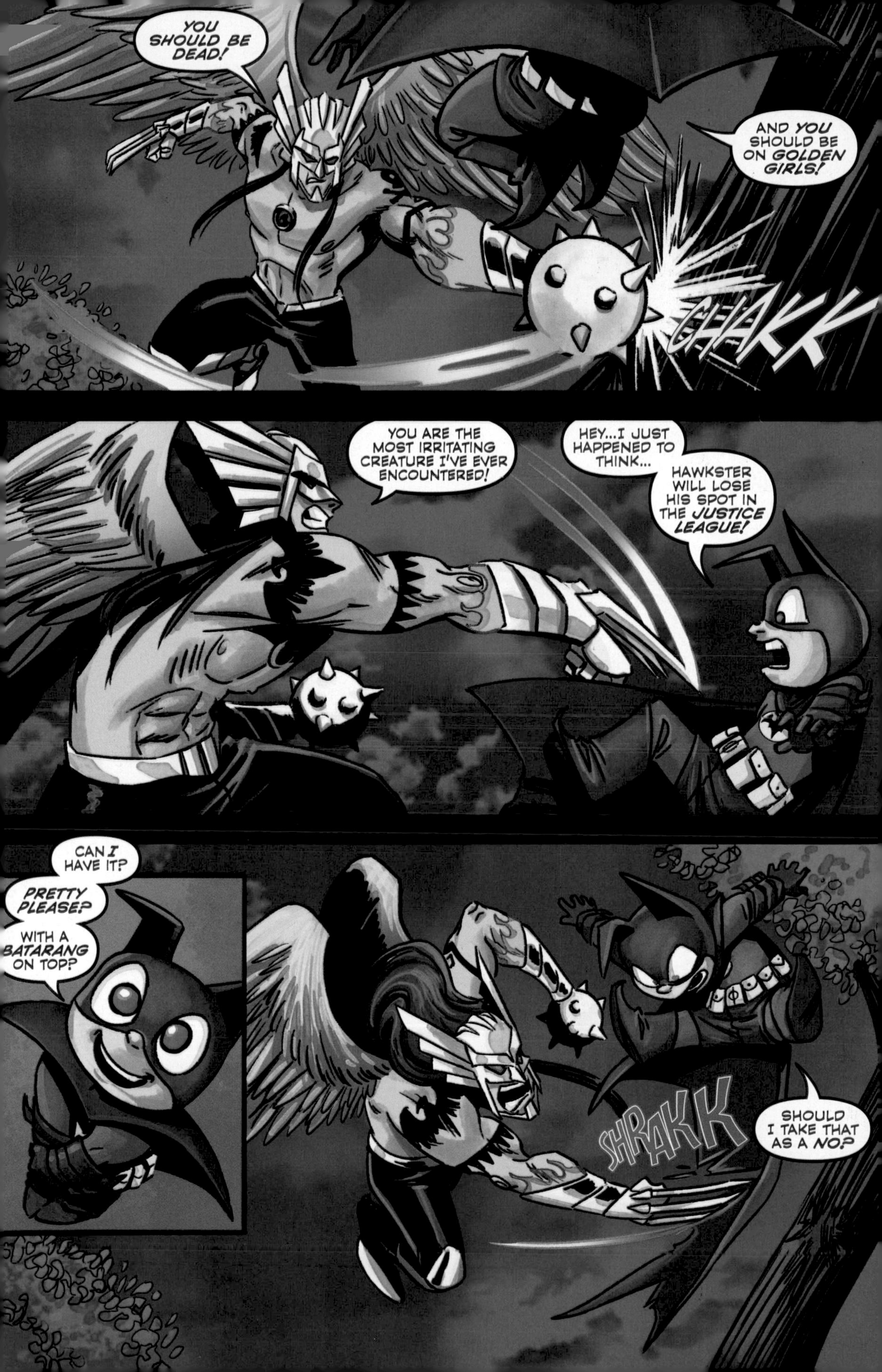
YOU SHOULD BE DEAD!
AND YOU SHOULD BE ON GOLDEN GIRLS!
CHAKK
YOU ARE THE MOST IRRITATING CREATURE I'VE EVER ENCOUNTERED!
HEY...I JUST HAPPENED TO THINK...
HAWKSTER WILL LOSE HIS SPOT IN THE JUSTICE LEAGUE!
CAN I HAVE IT?
PRETTY PLEASE?
WITH A BATARANG ON TOP?
SHRAKK
SHOULD I TAKE THAT AS A NO?

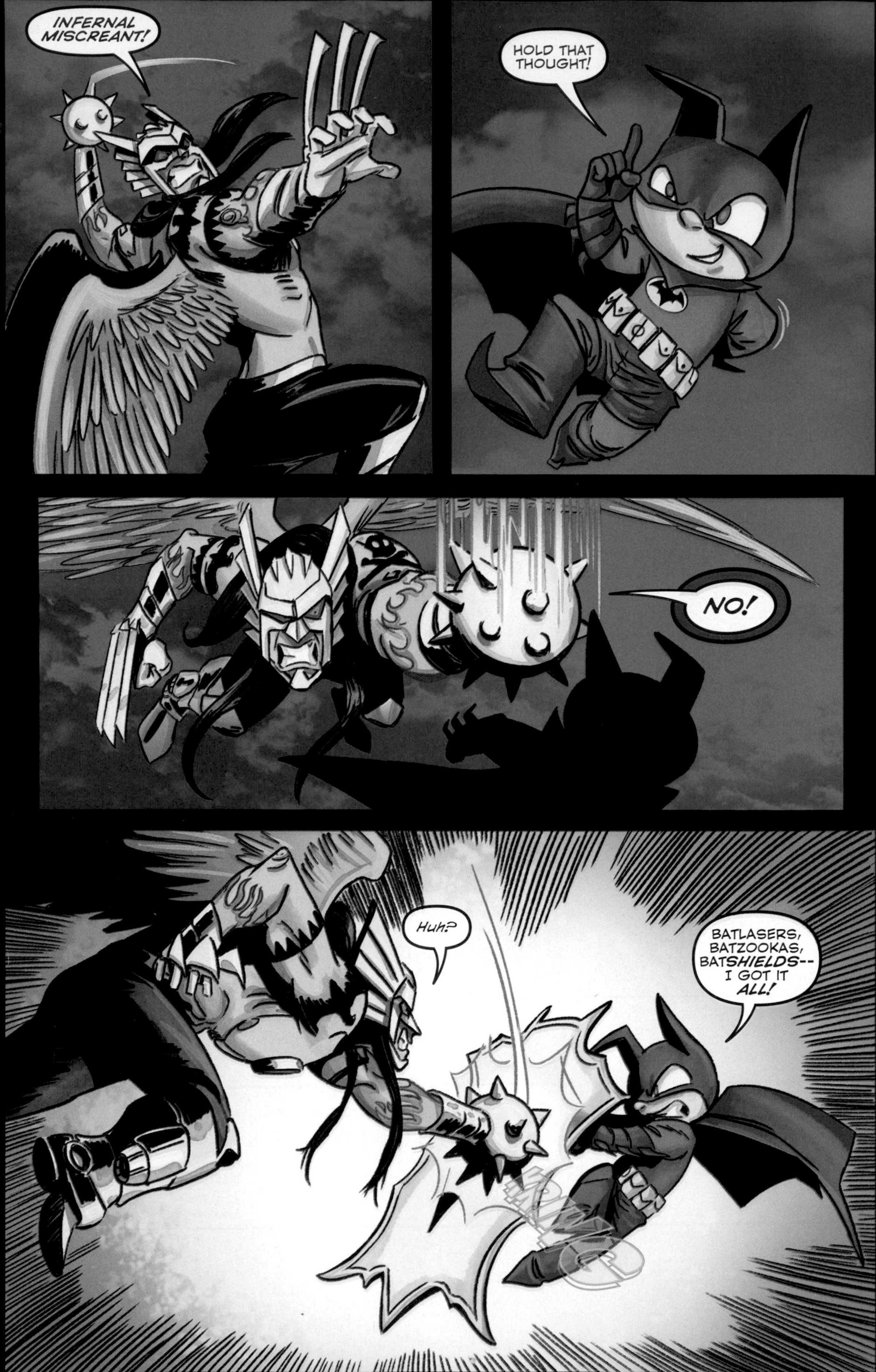
INFERNAL MISCREANT!
HOLD THAT THOUGHT!
NO!
Huh?
BATLASERS, BATZOOKAS, BATSHIELDS-- I GOT IT ALL!

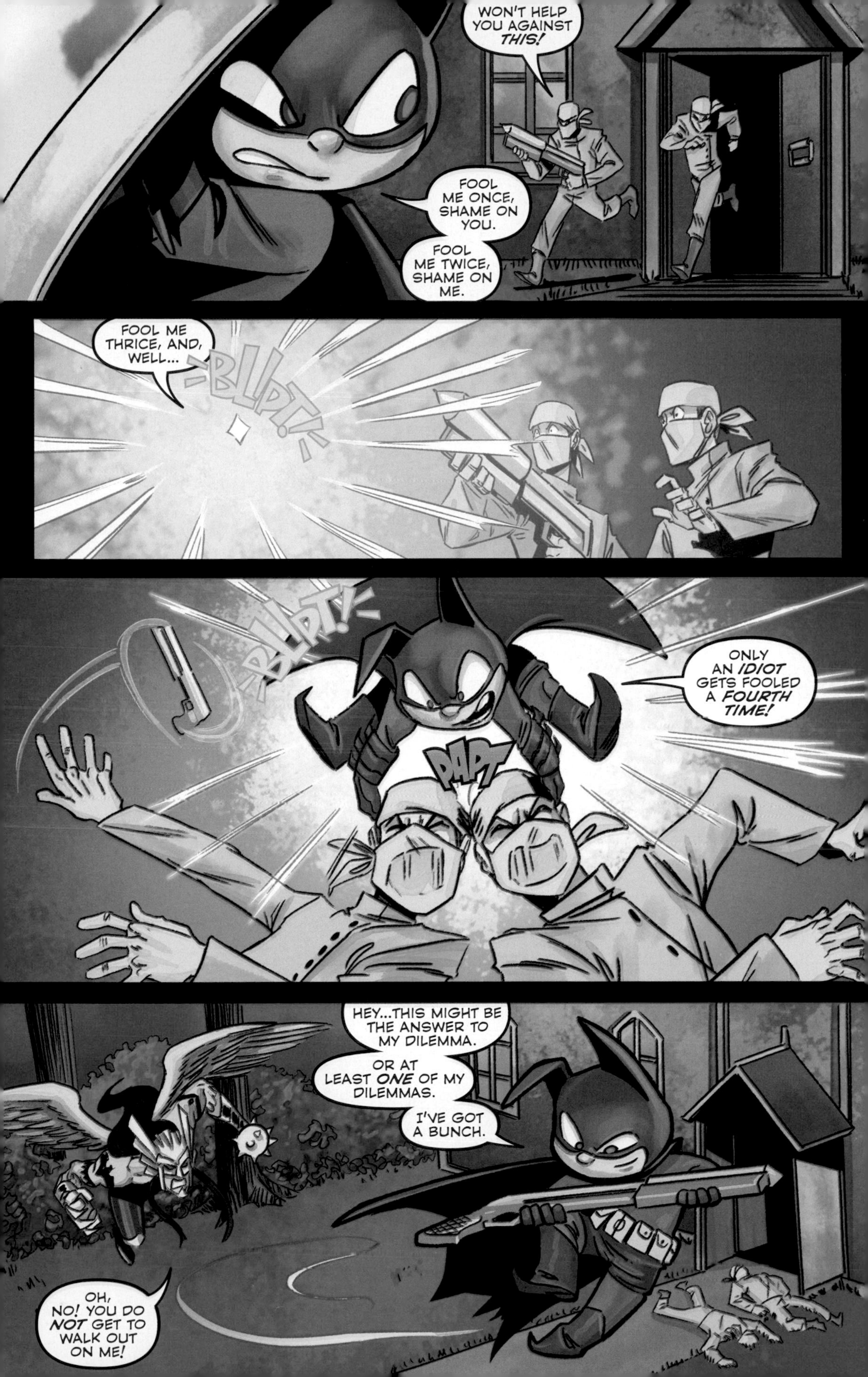
WON'T HELP YOU AGAINST *THIS!*
FOOL ME ONCE, SHAME ON YOU.
FOOL ME TWICE, SHAME ON ME.
FOOL ME THRICE, AND, WELL...
-BLIPT!
BLIPT!
ONLY AN *IDIOT* GETS FOOLED A *FOURTH TIME!*
DAPT
HEY...THIS MIGHT BE THE ANSWER TO MY DILEMMA.
OR AT LEAST *ONE* OF MY DILEMMAS.
I'VE GOT A BUNCH.
OH, NO! YOU DO ***NOT*** GET TO WALK OUT ON ME!

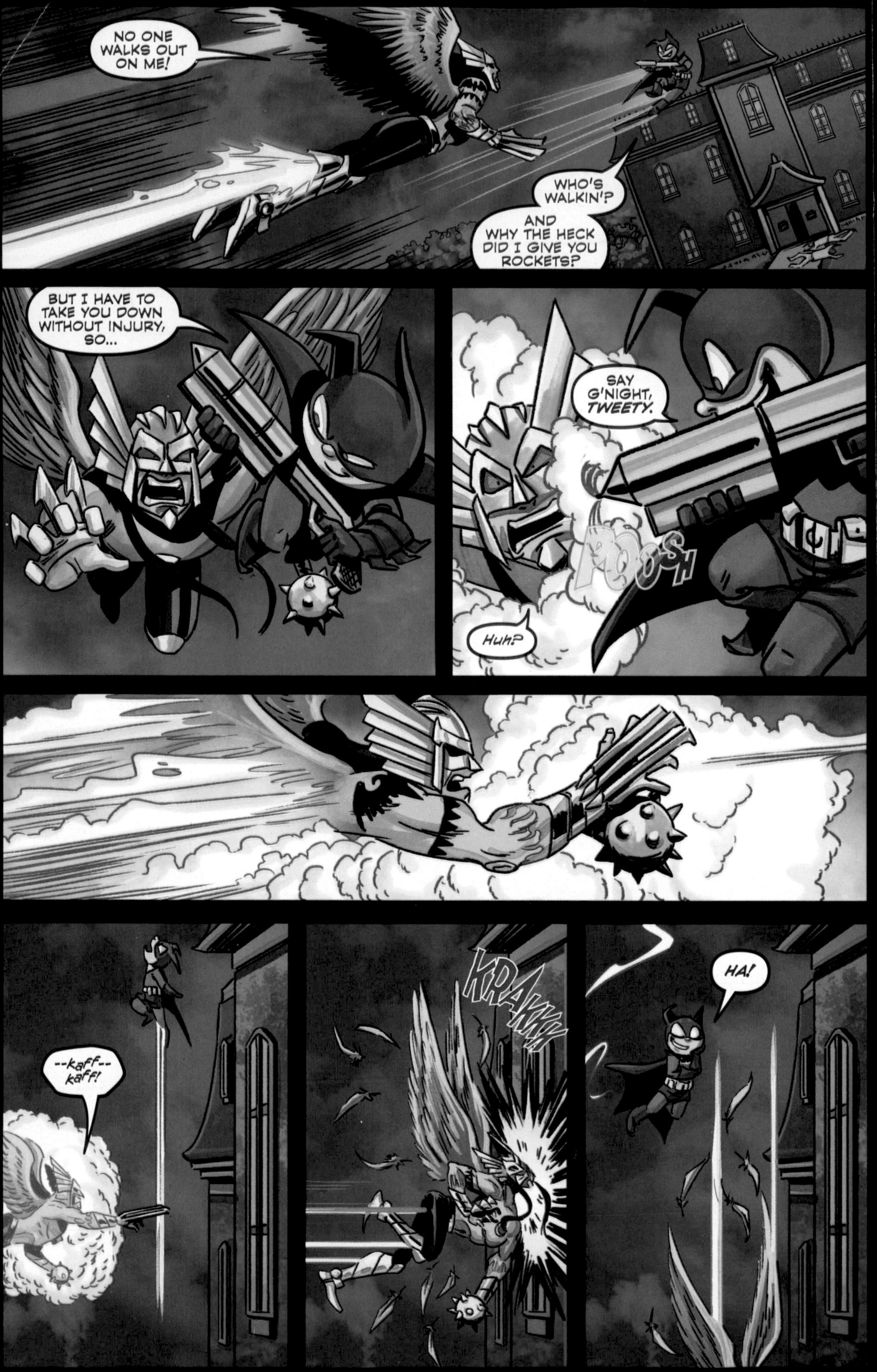
NO ONE WALKS OUT ON ME!
WHO'S WALKIN'?
AND WHY THE HECK DID I GIVE YOU ROCKETS?
BUT I HAVE TO TAKE YOU DOWN WITHOUT INJURY, SO...
SAY G'NIGHT, TWEETY.
POOSH
Huh?
--kaff-- kaff!
KRAKKK
HA!

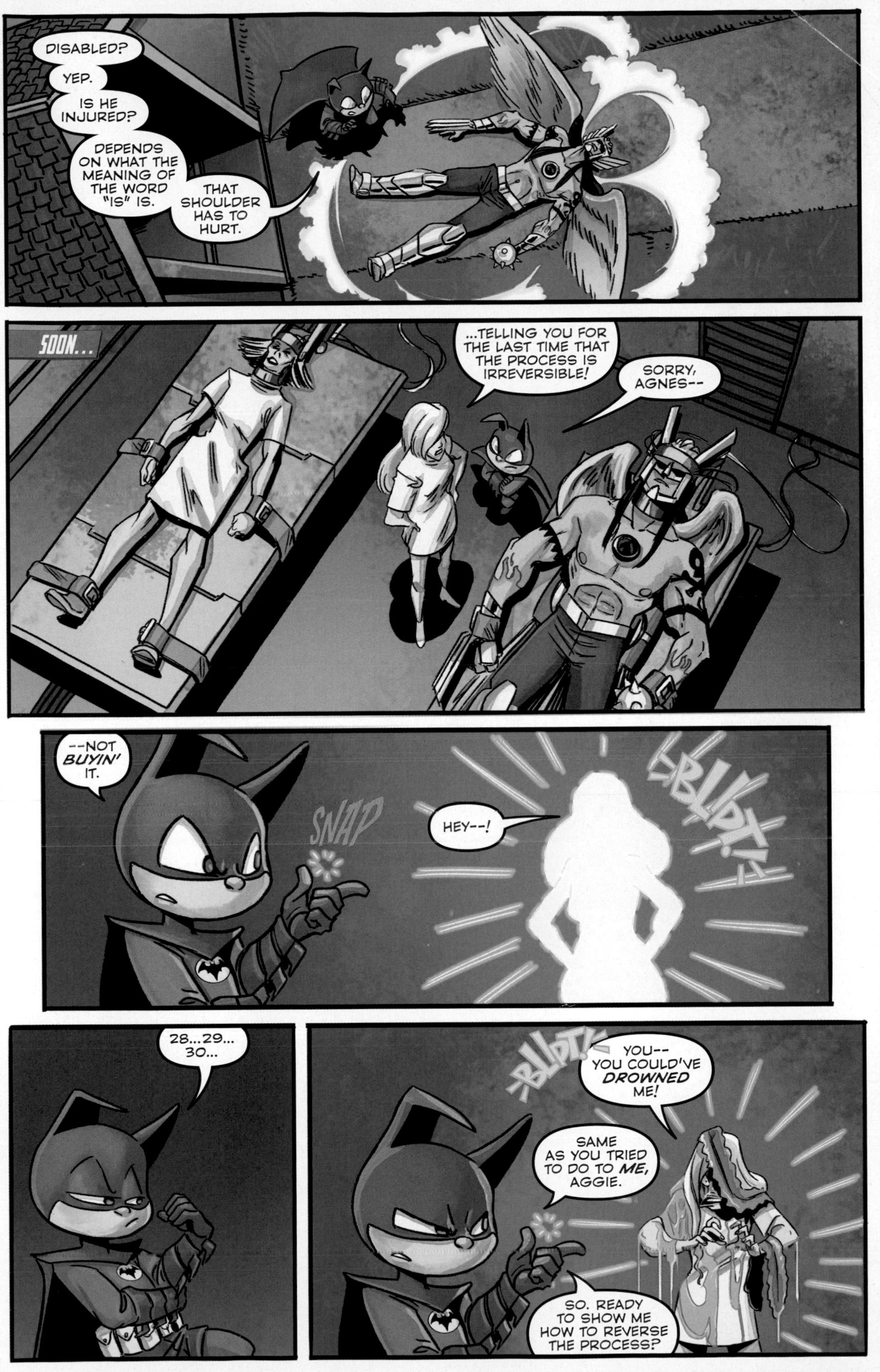

DISABLED?
YEP.
IS HE INJURED?
DEPENDS ON WHAT THE MEANING OF THE WORD "IS" IS.
THAT SHOULDER HAS TO HURT.
SOON...
...TELLING YOU FOR THE LAST TIME THAT THE PROCESS IS IRREVERSIBLE!
SORRY, AGNES--
--NOT *BUYIN'* IT.
SNAP
HEY--!
BLIPT!
28...29... 30...
BLIPT!
YOU-- YOU COULD'VE *DROWNED* ME!
SAME AS YOU TRIED TO DO TO *ME,* AGGIE.
SO. READY TO SHOW ME HOW TO REVERSE THE PROCESS?

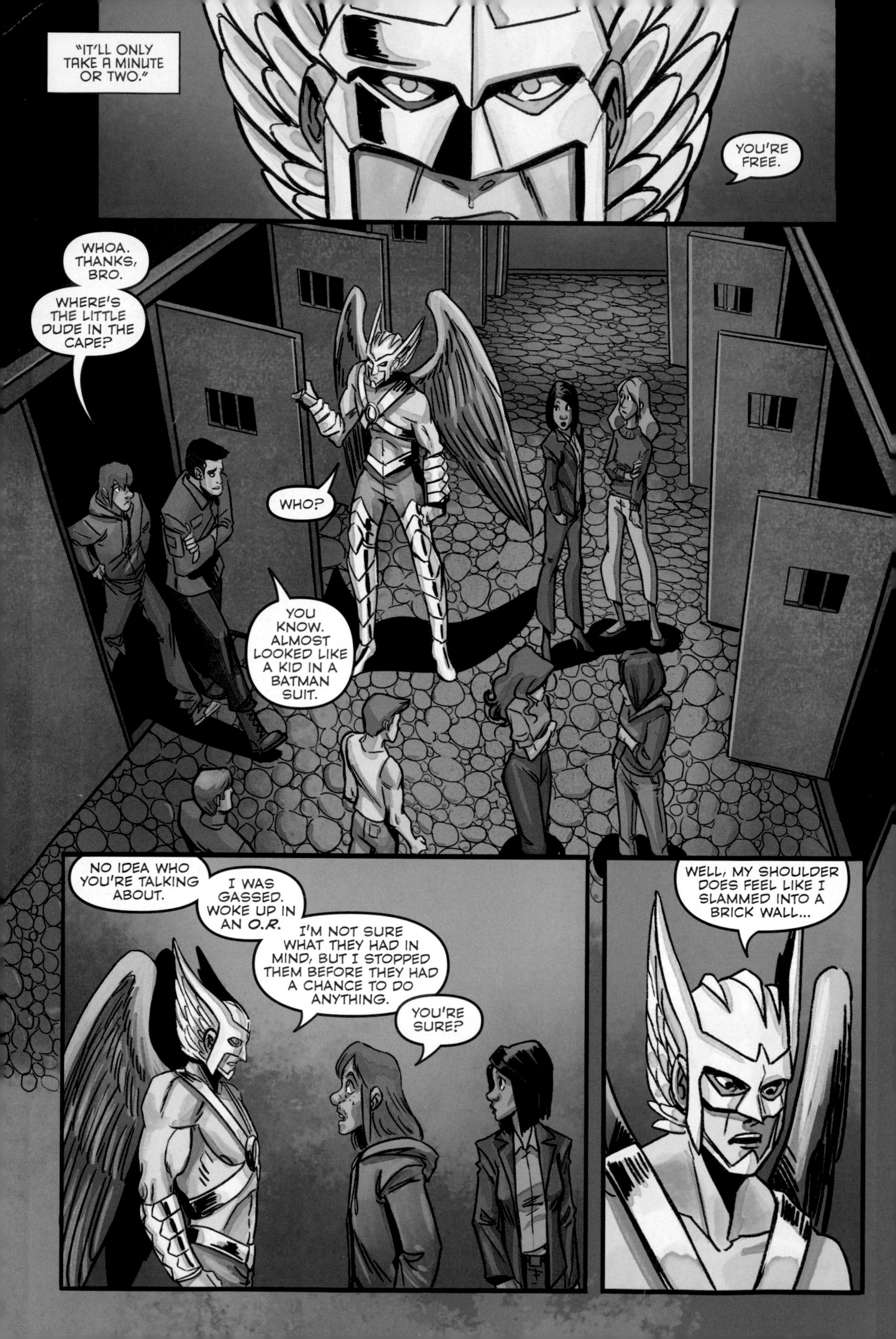
"IT'LL ONLY TAKE A MINUTE OR TWO."
YOU'RE FREE.
WHOA. THANKS, BRO.
WHERE'S THE LITTLE DUDE IN THE CAPE?
WHO?
YOU KNOW. ALMOST LOOKED LIKE A KID IN A BATMAN SUIT.
NO IDEA WHO YOU'RE TALKING ABOUT.
I WAS GASSED. WOKE UP IN AN *O.R.*
I'M NOT SURE WHAT THEY HAD IN MIND, BUT I STOPPED THEM BEFORE THEY HAD A CHANCE TO DO ANYTHING.
YOU'RE SURE?
WELL, MY SHOULDER DOES FEEL LIKE I SLAMMED INTO A BRICK WALL...

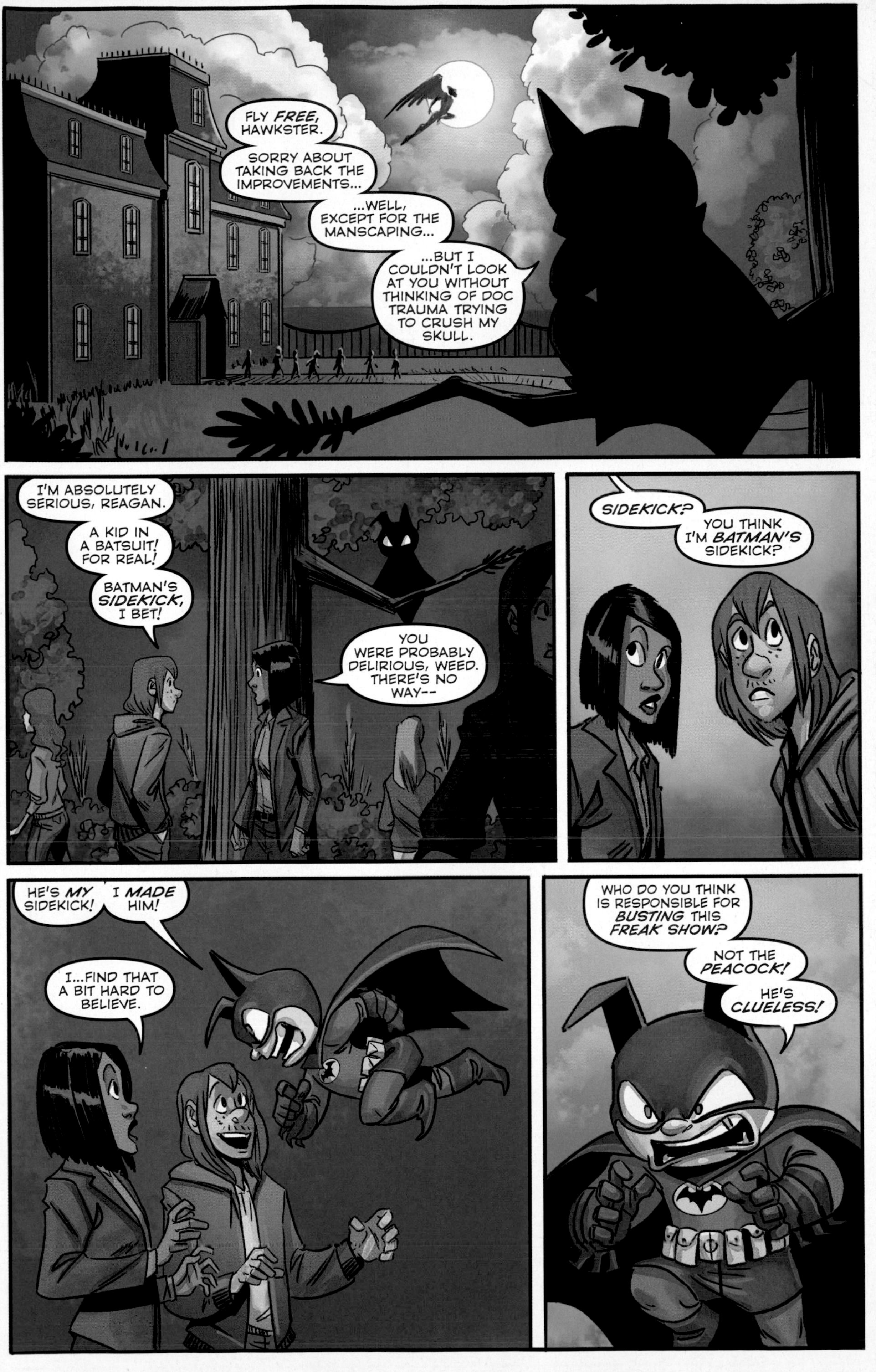
FLY FREE, HAWKSTER.
SORRY ABOUT TAKING BACK THE IMPROVEMENTS...
...WELL, EXCEPT FOR THE MANSCAPING...
...BUT I COULDN'T LOOK AT YOU WITHOUT THINKING OF DOC TRAUMA TRYING TO CRUSH MY SKULL.
I'M ABSOLUTELY SERIOUS, REAGAN.
A KID IN A BATSUIT! FOR REAL!
BATMAN'S SIDEKICK, I BET!
YOU WERE PROBABLY DELIRIOUS, WEED. THERE'S NO WAY--
SIDEKICK?
YOU THINK I'M BATMAN'S SIDEKICK?
HE'S MY SIDEKICK!
I MADE HIM!
I...FIND THAT A BIT HARD TO BELIEVE.
WHO DO YOU THINK IS RESPONSIBLE FOR BUSTING THIS FREAK SHOW?
NOT THE PEACOCK!
HE'S CLUELESS!

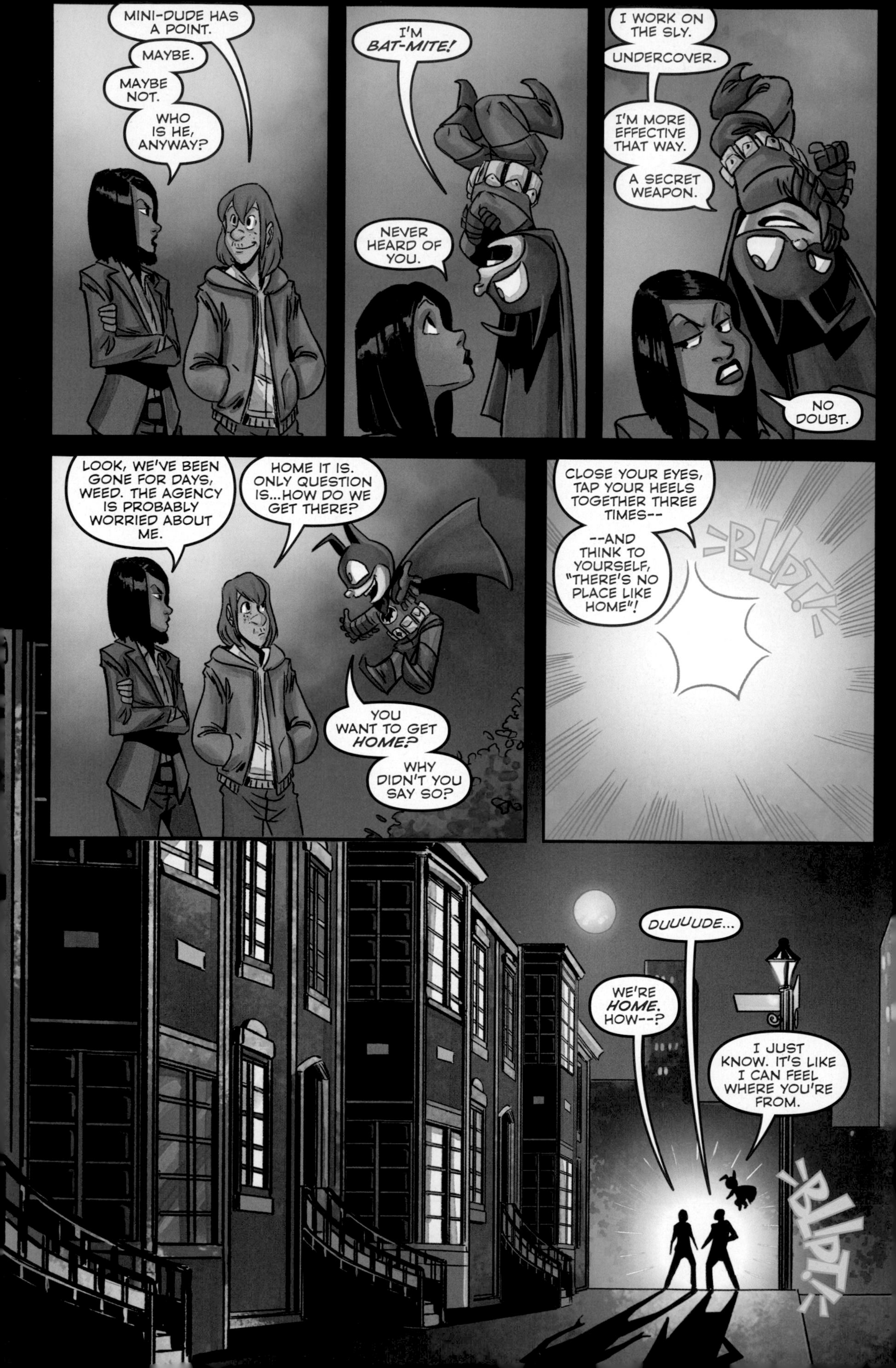

MINI-DUDE HAS A POINT.
MAYBE.
MAYBE NOT.
WHO IS HE, ANYWAY?
I'M *BAT-MITE!*
NEVER HEARD OF YOU.
I WORK ON THE SLY.
UNDERCOVER.
I'M MORE EFFECTIVE THAT WAY.
A SECRET WEAPON.
NO DOUBT.
LOOK, WE'VE BEEN GONE FOR DAYS, WEED. THE AGENCY IS PROBABLY WORRIED ABOUT ME.
HOME IT IS. ONLY QUESTION IS...HOW DO WE GET THERE?
YOU WANT TO GET *HOME?*
WHY DIDN'T YOU SAY SO?
CLOSE YOUR EYES, TAP YOUR HEELS TOGETHER THREE TIMES--
--AND THINK TO YOURSELF, "THERE'S NO PLACE LIKE HOME"!
-BLIPT!-
DUUUUDE...
WE'RE *HOME.* HOW--?
I JUST KNOW. IT'S LIKE I CAN FEEL WHERE YOU'RE FROM.
-BLIPT!-

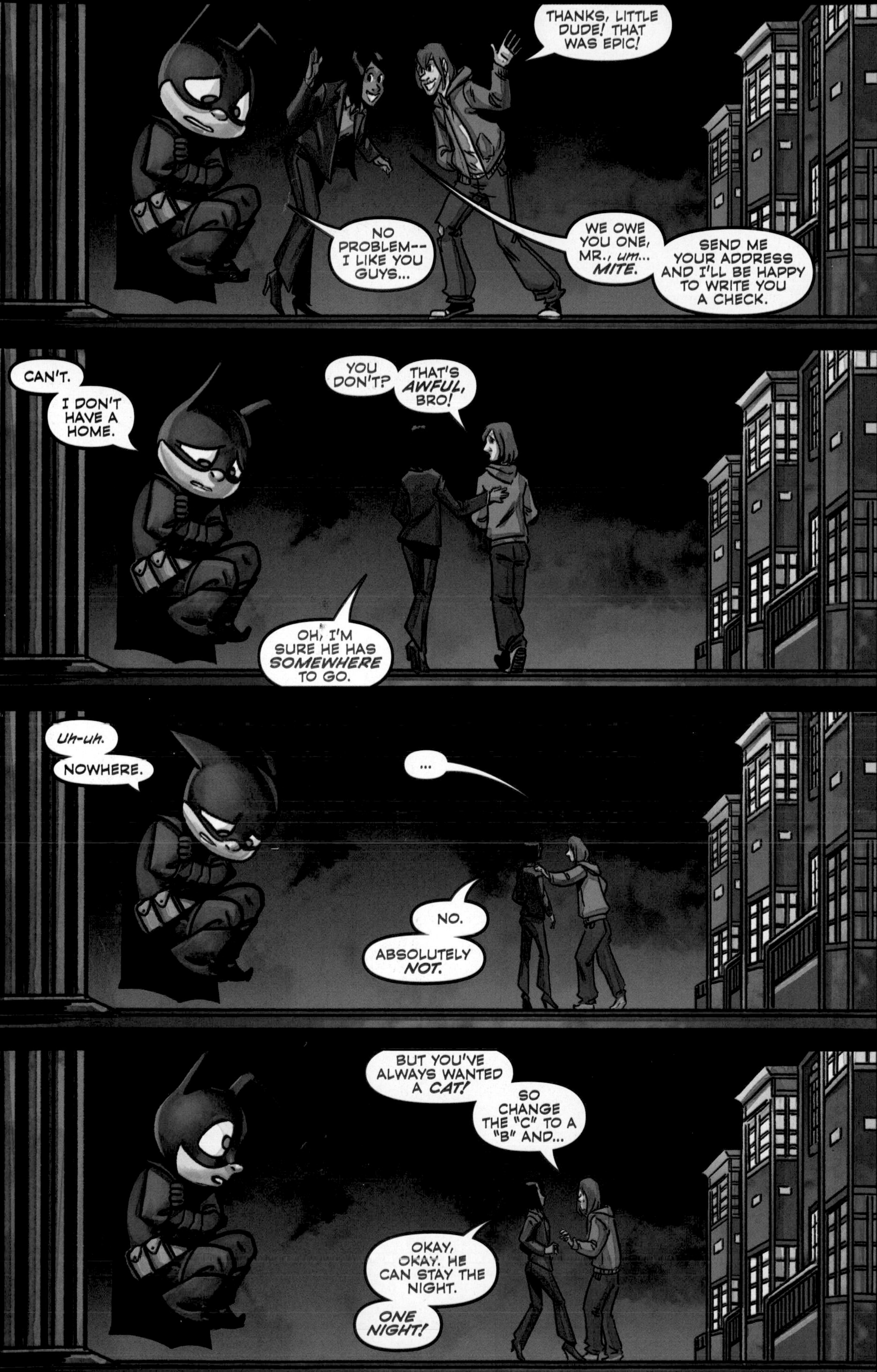
THANKS, LITTLE DUDE! THAT WAS EPIC!
NO PROBLEM-- I LIKE YOU GUYS...
WE OWE YOU ONE, MR., *um*... *MITE*.
SEND ME YOUR ADDRESS AND I'LL BE HAPPY TO WRITE YOU A CHECK.
CAN'T.
I DON'T HAVE A HOME.
YOU DON'T?
THAT'S *AWFUL*, BRO!
OH, I'M SURE HE HAS *SOMEWHERE* TO GO.
Uh-uh.
NOWHERE.
...
NO.
ABSOLUTELY *NOT*.
BUT YOU'VE ALWAYS WANTED A *CAT!*
SO CHANGE THE "C" TO A "B" AND...
OKAY, OKAY. HE CAN STAY THE NIGHT.
ONE NIGHT!

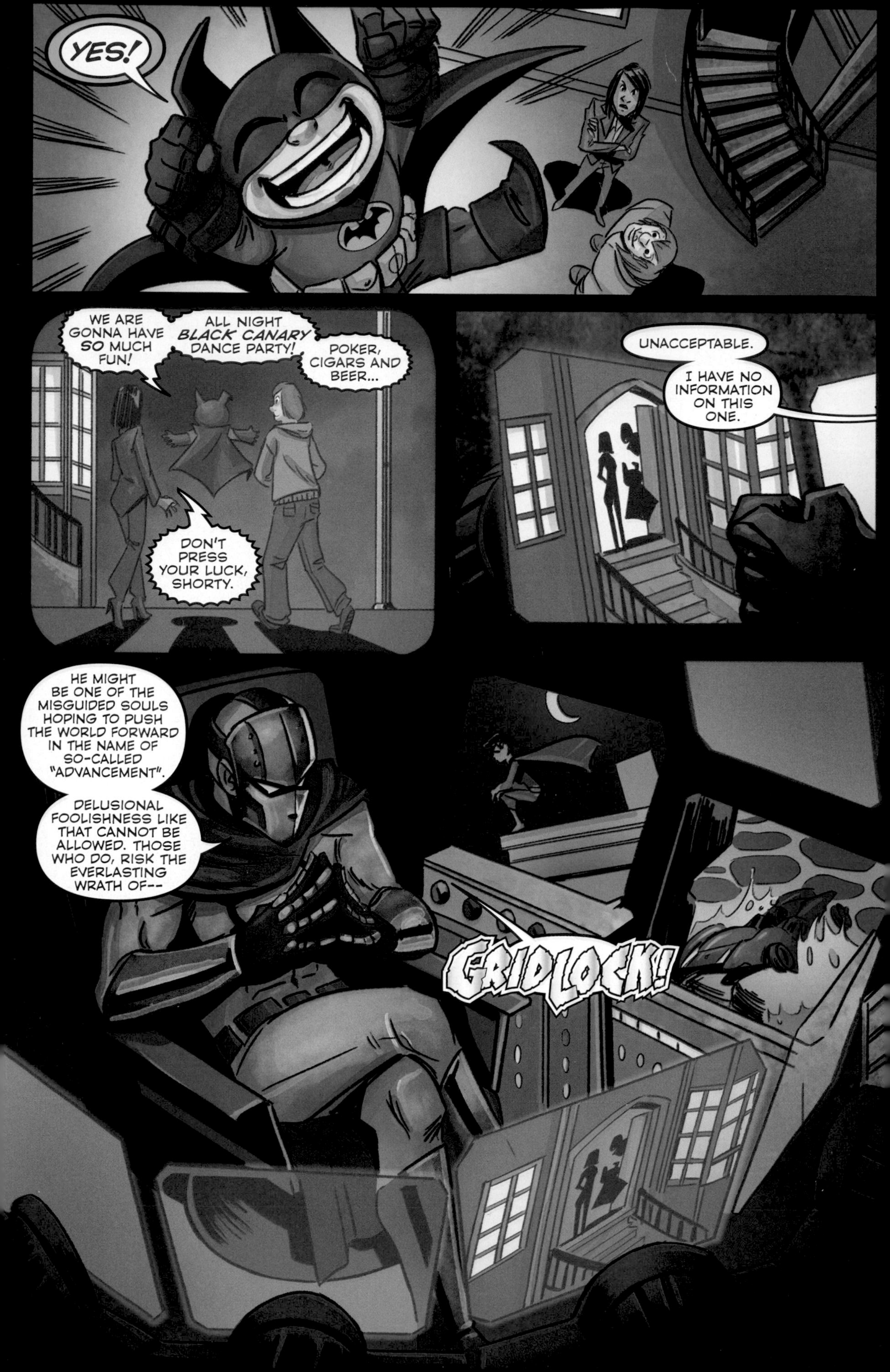
YES!
WE ARE GONNA HAVE SO MUCH FUN!
ALL NIGHT BLACK CANARY DANCE PARTY!
POKER, CIGARS AND BEER...
DON'T PRESS YOUR LUCK, SHORTY.
UNACCEPTABLE.
I HAVE NO INFORMATION ON THIS ONE.
HE MIGHT BE ONE OF THE MISGUIDED SOULS HOPING TO PUSH THE WORLD FORWARD IN THE NAME OF SO-CALLED "ADVANCEMENT".
DELUSIONAL FOOLISHNESS LIKE THAT CANNOT BE ALLOWED. THOSE WHO DO, RISK THE EVERLASTING WRATH OF--
GRIDLOCK!

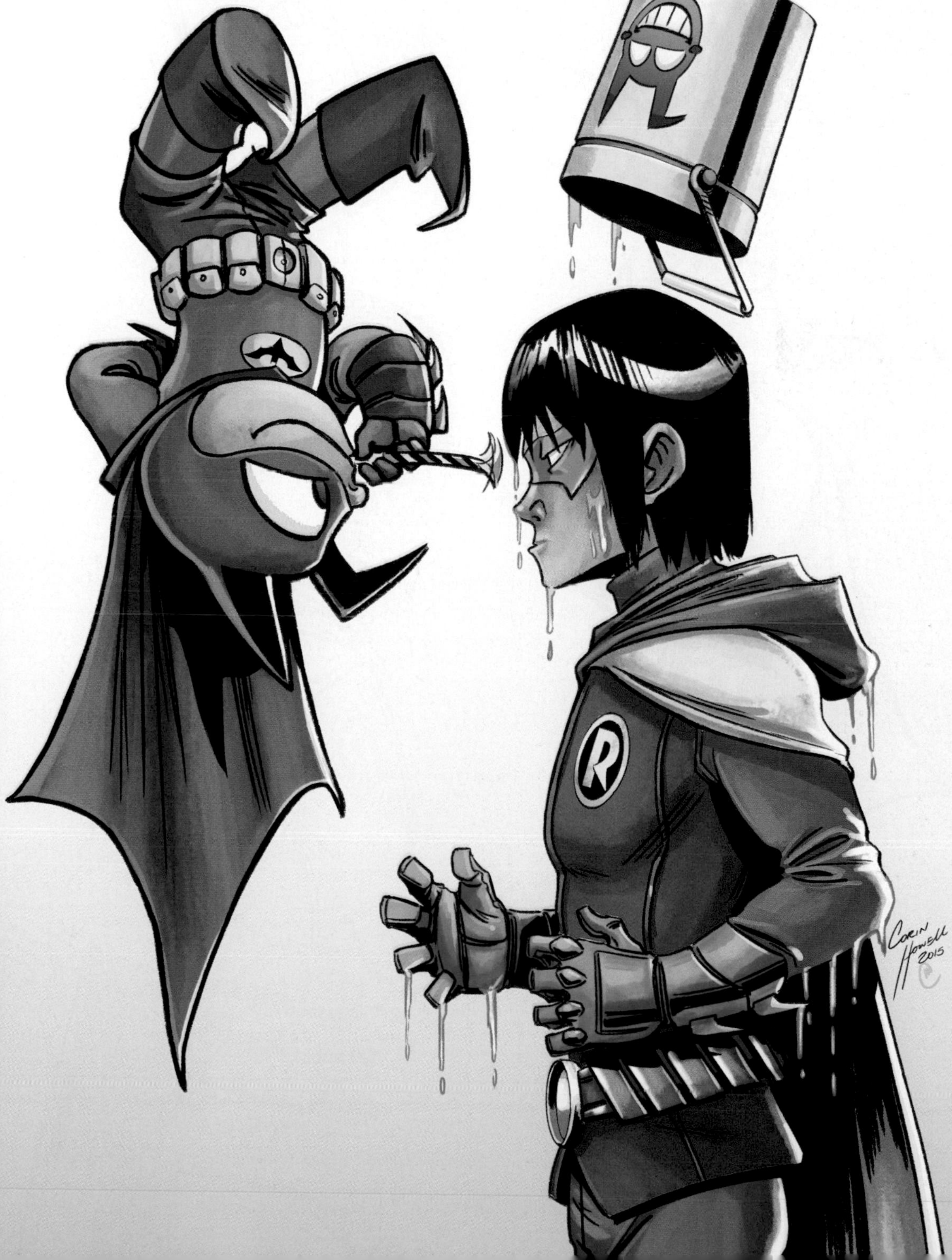
CORIN HOWELL 2015

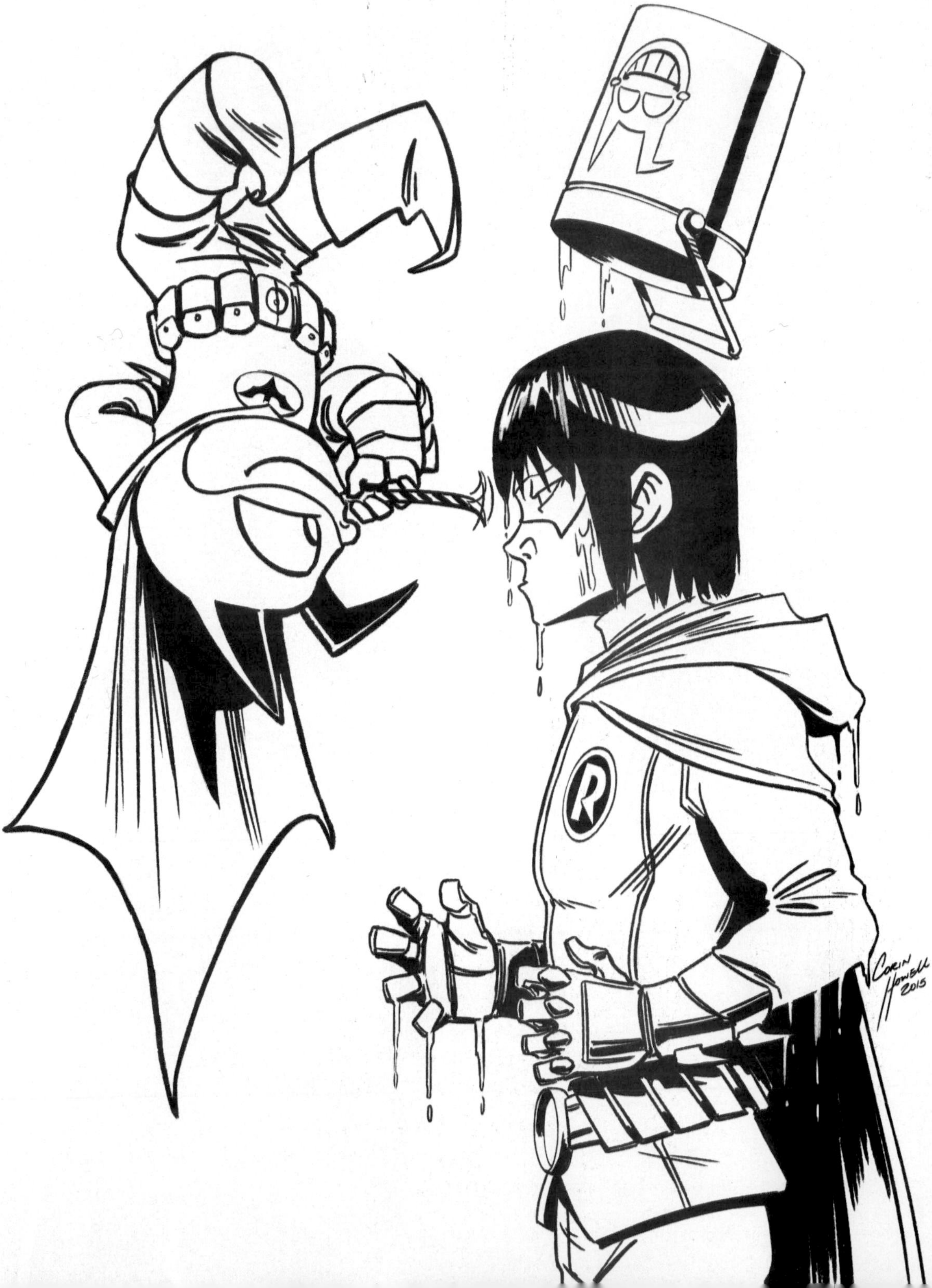
CORIN HOWELL 2015

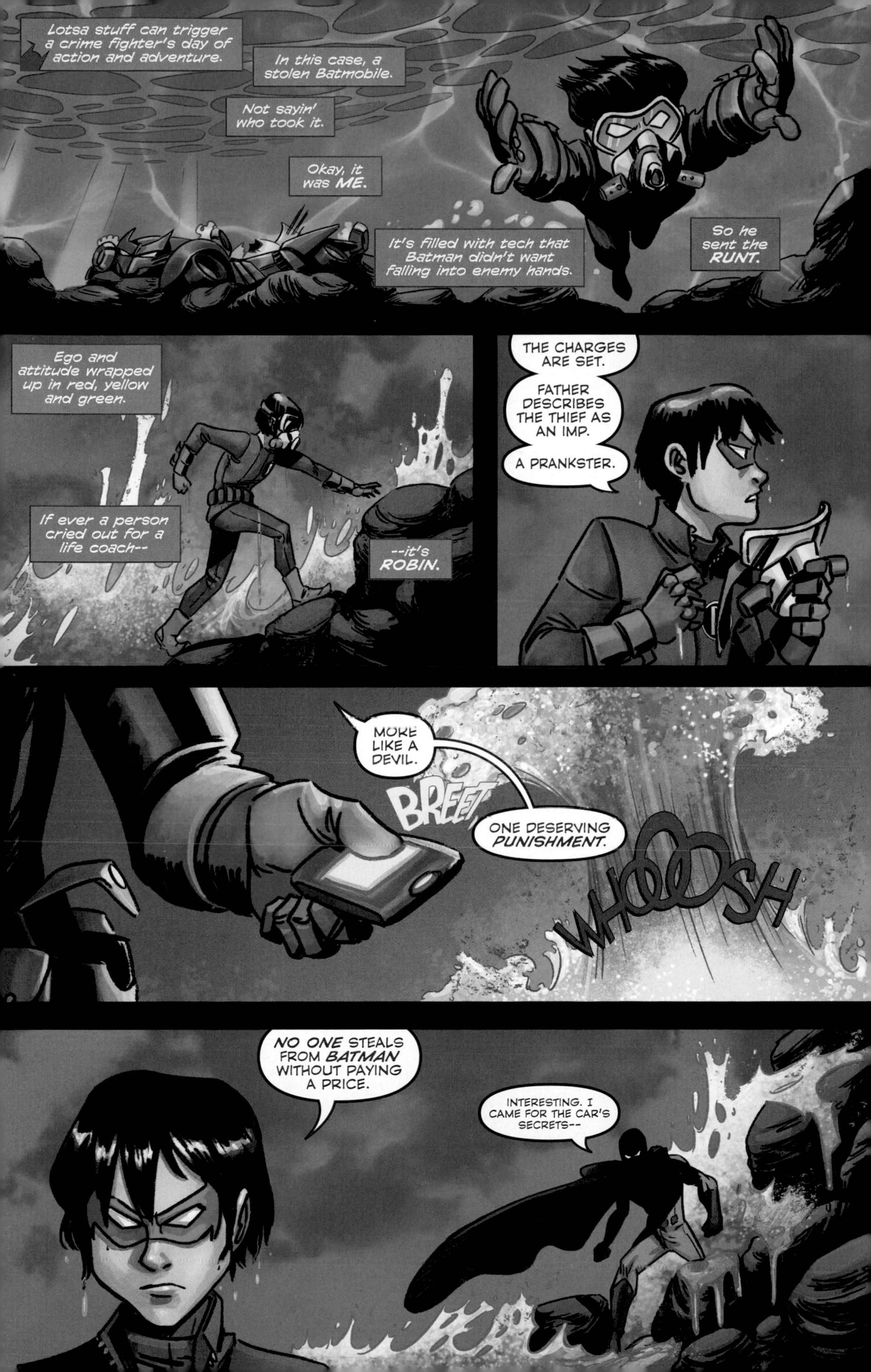

Lotsa stuff can trigger a crime fighter's day of action and adventure.
In this case, a stolen Batmobile.
Not sayin' who took it.
Okay, it was ME.
It's filled with tech that Batman didn't want falling into enemy hands.
So he sent the RUNT.
Ego and attitude wrapped up in red, yellow and green.
If ever a person cried out for a life coach--
--it's ROBIN.
THE CHARGES ARE SET.
FATHER DESCRIBES THE THIEF AS AN IMP.
A PRANKSTER.
MORE LIKE A DEVIL.
BREET
ONE DESERVING PUNISHMENT.
WHOOOSH
NO ONE STEALS FROM BATMAN WITHOUT PAYING A PRICE.
INTERESTING. I CAME FOR THE CAR'S SECRETS--

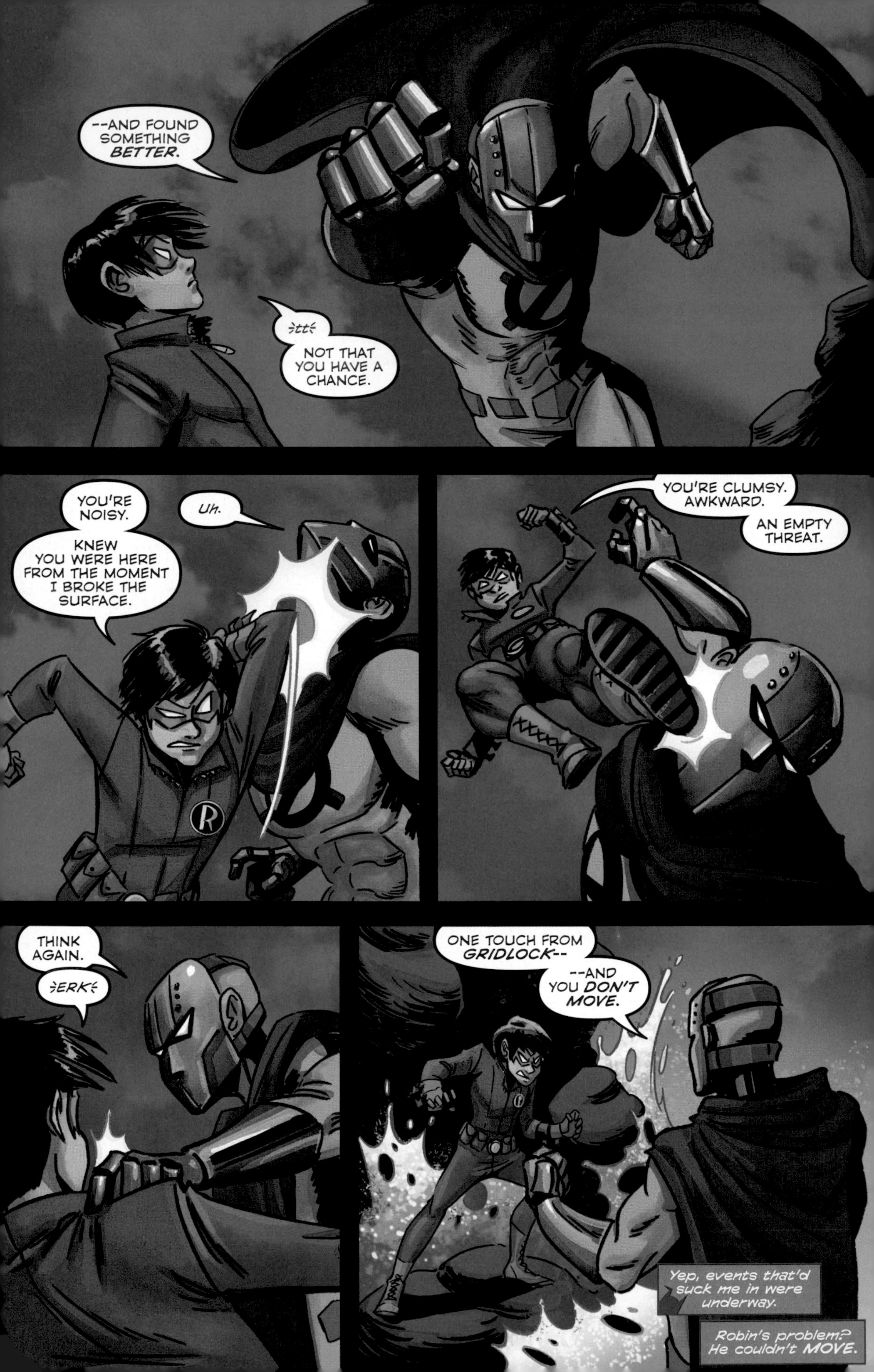
--AND FOUND SOMETHING *BETTER*.
TT
NOT THAT YOU HAVE A CHANCE.
YOU'RE NOISY.
Uh.
KNEW YOU WERE HERE FROM THE MOMENT I BROKE THE SURFACE.
YOU'RE CLUMSY. AWKWARD.
AN EMPTY THREAT.
THINK AGAIN.
ERK
ONE TOUCH FROM *GRIDLOCK*--
--AND YOU *DON'T MOVE*.
Yep, events that'd suck me in were underway.
Robin's problem? He couldn't **MOVE**.

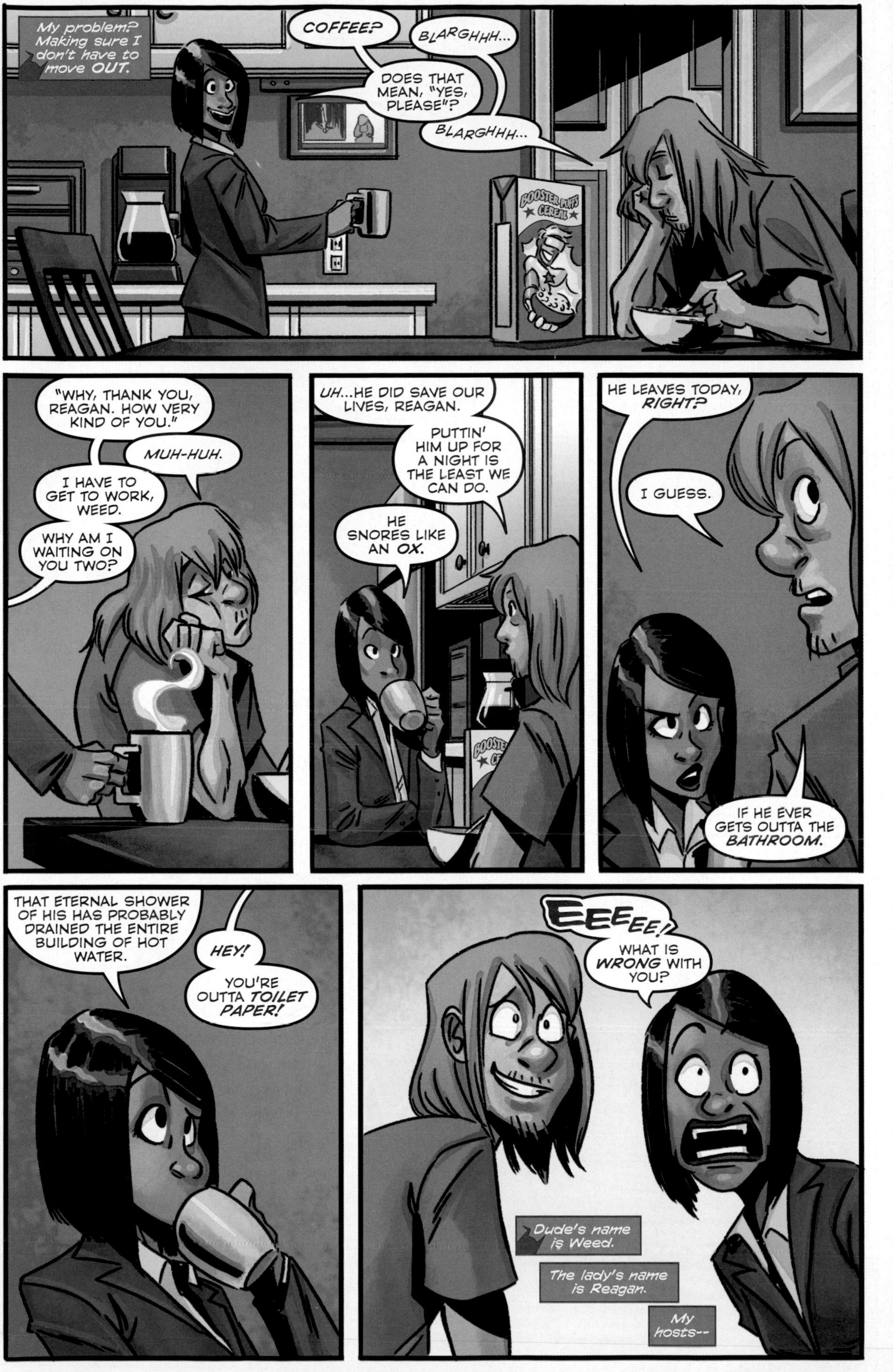
My problem? Making sure I don't have to move OUT.
COFFEE?
BLARGHHH...
DOES THAT MEAN, "YES, PLEASE"?
BLARGHHH...
BOOSTER PUFFS CEREAL
"WHY, THANK YOU, REAGAN. HOW VERY KIND OF YOU."
MUH-HUH.
I HAVE TO GET TO WORK, WEED.
WHY AM I WAITING ON YOU TWO?
UH...HE DID SAVE OUR LIVES, REAGAN.
PUTTIN' HIM UP FOR A NIGHT IS THE LEAST WE CAN DO.
HE SNORES LIKE AN OX.
HE LEAVES TODAY, RIGHT?
I GUESS.
IF HE EVER GETS OUTTA THE BATHROOM.
THAT ETERNAL SHOWER OF HIS HAS PROBABLY DRAINED THE ENTIRE BUILDING OF HOT WATER.
HEY!
YOU'RE OUTTA TOILET PAPER!
EEEEEE!
WHAT IS WRONG WITH YOU?
Dude's name is Weed.
The lady's name is Reagan.
My hosts--

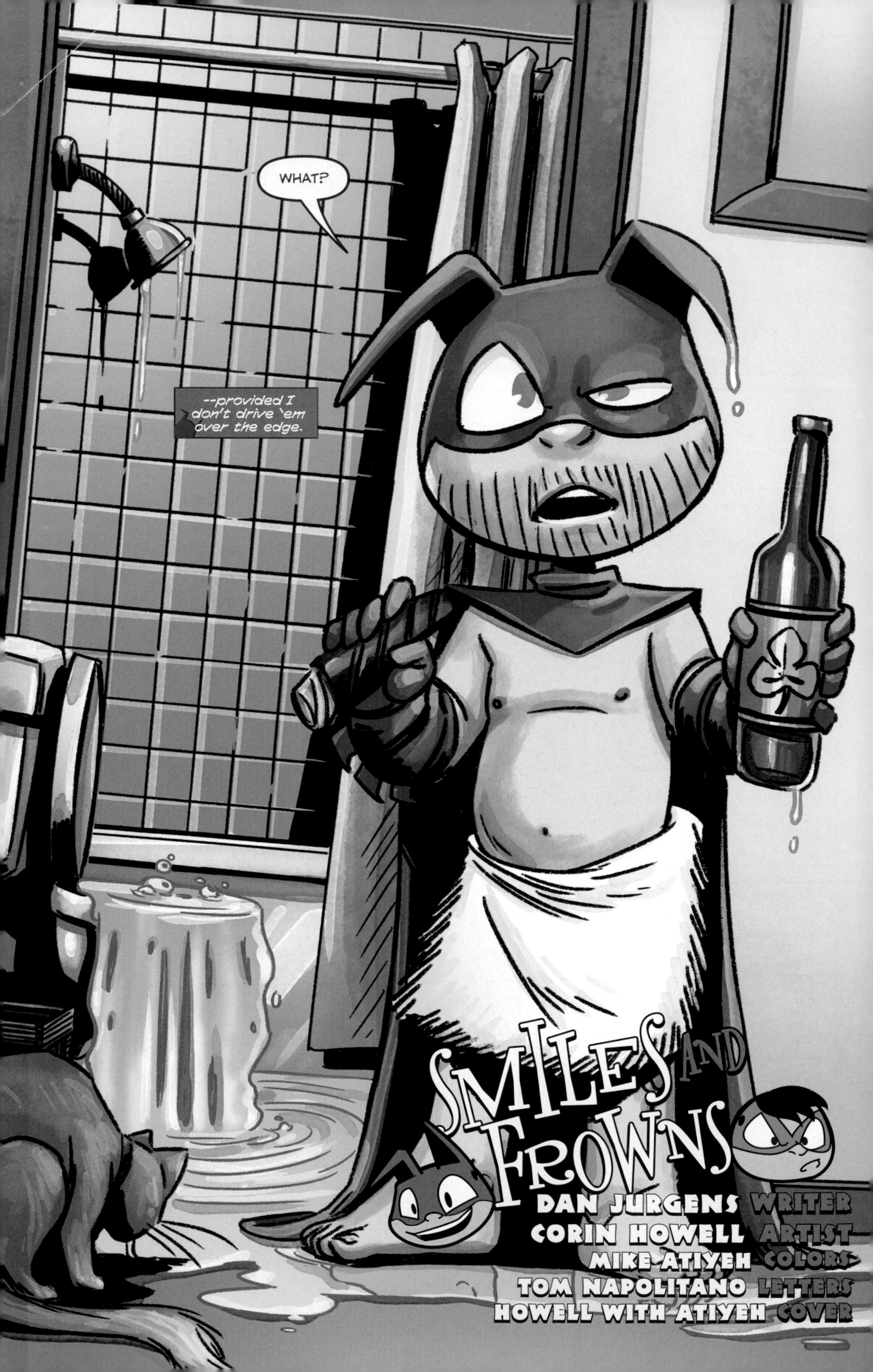
WHAT?
--provided I don't drive 'em over the edge.
SMILES AND FROWNS
DAN JURGENS WRITER
CORIN HOWELL ARTIST
MIKE ATIYEH COLORS
TOM NAPOLITANO LETTERS
HOWELL WITH ATIYEH COVER

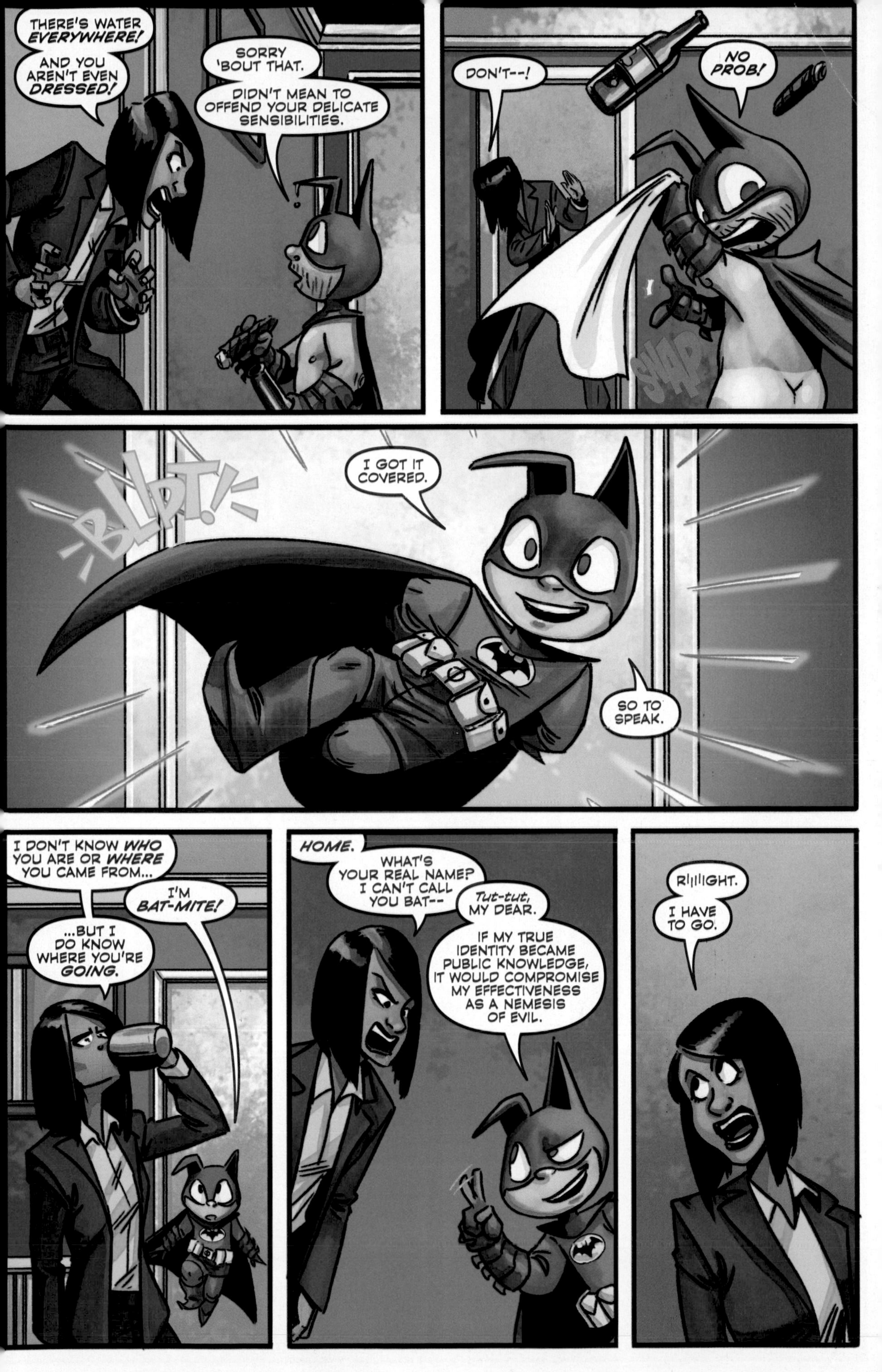

THERE'S WATER *EVERYWHERE!*
AND YOU AREN'T EVEN *DRESSED!*
SORRY 'BOUT THAT.
DIDN'T MEAN TO OFFEND YOUR DELICATE SENSIBILITIES.
DON'T--!
NO PROB!
SNAP
BLIPT!
I GOT IT COVERED.
SO TO SPEAK.
I DON'T KNOW *WHO* YOU ARE OR *WHERE* YOU CAME FROM...
I'M *BAT-MITE!*
...BUT I DO KNOW WHERE YOU'RE *GOING.*
HOME.
WHAT'S YOUR REAL NAME? I CAN'T CALL YOU BAT--
Tut-tut, MY DEAR.
IF MY TRUE IDENTITY BECAME PUBLIC KNOWLEDGE, IT WOULD COMPROMISE MY EFFECTIVENESS AS A NEMESIS OF EVIL.
RIIIIGHT.
I HAVE TO GO.

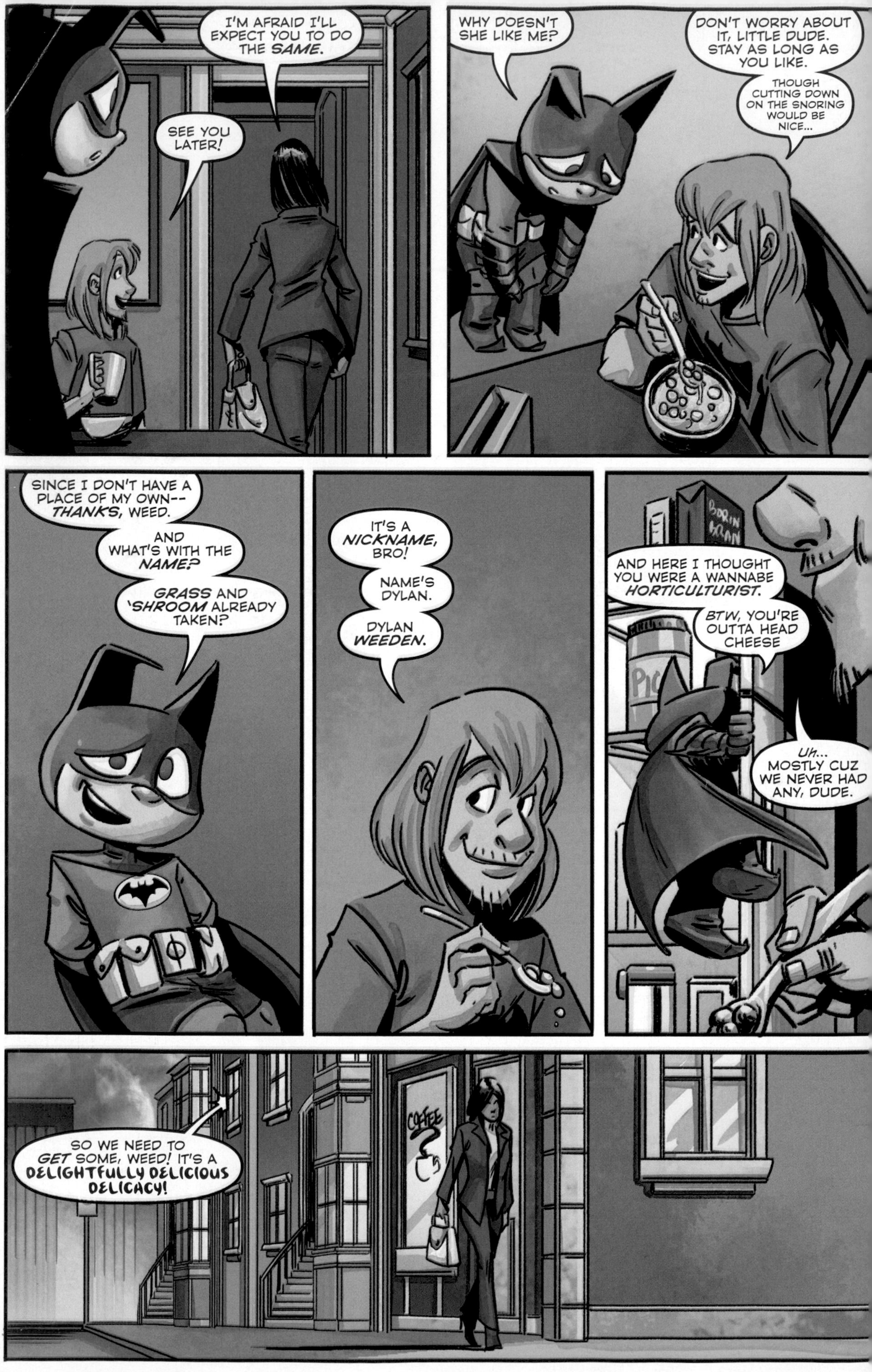

I'M AFRAID I'LL EXPECT YOU TO DO THE SAME.
SEE YOU LATER!
WHY DOESN'T SHE LIKE ME?
DON'T WORRY ABOUT IT, LITTLE DUDE. STAY AS LONG AS YOU LIKE.
THOUGH CUTTING DOWN ON THE SNORING WOULD BE NICE...
SINCE I DON'T HAVE A PLACE OF MY OWN-- THANKS, WEED.
AND WHAT'S WITH THE NAME?
GRASS AND 'SHROOM ALREADY TAKEN?
IT'S A NICKNAME, BRO!
NAME'S DYLAN.
DYLAN WEEDEN.
AND HERE I THOUGHT YOU WERE A WANNABE HORTICULTURIST.
BTW, YOU'RE OUTTA HEAD CHEESE
Uh... MOSTLY CUZ WE NEVER HAD ANY, DUDE.
SO WE NEED TO GET SOME, WEED! IT'S A DELIGHTFULLY DELICIOUS DELICACY!
COFFEE

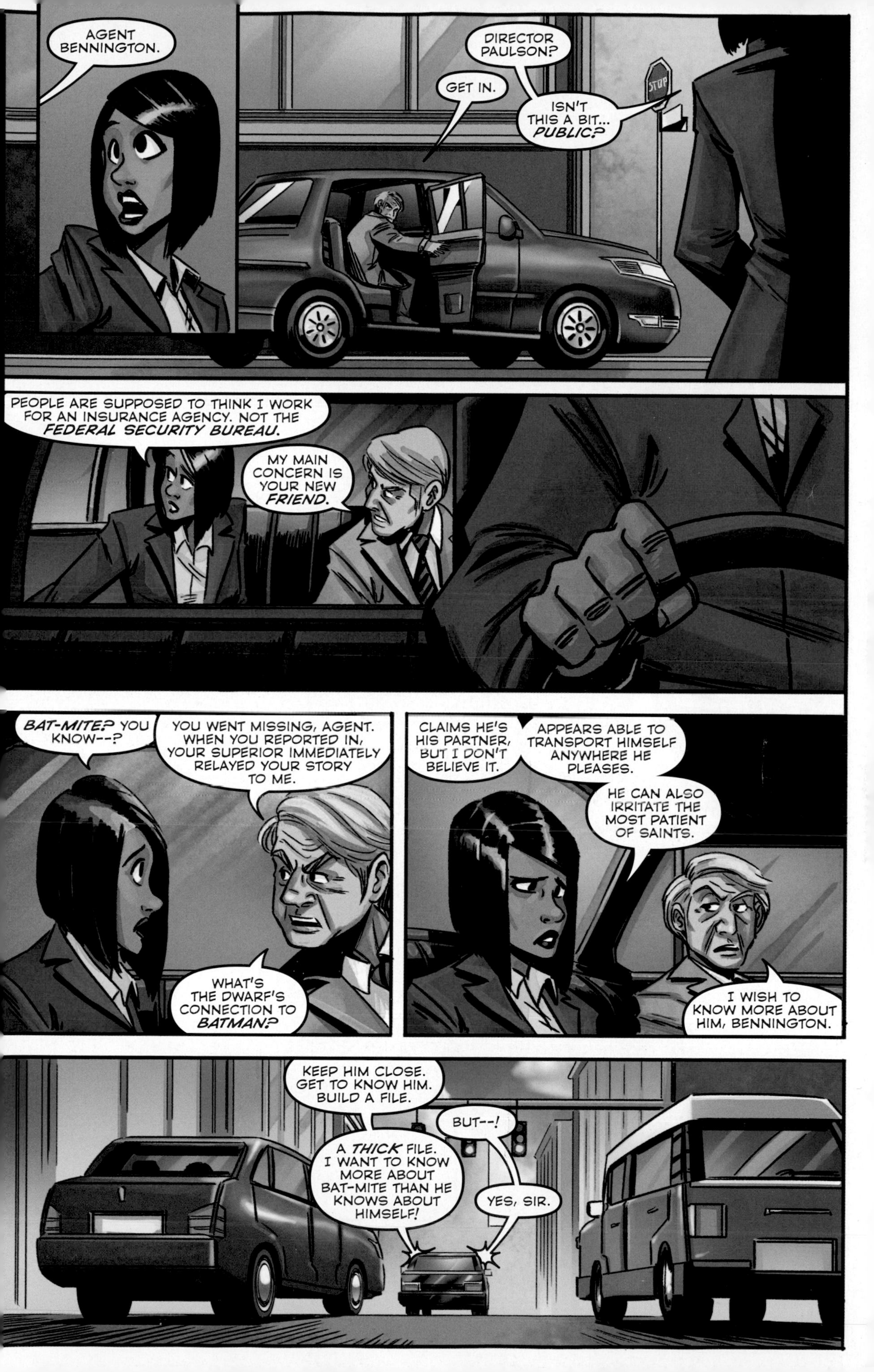
AGENT BENNINGTON.
DIRECTOR PAULSON?
GET IN.
ISN'T THIS A BIT... *PUBLIC?*
PEOPLE ARE SUPPOSED TO THINK I WORK FOR AN INSURANCE AGENCY. NOT THE *FEDERAL SECURITY BUREAU.*
MY MAIN CONCERN IS YOUR NEW *FRIEND.*
BAT-MITE? YOU KNOW--?
YOU WENT MISSING, AGENT. WHEN YOU REPORTED IN, YOUR SUPERIOR IMMEDIATELY RELAYED YOUR STORY TO ME.
WHAT'S THE DWARF'S CONNECTION TO *BATMAN?*
CLAIMS HE'S HIS PARTNER, BUT I DON'T BELIEVE IT.
APPEARS ABLE TO TRANSPORT HIMSELF ANYWHERE HE PLEASES.
HE CAN ALSO IRRITATE THE MOST PATIENT OF SAINTS.
I WISH TO KNOW MORE ABOUT HIM, BENNINGTON.
KEEP HIM CLOSE. GET TO KNOW HIM. BUILD A FILE.
BUT--!
A *THICK* FILE. I WANT TO KNOW MORE ABOUT BAT-MITE THAN HE KNOWS ABOUT HIMSELF!
YES, SIR.

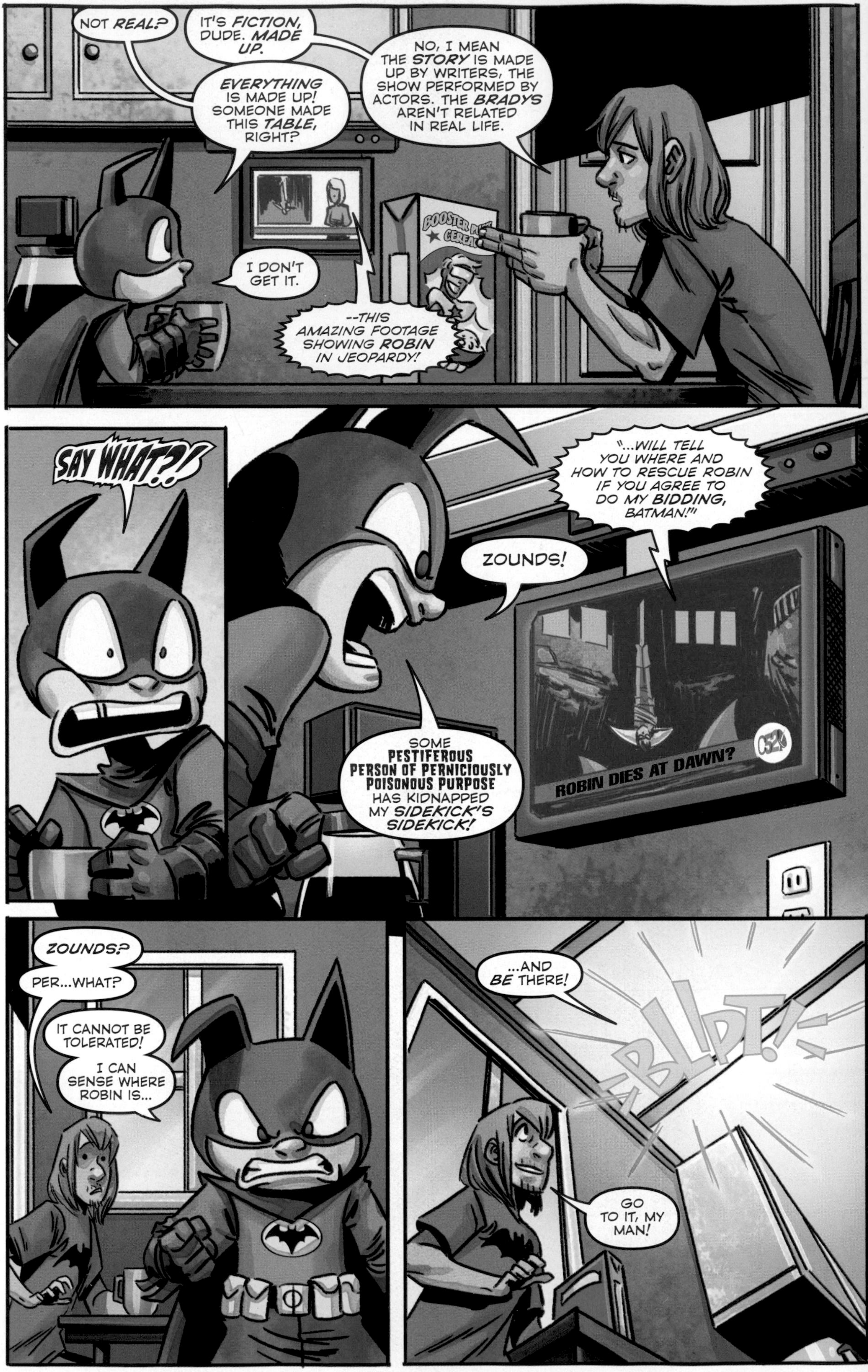

NOT REAL?
IT'S FICTION, DUDE. MADE UP.
EVERYTHING IS MADE UP! SOMEONE MADE THIS TABLE, RIGHT?
NO, I MEAN THE STORY IS MADE UP BY WRITERS, THE SHOW PERFORMED BY ACTORS. THE BRADYS AREN'T RELATED IN REAL LIFE.
BOOSTER PUFF CEREAL
I DON'T GET IT.
--THIS AMAZING FOOTAGE SHOWING ROBIN IN JEOPARDY!
SAY WHAT?!
"...WILL TELL YOU WHERE AND HOW TO RESCUE ROBIN IF YOU AGREE TO DO MY BIDDING, BATMAN!"
ZOUNDS!
ROBIN DIES AT DAWN?
SOME PESTIFEROUS PERSON OF PERNICIOUSLY POISONOUS PURPOSE HAS KIDNAPPED MY SIDEKICK'S SIDEKICK!
ZOUNDS?
PER...WHAT?
IT CANNOT BE TOLERATED!
I CAN SENSE WHERE ROBIN IS...
...AND BE THERE!
BLIPT!
GO TO IT, MY MAN!

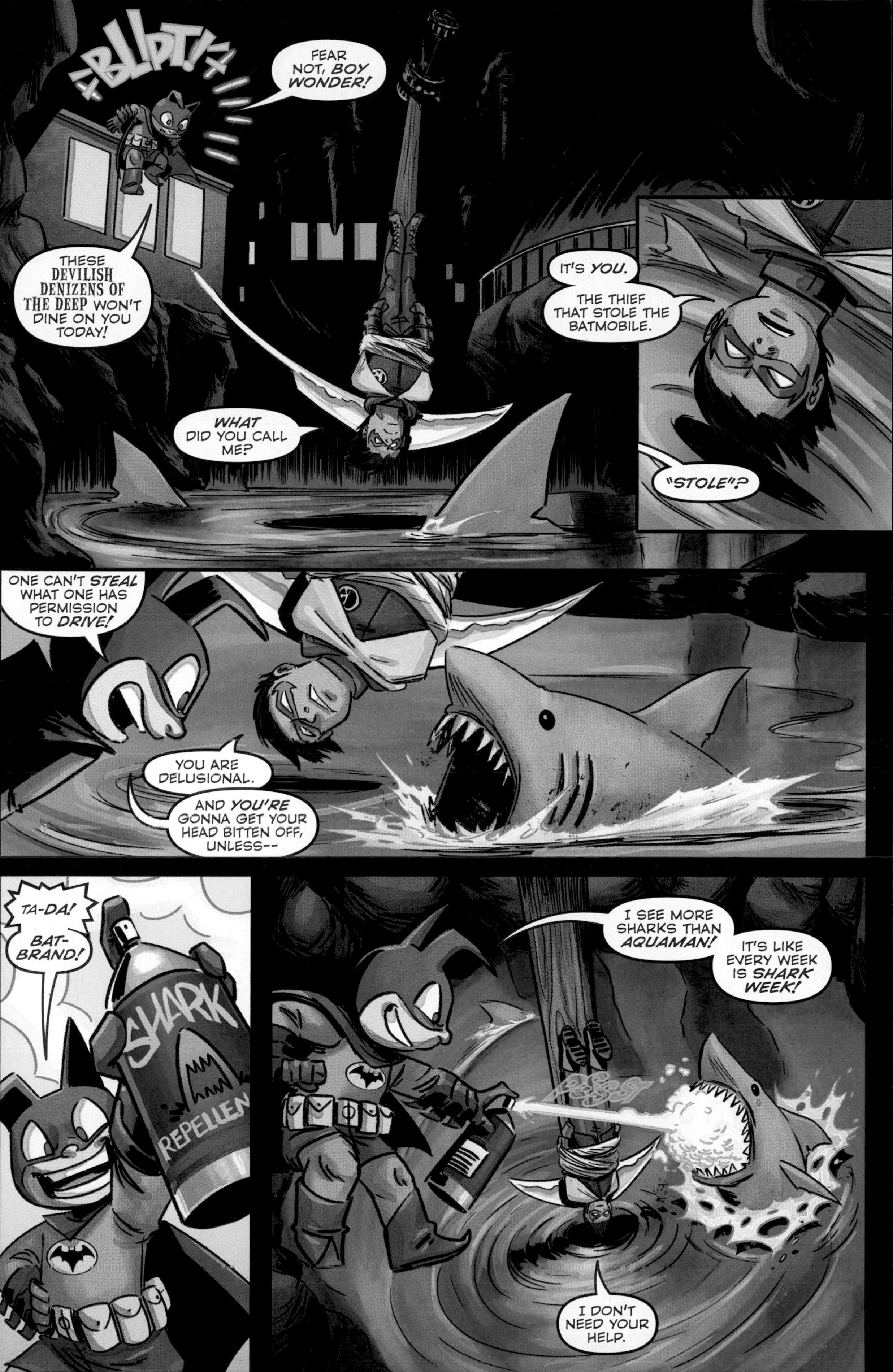
BLIPT!
FEAR NOT, BOY WONDER!
THESE DEVILISH DENIZENS OF THE DEEP WON'T DINE ON YOU TODAY!
WHAT DID YOU CALL ME?
IT'S YOU.
THE THIEF THAT STOLE THE BATMOBILE.
"STOLE"?
ONE CAN'T STEAL WHAT ONE HAS PERMISSION TO DRIVE!
YOU ARE DELUSIONAL.
AND YOU'RE GONNA GET YOUR HEAD BITTEN OFF, UNLESS--
TA-DA!
BAT-BRAND!
SHARK
REPELLEN
I SEE MORE SHARKS THAN AQUAMAN!
IT'S LIKE EVERY WEEK IS SHARK WEEK!
I DON'T NEED YOUR HELP.

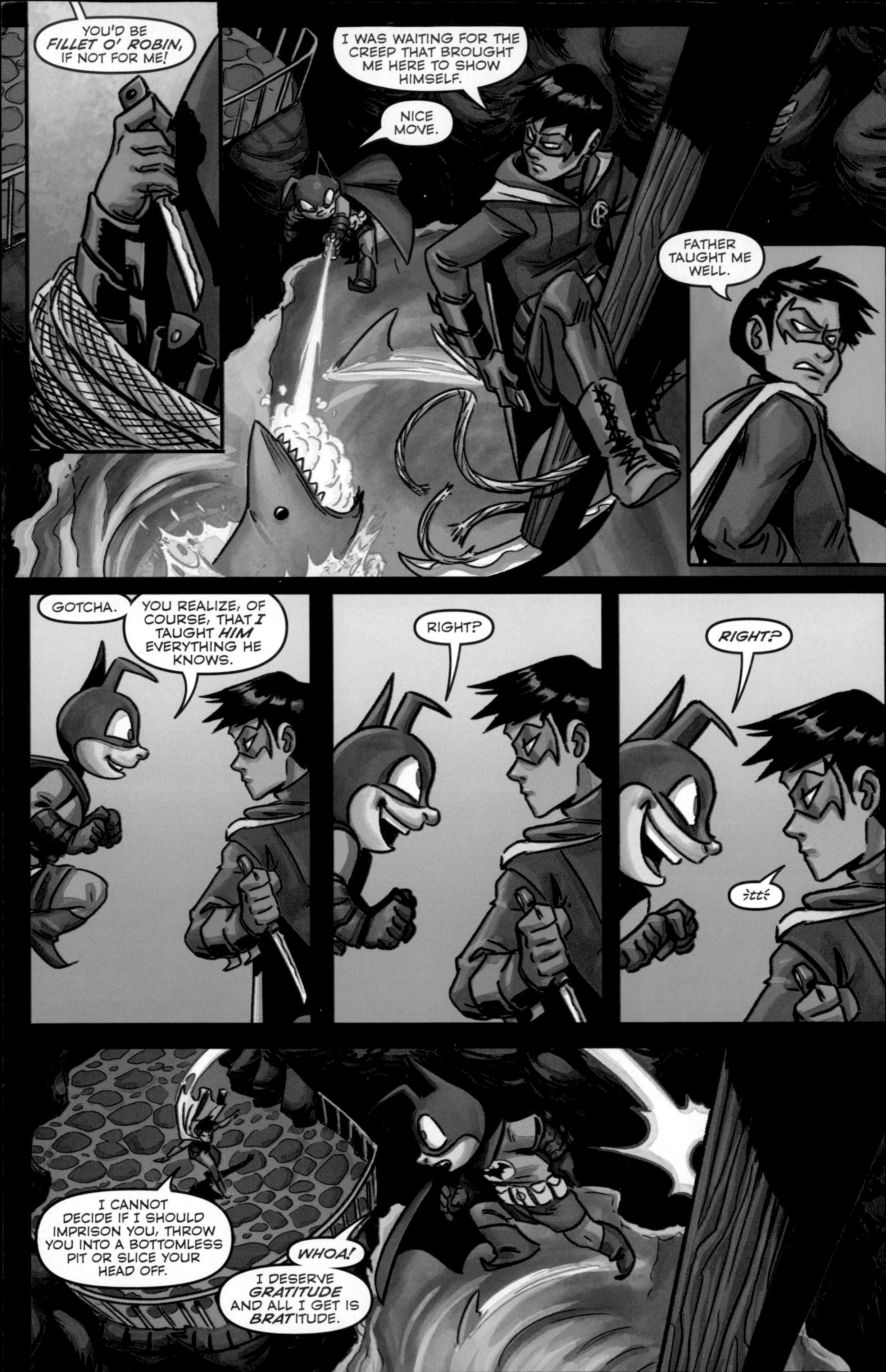
YOU'D BE *FILLET O' ROBIN,* IF NOT FOR ME!
I WAS WAITING FOR THE CREEP THAT BROUGHT ME HERE TO SHOW HIMSELF.
NICE MOVE.
FATHER TAUGHT ME WELL.
GOTCHA.
YOU REALIZE, OF COURSE, THAT *I* TAUGHT *HIM* EVERYTHING HE KNOWS.
RIGHT?
RIGHT?
TT
I CANNOT DECIDE IF I SHOULD IMPRISON YOU, THROW YOU INTO A BOTTOMLESS PIT OR SLICE YOUR HEAD OFF.
WHOA!
I DESERVE *GRATITUDE* AND ALL I GET IS *BRAT*ITUDE.

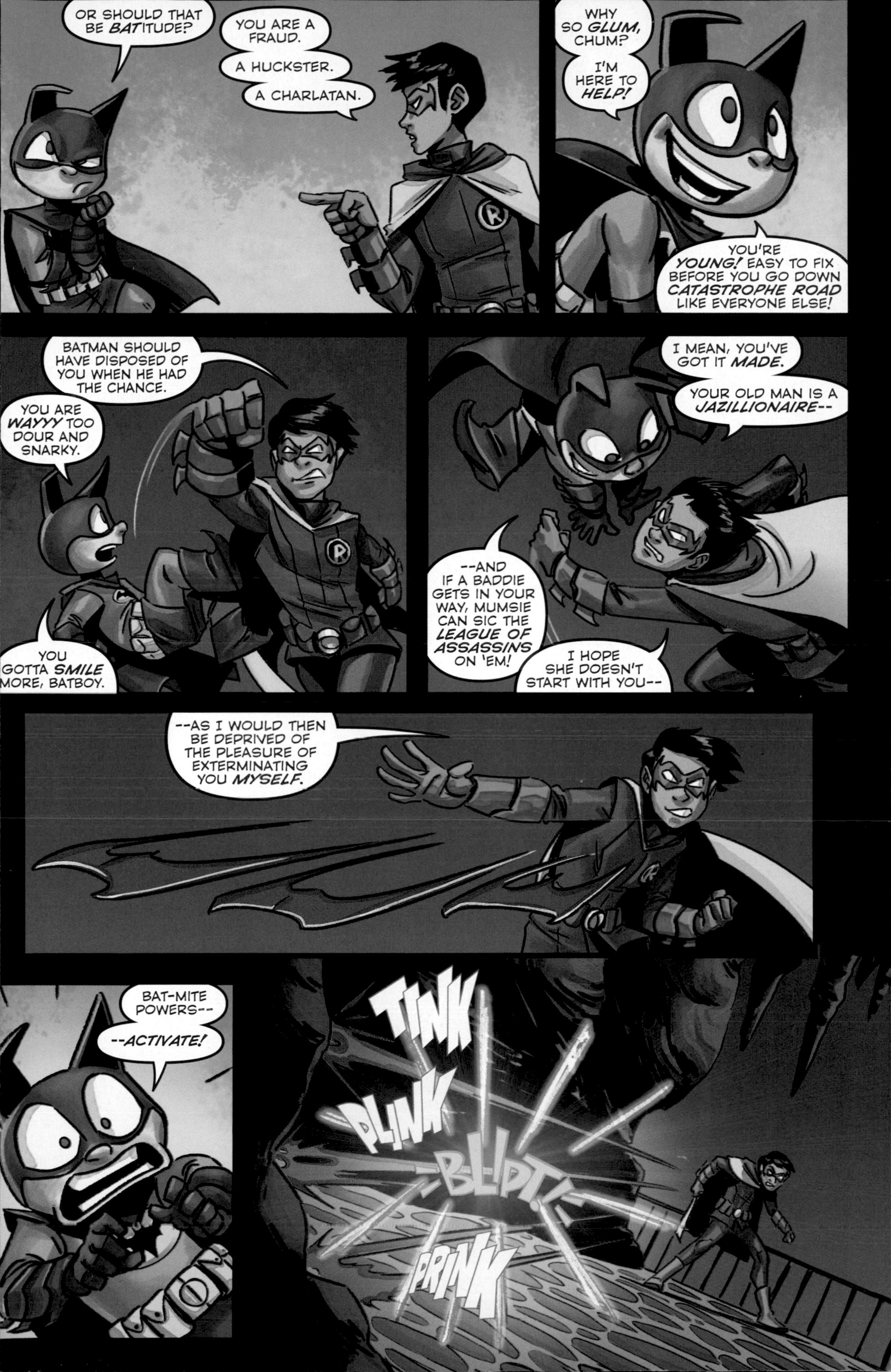
OR SHOULD THAT BE *BAT*ITUDE?
YOU ARE A FRAUD.
A HUCKSTER.
A CHARLATAN.
WHY SO *GLUM*, CHUM?
I'M HERE TO *HELP!*
YOU'RE *YOUNG!* EASY TO FIX BEFORE YOU GO DOWN *CATASTROPHE ROAD* LIKE EVERYONE ELSE!
BATMAN SHOULD HAVE DISPOSED OF YOU WHEN HE HAD THE CHANCE.
YOU ARE *WAYYY* TOO DOUR AND SNARKY.
YOU GOTTA *SMILE* MORE, BATBOY.
I MEAN, YOU'VE GOT IT *MADE*.
YOUR OLD MAN IS A *JAZILLIONAIRE*--
--AND IF A BADDIE GETS IN YOUR WAY, MUMSIE CAN SIC THE *LEAGUE OF ASSASSINS* ON 'EM!
I HOPE SHE DOESN'T START WITH YOU--
--AS I WOULD THEN BE DEPRIVED OF THE PLEASURE OF EXTERMINATING YOU *MYSELF*.
BAT-MITE POWERS--
--*ACTIVATE!*
TINK
PLINK
BLIPT
PRINK

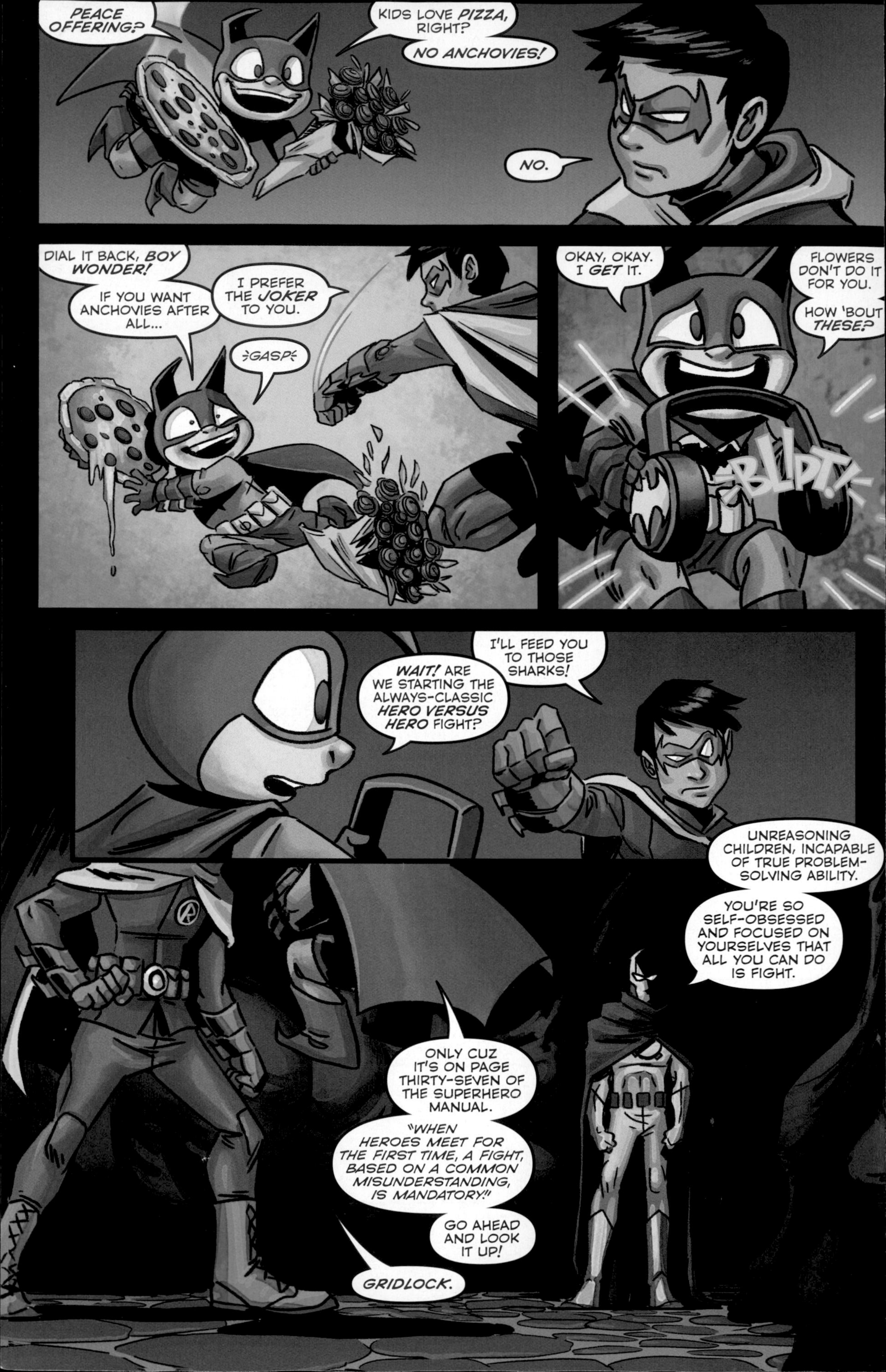
PEACE OFFERING?
KIDS LOVE PIZZA, RIGHT?
NO ANCHOVIES!
NO.
DIAL IT BACK, BOY WONDER!
IF YOU WANT ANCHOVIES AFTER ALL...
I PREFER THE JOKER TO YOU.
GASP
OKAY, OKAY. I GET IT.
FLOWERS DON'T DO IT FOR YOU.
HOW 'BOUT THESE?
BLIPT!
I'LL FEED YOU TO THOSE SHARKS!
WAIT! ARE WE STARTING THE ALWAYS-CLASSIC HERO VERSUS HERO FIGHT?
UNREASONING CHILDREN, INCAPABLE OF TRUE PROBLEM-SOLVING ABILITY.
YOU'RE SO SELF-OBSESSED AND FOCUSED ON YOURSELVES THAT ALL YOU CAN DO IS FIGHT.
ONLY CUZ IT'S ON PAGE THIRTY-SEVEN OF THE SUPERHERO MANUAL.
"WHEN HEROES MEET FOR THE FIRST TIME, A FIGHT, BASED ON A COMMON MISUNDERSTANDING, IS MANDATORY!"
GO AHEAD AND LOOK IT UP!
GRIDLOCK.

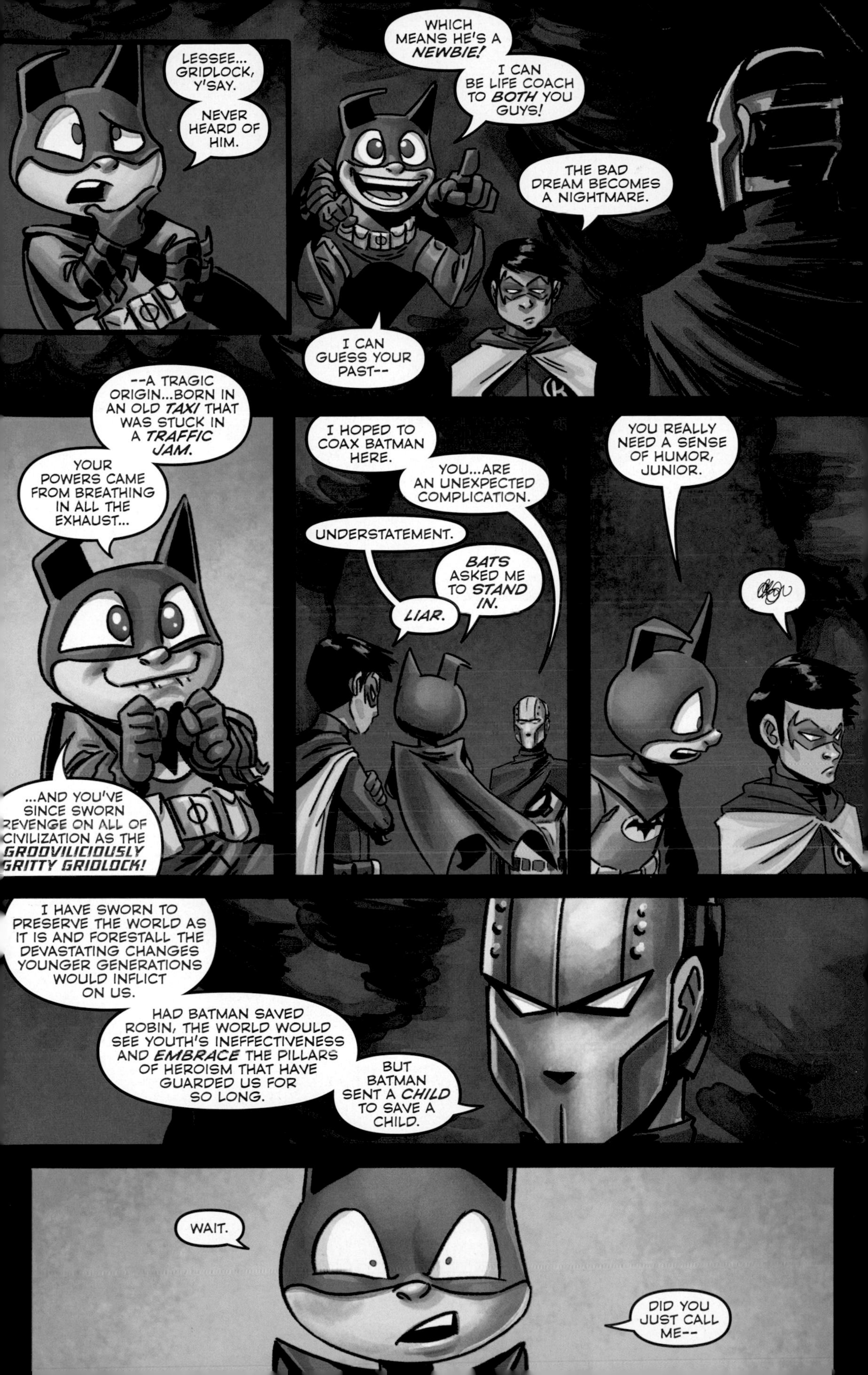
LESSEE... GRIDLOCK, Y'SAY.
NEVER HEARD OF HIM.
WHICH MEANS HE'S A NEWBIE!
I CAN BE LIFE COACH TO BOTH YOU GUYS!
THE BAD DREAM BECOMES A NIGHTMARE.
I CAN GUESS YOUR PAST--
--A TRAGIC ORIGIN...BORN IN AN OLD TAXI THAT WAS STUCK IN A TRAFFIC JAM.
YOUR POWERS CAME FROM BREATHING IN ALL THE EXHAUST...
...AND YOU'VE SINCE SWORN REVENGE ON ALL OF CIVILIZATION AS THE GROOVILICIOUSLY GRITTY GRIDLOCK!
I HOPED TO COAX BATMAN HERE.
YOU...ARE AN UNEXPECTED COMPLICATION.
UNDERSTATEMENT.
BATS ASKED ME TO STAND IN.
LIAR.
YOU REALLY NEED A SENSE OF HUMOR, JUNIOR.
I HAVE SWORN TO PRESERVE THE WORLD AS IT IS AND FORESTALL THE DEVASTATING CHANGES YOUNGER GENERATIONS WOULD INFLICT ON US.
HAD BATMAN SAVED ROBIN, THE WORLD WOULD SEE YOUTH'S INEFFECTIVENESS AND EMBRACE THE PILLARS OF HEROISM THAT HAVE GUARDED US FOR SO LONG.
BUT BATMAN SENT A CHILD TO SAVE A CHILD.
WAIT.
DID YOU JUST CALL ME--

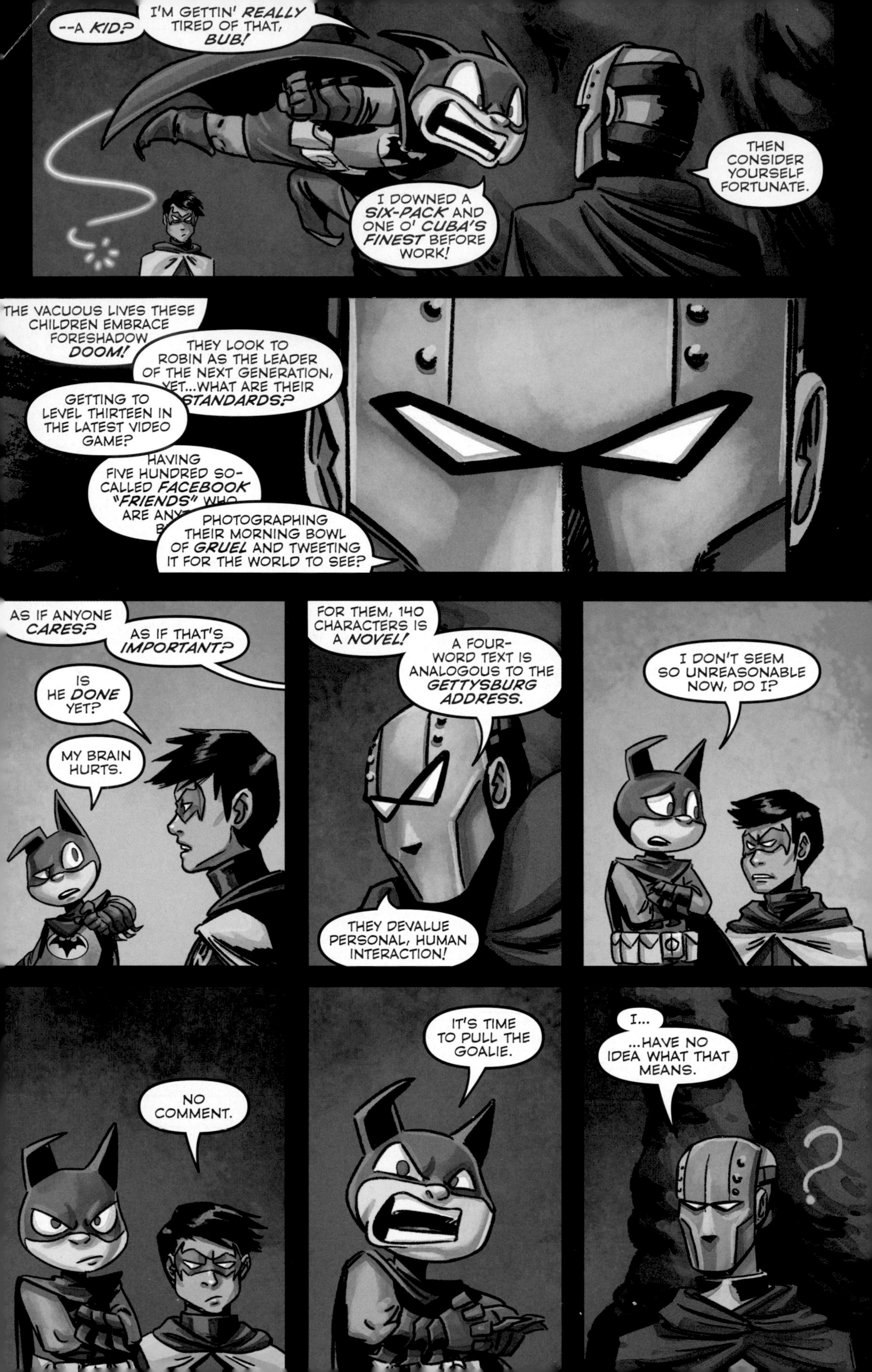
--A KID?
I'M GETTIN' REALLY TIRED OF THAT, BUB!
I DOWNED A SIX-PACK AND ONE O' CUBA'S FINEST BEFORE WORK!
THEN CONSIDER YOURSELF FORTUNATE.
THE VACUOUS LIVES THESE CHILDREN EMBRACE FORESHADOW DOOM!
THEY LOOK TO ROBIN AS THE LEADER OF THE NEXT GENERATION, YET...WHAT ARE THEIR STANDARDS?
GETTING TO LEVEL THIRTEEN IN THE LATEST VIDEO GAME?
HAVING FIVE HUNDRED SO-CALLED FACEBOOK "FRIENDS" WHO ARE
PHOTOGRAPHING THEIR MORNING BOWL OF GRUEL AND TWEETING IT FOR THE WORLD TO SEE?
AS IF ANYONE CARES?
AS IF THAT'S IMPORTANT?
IS HE DONE YET?
MY BRAIN HURTS.
FOR THEM, 140 CHARACTERS IS A NOVEL!
A FOUR-WORD TEXT IS ANALOGOUS TO THE GETTYSBURG ADDRESS.
THEY DEVALUE PERSONAL, HUMAN INTERACTION!
I DON'T SEEM SO UNREASONABLE NOW, DO I?
NO COMMENT.
IT'S TIME TO PULL THE GOALIE.
I...
...HAVE NO IDEA WHAT THAT MEANS.

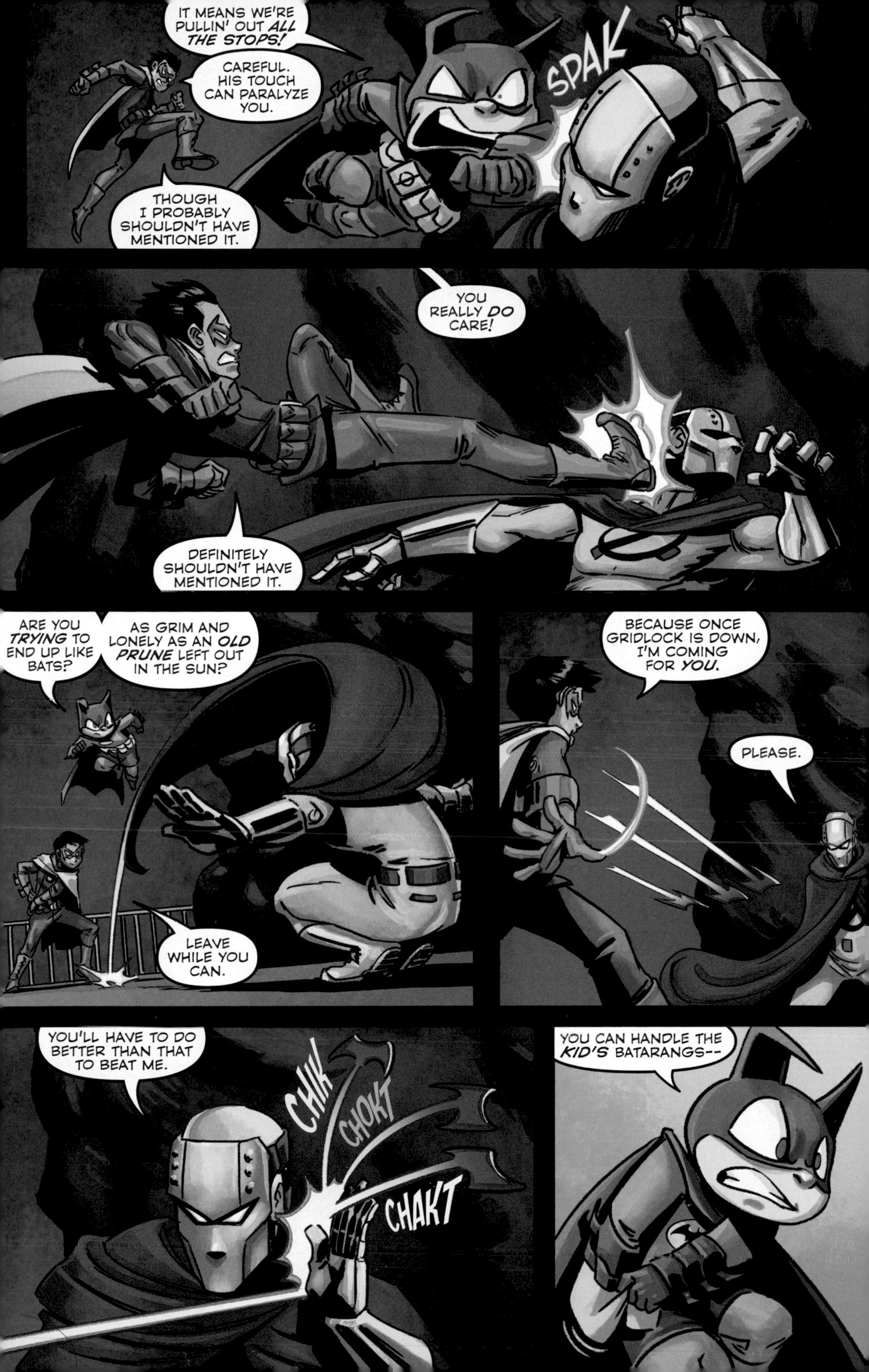
IT MEANS WE'RE PULLIN' OUT ALL THE STOPS!
CAREFUL. HIS TOUCH CAN PARALYZE YOU.
SPAK
THOUGH I PROBABLY SHOULDN'T HAVE MENTIONED IT.
YOU REALLY DO CARE!
DEFINITELY SHOULDN'T HAVE MENTIONED IT.
ARE YOU TRYING TO END UP LIKE BATS?
AS GRIM AND LONELY AS AN OLD PRUNE LEFT OUT IN THE SUN?
LEAVE WHILE YOU CAN.
BECAUSE ONCE GRIDLOCK IS DOWN, I'M COMING FOR YOU.
PLEASE.
YOU'LL HAVE TO DO BETTER THAN THAT TO BEAT ME.
CHIK
CHOKT
CHAKT
YOU CAN HANDLE THE KID'S BATARANGS--

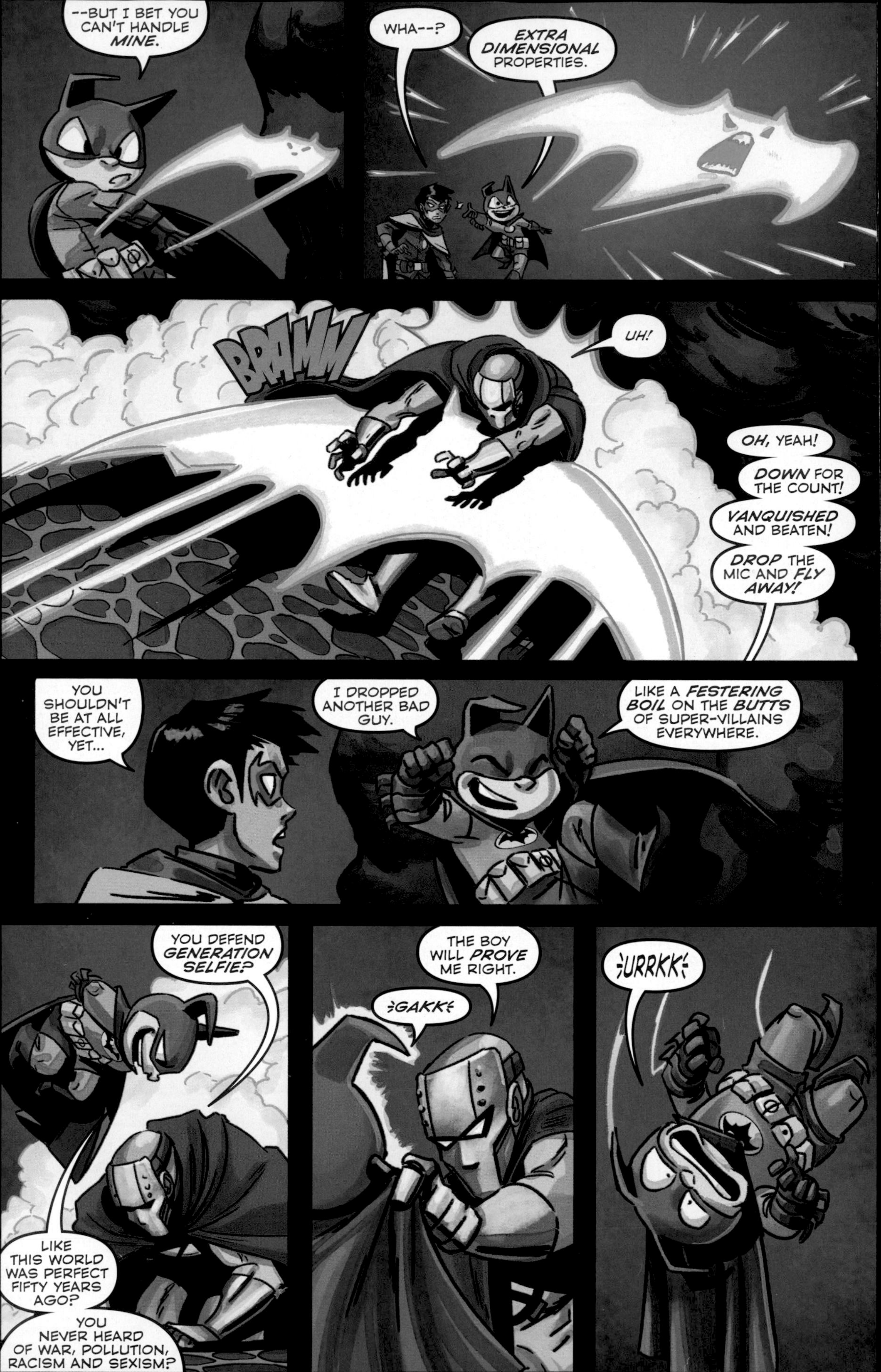
--BUT I BET YOU CAN'T HANDLE MINE.
WHA--?
EXTRA DIMENSIONAL PROPERTIES.
BRAMM
UH!
OH, YEAH!
DOWN FOR THE COUNT!
VANQUISHED AND BEATEN!
DROP THE MIC AND FLY AWAY!
YOU SHOULDN'T BE AT ALL EFFECTIVE, YET...
I DROPPED ANOTHER BAD GUY.
LIKE A FESTERING BOIL ON THE BUTTS OF SUPER-VILLAINS EVERYWHERE.
YOU DEFEND GENERATION SELFIE?
LIKE THIS WORLD WAS PERFECT FIFTY YEARS AGO?
YOU NEVER HEARD OF WAR, POLLUTION, RACISM AND SEXISM?
THE BOY WILL PROVE ME RIGHT.
GAKK
URRKK

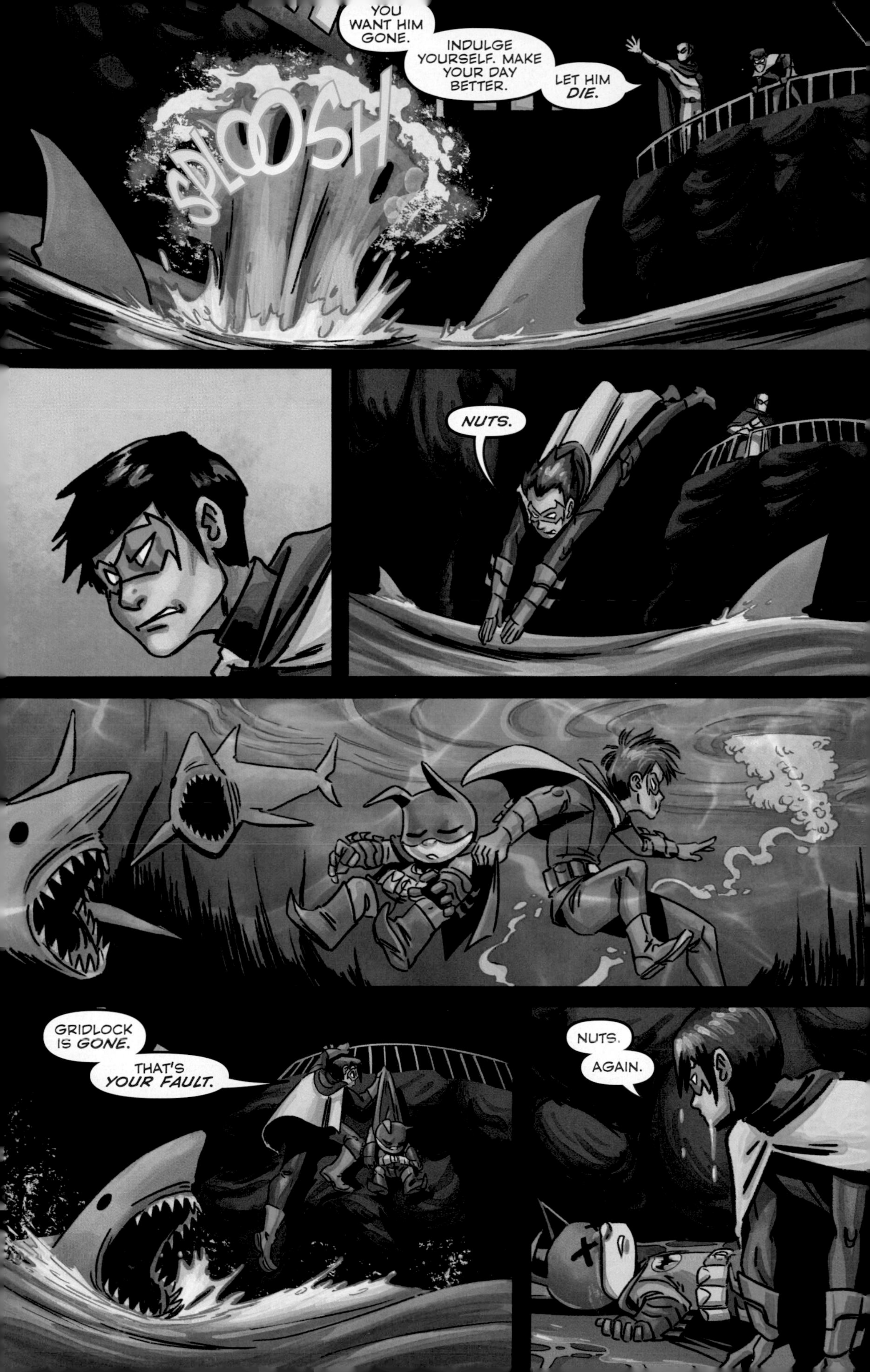
YOU WANT HIM GONE.
INDULGE YOURSELF. MAKE YOUR DAY BETTER.
LET HIM DIE.
SPLOOSH
NUTS.
GRIDLOCK IS GONE.
THAT'S YOUR FAULT.
NUTS.
AGAIN.

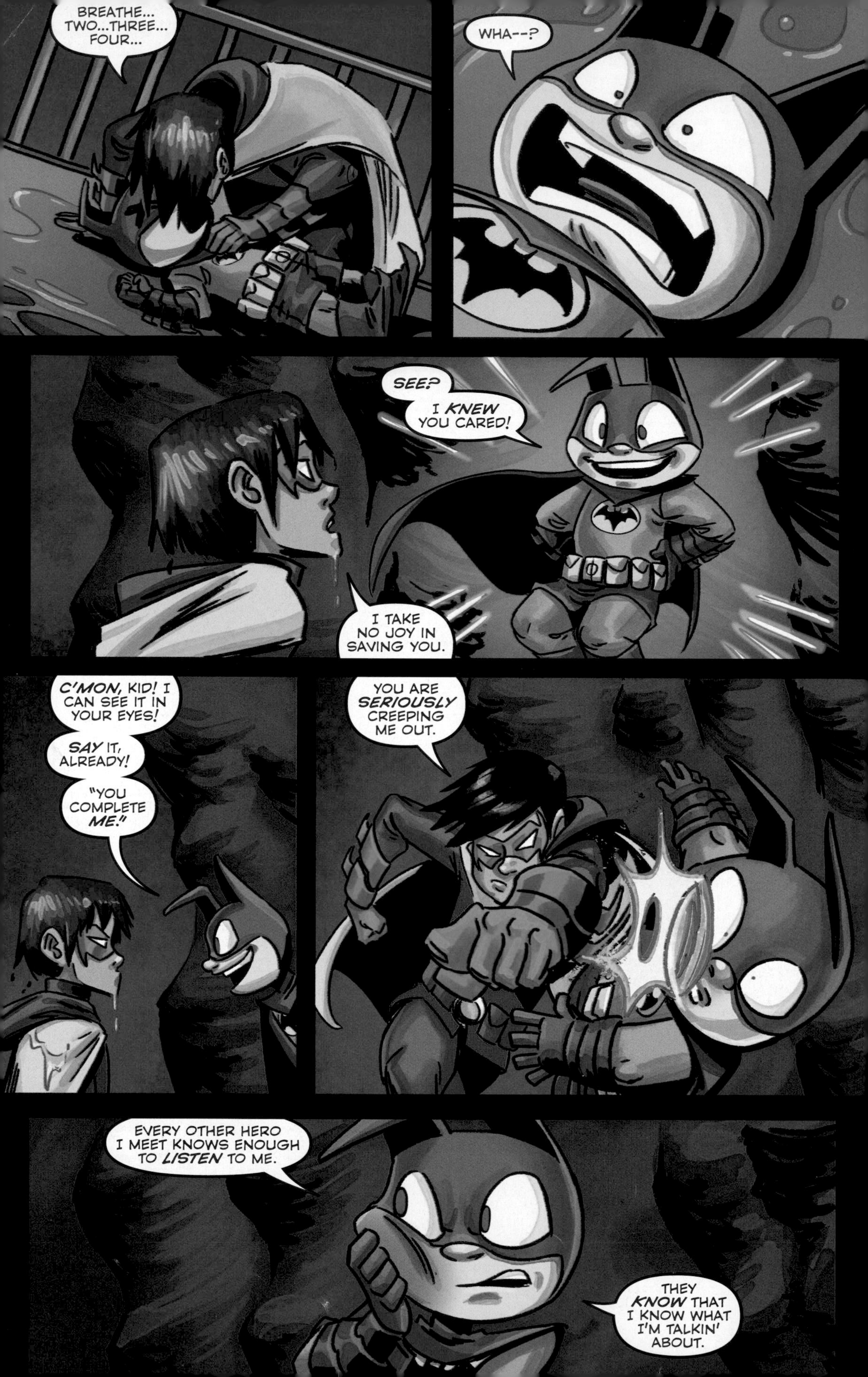
BREATHE... TWO...THREE... FOUR...
WHA--?
SEE?
I *KNEW* YOU CARED!
I TAKE NO JOY IN SAVING YOU.
C'MON, KID! I CAN SEE IT IN YOUR EYES!
SAY IT, ALREADY!
"YOU COMPLETE *ME.*"
YOU ARE *SERIOUSLY* CREEPING ME OUT.
EVERY OTHER HERO I MEET KNOWS ENOUGH TO *LISTEN* TO ME.
THEY *KNOW* THAT I KNOW WHAT I'M TALKIN' ABOUT.

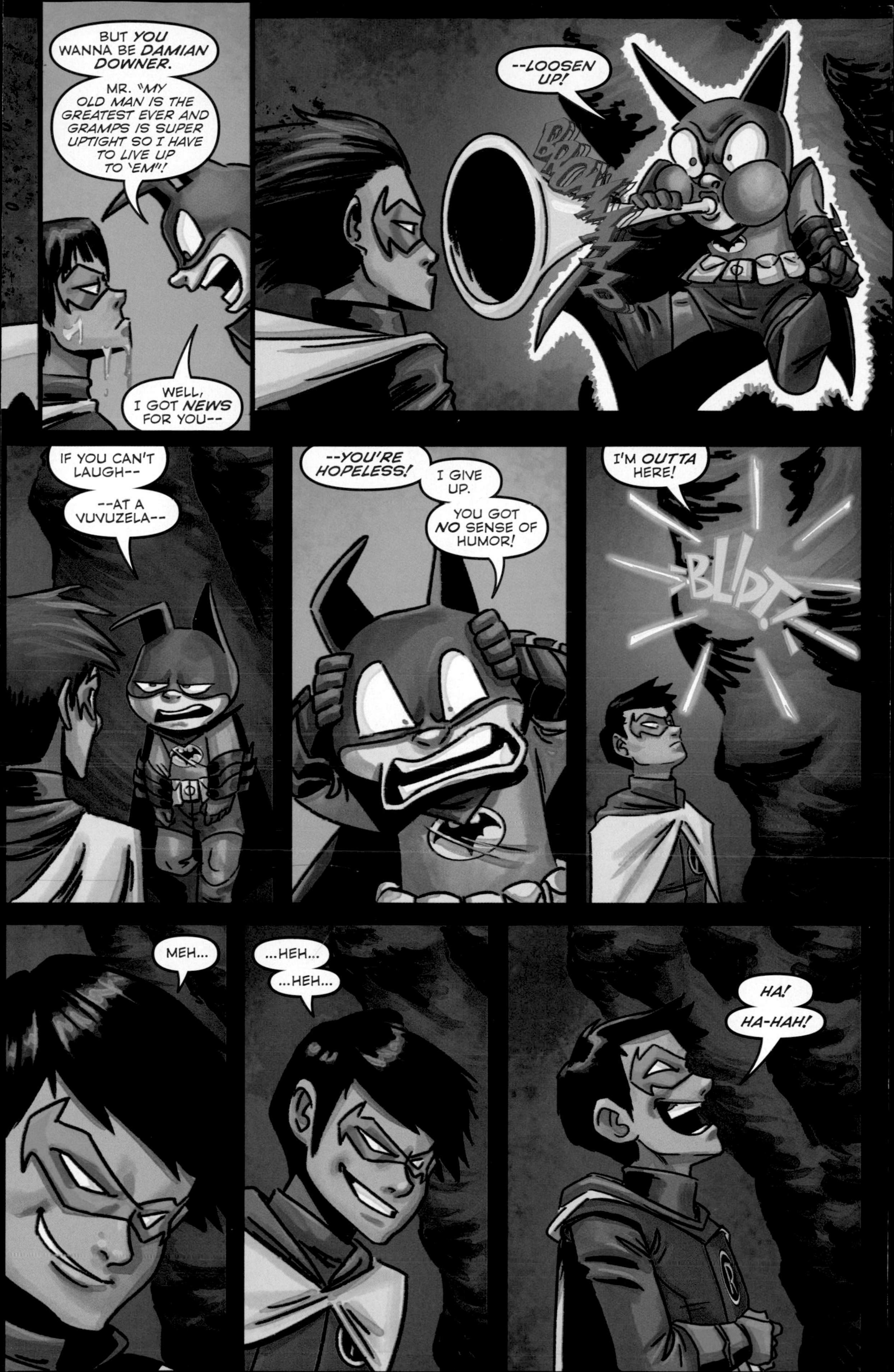
BUT YOU WANNA BE DAMIAN DOWNER.
MR. "MY OLD MAN IS THE GREATEST EVER AND GRAMPS IS SUPER UPTIGHT SO I HAVE TO LIVE UP TO 'EM"!
WELL, I GOT NEWS FOR YOU--
--LOOSEN UP!
IF YOU CAN'T LAUGH--
--AT A VUVUZELA--
--YOU'RE HOPELESS!
I GIVE UP.
YOU GOT NO SENSE OF HUMOR!
I'M OUTTA HERE!
BLIPT!
MEH...
...HEH...
...HEH...
HA!
HA-HAH!

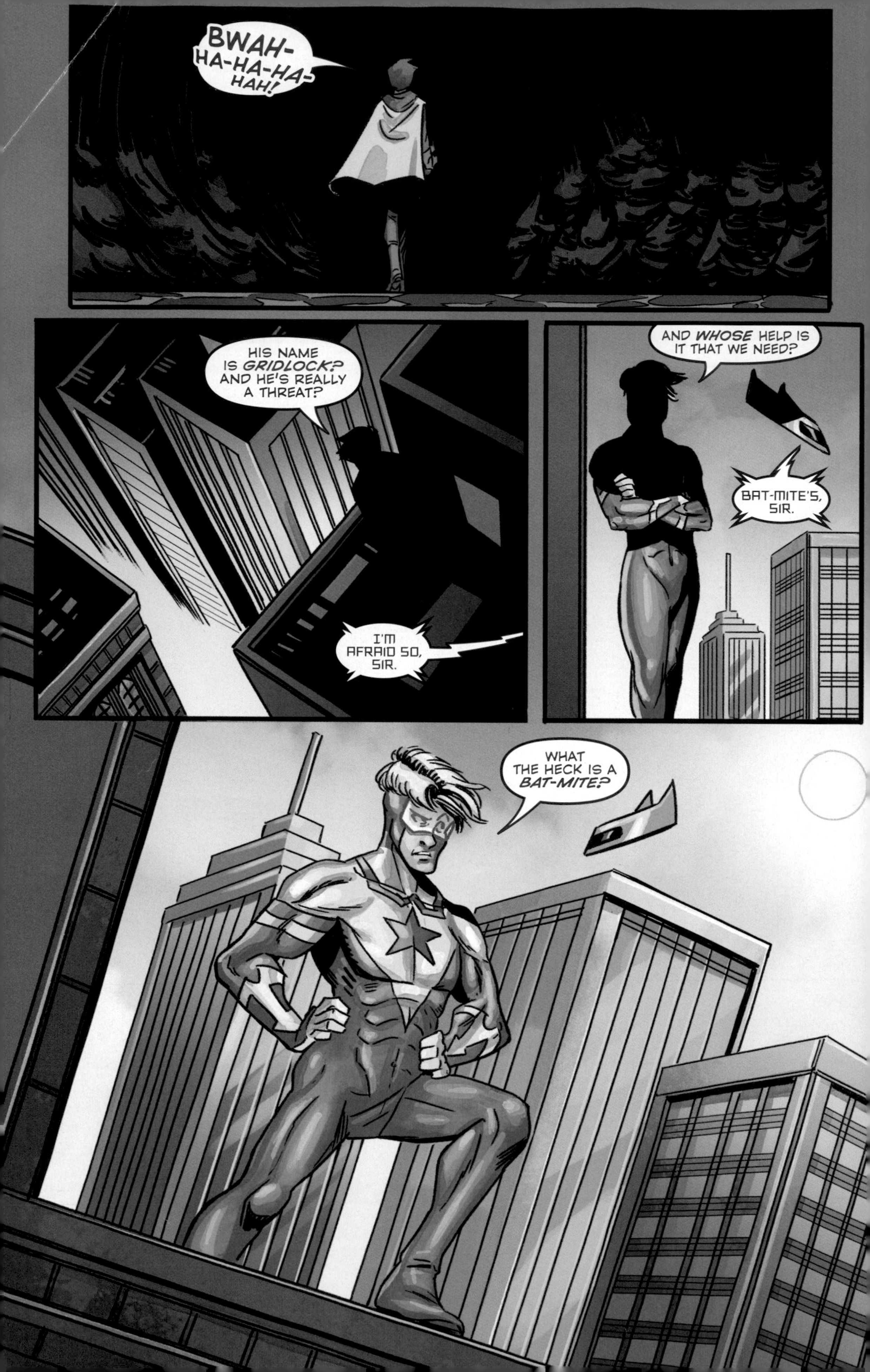
BWAH-HA-HA-HA-HAH!
HIS NAME IS GRIDLOCK? AND HE'S REALLY A THREAT?
I'M AFRAID SO, SIR.
AND WHOSE HELP IS IT THAT WE NEED?
BAT-MITE'S, SIR.
WHAT THE HECK IS A BAT-MITE?

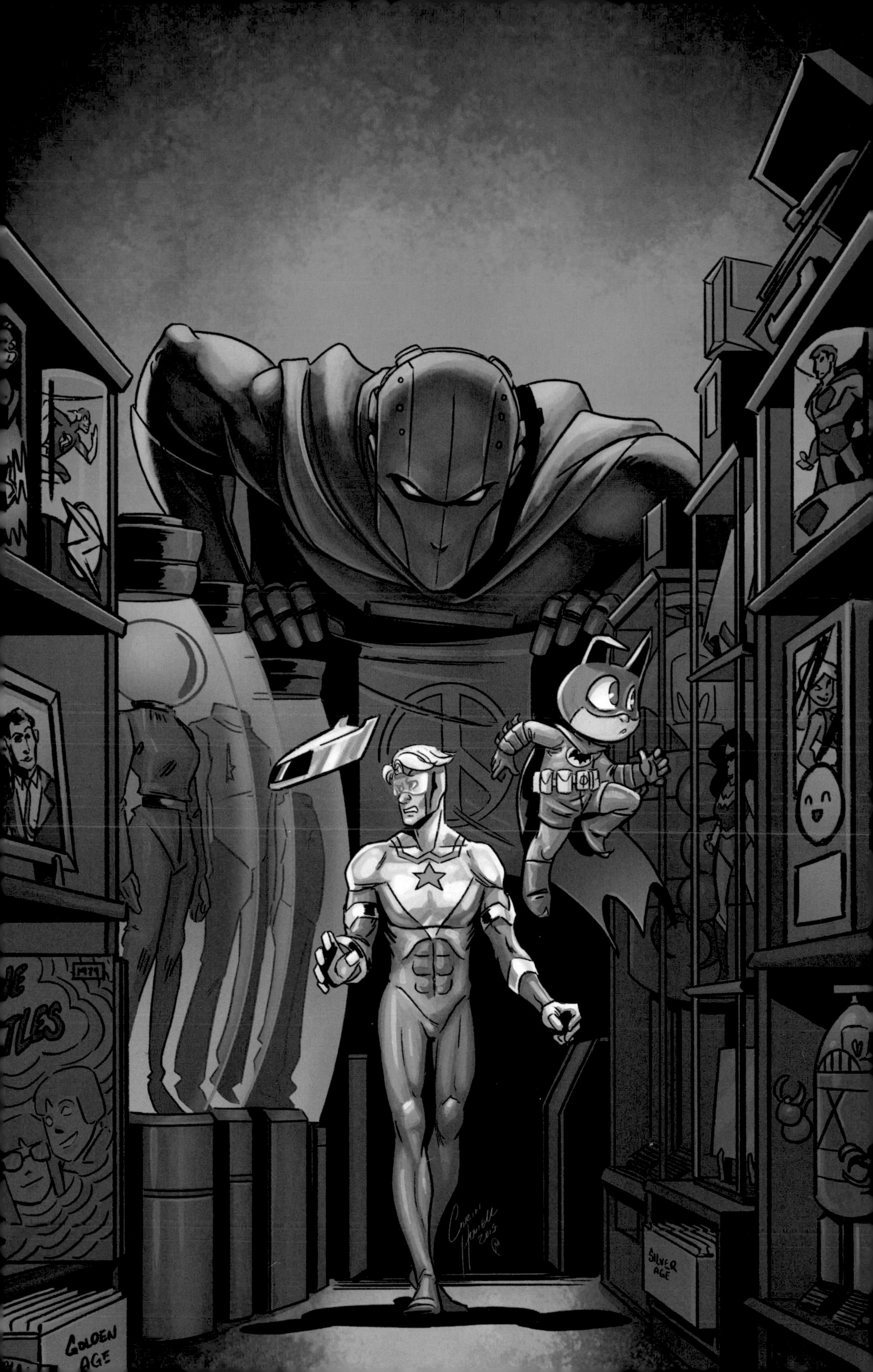
SILVER AGE
GOLDEN AGE

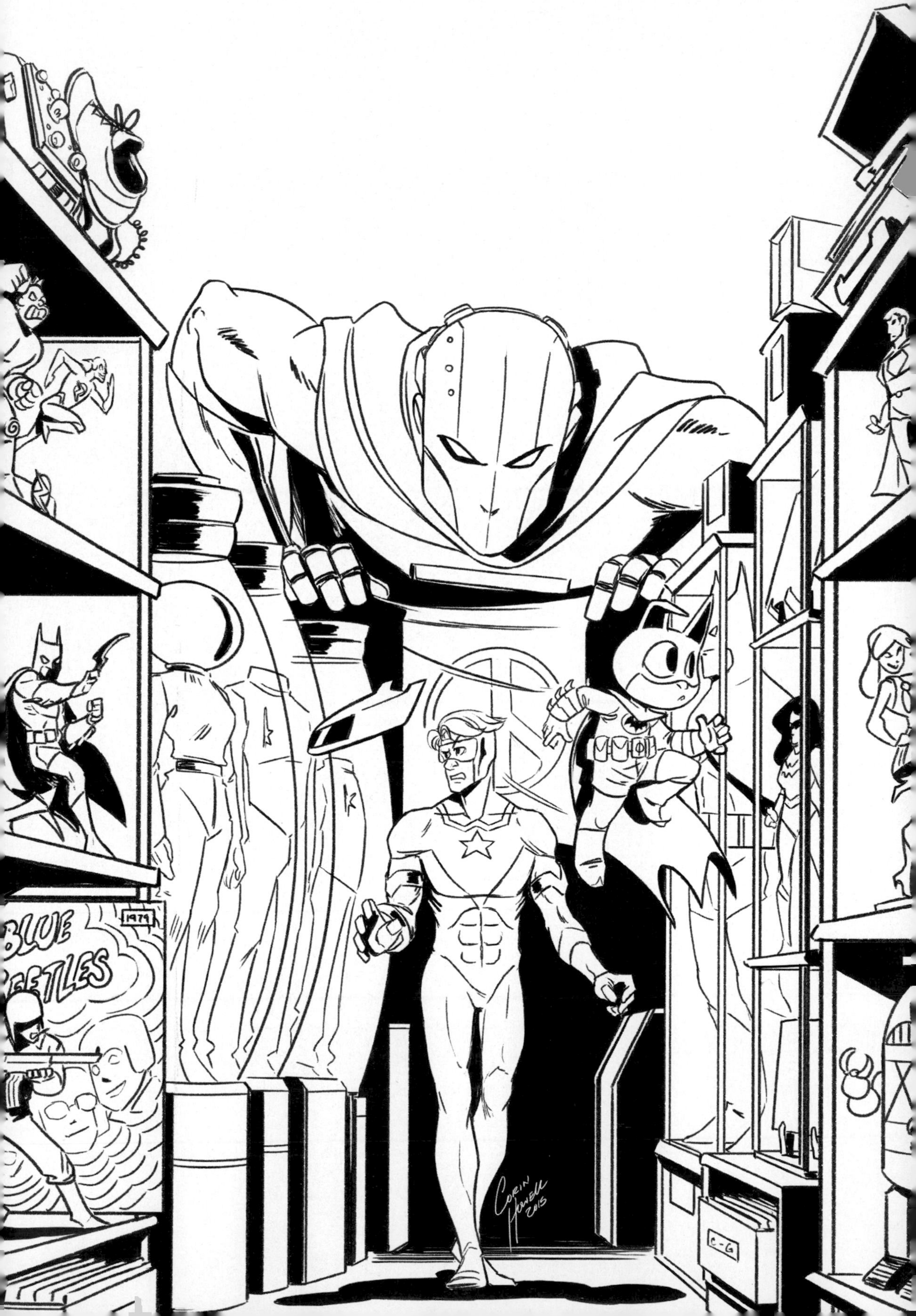
BLUE
1979
C-G
Corin Howell 2015

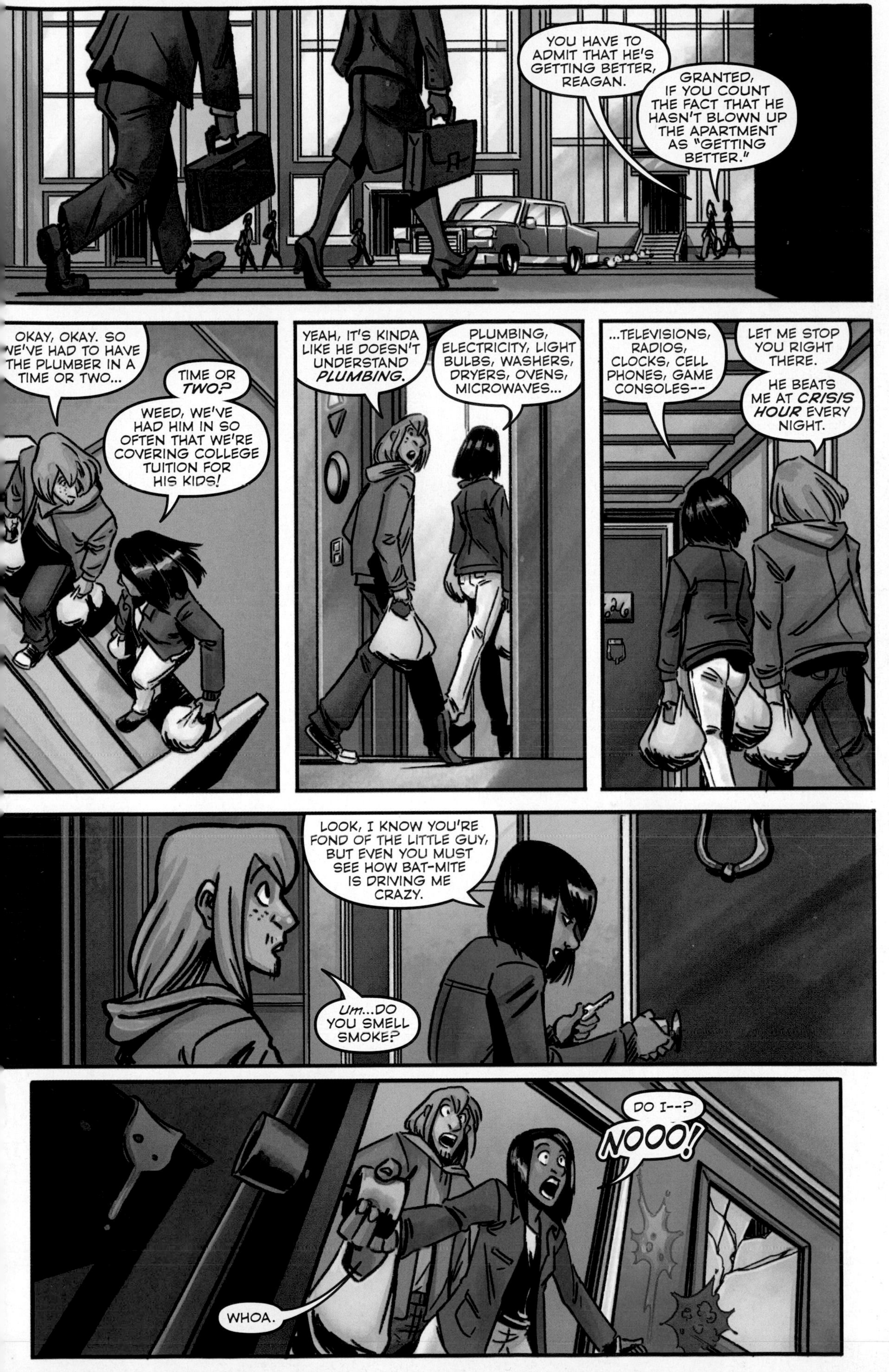

YOU HAVE TO ADMIT THAT HE'S GETTING BETTER, REAGAN.
GRANTED, IF YOU COUNT THE FACT THAT HE HASN'T BLOWN UP THE APARTMENT AS "GETTING BETTER."
OKAY, OKAY. SO WE'VE HAD TO HAVE THE PLUMBER IN A TIME OR TWO...
TIME OR *TWO?*
WEED, WE'VE HAD HIM IN SO OFTEN THAT WE'RE COVERING COLLEGE TUITION FOR HIS KIDS!
YEAH, IT'S KINDA LIKE HE DOESN'T UNDERSTAND *PLUMBING.*
PLUMBING, ELECTRICITY, LIGHT BULBS, WASHERS, DRYERS, OVENS, MICROWAVES...
...TELEVISIONS, RADIOS, CLOCKS, CELL PHONES, GAME CONSOLES--
LET ME STOP YOU RIGHT THERE.
HE BEATS ME AT *CRISIS HOUR* EVERY NIGHT.
LOOK, I KNOW YOU'RE FOND OF THE LITTLE GUY, BUT EVEN YOU MUST SEE HOW BAT-MITE IS DRIVING ME CRAZY.
UM...DO YOU SMELL SMOKE?
DO I--?
NOOO!
WHOA.

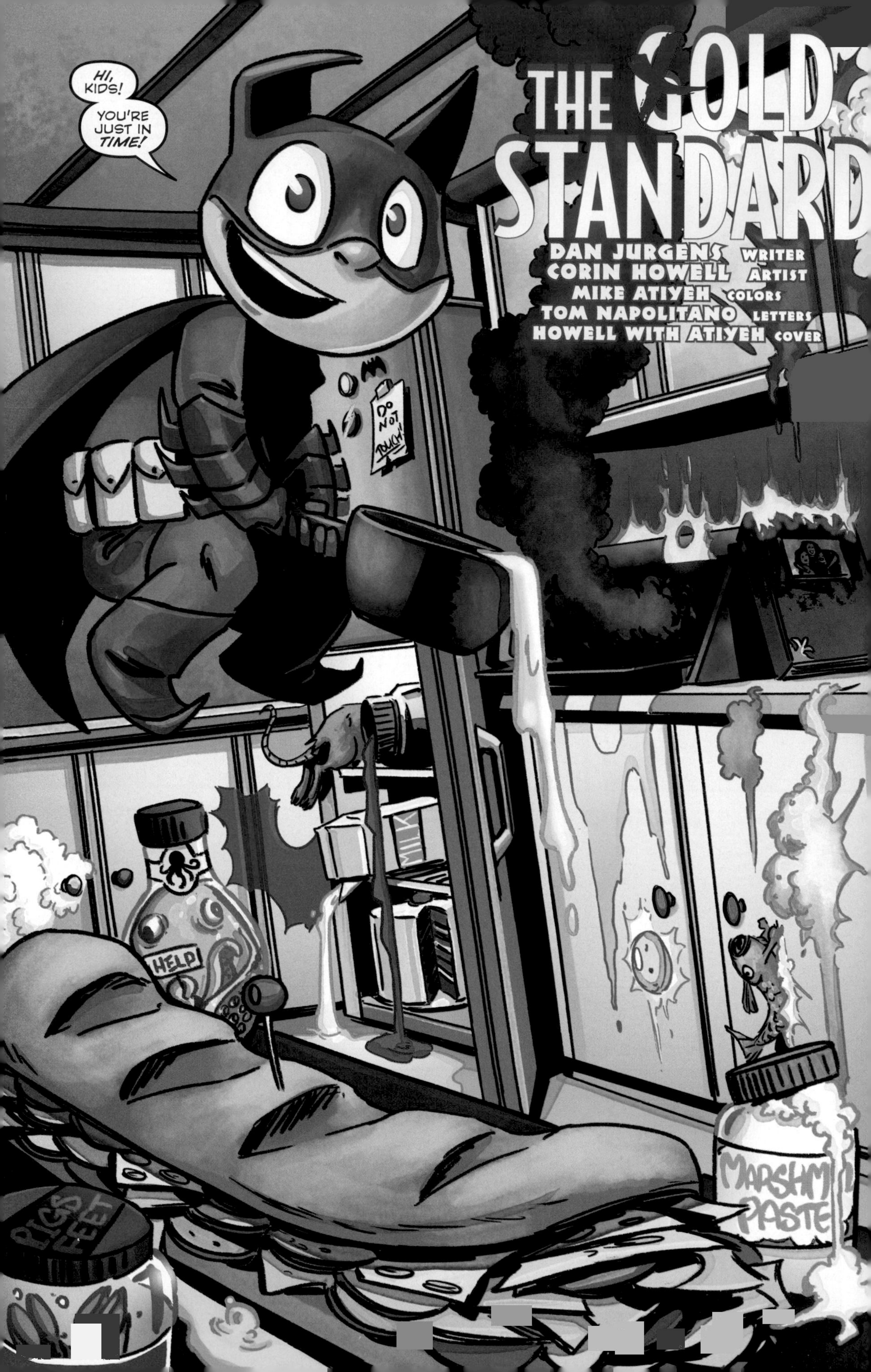
HI, KIDS!
YOU'RE JUST IN *TIME!*
THE GOLD STANDARD
DAN JURGENS WRITER
CORIN HOWELL ARTIST
MIKE ATIYEH COLORS
TOM NAPOLITANO LETTERS
HOWELL WITH ATIYEH COVER
DO NOT TOUCH!
MILK
HELP!
MARSHM PASTE
PIGS FEET

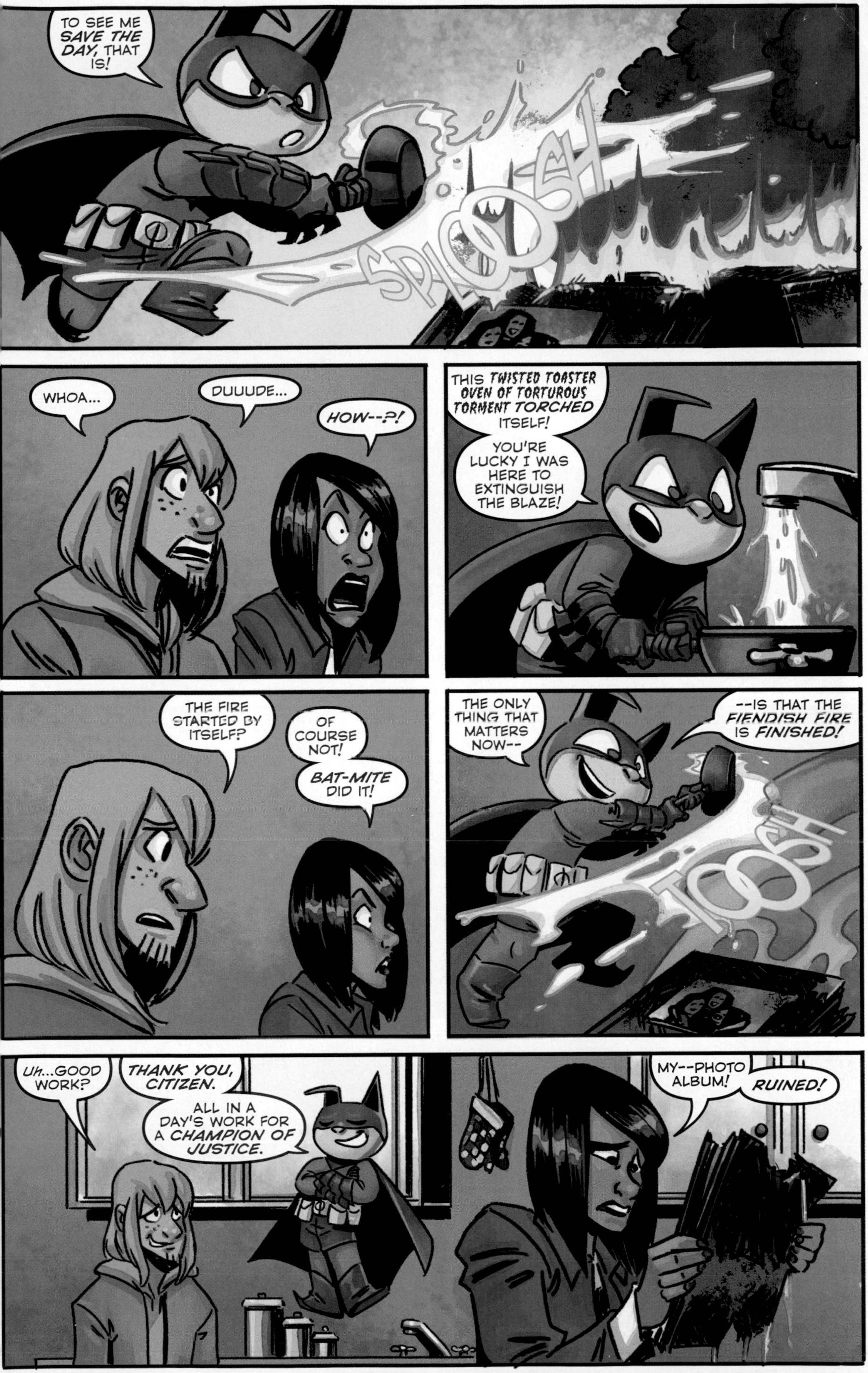
TO SEE ME SAVE THE DAY, THAT IS!
SPLOOOSH
WHOA...
DUUUDE...
HOW--?!
THIS TWISTED TOASTER OVEN OF TORTUROUS TORMENT TORCHED ITSELF!
YOU'RE LUCKY I WAS HERE TO EXTINGUISH THE BLAZE!
THE FIRE STARTED BY ITSELF?
OF COURSE NOT!
BAT-MITE DID IT!
THE ONLY THING THAT MATTERS NOW--
--IS THAT THE FIENDISH FIRE IS FINISHED!
TOOSH
Uh...GOOD WORK?
THANK YOU, CITIZEN.
ALL IN A DAY'S WORK FOR A CHAMPION OF JUSTICE.
MY--PHOTO ALBUM!
RUINED!

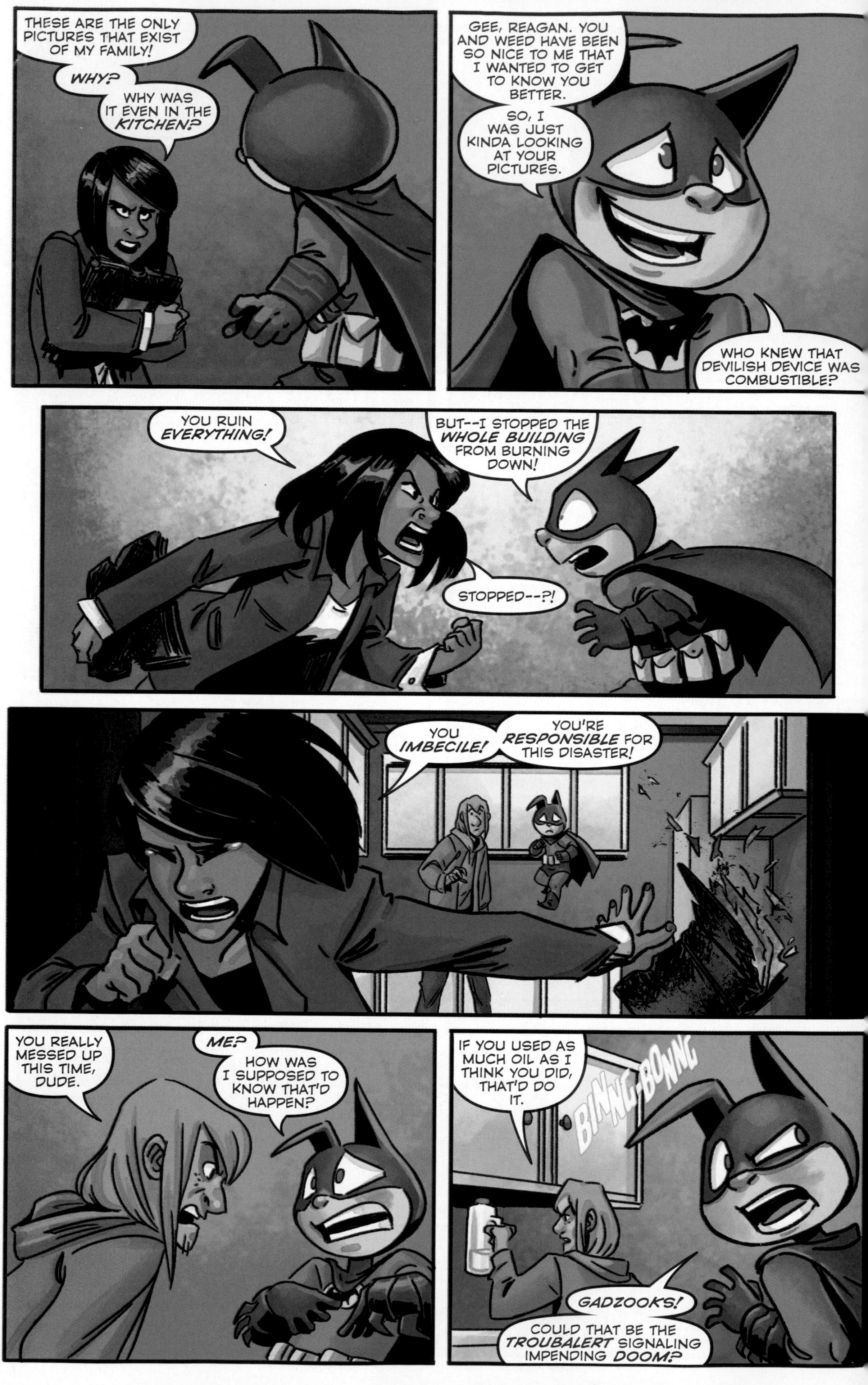
THESE ARE THE ONLY PICTURES THAT EXIST OF MY FAMILY!
WHY?
WHY WAS IT EVEN IN THE KITCHEN?
GEE, REAGAN. YOU AND WEED HAVE BEEN SO NICE TO ME THAT I WANTED TO GET TO KNOW YOU BETTER.
SO, I WAS JUST KINDA LOOKING AT YOUR PICTURES.
WHO KNEW THAT DEVILISH DEVICE WAS COMBUSTIBLE?
YOU RUIN EVERYTHING!
BUT--I STOPPED THE WHOLE BUILDING FROM BURNING DOWN!
STOPPED--?!
YOU IMBECILE!
YOU'RE RESPONSIBLE FOR THIS DISASTER!
YOU REALLY MESSED UP THIS TIME, DUDE.
ME?
HOW WAS I SUPPOSED TO KNOW THAT'D HAPPEN?
IF YOU USED AS MUCH OIL AS I THINK YOU DID, THAT'D DO IT.
BINNG-BONNG
GADZOOKS!
COULD THAT BE THE TROUBALERT SIGNALING IMPENDING DOOM?

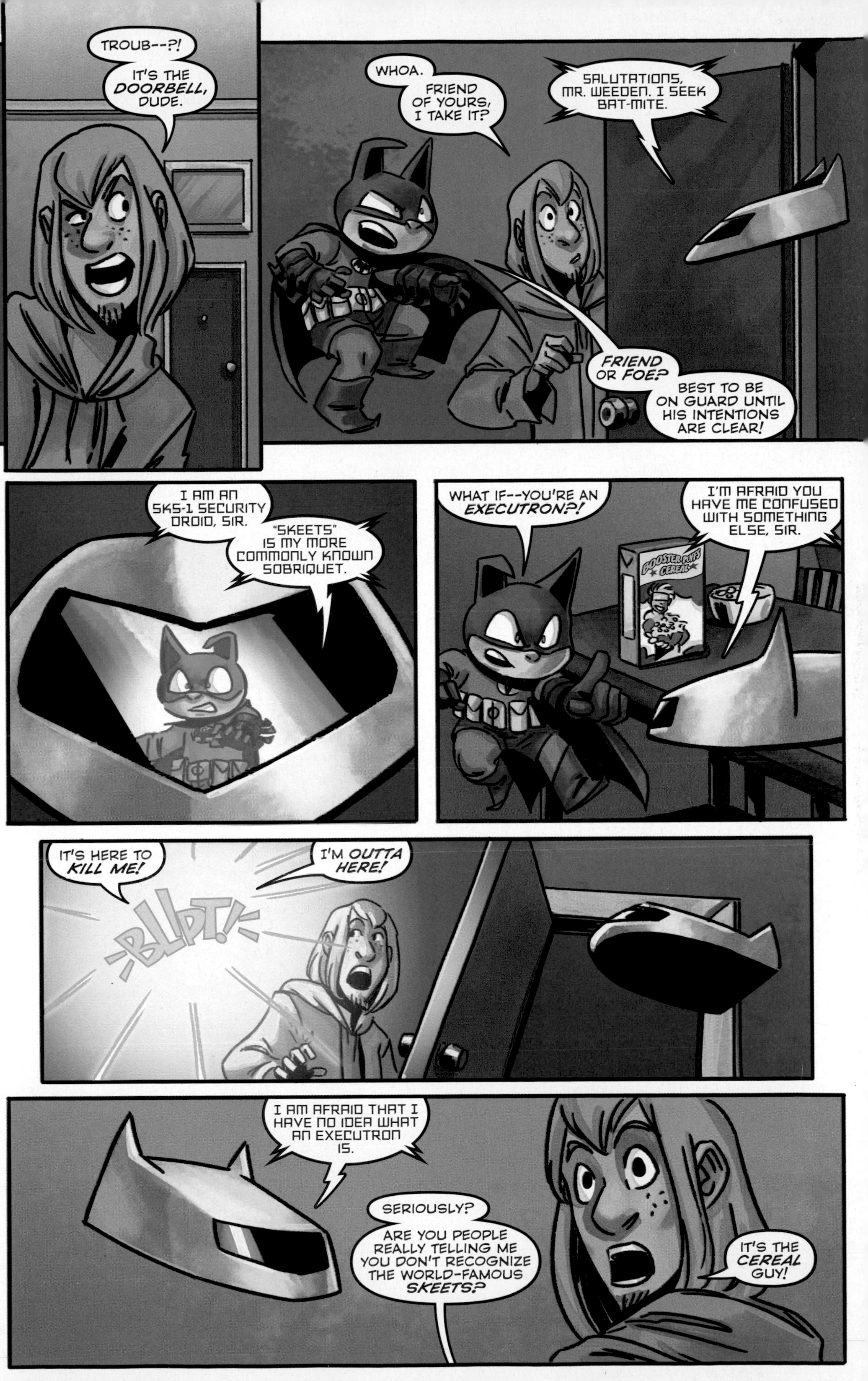

TROUB--?!
IT'S THE *DOORBELL,* DUDE.
WHOA. FRIEND OF YOURS, I TAKE IT?
SALUTATIONS, MR. WEEDEN. I SEEK BAT-MITE.
FRIEND OR *FOE?*
BEST TO BE ON GUARD UNTIL HIS INTENTIONS ARE CLEAR!
I AM AN SKS-1 SECURITY DROID, SIR.
"SKEETS" IS MY MORE COMMONLY KNOWN SOBRIQUET.
WHAT IF--YOU'RE AN *EXECUTRON?!*
I'M AFRAID YOU HAVE ME CONFUSED WITH SOMETHING ELSE, SIR.
BOOSTER PUFFS CEREAL
IT'S HERE TO *KILL ME!*
BLIPT!
I'M *OUTTA HERE!*
I AM AFRAID THAT I HAVE NO IDEA WHAT AN EXECUTRON IS.
SERIOUSLY?
ARE YOU PEOPLE REALLY TELLING ME YOU DON'T RECOGNIZE THE WORLD-FAMOUS *SKEETS?*
IT'S THE *CEREAL* GUY!

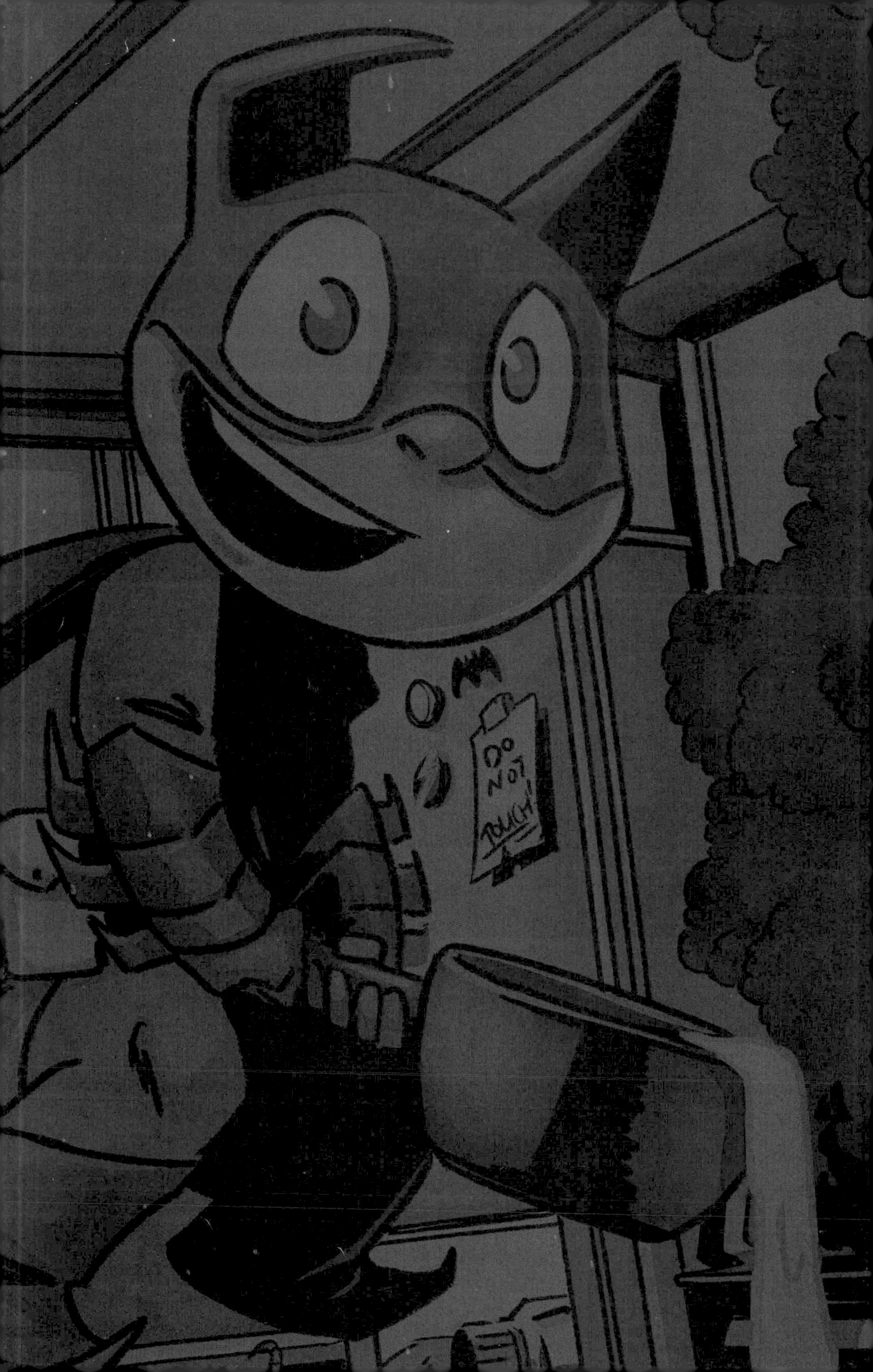
DO NOT TOUCH!

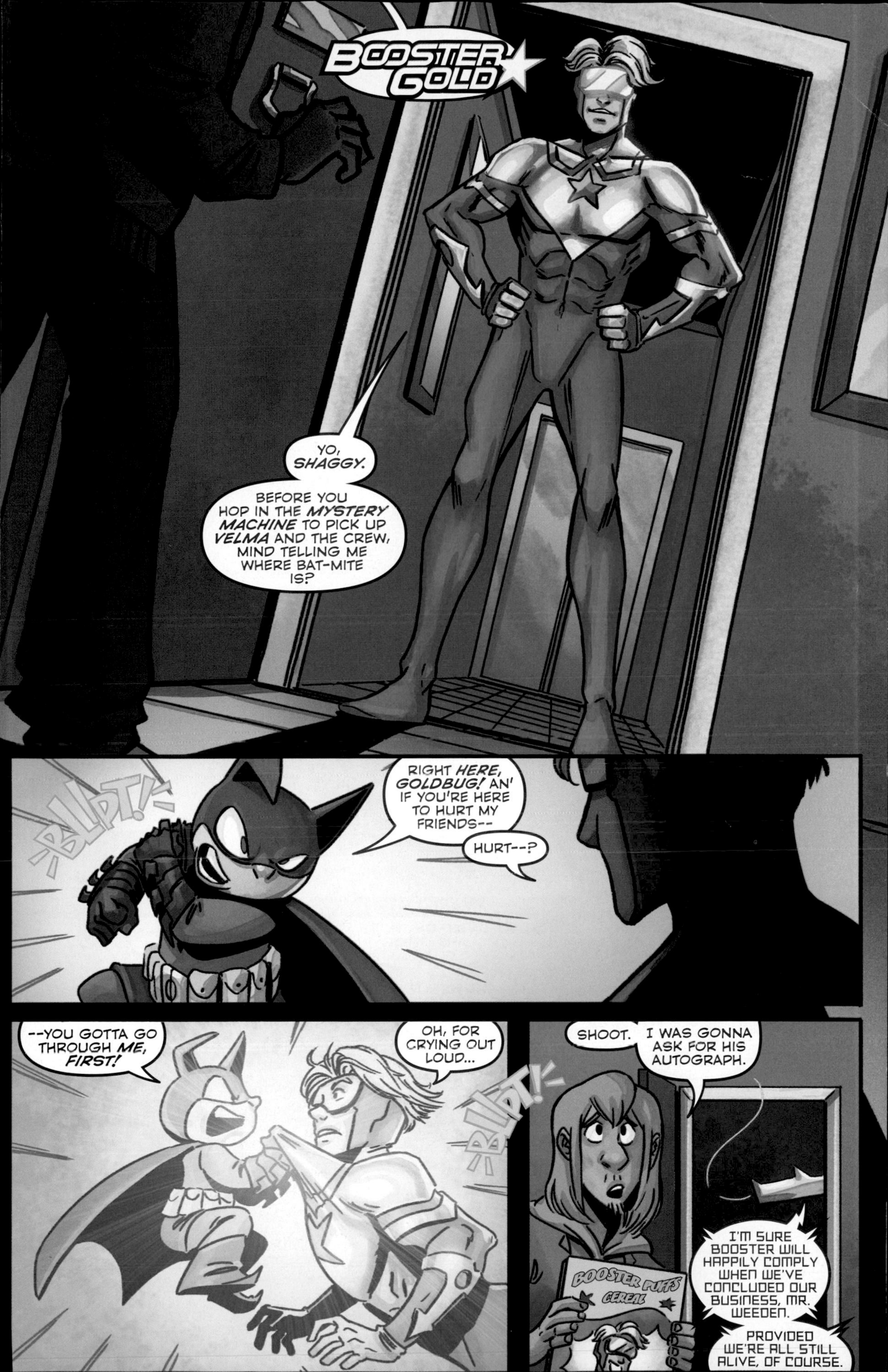

BOOSTER GOLD
YO, SHAGGY.
BEFORE YOU HOP IN THE MYSTERY MACHINE TO PICK UP VELMA AND THE CREW, MIND TELLING ME WHERE BAT-MITE IS?
BLIPT!
RIGHT HERE, GOLDBUG! AN' IF YOU'RE HERE TO HURT MY FRIENDS--
HURT--?
--YOU GOTTA GO THROUGH ME, FIRST!
OH, FOR CRYING OUT LOUD...
BLIPT!
SHOOT. I WAS GONNA ASK FOR HIS AUTOGRAPH.
BOOSTER PUFFS CEREAL
I'M SURE BOOSTER WILL HAPPILY COMPLY WHEN WE'VE CONCLUDED OUR BUSINESS, MR. WEEDEN.
PROVIDED WE'RE ALL STILL ALIVE, OF COURSE.

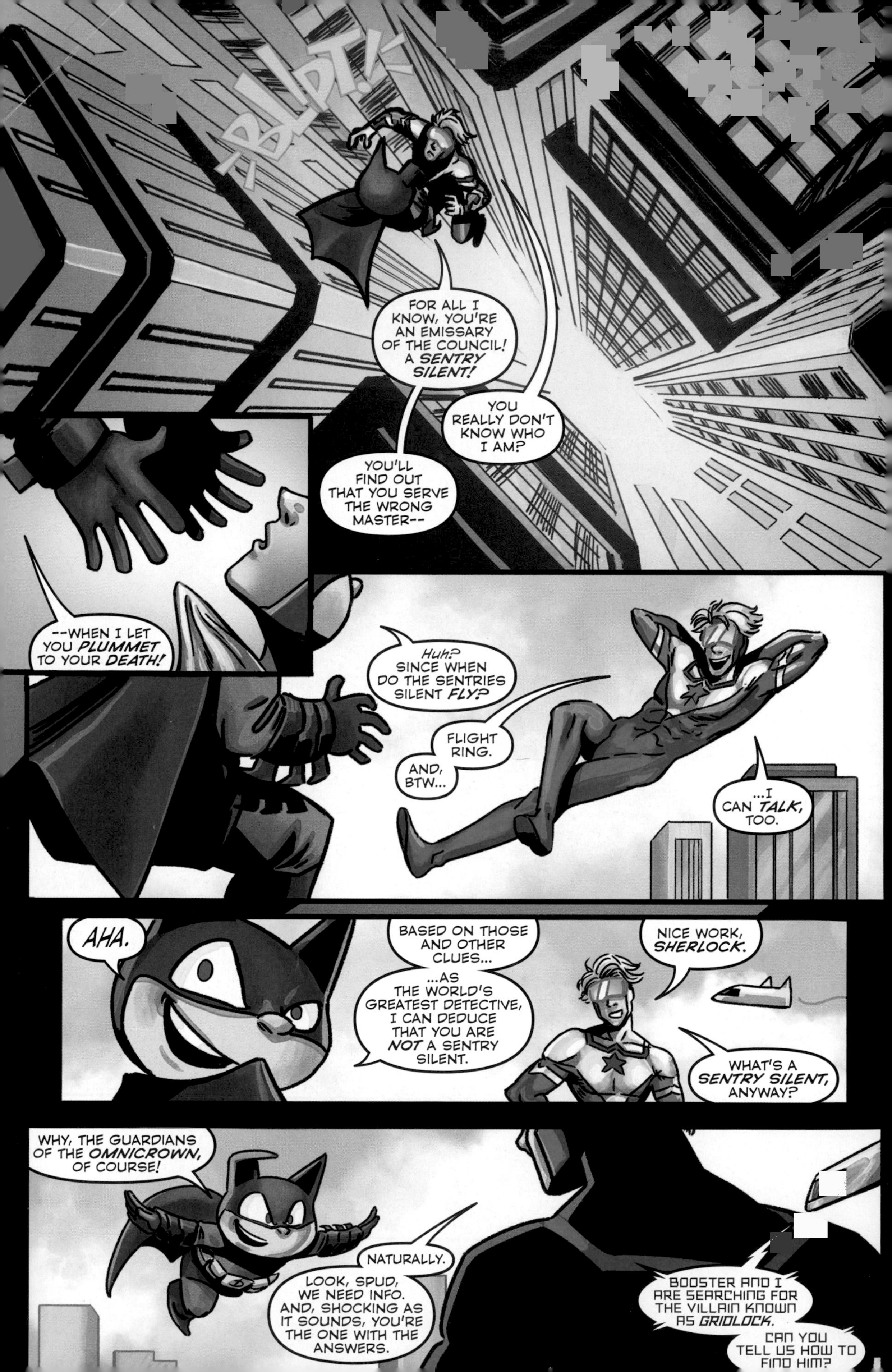
FOR ALL I KNOW, YOU'RE AN EMISSARY OF THE COUNCIL! A *SENTRY SILENT!*
YOU REALLY DON'T KNOW WHO I AM?
YOU'LL FIND OUT THAT YOU SERVE THE WRONG MASTER--
--WHEN I LET YOU *PLUMMET* TO YOUR *DEATH!*
Huh? SINCE WHEN DO THE SENTRIES SILENT *FLY?*
FLIGHT RING.
AND, BTW...
...I CAN *TALK,* TOO.
AHA.
BASED ON THOSE AND OTHER CLUES...
...AS THE WORLD'S GREATEST DETECTIVE, I CAN DEDUCE THAT YOU ARE *NOT* A SENTRY SILENT.
NICE WORK, *SHERLOCK.*
WHAT'S A *SENTRY SILENT,* ANYWAY?
WHY, THE GUARDIANS OF THE *OMNICROWN,* OF COURSE!
NATURALLY.
LOOK, SPUD, WE NEED INFO. AND, SHOCKING AS IT SOUNDS, YOU'RE THE ONE WITH THE ANSWERS.
BOOSTER AND I ARE SEARCHING FOR THE VILLAIN KNOWN AS *GRIDLOCK.*
CAN YOU TELL US HOW TO FIND HIM?

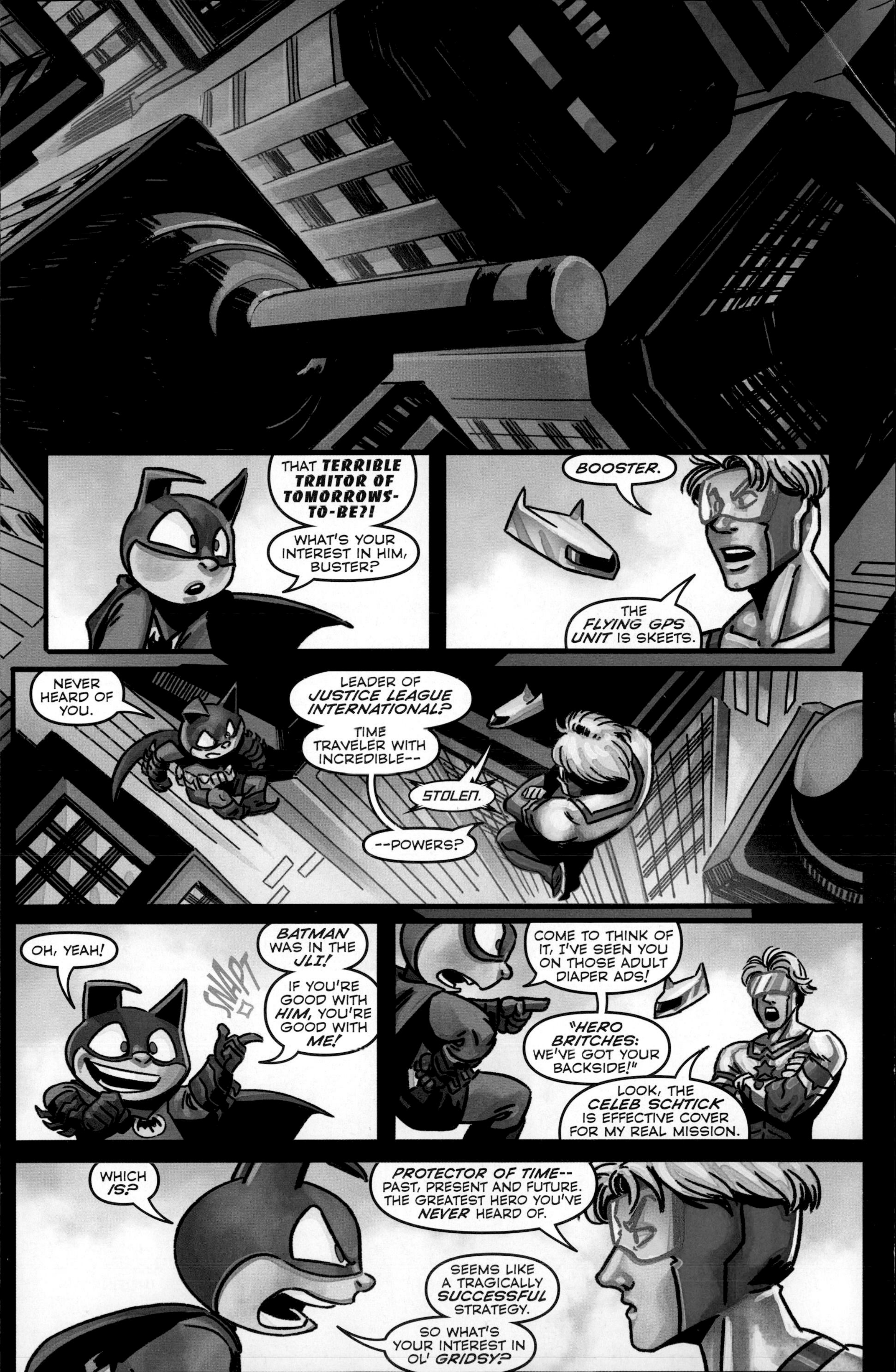

THAT TERRIBLE TRAITOR OF TOMORROWS-TO-BE?!
WHAT'S YOUR INTEREST IN HIM, BUSTER?
BOOSTER.
THE FLYING GPS UNIT IS SKEETS.
NEVER HEARD OF YOU.
LEADER OF JUSTICE LEAGUE INTERNATIONAL?
TIME TRAVELER WITH INCREDIBLE--
STOLEN.
--POWERS?
OH, YEAH!
BATMAN WAS IN THE JLI!
IF YOU'RE GOOD WITH HIM, YOU'RE GOOD WITH ME!
SNAP!
COME TO THINK OF IT, I'VE SEEN YOU ON THOSE ADULT DIAPER ADS!
"HERO BRITCHES: WE'VE GOT YOUR BACKSIDE!"
LOOK, THE CELEB SCHTICK IS EFFECTIVE COVER FOR MY REAL MISSION.
WHICH IS?
PROTECTOR OF TIME-- PAST, PRESENT AND FUTURE. THE GREATEST HERO YOU'VE NEVER HEARD OF.
SEEMS LIKE A TRAGICALLY SUCCESSFUL STRATEGY.
SO WHAT'S YOUR INTEREST IN OL' GRIDSY?

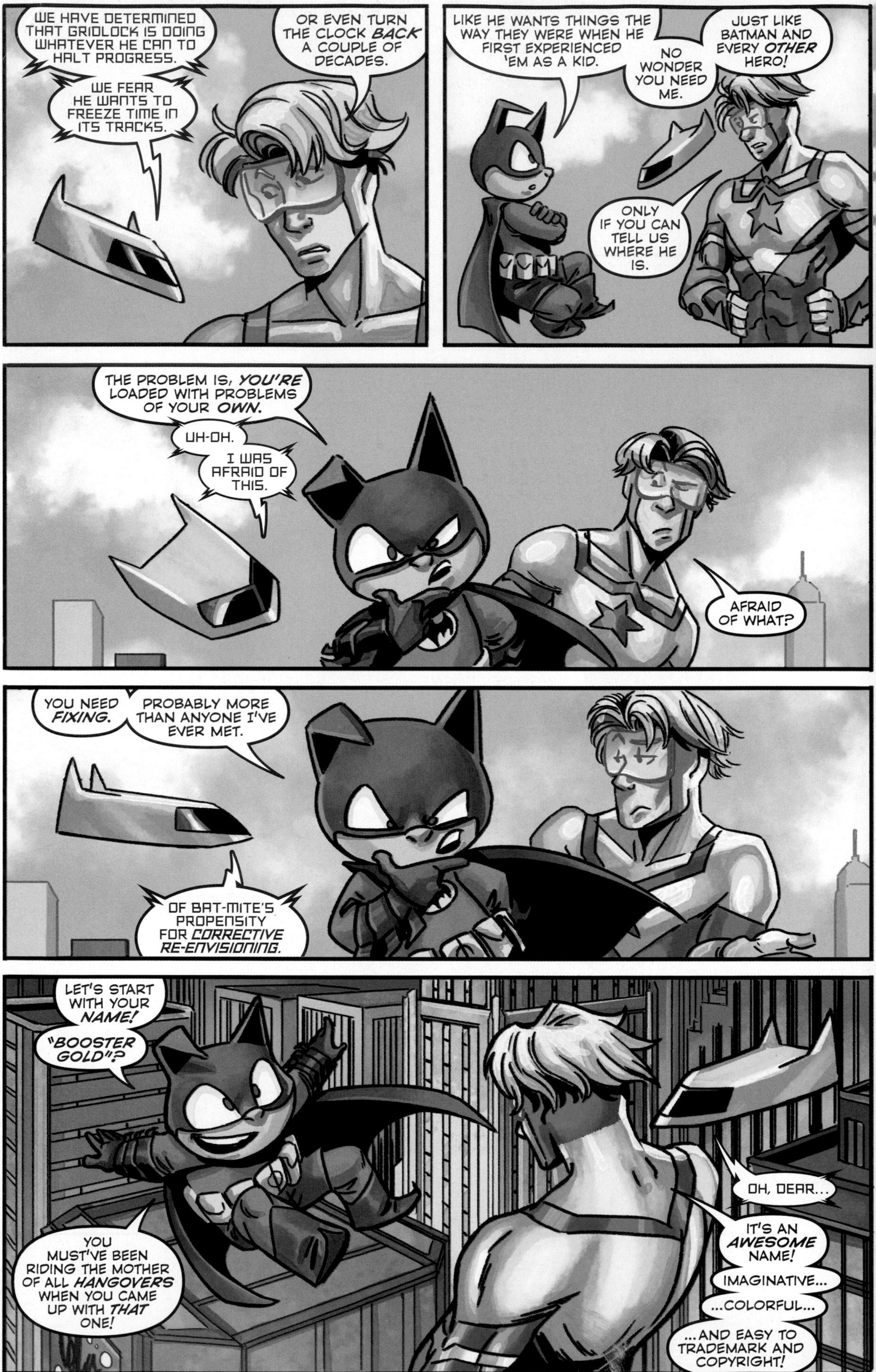
WE HAVE DETERMINED THAT GRIDLOCK IS DOING WHATEVER HE CAN TO HALT PROGRESS.
WE FEAR HE WANTS TO FREEZE TIME IN ITS TRACKS.
OR EVEN TURN THE CLOCK BACK A COUPLE OF DECADES.
LIKE HE WANTS THINGS THE WAY THEY WERE WHEN HE FIRST EXPERIENCED 'EM AS A KID.
JUST LIKE BATMAN AND EVERY OTHER HERO!
NO WONDER YOU NEED ME.
ONLY IF YOU CAN TELL US WHERE HE IS.
THE PROBLEM IS, YOU'RE LOADED WITH PROBLEMS OF YOUR OWN.
UH-OH.
I WAS AFRAID OF THIS.
AFRAID OF WHAT?
YOU NEED FIXING.
PROBABLY MORE THAN ANYONE I'VE EVER MET.
OF BAT-MITE'S PROPENSITY FOR CORRECTIVE RE-ENVISIONING.
LET'S START WITH YOUR NAME!
"BOOSTER GOLD"?
YOU MUST'VE BEEN RIDING THE MOTHER OF ALL HANGOVERS WHEN YOU CAME UP WITH THAT ONE!
OH, DEAR...
IT'S AN AWESOME NAME!
IMAGINATIVE...
...COLORFUL...
...AND EASY TO TRADEMARK AND COPYRIGHT!

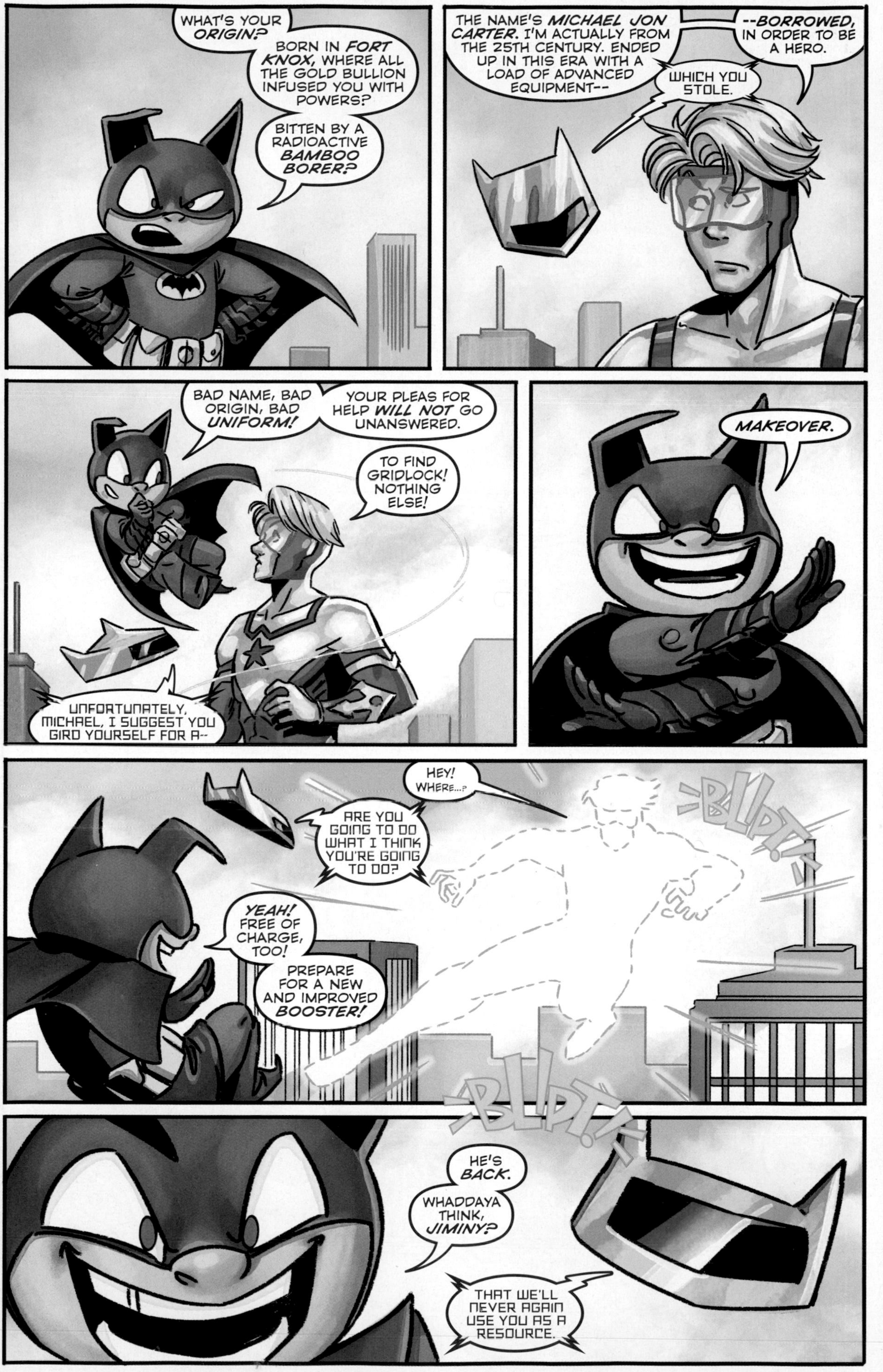
WHAT'S YOUR ORIGIN?
BORN IN FORT KNOX, WHERE ALL THE GOLD BULLION INFUSED YOU WITH POWERS?
BITTEN BY A RADIOACTIVE BAMBOO BORER?
THE NAME'S MICHAEL JON CARTER. I'M ACTUALLY FROM THE 25TH CENTURY. ENDED UP IN THIS ERA WITH A LOAD OF ADVANCED EQUIPMENT--
WHICH YOU STOLE.
--BORROWED, IN ORDER TO BE A HERO.
BAD NAME, BAD ORIGIN, BAD UNIFORM!
YOUR PLEAS FOR HELP WILL NOT GO UNANSWERED.
TO FIND GRIDLOCK! NOTHING ELSE!
UNFORTUNATELY, MICHAEL, I SUGGEST YOU GIRD YOURSELF FOR A--
MAKEOVER.
HEY! WHERE...?
ARE YOU GOING TO DO WHAT I THINK YOU'RE GOING TO DO?
YEAH! FREE OF CHARGE, TOO!
PREPARE FOR A NEW AND IMPROVED BOOSTER!
BLIPT!
BLIPT!
HE'S BACK.
WHADDAYA THINK, JIMINY?
THAT WE'LL NEVER AGAIN USE YOU AS A RESOURCE.

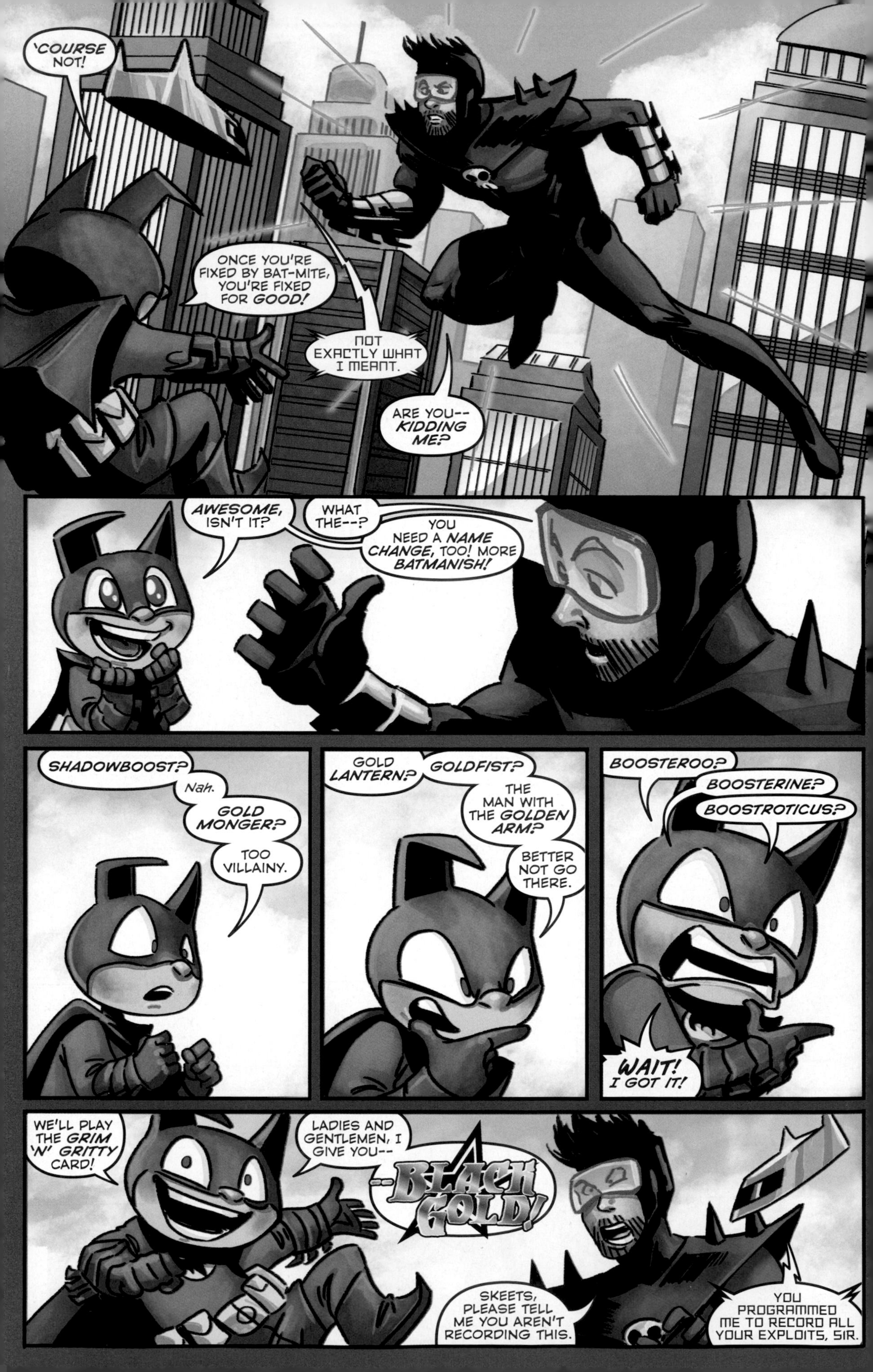
'COURSE NOT!
ONCE YOU'RE FIXED BY BAT-MITE, YOU'RE FIXED FOR GOOD!
NOT EXACTLY WHAT I MEANT.
ARE YOU--KIDDING ME?
AWESOME, ISN'T IT?
WHAT THE--?
YOU NEED A NAME CHANGE, TOO! MORE BATMANISH!
SHADOWBOOST?
Nah.
GOLD MONGER?
TOO VILLAINY.
GOLD LANTERN?
GOLDFIST?
THE MAN WITH THE GOLDEN ARM?
BETTER NOT GO THERE.
BOOSTEROO?
BOOSTERINE?
BOOSTROTICUS?
WAIT! I GOT IT!
WE'LL PLAY THE GRIM 'N' GRITTY CARD!
LADIES AND GENTLEMEN, I GIVE YOU--
--BLACK GOLD!
SKEETS, PLEASE TELL ME YOU AREN'T RECORDING THIS.
YOU PROGRAMMED ME TO RECORD ALL YOUR EXPLOITS, SIR.

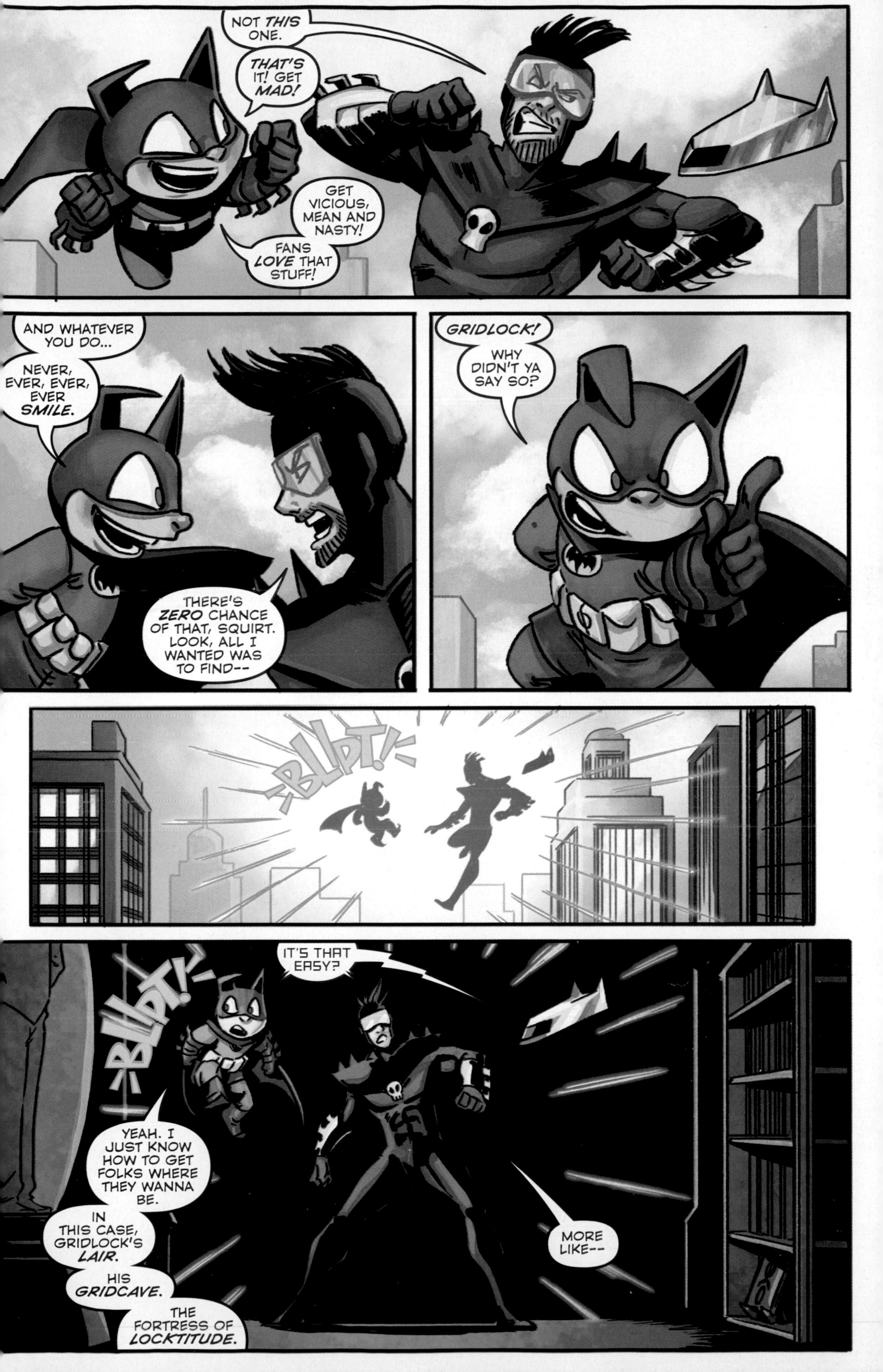
NOT *THIS* ONE.
THAT'S IT! GET *MAD!*
GET VICIOUS, MEAN AND NASTY!
FANS *LOVE* THAT STUFF!
AND WHATEVER YOU DO...
NEVER, EVER, EVER, EVER *SMILE*.
THERE'S *ZERO* CHANCE OF THAT, SQUIRT. LOOK, ALL I WANTED WAS TO FIND--
GRIDLOCK!
WHY DIDN'T YA SAY SO?
BLIPT!
BLIPT!
IT'S THAT EASY?
YEAH. I JUST KNOW HOW TO GET FOLKS WHERE THEY WANNA BE.
IN THIS CASE, GRIDLOCK'S *LAIR*.
HIS *GRIDCAVE*.
THE FORTRESS OF *LOCKTITUDE*.
MORE LIKE--

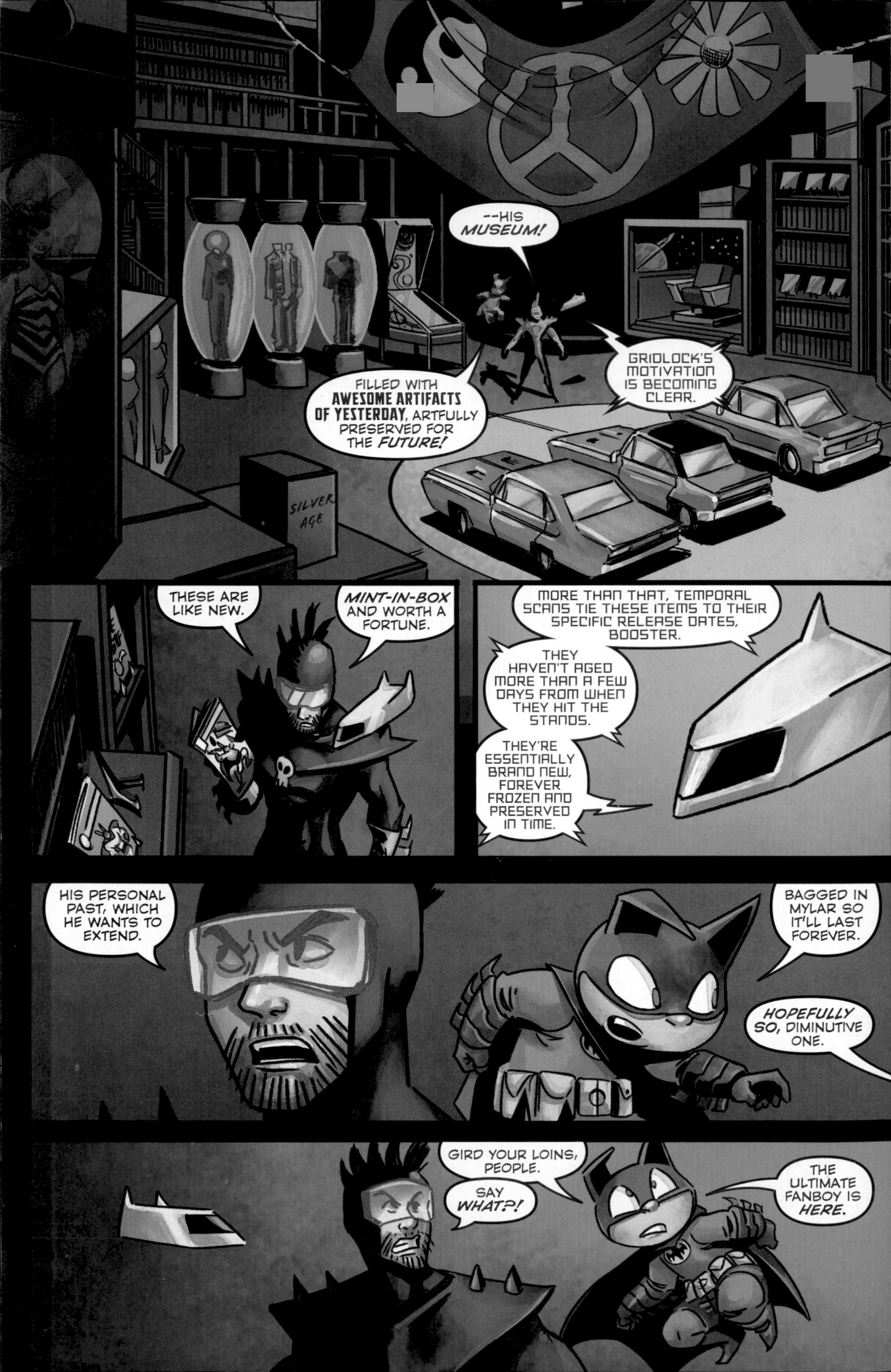
--HIS MUSEUM!
FILLED WITH AWESOME ARTIFACTS OF YESTERDAY, ARTFULLY PRESERVED FOR THE FUTURE!
GRIDLOCK'S MOTIVATION IS BECOMING CLEAR.
SILVER AGE
THESE ARE LIKE NEW.
MINT-IN-BOX AND WORTH A FORTUNE.
MORE THAN THAT, TEMPORAL SCANS TIE THESE ITEMS TO THEIR SPECIFIC RELEASE DATES, BOOSTER.
THEY HAVEN'T AGED MORE THAN A FEW DAYS FROM WHEN THEY HIT THE STANDS.
THEY'RE ESSENTIALLY BRAND NEW, FOREVER FROZEN AND PRESERVED IN TIME.
HIS PERSONAL PAST, WHICH HE WANTS TO EXTEND.
BAGGED IN MYLAR SO IT'LL LAST FOREVER.
HOPEFULLY SO, DIMINUTIVE ONE.
GIRD YOUR LOINS, PEOPLE.
SAY WHAT?!
THE ULTIMATE FANBOY IS HERE.

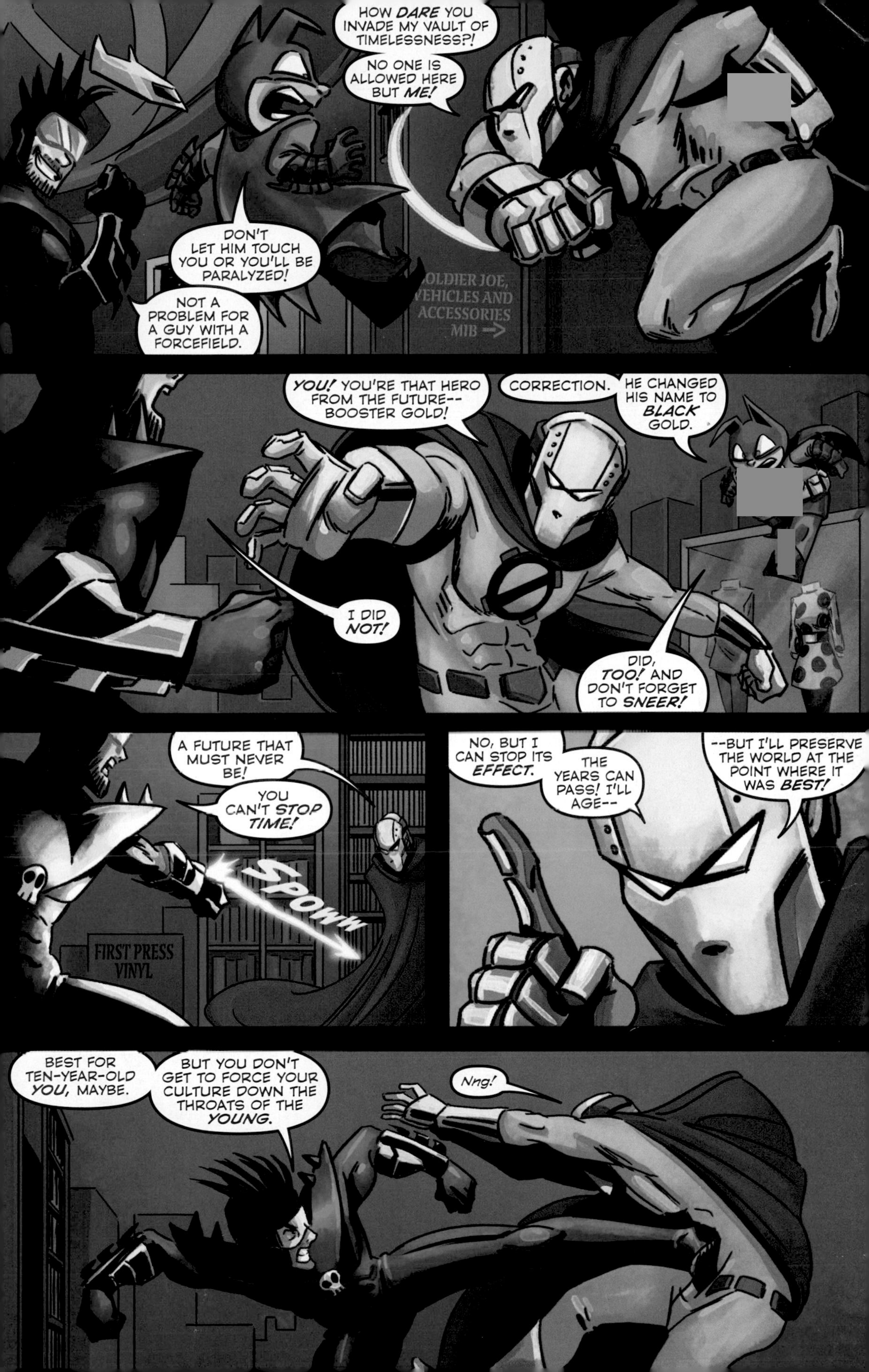
HOW DARE YOU INVADE MY VAULT OF TIMELESSNESS?!
NO ONE IS ALLOWED HERE BUT ME!
DON'T LET HIM TOUCH YOU OR YOU'LL BE PARALYZED!
NOT A PROBLEM FOR A GUY WITH A FORCEFIELD.
OLDIER JOE, VEHICLES AND ACCESSORIES MIB
YOU! YOU'RE THAT HERO FROM THE FUTURE-- BOOSTER GOLD!
CORRECTION.
HE CHANGED HIS NAME TO BLACK GOLD.
I DID NOT!
DID, TOO! AND DON'T FORGET TO SNEER!
A FUTURE THAT MUST NEVER BE!
YOU CAN'T STOP TIME!
SPOWW
FIRST PRESS VINYL
NO, BUT I CAN STOP ITS EFFECT.
THE YEARS CAN PASS! I'LL AGE--
--BUT I'LL PRESERVE THE WORLD AT THE POINT WHERE IT WAS BEST!
BEST FOR TEN-YEAR-OLD YOU, MAYBE.
BUT YOU DON'T GET TO FORCE YOUR CULTURE DOWN THE THROATS OF THE YOUNG.
Nng!

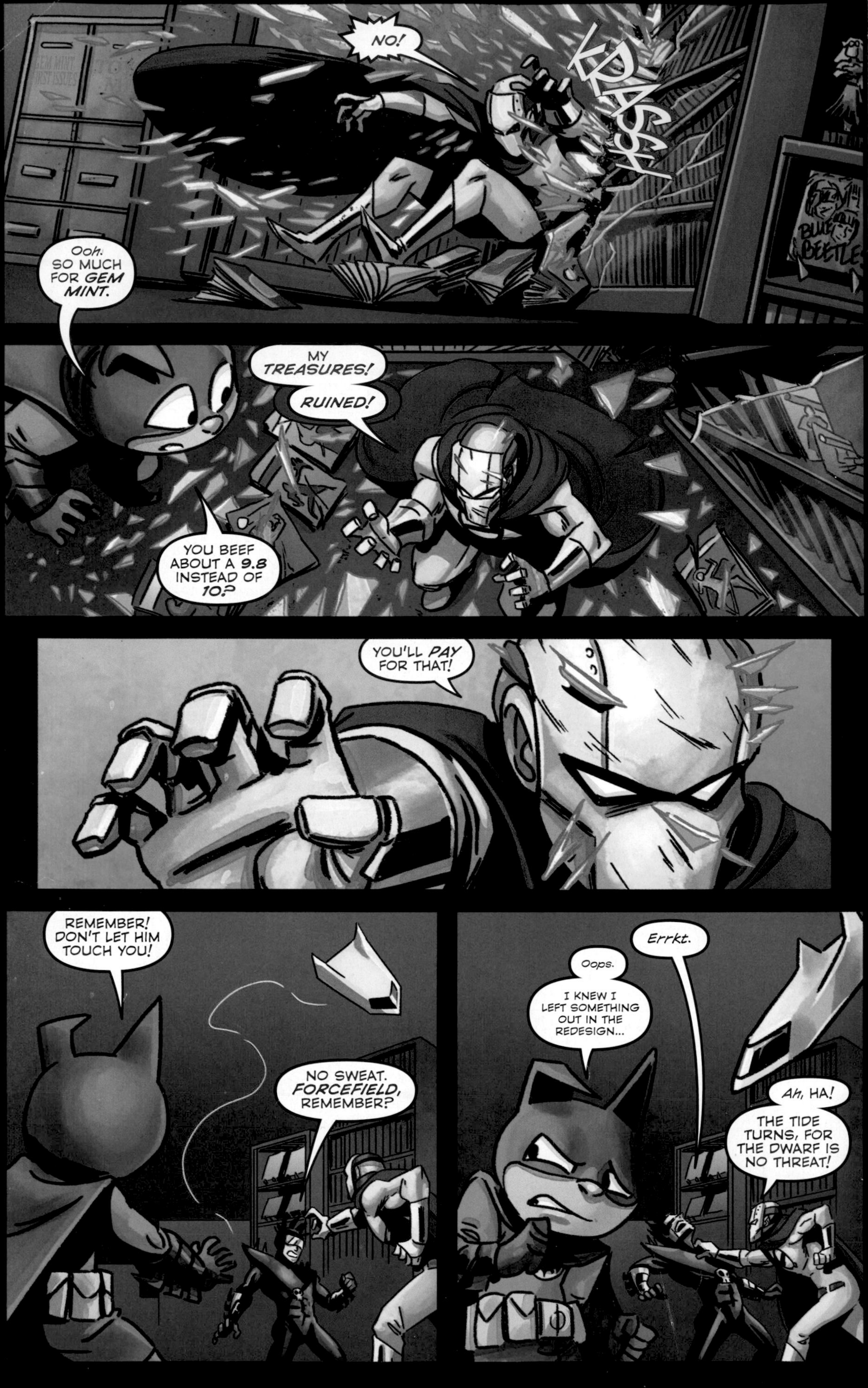
NO!
KRASSH
Ooh. SO MUCH FOR GEM MINT.
MY TREASURES!
RUINED!
YOU BEEF ABOUT A 9.8 INSTEAD OF 10?
YOU'LL PAY FOR THAT!
REMEMBER! DON'T LET HIM TOUCH YOU!
NO SWEAT. FORCEFIELD, REMEMBER?
Errkt.
Oops.
I KNEW I LEFT SOMETHING OUT IN THE REDESIGN...
Ah, HA!
THE TIDE TURNS, FOR THE DWARF IS NO THREAT!

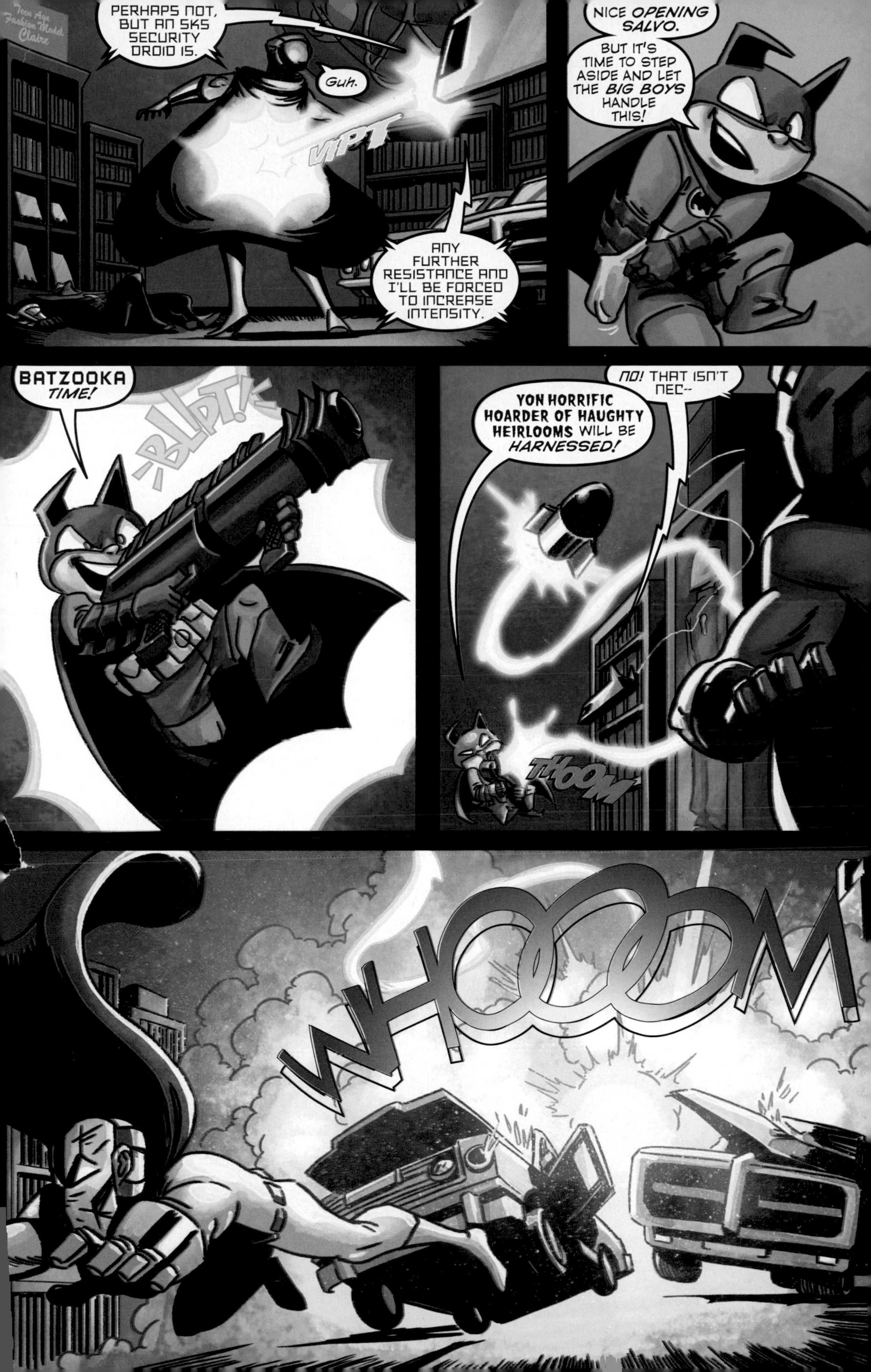

Icon Age Fashion Model Claire
PERHAPS NOT, BUT AN SKS SECURITY DROID IS.
Guh.
VIPT
ANY FURTHER RESISTANCE AND I'LL BE FORCED TO INCREASE INTENSITY.
NICE OPENING SALVO.
BUT IT'S TIME TO STEP ASIDE AND LET THE BIG BOYS HANDLE THIS!
BATZOOKA TIME!
BLIPT!
NO! THAT ISN'T NEC--
YON HORRIFIC HOARDER OF HAUGHTY HEIRLOOMS WILL BE HARNESSED!
THOOM
WHOOOOM

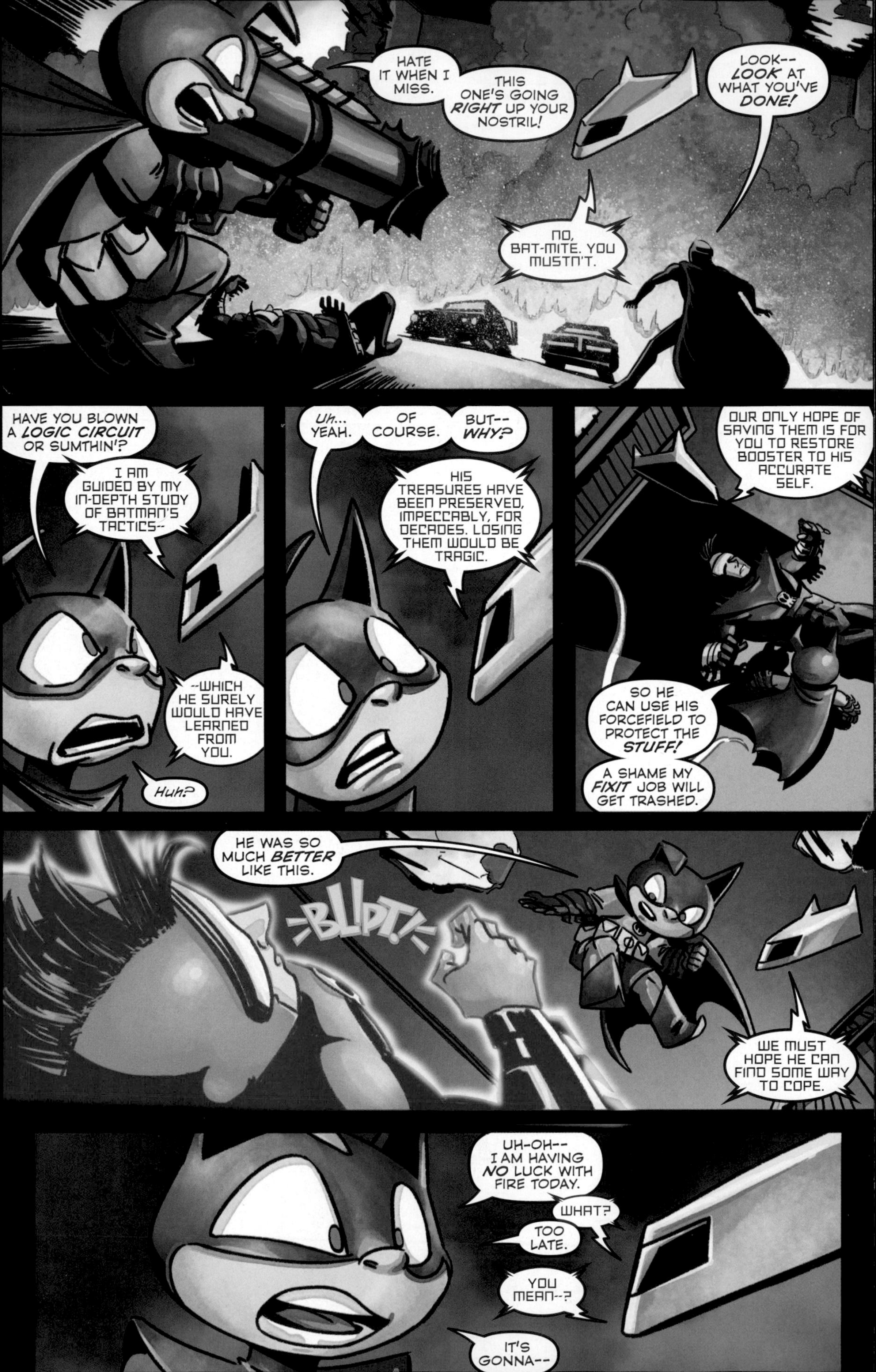
HATE IT WHEN I MISS.
THIS ONE'S GOING *RIGHT* UP YOUR NOSTRIL!
LOOK-- *LOOK* AT WHAT YOU'VE *DONE!*
NO, BAT-MITE. YOU MUSTN'T.
HAVE YOU BLOWN A *LOGIC CIRCUIT* OR SUMTHIN'?
I AM GUIDED BY MY IN-DEPTH STUDY OF BATMAN'S TACTICS--
--WHICH HE SURELY WOULD HAVE LEARNED FROM YOU.
Huh?
Uh... YEAH.
OF COURSE.
BUT-- *WHY?*
HIS TREASURES HAVE BEEN PRESERVED, IMPECCABLY, FOR DECADES. LOSING THEM WOULD BE TRAGIC.
OUR ONLY HOPE OF SAVING THEM IS FOR YOU TO RESTORE BOOSTER TO HIS ACCURATE SELF.
SO HE CAN USE HIS FORCEFIELD TO PROTECT THE *STUFF!*
A SHAME MY *FIXIT* JOB WILL GET TRASHED.
HE WAS SO MUCH *BETTER* LIKE THIS.
BLIPT!
WE MUST HOPE HE CAN FIND SOME WAY TO COPE.
UH-OH-- I AM HAVING *NO* LUCK WITH FIRE TODAY.
WHAT?
TOO LATE.
YOU MEAN--?
IT'S GONNA--

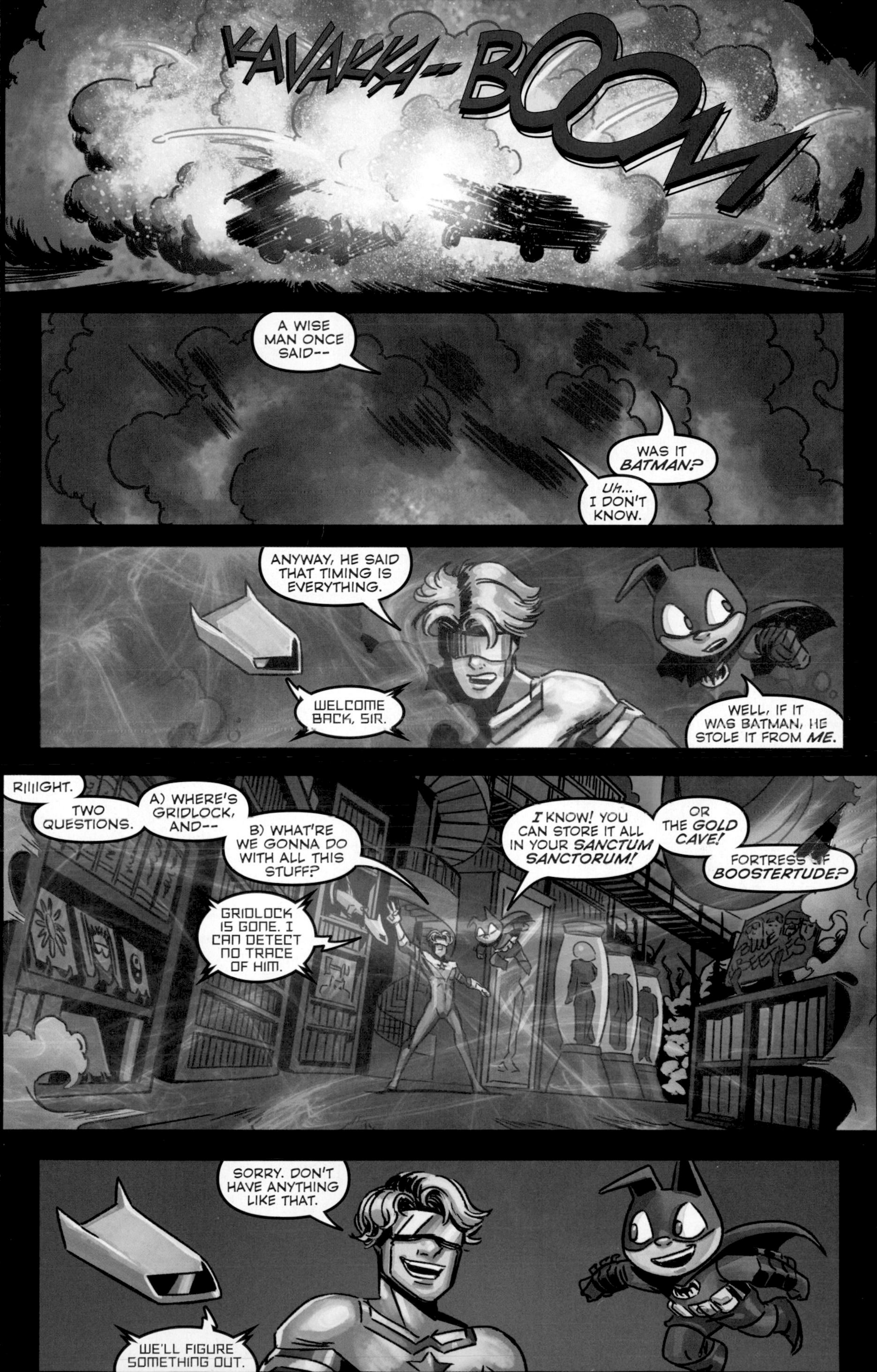
KAVAKKA-- BOOM
A WISE MAN ONCE SAID--
WAS IT BATMAN?
UH... I DON'T KNOW.
ANYWAY, HE SAID THAT TIMING IS EVERYTHING.
WELCOME BACK, SIR.
WELL, IF IT WAS BATMAN, HE STOLE IT FROM ME.
RIIIIGHT.
TWO QUESTIONS.
A) WHERE'S GRIDLOCK, AND--
B) WHAT'RE WE GONNA DO WITH ALL THIS STUFF?
GRIDLOCK IS GONE. I CAN DETECT NO TRACE OF HIM.
I KNOW! YOU CAN STORE IT ALL IN YOUR SANCTUM SANCTORUM!
OR THE GOLD CAVE!
FORTRESS OF BOOSTERTUDE?
BLUE BEETLES
SORRY. DON'T HAVE ANYTHING LIKE THAT.
WE'LL FIGURE SOMETHING OUT.

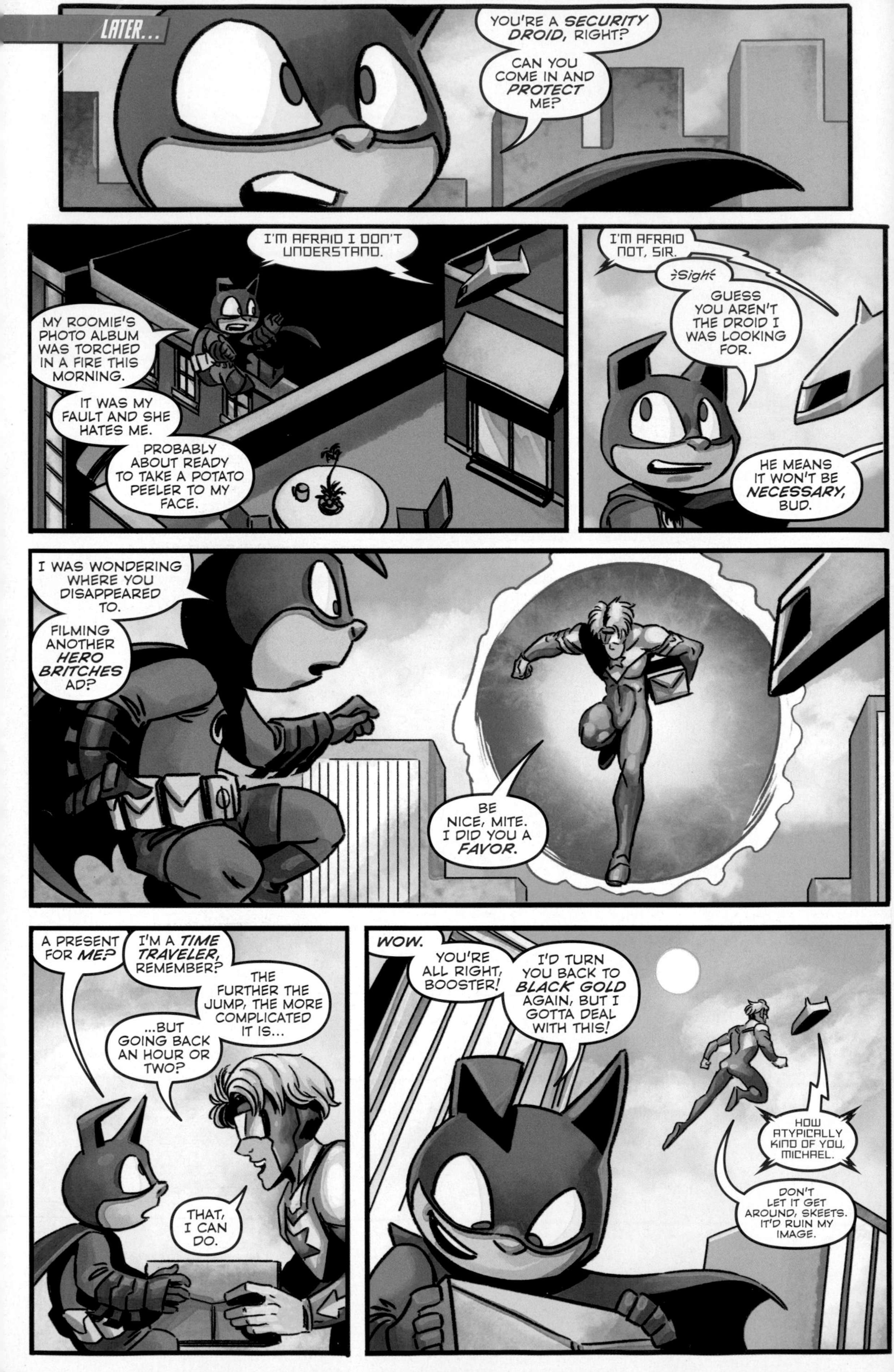
LATER...
YOU'RE A SECURITY DROID, RIGHT?
CAN YOU COME IN AND PROTECT ME?
I'M AFRAID I DON'T UNDERSTAND.
MY ROOMIE'S PHOTO ALBUM WAS TORCHED IN A FIRE THIS MORNING.
IT WAS MY FAULT AND SHE HATES ME.
PROBABLY ABOUT READY TO TAKE A POTATO PEELER TO MY FACE.
I'M AFRAID NOT, SIR.
Sigh
GUESS YOU AREN'T THE DROID I WAS LOOKING FOR.
HE MEANS IT WON'T BE NECESSARY, BUD.
I WAS WONDERING WHERE YOU DISAPPEARED TO.
FILMING ANOTHER HERO BRITCHES AD?
BE NICE, MITE. I DID YOU A FAVOR.
A PRESENT FOR ME?
I'M A TIME TRAVELER, REMEMBER?
THE FURTHER THE JUMP, THE MORE COMPLICATED IT IS...
...BUT GOING BACK AN HOUR OR TWO?
THAT, I CAN DO.
WOW.
YOU'RE ALL RIGHT, BOOSTER!
I'D TURN YOU BACK TO BLACK GOLD AGAIN, BUT I GOTTA DEAL WITH THIS!
HOW ATYPICALLY KIND OF YOU, MICHAEL.
DON'T LET IT GET AROUND, SKEETS. IT'D RUIN MY IMAGE.

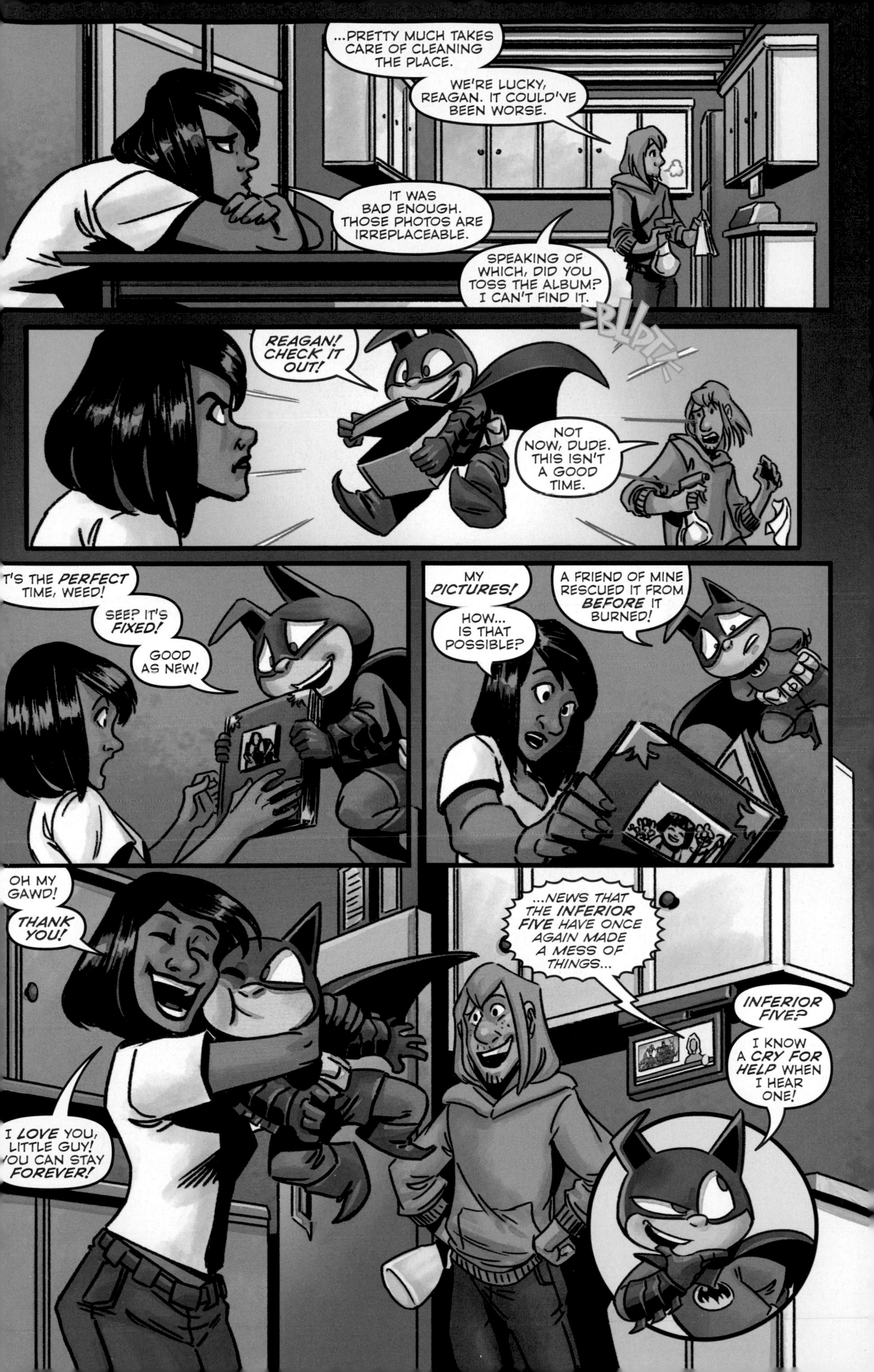

...PRETTY MUCH TAKES CARE OF CLEANING THE PLACE.
WE'RE LUCKY, REAGAN. IT COULD'VE BEEN WORSE.
IT WAS BAD ENOUGH. THOSE PHOTOS ARE IRREPLACEABLE.
SPEAKING OF WHICH, DID YOU TOSS THE ALBUM? I CAN'T FIND IT.
BLIPT!
REAGAN! CHECK IT OUT!
NOT NOW, DUDE. THIS ISN'T A GOOD TIME.
T'S THE PERFECT TIME, WEED!
SEE? IT'S FIXED!
GOOD AS NEW!
MY PICTURES!
HOW... IS THAT POSSIBLE?
A FRIEND OF MINE RESCUED IT FROM BEFORE IT BURNED!
OH MY GAWD!
THANK YOU!
...NEWS THAT THE INFERIOR FIVE HAVE ONCE AGAIN MADE A MESS OF THINGS...
INFERIOR FIVE?
I KNOW A CRY FOR HELP WHEN I HEAR ONE!
I LOVE YOU, LITTLE GUY! OU CAN STAY FOREVER!

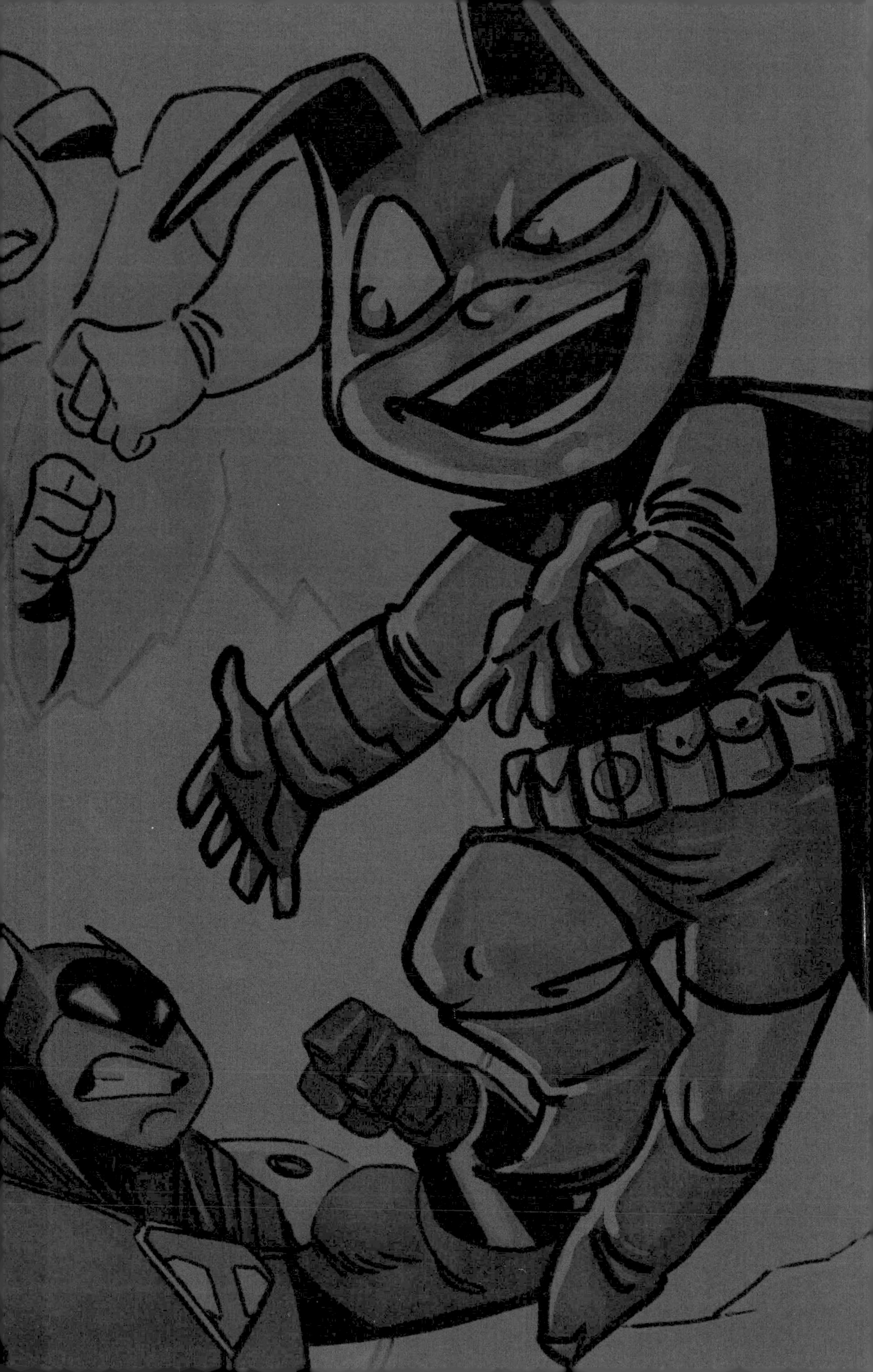

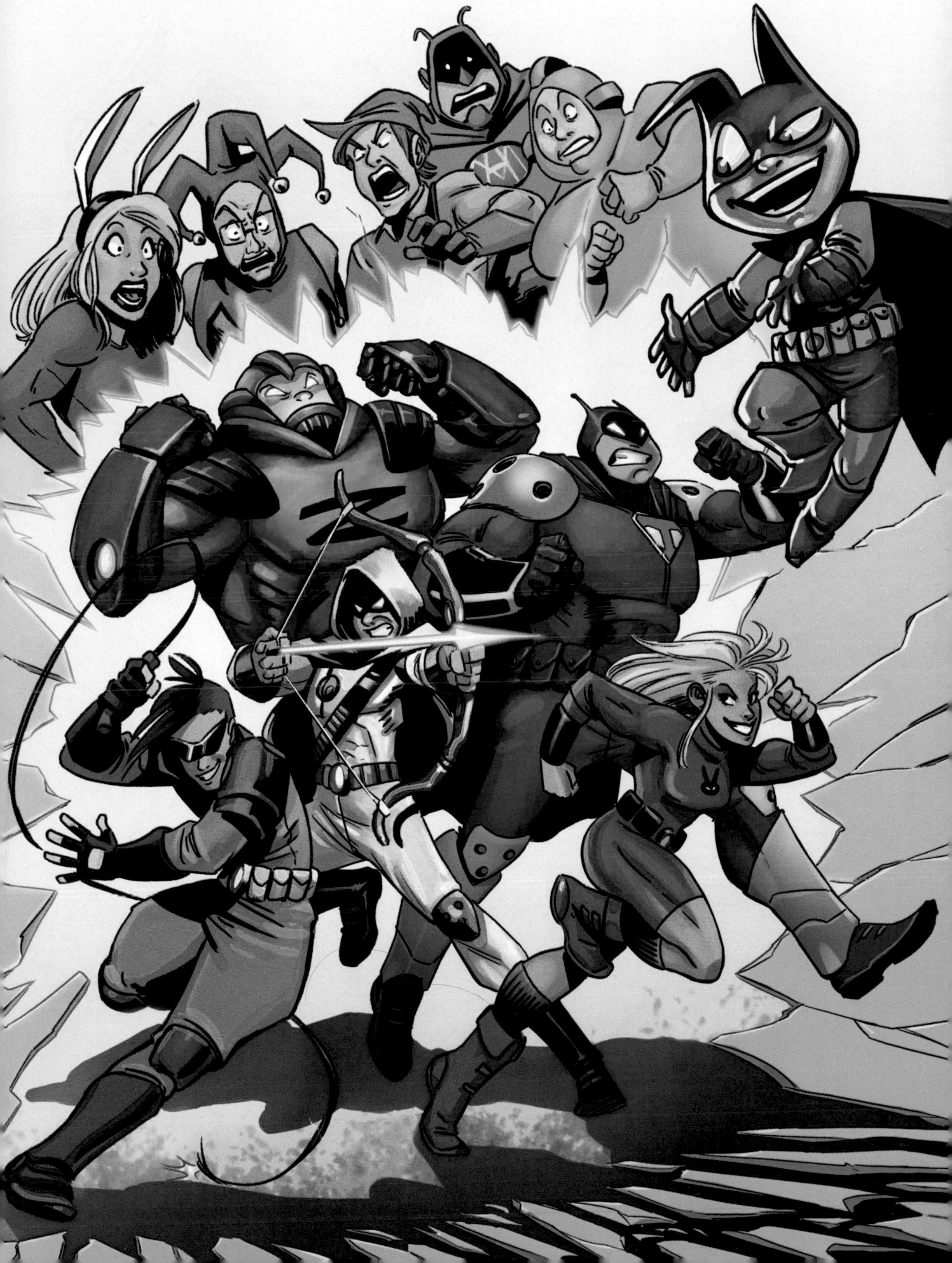

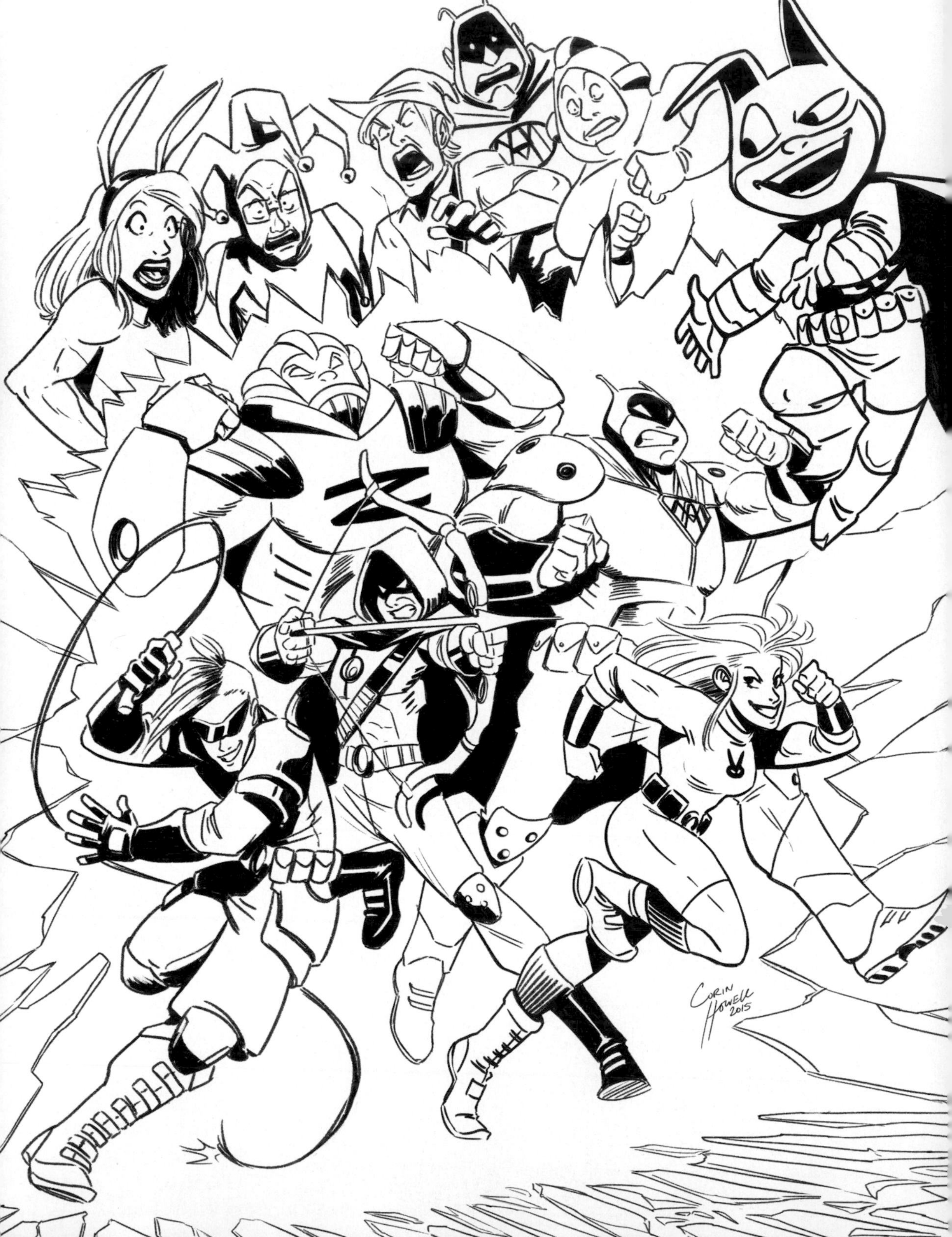
CORIN HOWELL 2015

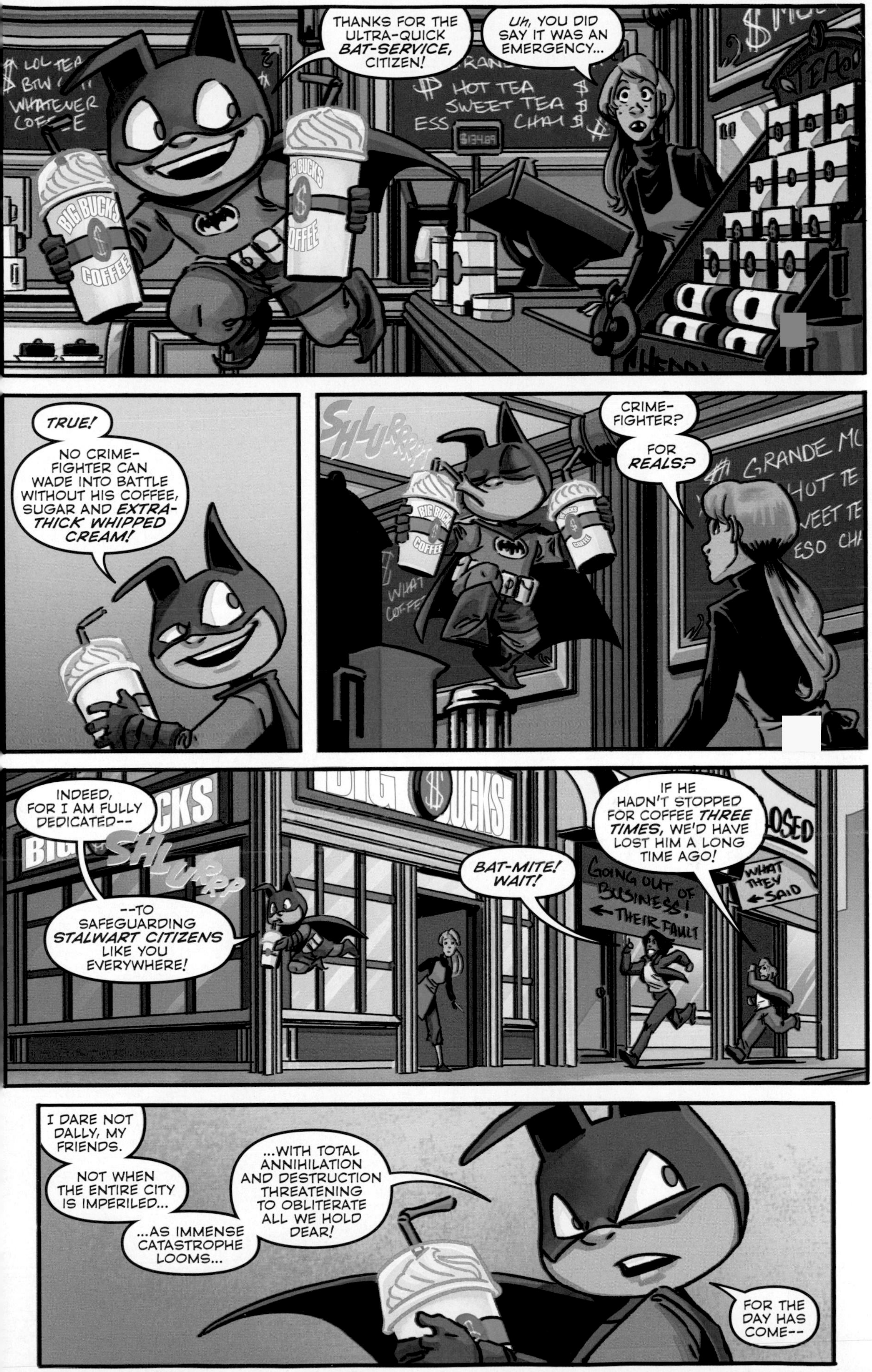
THANKS FOR THE ULTRA-QUICK *BAT-SERVICE,* CITIZEN!
Uh, YOU DID SAY IT WAS AN EMERGENCY...
HOT TEA
SWEET TEA
TRUE!
NO CRIME-FIGHTER CAN WADE INTO BATTLE WITHOUT HIS COFFEE, SUGAR AND *EXTRA-THICK WHIPPED CREAM!*
CRIME-FIGHTER?
FOR *REALS?*
INDEED, FOR I AM FULLY DEDICATED--
SHLURRP
--TO SAFEGUARDING *STALWART CITIZENS* LIKE YOU EVERYWHERE!
BAT-MITE! WAIT!
IF HE HADN'T STOPPED FOR COFFEE *THREE TIMES,* WE'D HAVE LOST HIM A LONG TIME AGO!
GOING OUT OF BUSINESS! ← THEIR FAULT
WHAT THEY ← SAID
I DARE NOT DALLY, MY FRIENDS.
NOT WHEN THE ENTIRE CITY IS IMPERILED...
...AS IMMENSE CATASTROPHE LOOMS...
...WITH TOTAL ANNIHILATION AND DESTRUCTION THREATENING TO OBLITERATE ALL WE HOLD DEAR!
FOR THE DAY HAS COME--

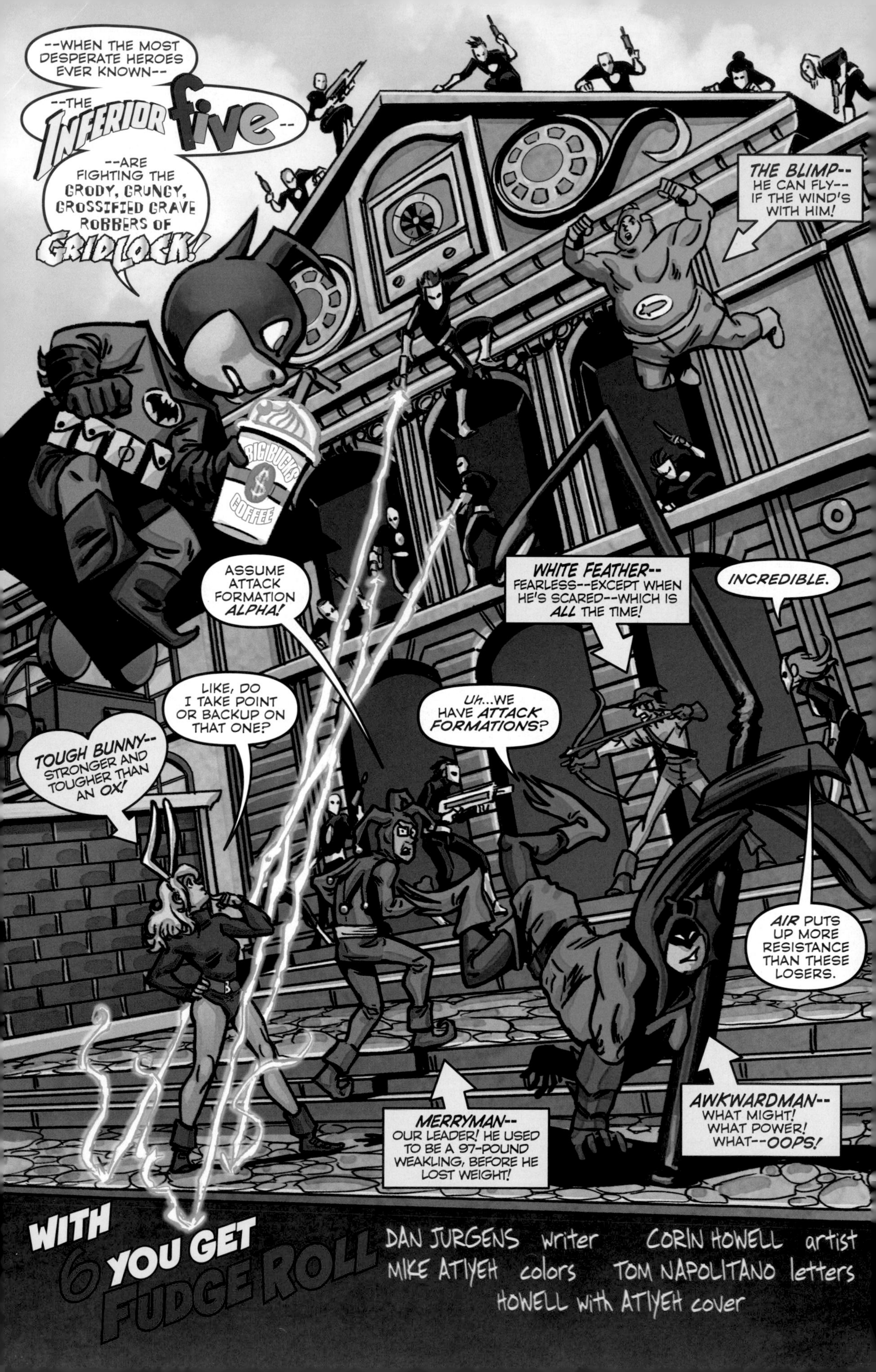
--WHEN THE MOST DESPERATE HEROES EVER KNOWN--
--THE INFERIOR FIVE--
--ARE FIGHTING THE GRODY, GRUNGY, GROSSIFIED GRAVE ROBBERS OF GRIDLOCK!
THE BLIMP-- HE CAN FLY-- IF THE WIND'S WITH HIM!
BIG BUCKS $ COFFEE
ASSUME ATTACK FORMATION ALPHA!
WHITE FEATHER-- FEARLESS--EXCEPT WHEN HE'S SCARED--WHICH IS ALL THE TIME!
INCREDIBLE.
LIKE, DO I TAKE POINT OR BACKUP ON THAT ONE?
UH...WE HAVE ATTACK FORMATIONS?
TOUGH BUNNY-- STRONGER AND TOUGHER THAN AN OX!
AIR PUTS UP MORE RESISTANCE THAN THESE LOSERS.
MERRYMAN-- OUR LEADER! HE USED TO BE A 97-POUND WEAKLING, BEFORE HE LOST WEIGHT!
AWKWARDMAN-- WHAT MIGHT! WHAT POWER! WHAT--OOPS!
WITH 6 YOU GET FUDGE ROLL
DAN JURGENS writer CORIN HOWELL artist
MIKE ATIYEH colors TOM NAPOLITANO letters
HOWELL with ATIYEH cover

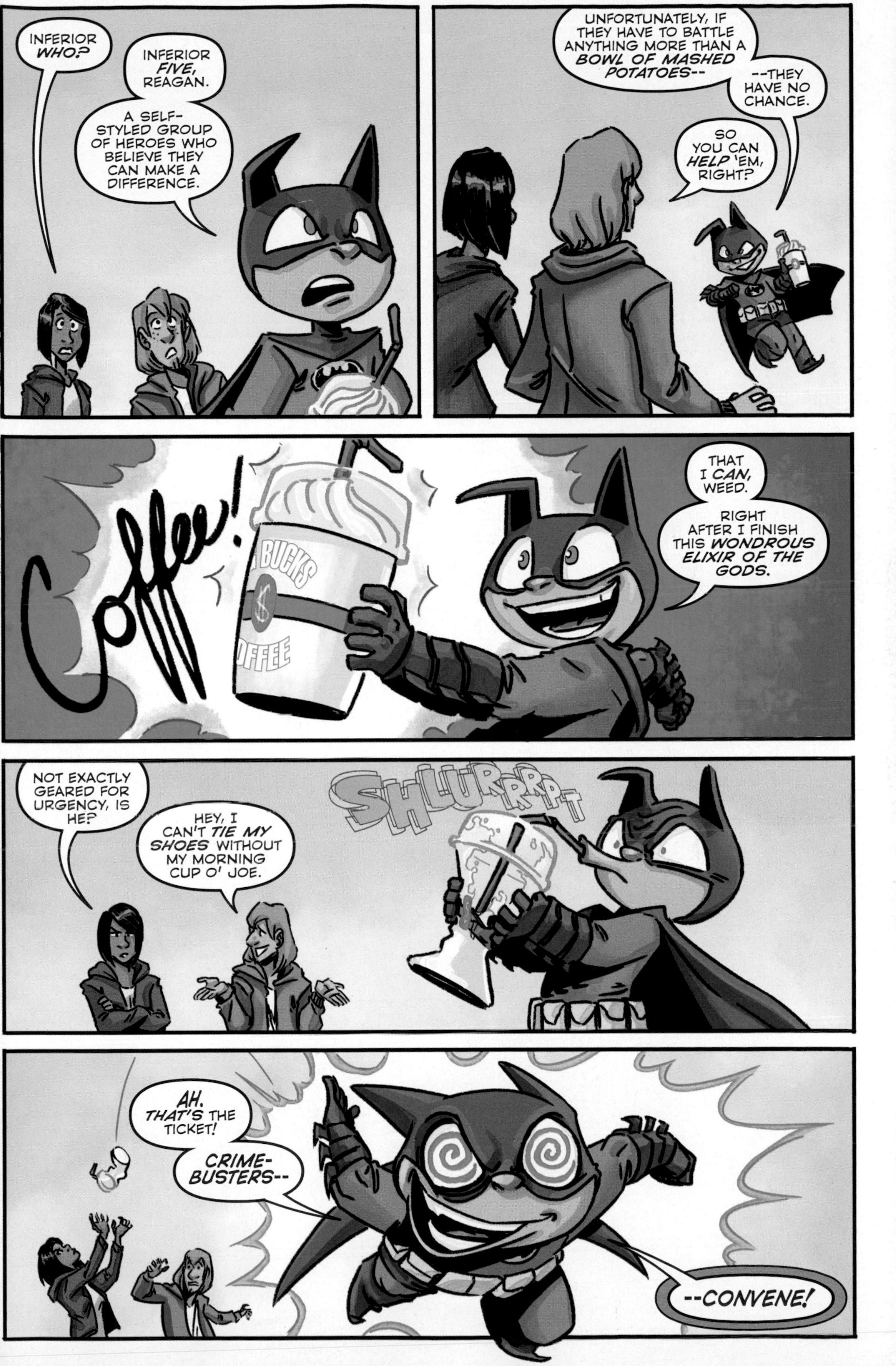

INFERIOR WHO?
INFERIOR FIVE, REAGAN.
A SELF-STYLED GROUP OF HEROES WHO BELIEVE THEY CAN MAKE A DIFFERENCE.
UNFORTUNATELY, IF THEY HAVE TO BATTLE ANYTHING MORE THAN A BOWL OF MASHED POTATOES--
--THEY HAVE NO CHANCE.
SO YOU CAN HELP 'EM, RIGHT?
Coffee!
THAT I CAN, WEED.
RIGHT AFTER I FINISH THIS WONDROUS ELIXIR OF THE GODS.
NOT EXACTLY GEARED FOR URGENCY, IS HE?
HEY, I CAN'T TIE MY SHOES WITHOUT MY MORNING CUP O' JOE.
SHLURRRPT
AH. THAT'S THE TICKET!
CRIME-BUSTERS--
--CONVENE!

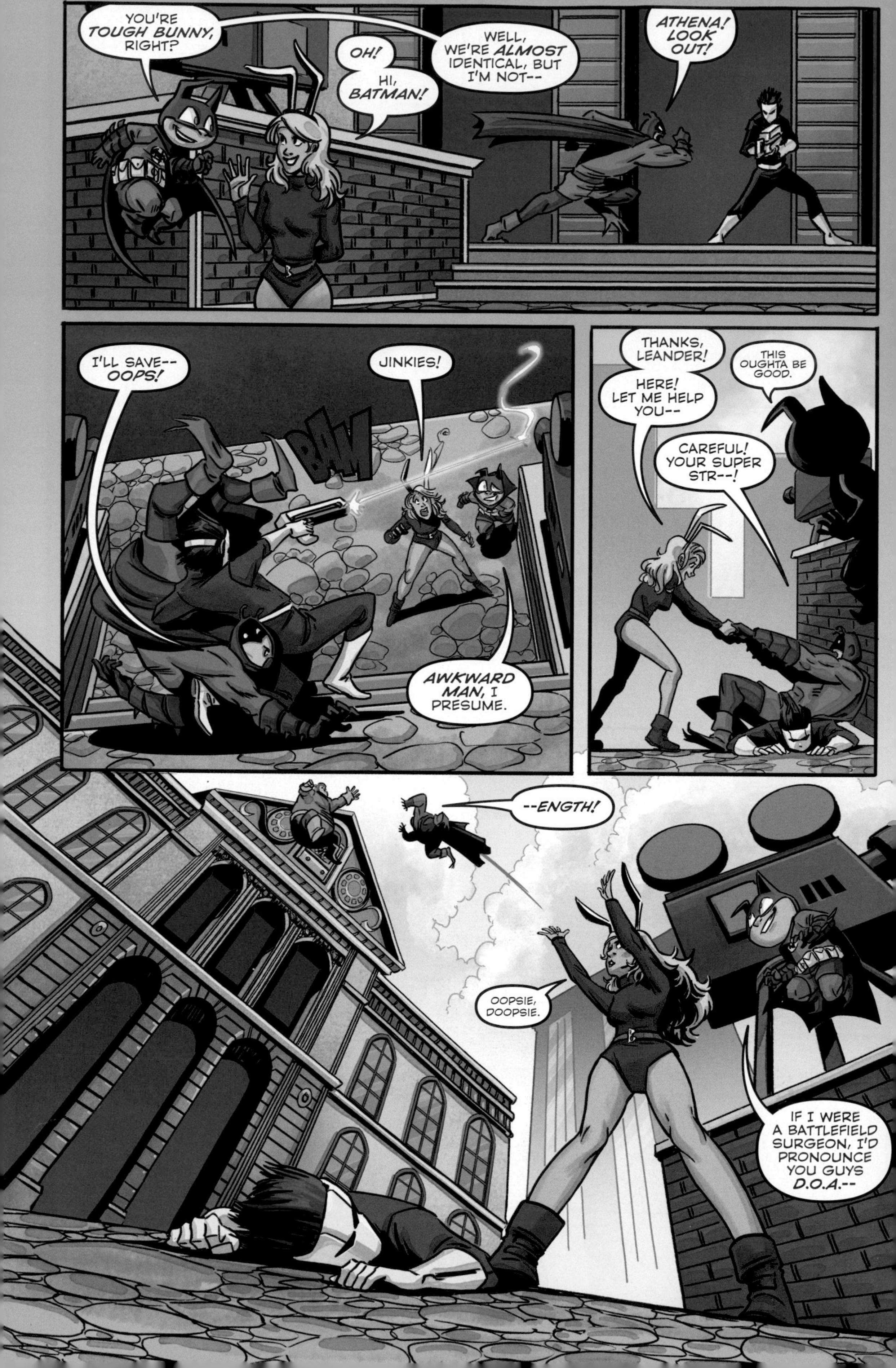
YOU'RE TOUGH BUNNY, RIGHT?
OH!
HI, BATMAN!
WELL, WE'RE ALMOST IDENTICAL, BUT I'M NOT--
ATHENA! LOOK OUT!
I'LL SAVE-- OOPS!
JINKIES!
BAM
AWKWARD MAN, I PRESUME.
THANKS, LEANDER!
HERE! LET ME HELP YOU--
THIS OUGHTA BE GOOD.
CAREFUL! YOUR SUPER STR--!
--ENGTH!
OOPSIE, DOOPSIE.
IF I WERE A BATTLEFIELD SURGEON, I'D PRONOUNCE YOU GUYS D.O.A.--

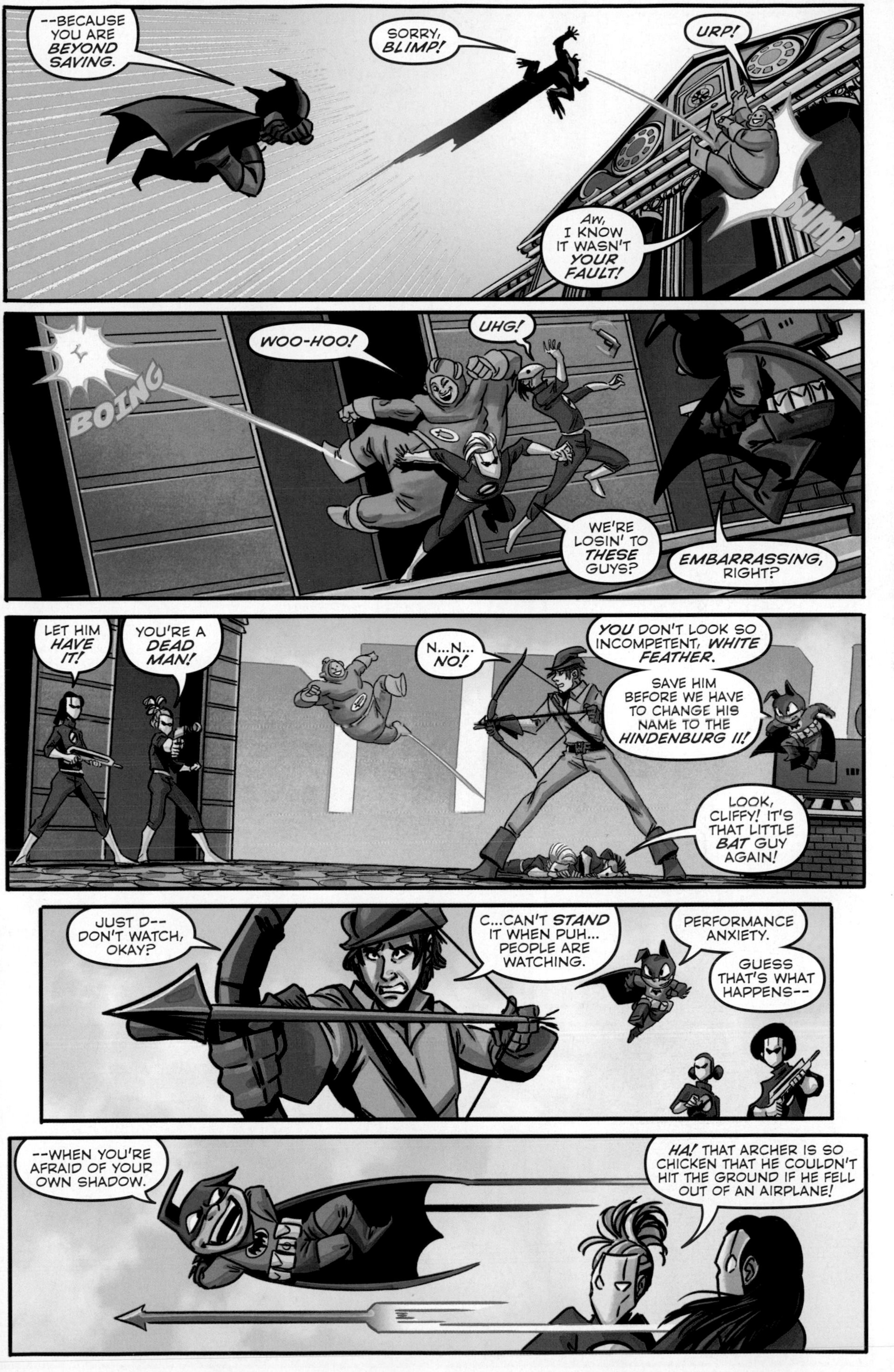
--BECAUSE YOU ARE BEYOND SAVING.
SORRY, BLIMP!
URP!
AW, I KNOW IT WASN'T YOUR FAULT!
BUMP
BOING
WOO-HOO!
UHG!
WE'RE LOSIN' TO THESE GUYS?
EMBARRASSING, RIGHT?
LET HIM HAVE IT!
YOU'RE A DEAD MAN!
N...N... NO!
YOU DON'T LOOK SO INCOMPETENT, WHITE FEATHER.
SAVE HIM BEFORE WE HAVE TO CHANGE HIS NAME TO THE HINDENBURG II!
LOOK, CLIFFY! IT'S THAT LITTLE BAT GUY AGAIN!
JUST D-- DON'T WATCH, OKAY?
C...CAN'T STAND IT WHEN PUH... PEOPLE ARE WATCHING.
PERFORMANCE ANXIETY.
GUESS THAT'S WHAT HAPPENS--
--WHEN YOU'RE AFRAID OF YOUR OWN SHADOW.
HA! THAT ARCHER IS SO CHICKEN THAT HE COULDN'T HIT THE GROUND IF HE FELL OUT OF AN AIRPLANE!

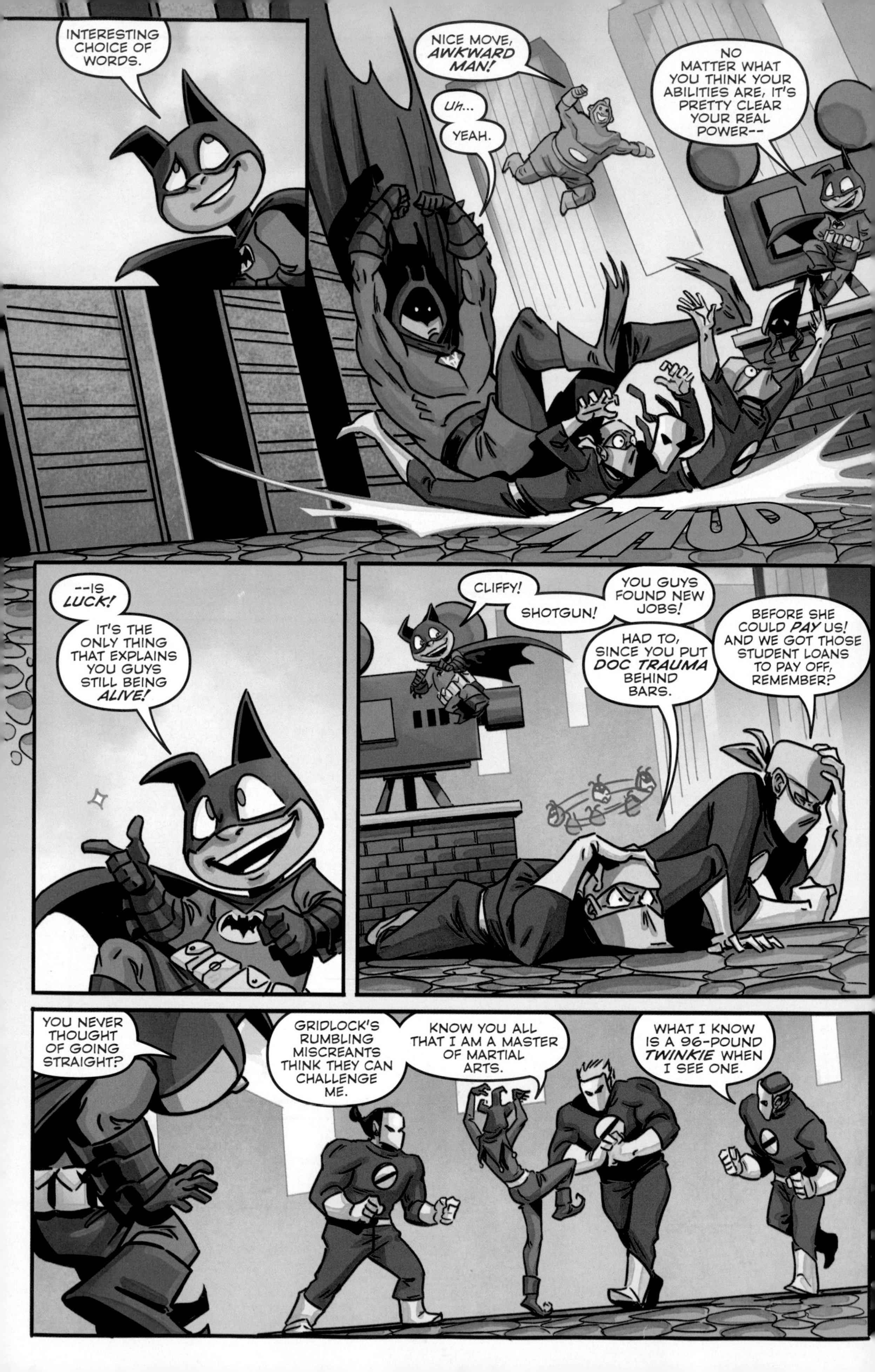
INTERESTING CHOICE OF WORDS.
NICE MOVE, AWKWARD MAN!
Uh...
YEAH.
NO MATTER WHAT YOU THINK YOUR ABILITIES ARE, IT'S PRETTY CLEAR YOUR REAL POWER--
WHUD
--IS LUCK!
IT'S THE ONLY THING THAT EXPLAINS YOU GUYS STILL BEING ALIVE!
CLIFFY!
SHOTGUN!
YOU GUYS FOUND NEW JOBS!
HAD TO, SINCE YOU PUT DOC TRAUMA BEHIND BARS.
BEFORE SHE COULD PAY US! AND WE GOT THOSE STUDENT LOANS TO PAY OFF, REMEMBER?
YOU NEVER THOUGHT OF GOING STRAIGHT?
GRIDLOCK'S RUMBLING MISCREANTS THINK THEY CAN CHALLENGE ME.
KNOW YOU ALL THAT I AM A MASTER OF MARTIAL ARTS.
WHAT I KNOW IS A 96-POUND TWINKIE WHEN I SEE ONE.

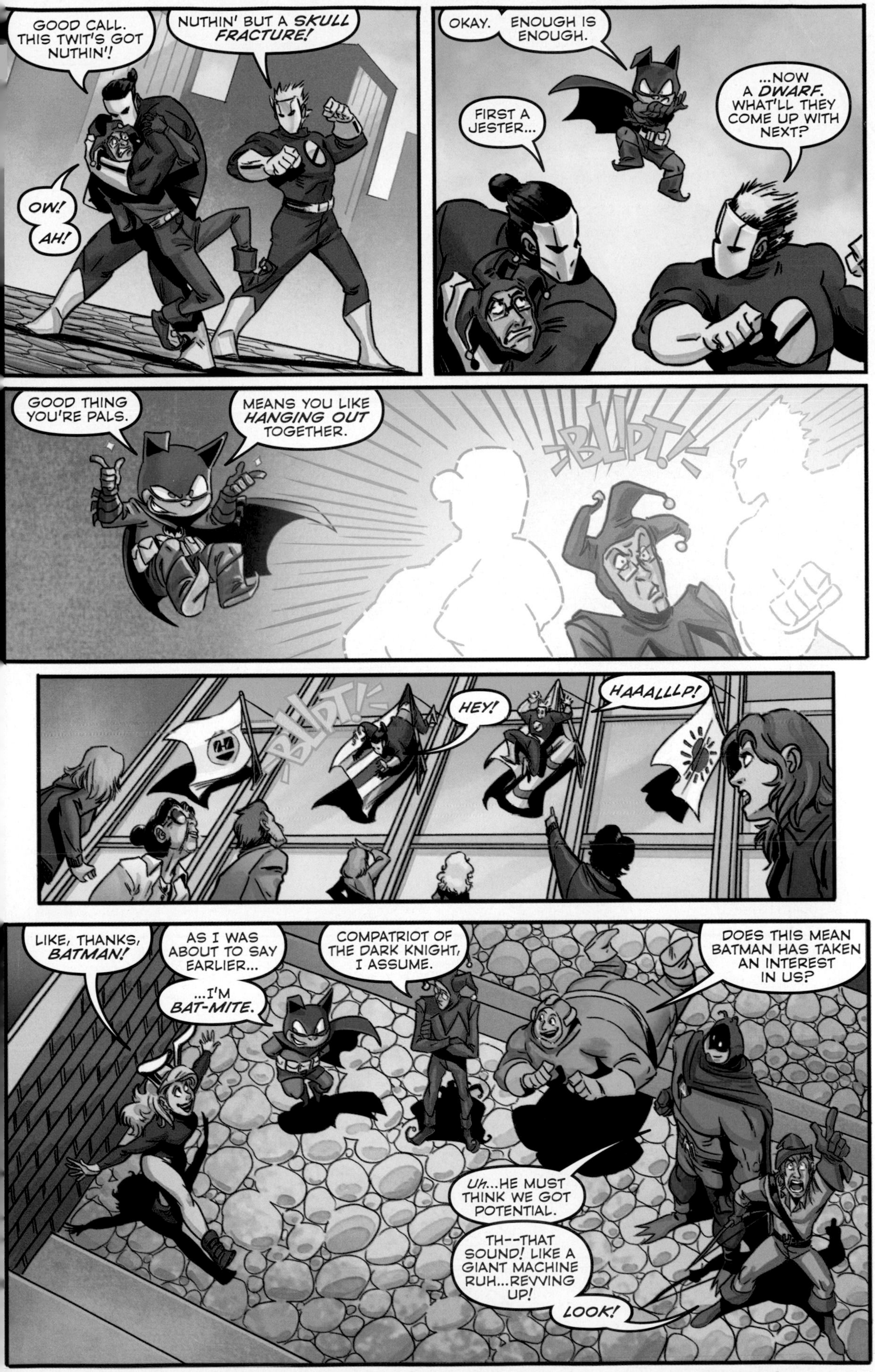
GOOD CALL. THIS TWIT'S GOT NUTHIN'!
NUTHIN' BUT A SKULL FRACTURE!
OW!
AH!
OKAY.
ENOUGH IS ENOUGH.
FIRST A JESTER...
...NOW A DWARF. WHAT'LL THEY COME UP WITH NEXT?
GOOD THING YOU'RE PALS.
MEANS YOU LIKE HANGING OUT TOGETHER.
BLIPT!
BLIPT!
HEY!
HAAALLLP!
LIKE, THANKS, BATMAN!
AS I WAS ABOUT TO SAY EARLIER...
...I'M BAT-MITE.
COMPATRIOT OF THE DARK KNIGHT, I ASSUME.
DOES THIS MEAN BATMAN HAS TAKEN AN INTEREST IN US?
Uh...HE MUST THINK WE GOT POTENTIAL.
TH--THAT SOUND! LIKE A GIANT MACHINE RUH...REVVING UP!
LOOK!

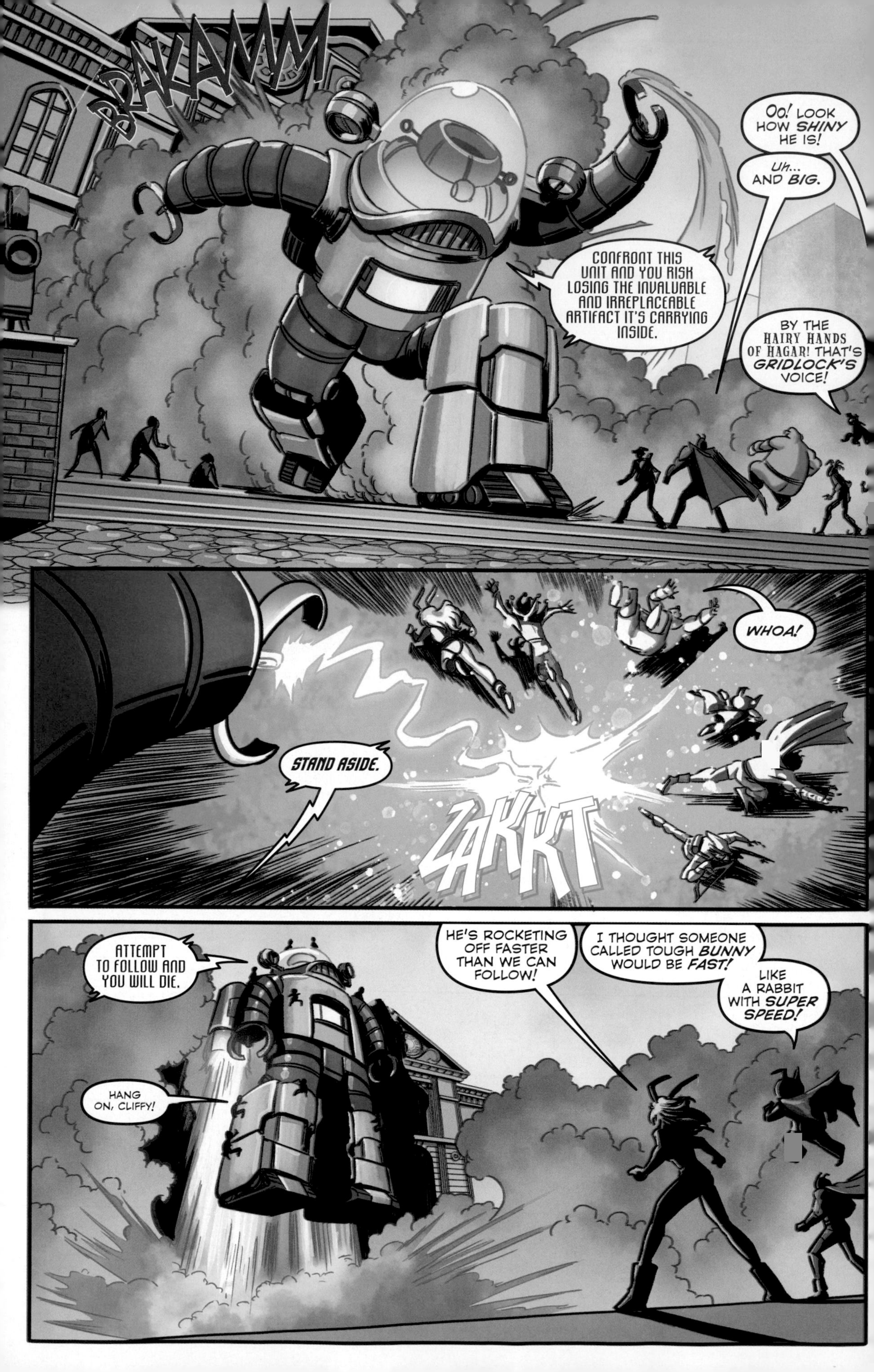
BRAKAMM
OO! LOOK HOW SHINY HE IS!
Uh... AND BIG.
CONFRONT THIS UNIT AND YOU RISK LOSING THE INVALUABLE AND IRREPLACEABLE ARTIFACT IT'S CARRYING INSIDE.
BY THE HAIRY HANDS OF HAGAR! THAT'S GRIDLOCK'S VOICE!
WHOA!
STAND ASIDE.
ZAKKT
ATTEMPT TO FOLLOW AND YOU WILL DIE.
HE'S ROCKETING OFF FASTER THAN WE CAN FOLLOW!
I THOUGHT SOMEONE CALLED TOUGH BUNNY WOULD BE FAST!
LIKE A RABBIT WITH SUPER SPEED!
HANG ON, CLIFFY!

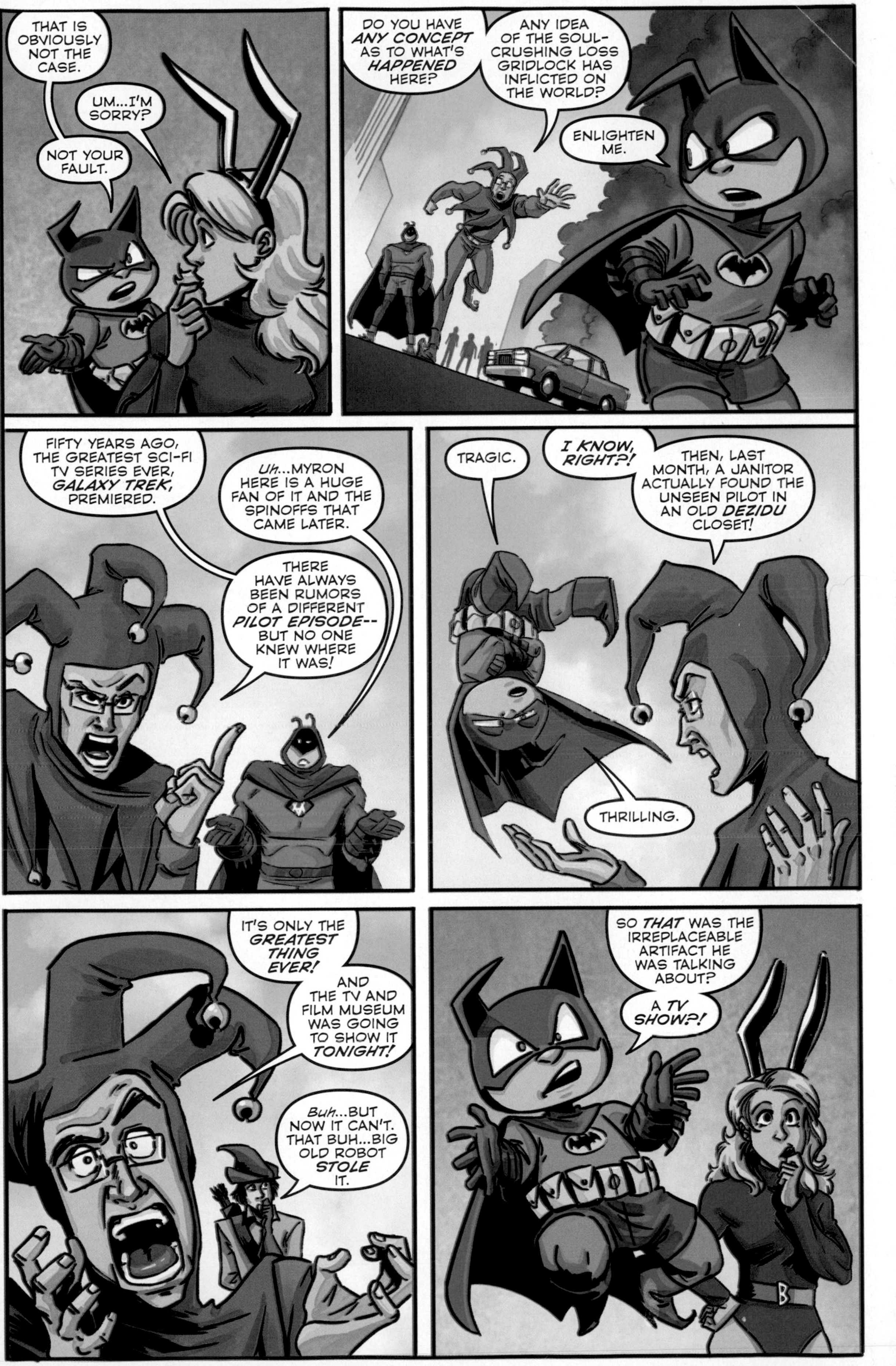
THAT IS OBVIOUSLY NOT THE CASE.
UM...I'M SORRY?
NOT YOUR FAULT.
DO YOU HAVE ANY CONCEPT AS TO WHAT'S HAPPENED HERE?
ANY IDEA OF THE SOUL-CRUSHING LOSS GRIDLOCK HAS INFLICTED ON THE WORLD?
ENLIGHTEN ME.
FIFTY YEARS AGO, THE GREATEST SCI-FI TV SERIES EVER, GALAXY TREK, PREMIERED.
Uh...MYRON HERE IS A HUGE FAN OF IT AND THE SPINOFFS THAT CAME LATER.
THERE HAVE ALWAYS BEEN RUMORS OF A DIFFERENT PILOT EPISODE--BUT NO ONE KNEW WHERE IT WAS!
TRAGIC.
I KNOW, RIGHT?!
THEN, LAST MONTH, A JANITOR ACTUALLY FOUND THE UNSEEN PILOT IN AN OLD DEZIDU CLOSET!
THRILLING.
IT'S ONLY THE GREATEST THING EVER!
AND THE TV AND FILM MUSEUM WAS GOING TO SHOW IT TONIGHT!
Buh...BUT NOW IT CAN'T. THAT BUH...BIG OLD ROBOT STOLE IT.
SO THAT WAS THE IRREPLACEABLE ARTIFACT HE WAS TALKING ABOUT?
A TV SHOW?!

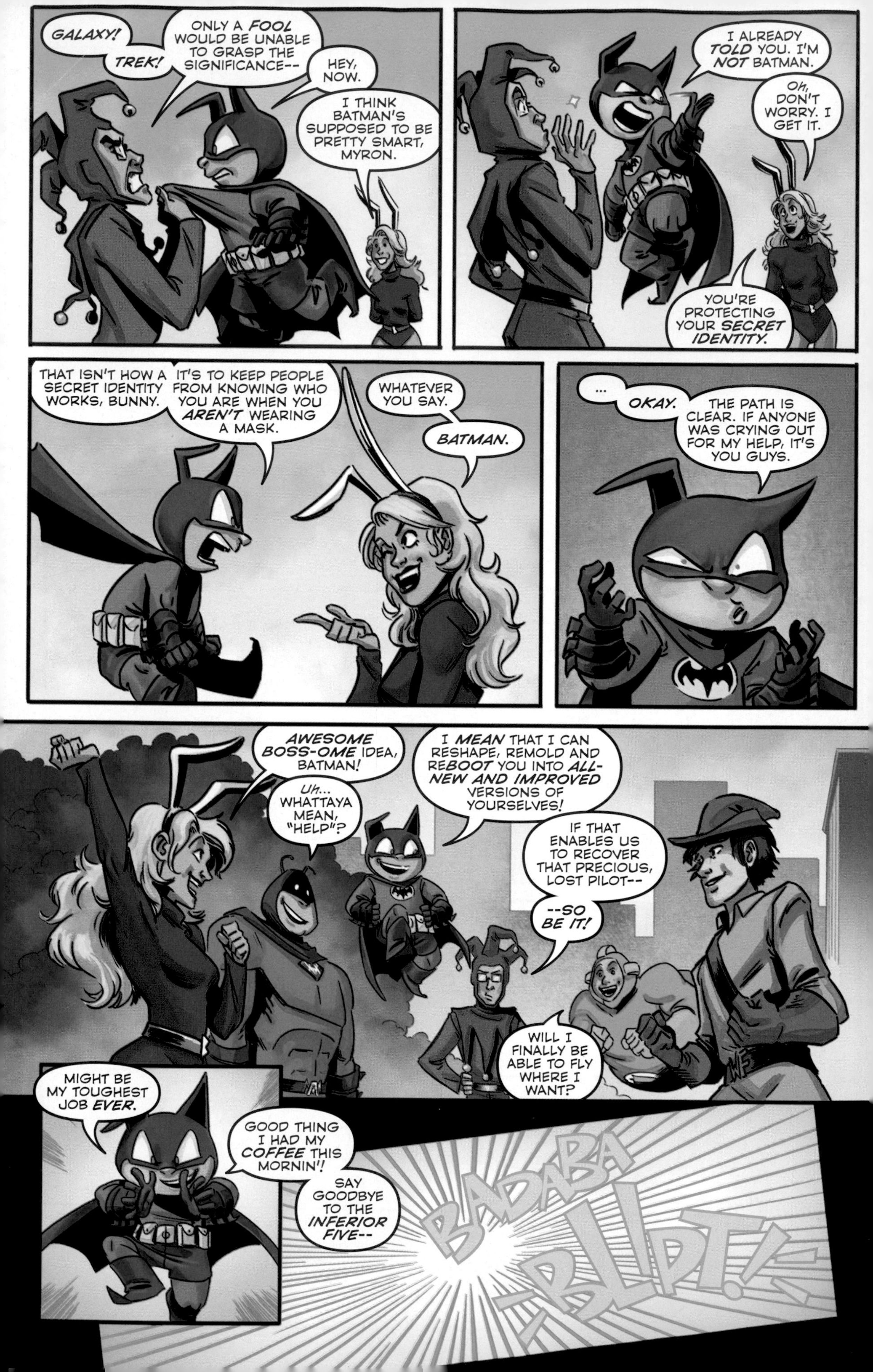

GALAXY!
TREK!
ONLY A FOOL WOULD BE UNABLE TO GRASP THE SIGNIFICANCE--
HEY, NOW.
I THINK BATMAN'S SUPPOSED TO BE PRETTY SMART, MYRON.
I ALREADY TOLD YOU. I'M NOT BATMAN.
Oh, DON'T WORRY. I GET IT.
YOU'RE PROTECTING YOUR SECRET IDENTITY.
THAT ISN'T HOW A SECRET IDENTITY WORKS, BUNNY.
IT'S TO KEEP PEOPLE FROM KNOWING WHO YOU ARE WHEN YOU AREN'T WEARING A MASK.
WHATEVER YOU SAY.
BATMAN.
...
OKAY.
THE PATH IS CLEAR. IF ANYONE WAS CRYING OUT FOR MY HELP, IT'S YOU GUYS.
AWESOME BOSS-OME IDEA, BATMAN!
Uh... WHATTAYA MEAN, "HELP"?
I MEAN THAT I CAN RESHAPE, REMOLD AND REBOOT YOU INTO ALL-NEW AND IMPROVED VERSIONS OF YOURSELVES!
IF THAT ENABLES US TO RECOVER THAT PRECIOUS, LOST PILOT--
--SO BE IT!
WILL I FINALLY BE ABLE TO FLY WHERE I WANT?
MIGHT BE MY TOUGHEST JOB EVER.
GOOD THING I HAD MY COFFEE THIS MORNIN'!
SAY GOODBYE TO THE INFERIOR FIVE--
BADABA -BLIPT!

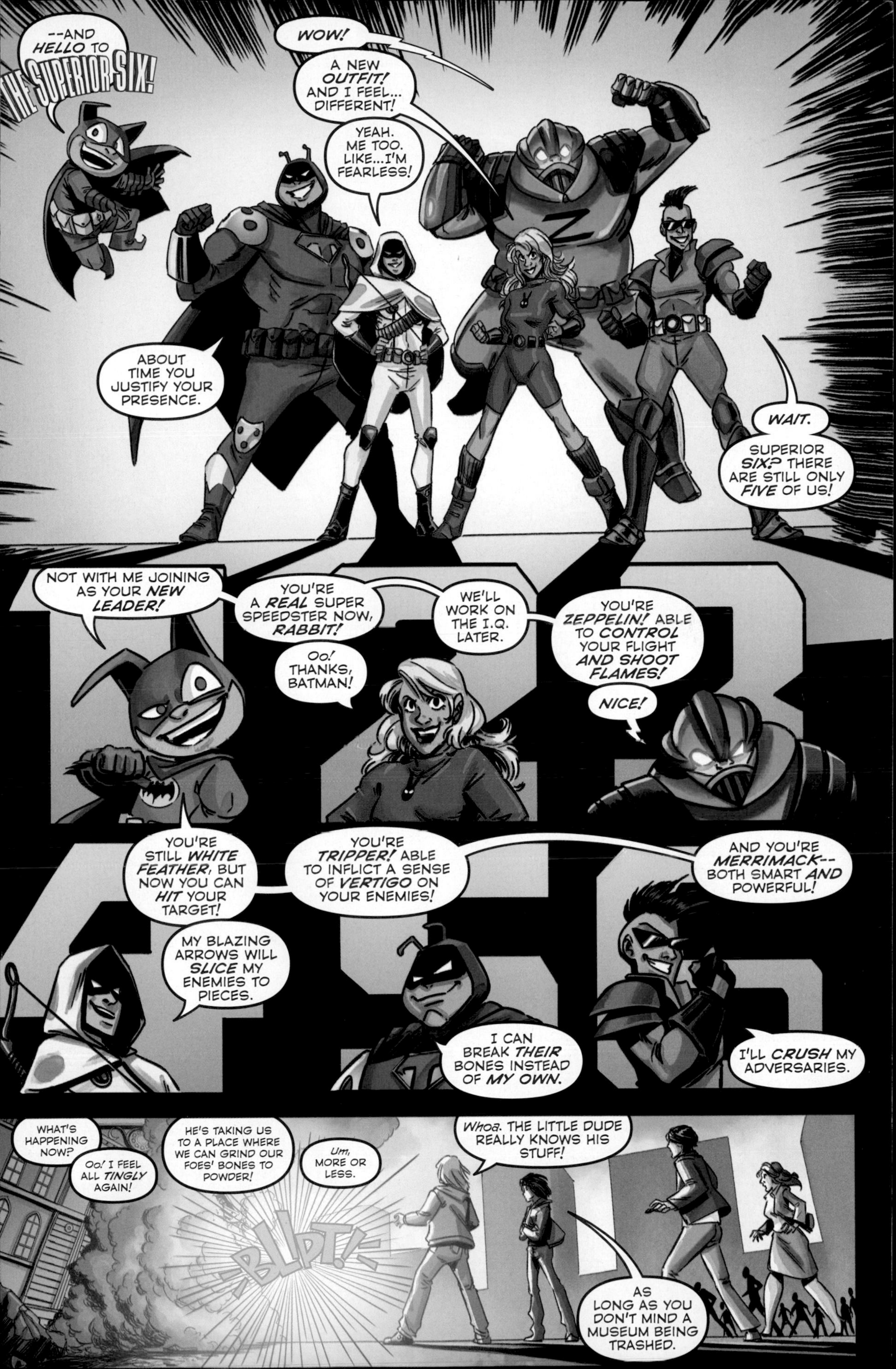
--AND HELLO TO
THE SUPERIOR SIX!
WOW!
A NEW OUTFIT! AND I FEEL... DIFFERENT!
YEAH. ME TOO. LIKE...I'M FEARLESS!
ABOUT TIME YOU JUSTIFY YOUR PRESENCE.
WAIT.
SUPERIOR SIX? THERE ARE STILL ONLY FIVE OF US!
NOT WITH ME JOINING AS YOUR NEW LEADER!
YOU'RE A REAL SUPER SPEEDSTER NOW, RABBIT!
Oo! THANKS, BATMAN!
WE'LL WORK ON THE I.Q. LATER.
YOU'RE ZEPPELIN! ABLE TO CONTROL YOUR FLIGHT AND SHOOT FLAMES!
NICE!
YOU'RE STILL WHITE FEATHER, BUT NOW YOU CAN HIT YOUR TARGET!
MY BLAZING ARROWS WILL SLICE MY ENEMIES TO PIECES.
YOU'RE TRIPPER! ABLE TO INFLICT A SENSE OF VERTIGO ON YOUR ENEMIES!
I CAN BREAK THEIR BONES INSTEAD OF MY OWN.
AND YOU'RE MERRIMACK-- BOTH SMART AND POWERFUL!
I'LL CRUSH MY ADVERSARIES.
WHAT'S HAPPENING NOW?
Oo! I FEEL ALL TINGLY AGAIN!
HE'S TAKING US TO A PLACE WHERE WE CAN GRIND OUR FOES' BONES TO POWDER!
Um, MORE OR LESS.
-BLIPT!-
Whoa. THE LITTLE DUDE REALLY KNOWS HIS STUFF!
AS LONG AS YOU DON'T MIND A MUSEUM BEING TRASHED.

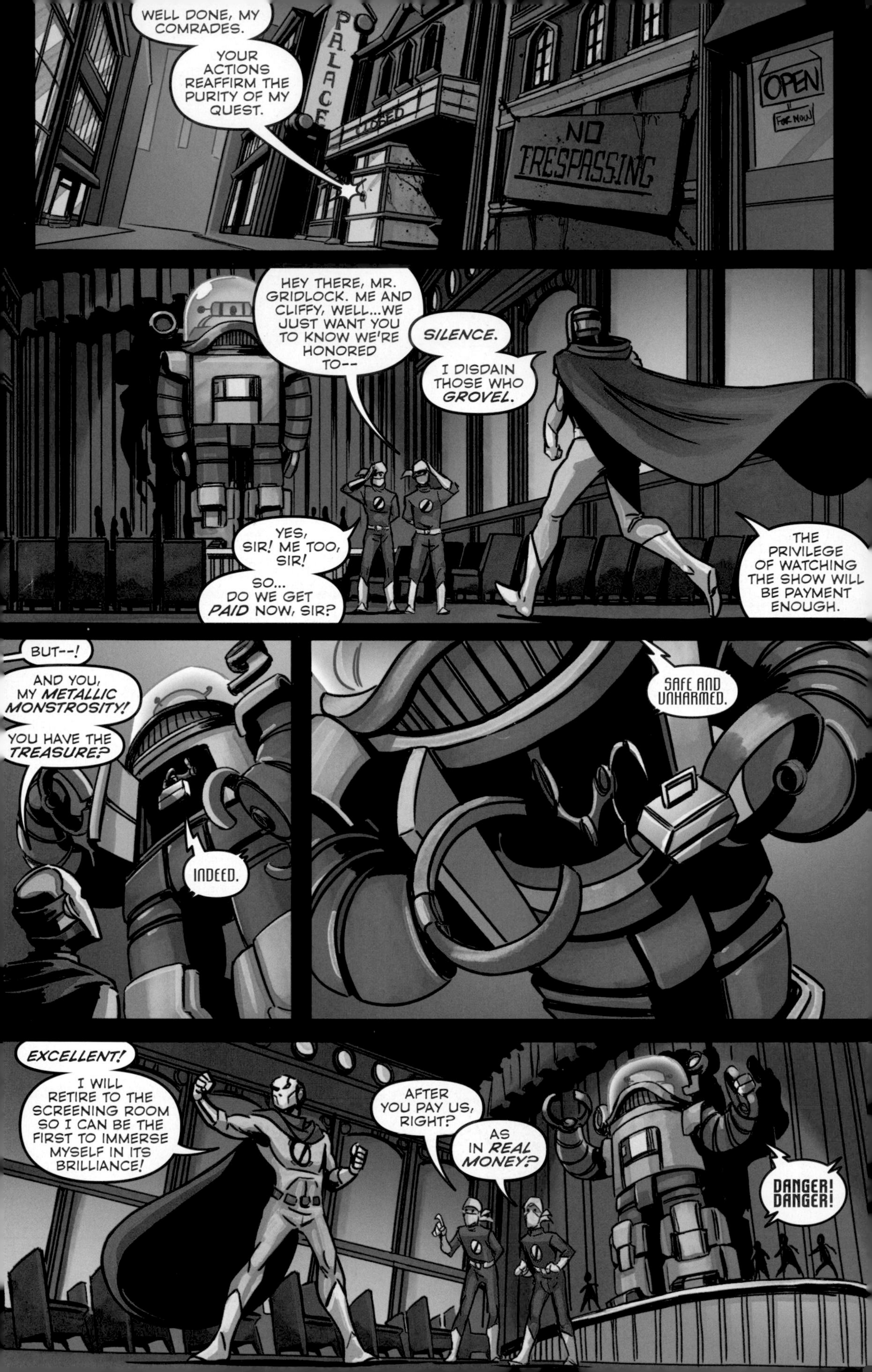
WELL DONE, MY COMRADES.
YOUR ACTIONS REAFFIRM THE PURITY OF MY QUEST.
PALACE
CLOSED
NO TRESPASSING
OPEN
FOR NOW
HEY THERE, MR. GRIDLOCK. ME AND CLIFFY, WELL...WE JUST WANT YOU TO KNOW WE'RE HONORED TO--
SILENCE.
I DISDAIN THOSE WHO GROVEL.
YES, SIR! ME TOO, SIR!
SO... DO WE GET PAID NOW, SIR?
THE PRIVILEGE OF WATCHING THE SHOW WILL BE PAYMENT ENOUGH.
BUT--!
AND YOU, MY METALLIC MONSTROSITY!
YOU HAVE THE TREASURE?
INDEED.
SAFE AND UNHARMED.
EXCELLENT!
I WILL RETIRE TO THE SCREENING ROOM SO I CAN BE THE FIRST TO IMMERSE MYSELF IN ITS BRILLIANCE!
AFTER YOU PAY US, RIGHT?
AS IN REAL MONEY?
DANGER! DANGER!

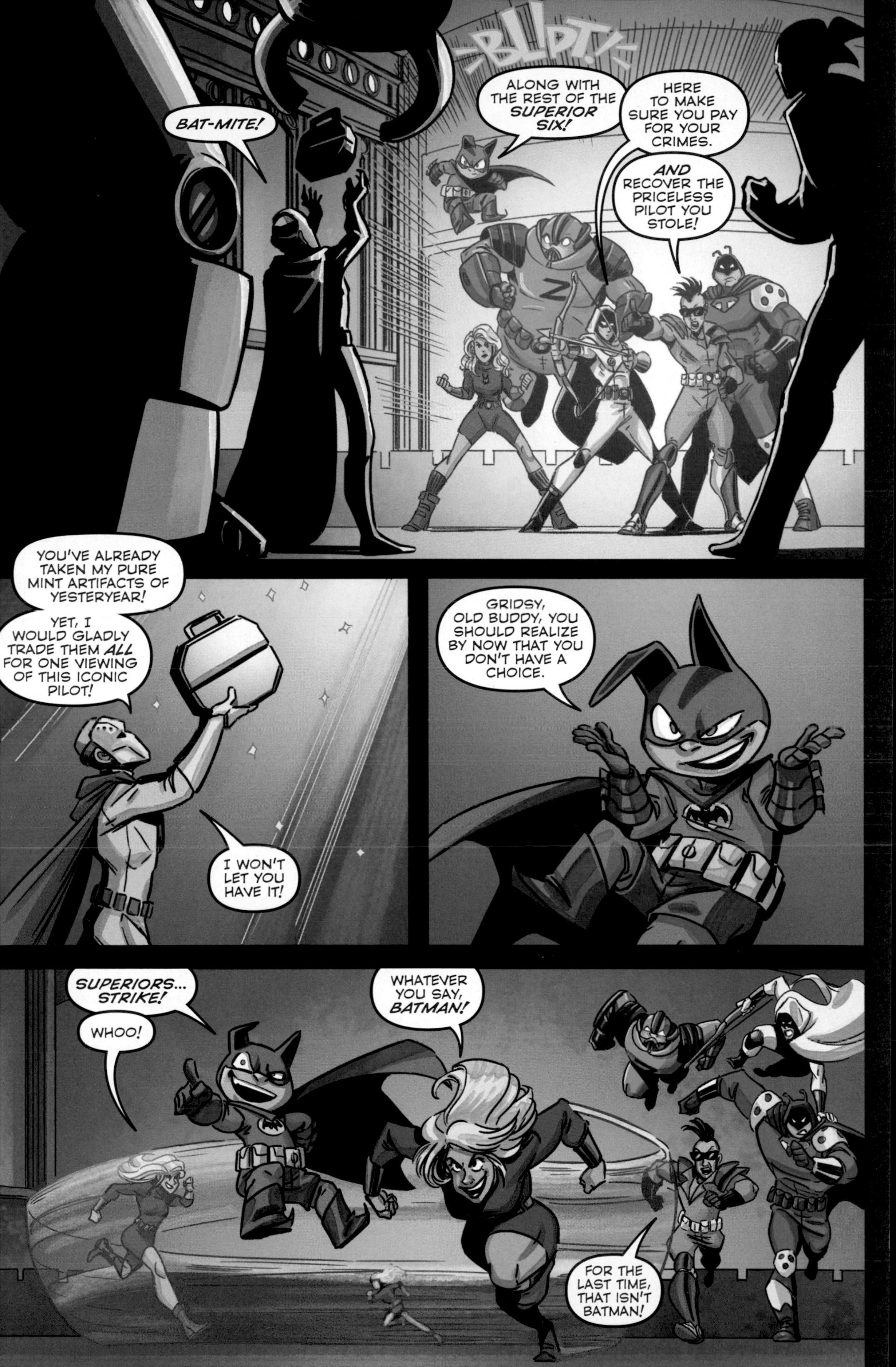
BLIPT!
BAT-MITE!
ALONG WITH THE REST OF THE SUPERIOR SIX!
HERE TO MAKE SURE YOU PAY FOR YOUR CRIMES.
AND RECOVER THE PRICELESS PILOT YOU STOLE!
YOU'VE ALREADY TAKEN MY PURE MINT ARTIFACTS OF YESTERYEAR!
YET, I WOULD GLADLY TRADE THEM ALL FOR ONE VIEWING OF THIS ICONIC PILOT!
I WON'T LET YOU HAVE IT!
GRIDSY, OLD BUDDY, YOU SHOULD REALIZE BY NOW THAT YOU DON'T HAVE A CHOICE.
SUPERIORS... STRIKE!
WHOO!
WHATEVER YOU SAY, BATMAN!
FOR THE LAST TIME, THAT ISN'T BATMAN!

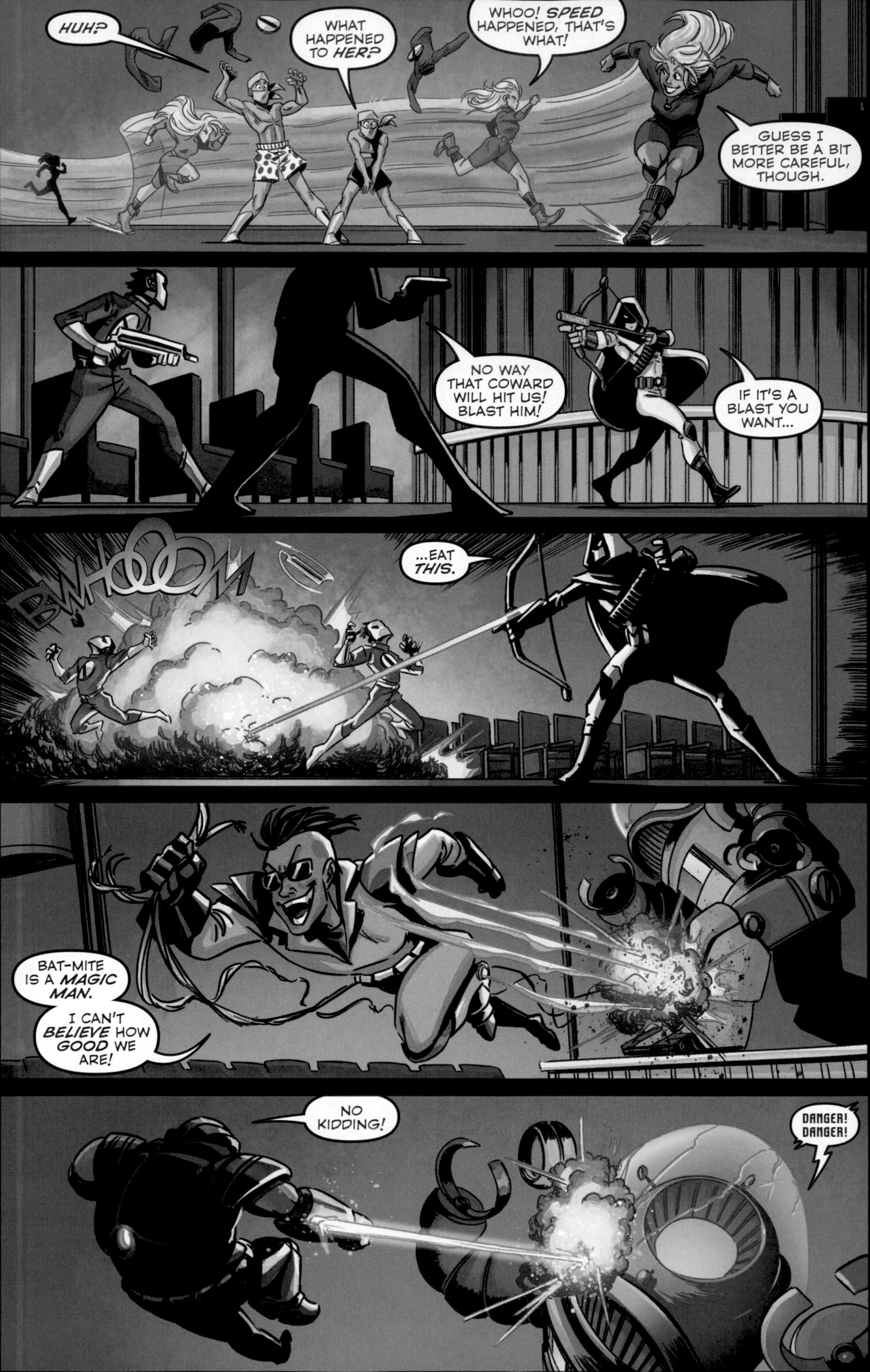
HUH?
WHAT HAPPENED TO HER?
WHOO! SPEED HAPPENED, THAT'S WHAT!
GUESS I BETTER BE A BIT MORE CAREFUL, THOUGH.
NO WAY THAT COWARD WILL HIT US! BLAST HIM!
IF IT'S A BLAST YOU WANT...
BWHOOOM
...EAT THIS.
BAT-MITE IS A MAGIC MAN.
I CAN'T BELIEVE HOW GOOD WE ARE!
NO KIDDING!
DANGER! DANGER!

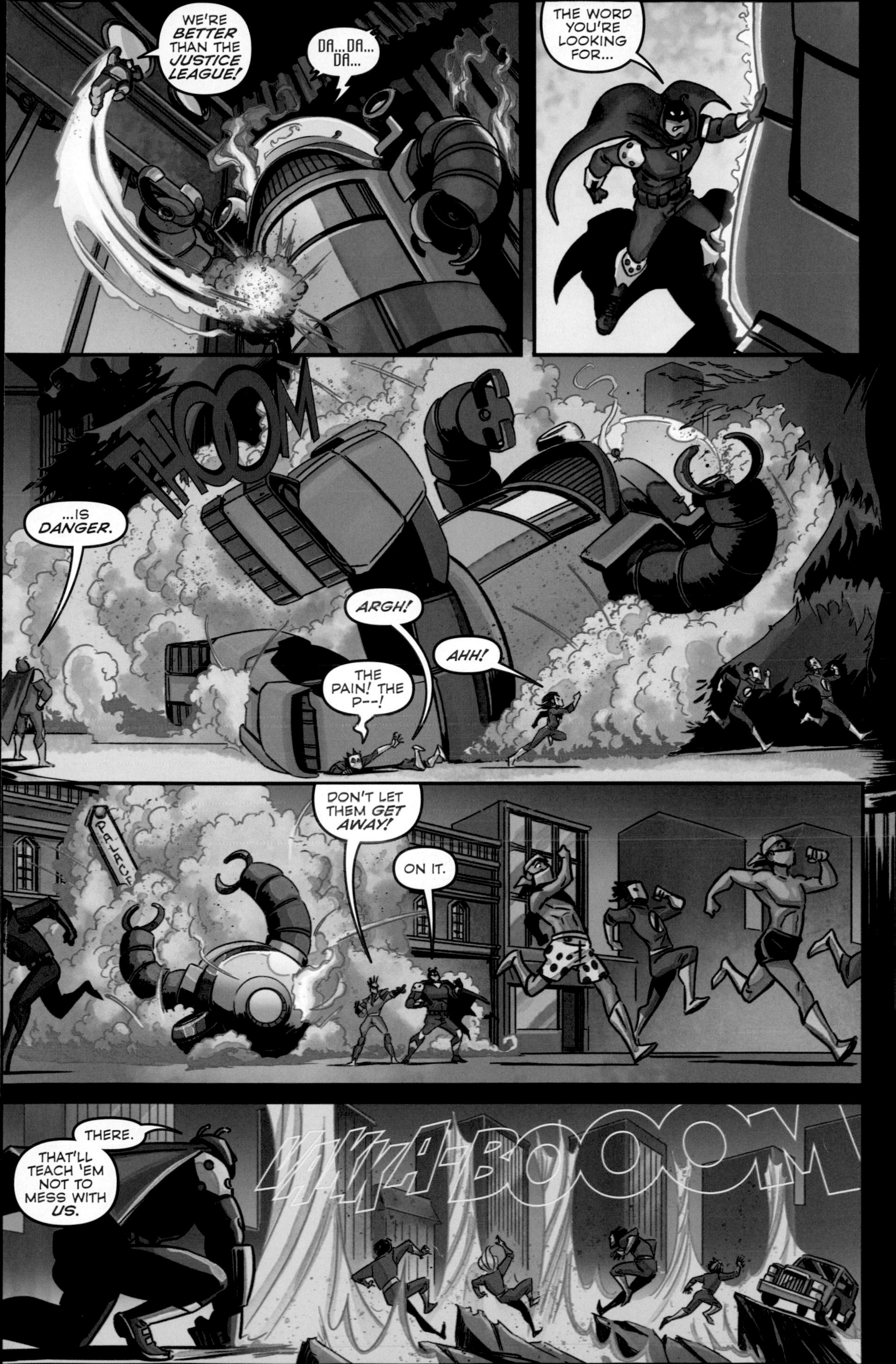
WE'RE *BETTER* THAN THE *JUSTICE LEAGUE!*
DA...DA... DA...
THE WORD YOU'RE LOOKING FOR...
THOOM
...IS *DANGER*.
ARGH!
THE PAIN! THE P--!
AHH!
PALACE
DON'T LET THEM *GET AWAY!*
ON IT.
THERE.
THAT'LL TEACH 'EM NOT TO MESS WITH *US*.

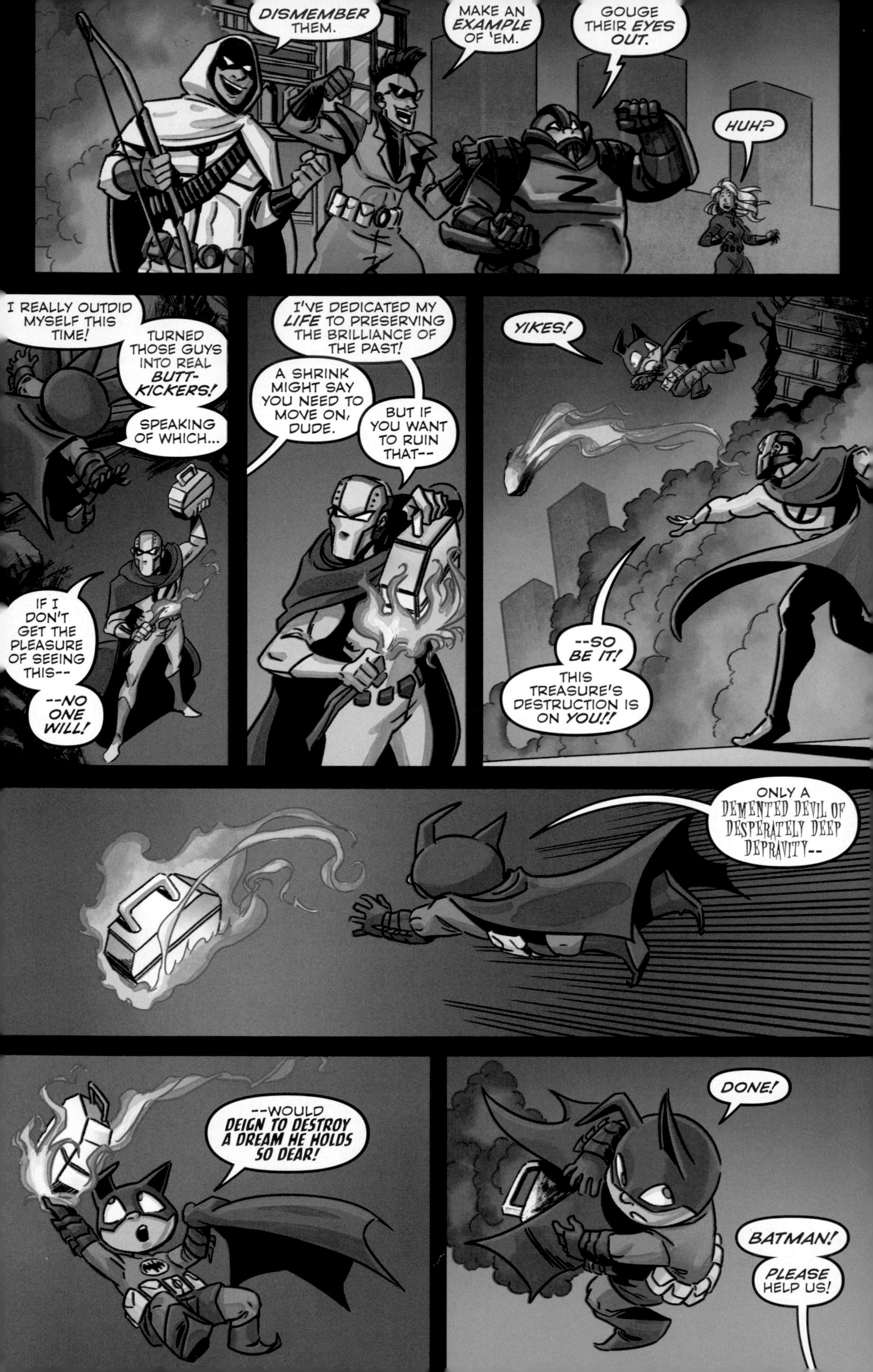
DISMEMBER THEM.
MAKE AN EXAMPLE OF 'EM.
GOUGE THEIR EYES OUT.
HUH?
I REALLY OUTDID MYSELF THIS TIME!
TURNED THOSE GUYS INTO REAL BUTT-KICKERS!
SPEAKING OF WHICH...
IF I DON'T GET THE PLEASURE OF SEEING THIS--
--NO ONE WILL!
I'VE DEDICATED MY LIFE TO PRESERVING THE BRILLIANCE OF THE PAST!
A SHRINK MIGHT SAY YOU NEED TO MOVE ON, DUDE.
BUT IF YOU WANT TO RUIN THAT--
YIKES!
--SO BE IT!
THIS TREASURE'S DESTRUCTION IS ON YOU!!
ONLY A DEMENTED DEVIL OF DESPERATELY DEEP DEPRAVITY--
--WOULD DEIGN TO DESTROY A DREAM HE HOLDS SO DEAR!
DONE!
BATMAN!
PLEASE HELP US!

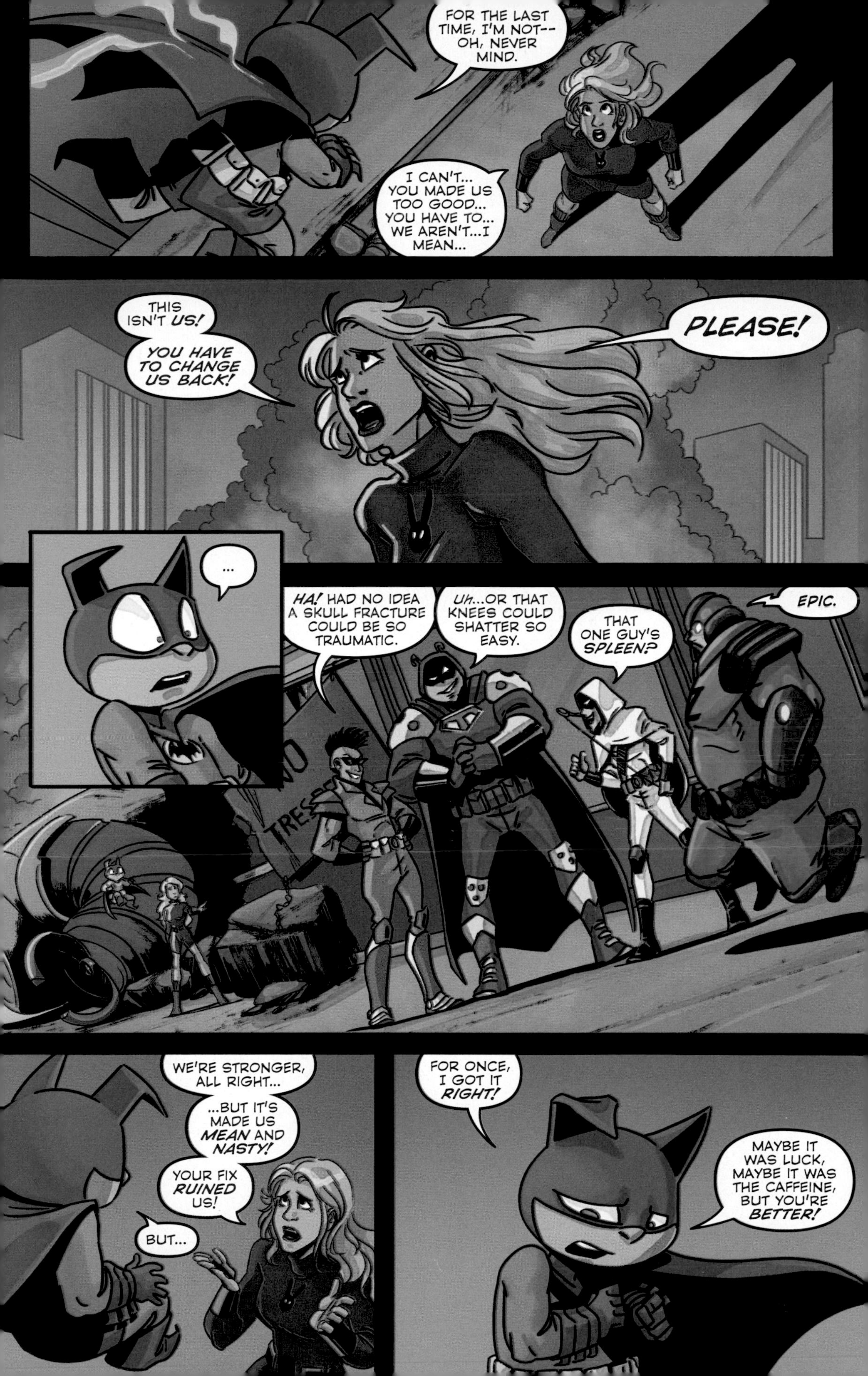
FOR THE LAST TIME, I'M NOT-- OH, NEVER MIND.
I CAN'T... YOU MADE US TOO GOOD... YOU HAVE TO... WE AREN'T...I MEAN...
THIS ISN'T *US!*
YOU HAVE TO CHANGE US BACK!
PLEASE!
...
HA! HAD NO IDEA A SKULL FRACTURE COULD BE SO TRAUMATIC.
Uh...OR THAT KNEES COULD SHATTER SO EASY.
THAT ONE GUY'S *SPLEEN?*
EPIC.
TRES
WE'RE STRONGER, ALL RIGHT...
...BUT IT'S MADE US *MEAN* AND *NASTY!*
YOUR FIX *RUINED* US!
BUT...
FOR ONCE, I GOT IT *RIGHT!*
MAYBE IT WAS LUCK, MAYBE IT WAS THE CAFFEINE, BUT YOU'RE *BETTER!*

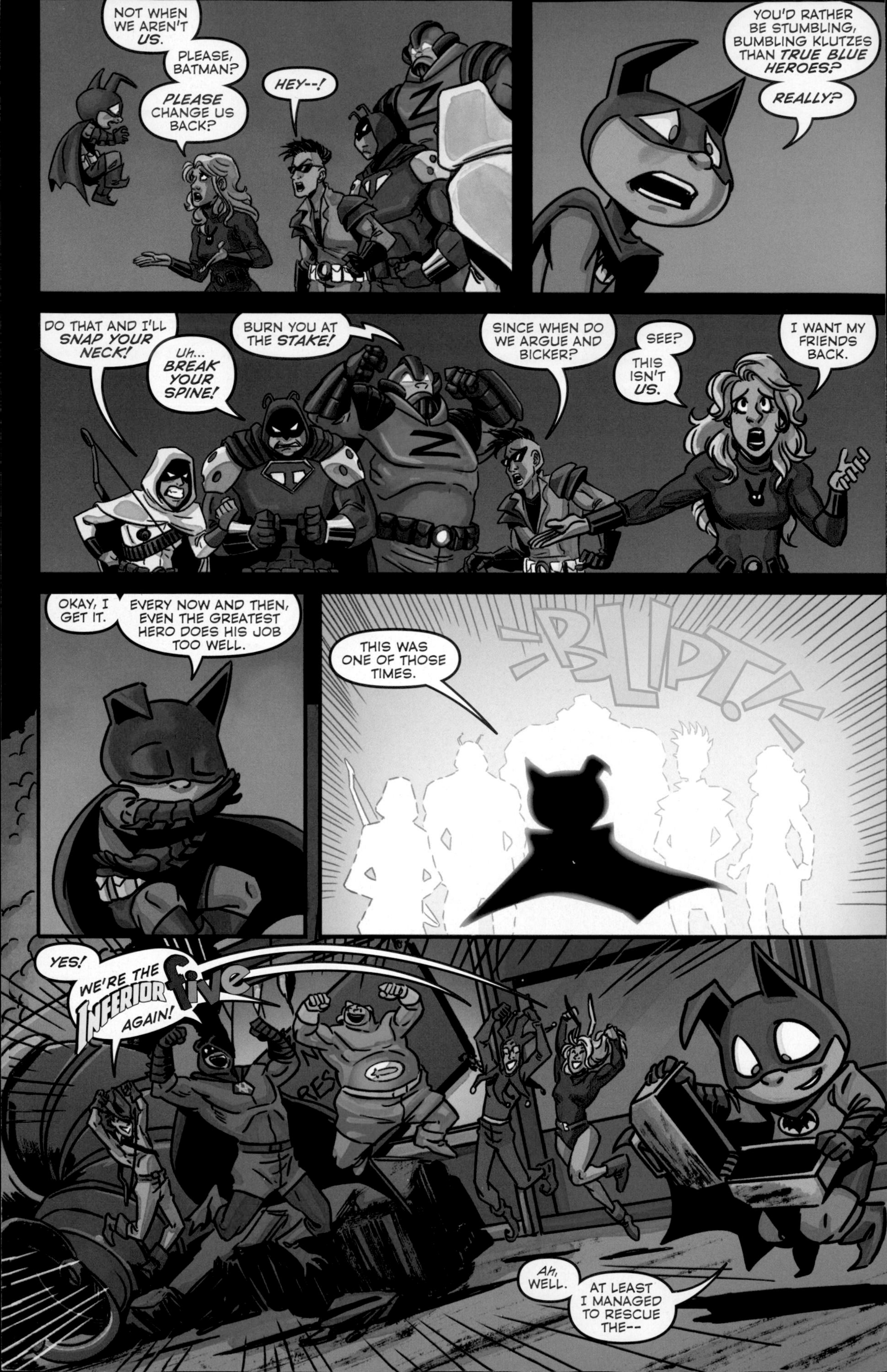
NOT WHEN WE AREN'T US.
PLEASE, BATMAN?
PLEASE CHANGE US BACK?
HEY--!
YOU'D RATHER BE STUMBLING, BUMBLING KLUTZES THAN TRUE BLUE HEROES?
REALLY?
DO THAT AND I'LL SNAP YOUR NECK!
Uh... BREAK YOUR SPINE!
BURN YOU AT THE STAKE!
SINCE WHEN DO WE ARGUE AND BICKER?
SEE?
THIS ISN'T US.
I WANT MY FRIENDS BACK.
OKAY, I GET IT.
EVERY NOW AND THEN, EVEN THE GREATEST HERO DOES HIS JOB TOO WELL.
THIS WAS ONE OF THOSE TIMES.
-BLIPT!-
YES!
WE'RE THE INFERIOR five AGAIN!
Ah, WELL.
AT LEAST I MANAGED TO RESCUE THE--

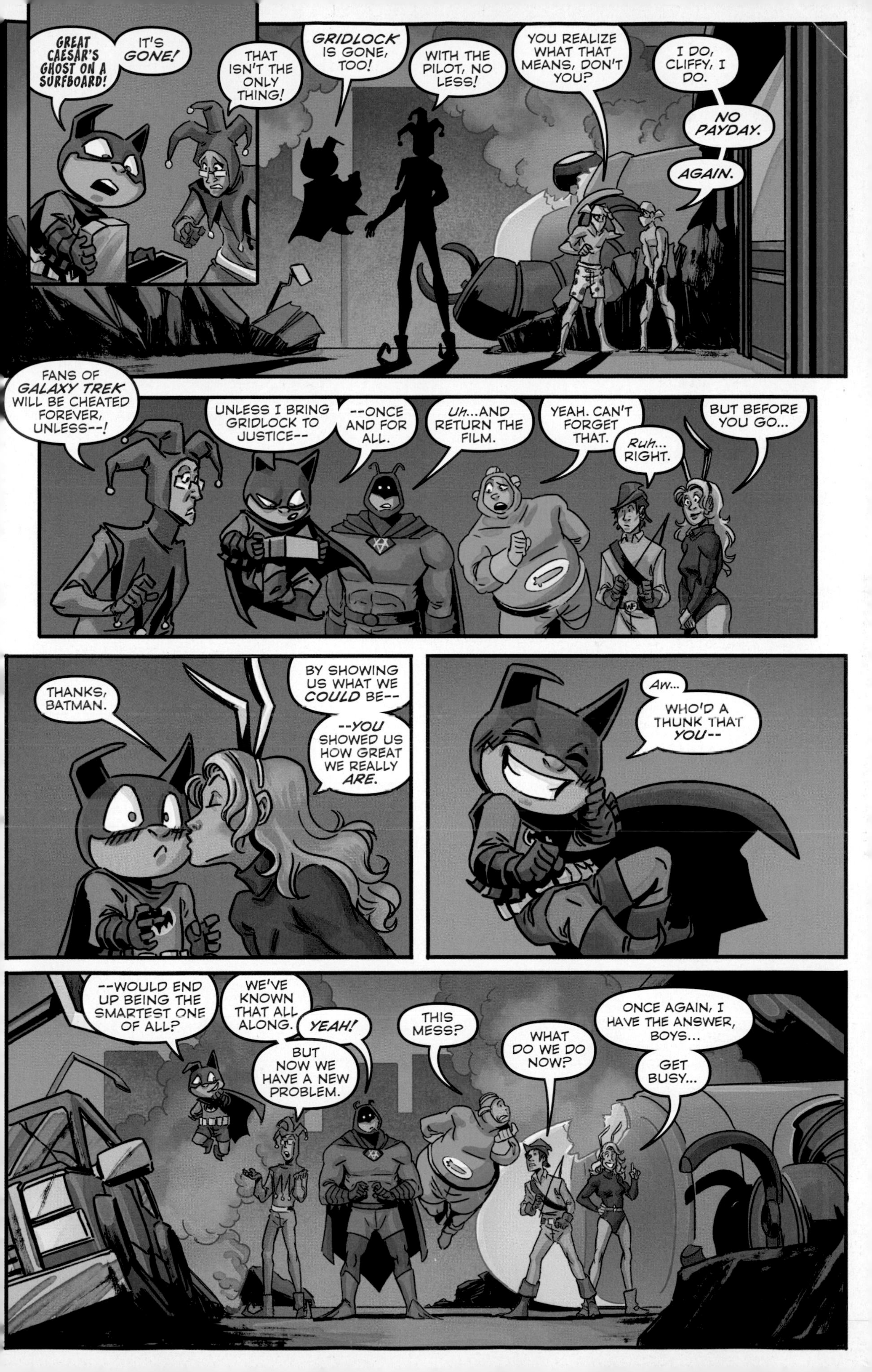
GREAT CAESAR'S GHOST ON A SURFBOARD!
IT'S GONE!
THAT ISN'T THE ONLY THING!
GRIDLOCK IS GONE, TOO!
WITH THE PILOT, NO LESS!
YOU REALIZE WHAT THAT MEANS, DON'T YOU?
I DO, CLIFFY, I DO.
NO PAYDAY.
AGAIN.
FANS OF GALAXY TREK WILL BE CHEATED FOREVER, UNLESS--!
UNLESS I BRING GRIDLOCK TO JUSTICE--
--ONCE AND FOR ALL.
Uh...AND RETURN THE FILM.
YEAH. CAN'T FORGET THAT.
Ruh... RIGHT.
BUT BEFORE YOU GO...
THANKS, BATMAN.
BY SHOWING US WHAT WE COULD BE--
--YOU SHOWED US HOW GREAT WE REALLY ARE.
Aw...
WHO'D A THUNK THAT YOU--
--WOULD END UP BEING THE SMARTEST ONE OF ALL?
WE'VE KNOWN THAT ALL ALONG.
YEAH!
BUT NOW WE HAVE A NEW PROBLEM.
THIS MESS?
WHAT DO WE DO NOW?
ONCE AGAIN, I HAVE THE ANSWER, BOYS...
GET BUSY...

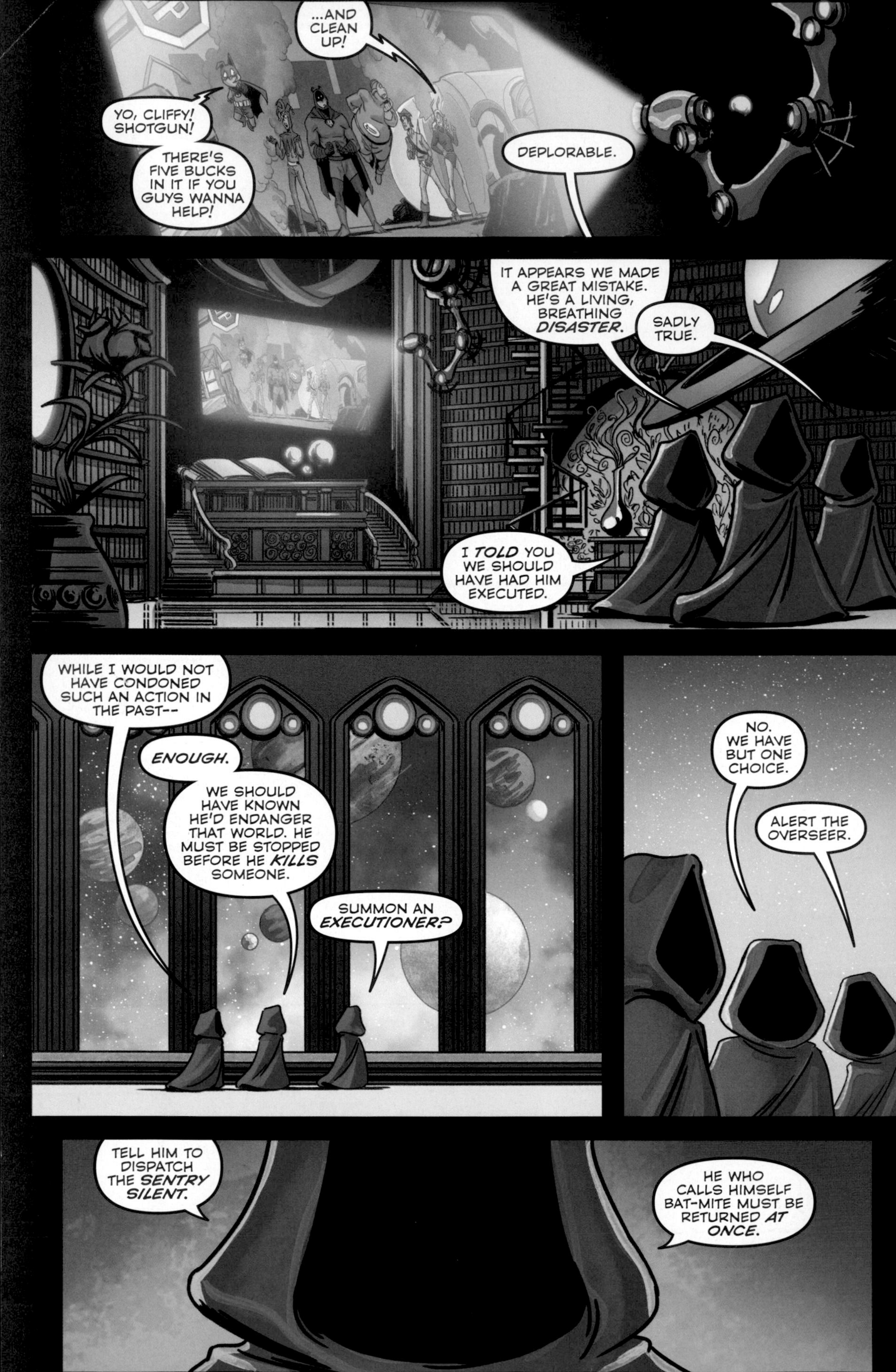
...AND CLEAN UP!
YO, CLIFFY! SHOTGUN!
THERE'S FIVE BUCKS IN IT IF YOU GUYS WANNA HELP!
DEPLORABLE.
IT APPEARS WE MADE A GREAT MISTAKE. HE'S A LIVING, BREATHING DISASTER.
SADLY TRUE.
I TOLD YOU WE SHOULD HAVE HAD HIM EXECUTED.
WHILE I WOULD NOT HAVE CONDONED SUCH AN ACTION IN THE PAST--
ENOUGH.
WE SHOULD HAVE KNOWN HE'D ENDANGER THAT WORLD. HE MUST BE STOPPED BEFORE HE KILLS SOMEONE.
SUMMON AN EXECUTIONER?
NO. WE HAVE BUT ONE CHOICE.
ALERT THE OVERSEER.
TELL HIM TO DISPATCH THE SENTRY SILENT.
HE WHO CALLS HIMSELF BAT-MITE MUST BE RETURNED AT ONCE.

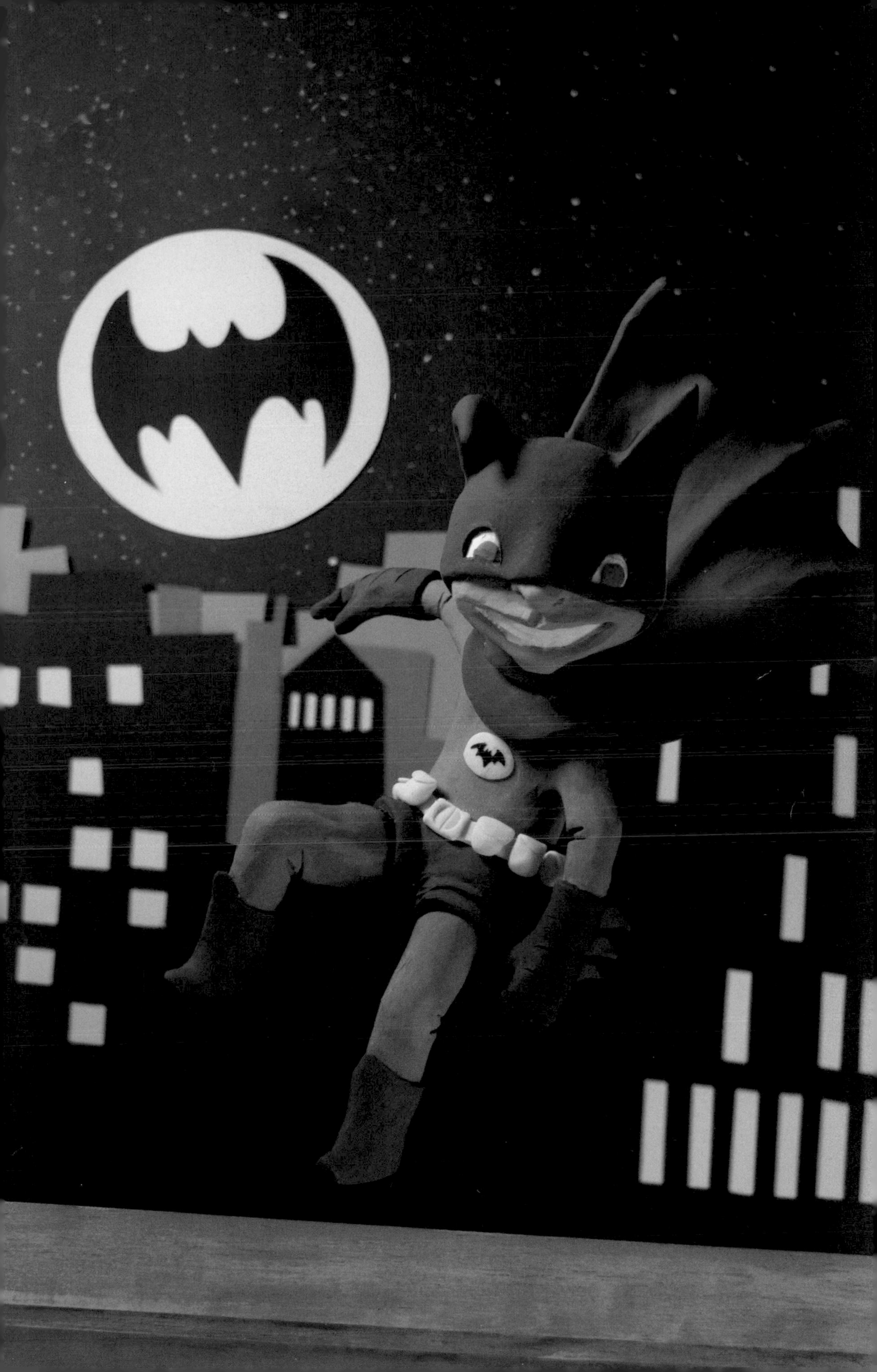

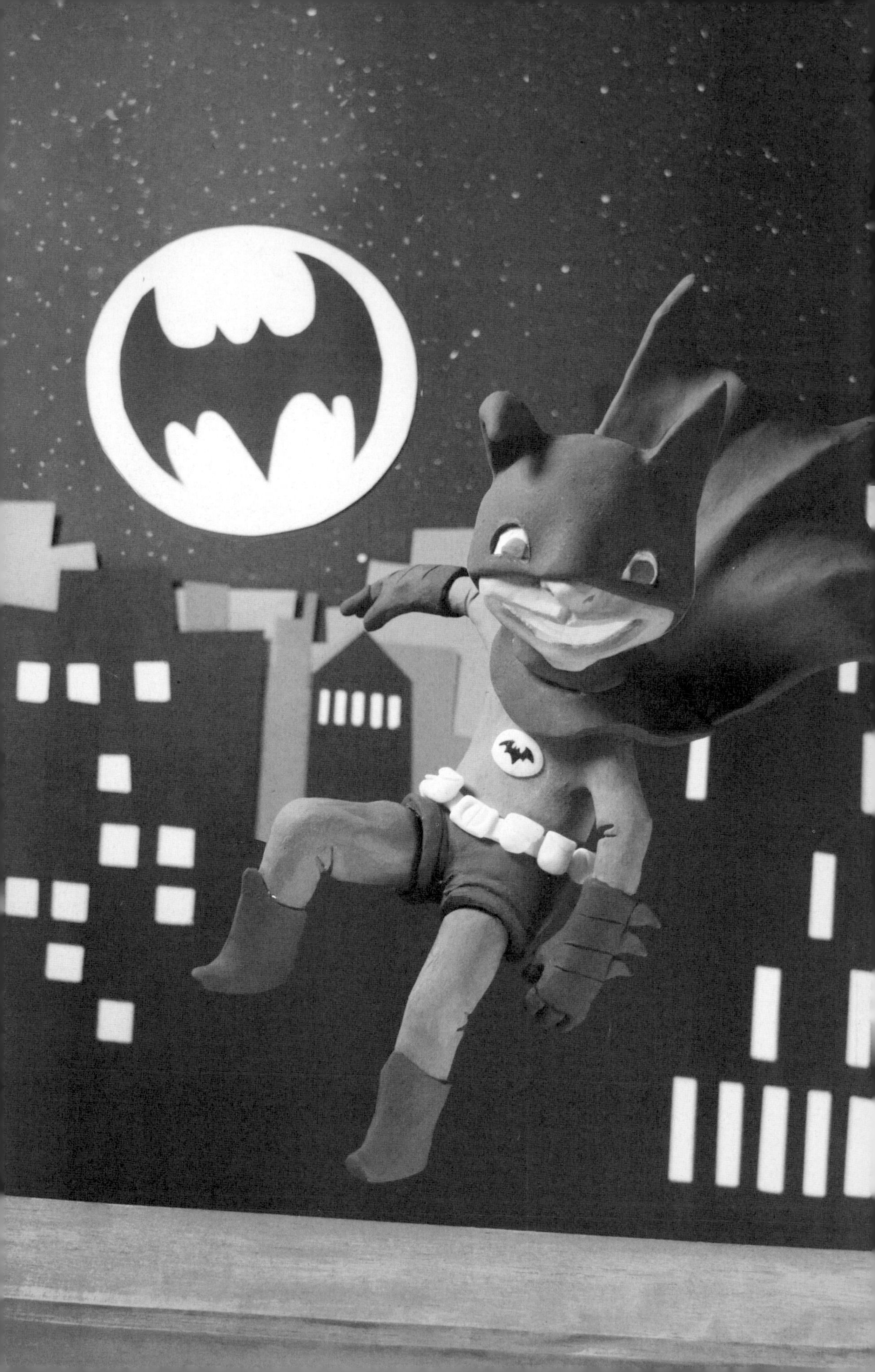

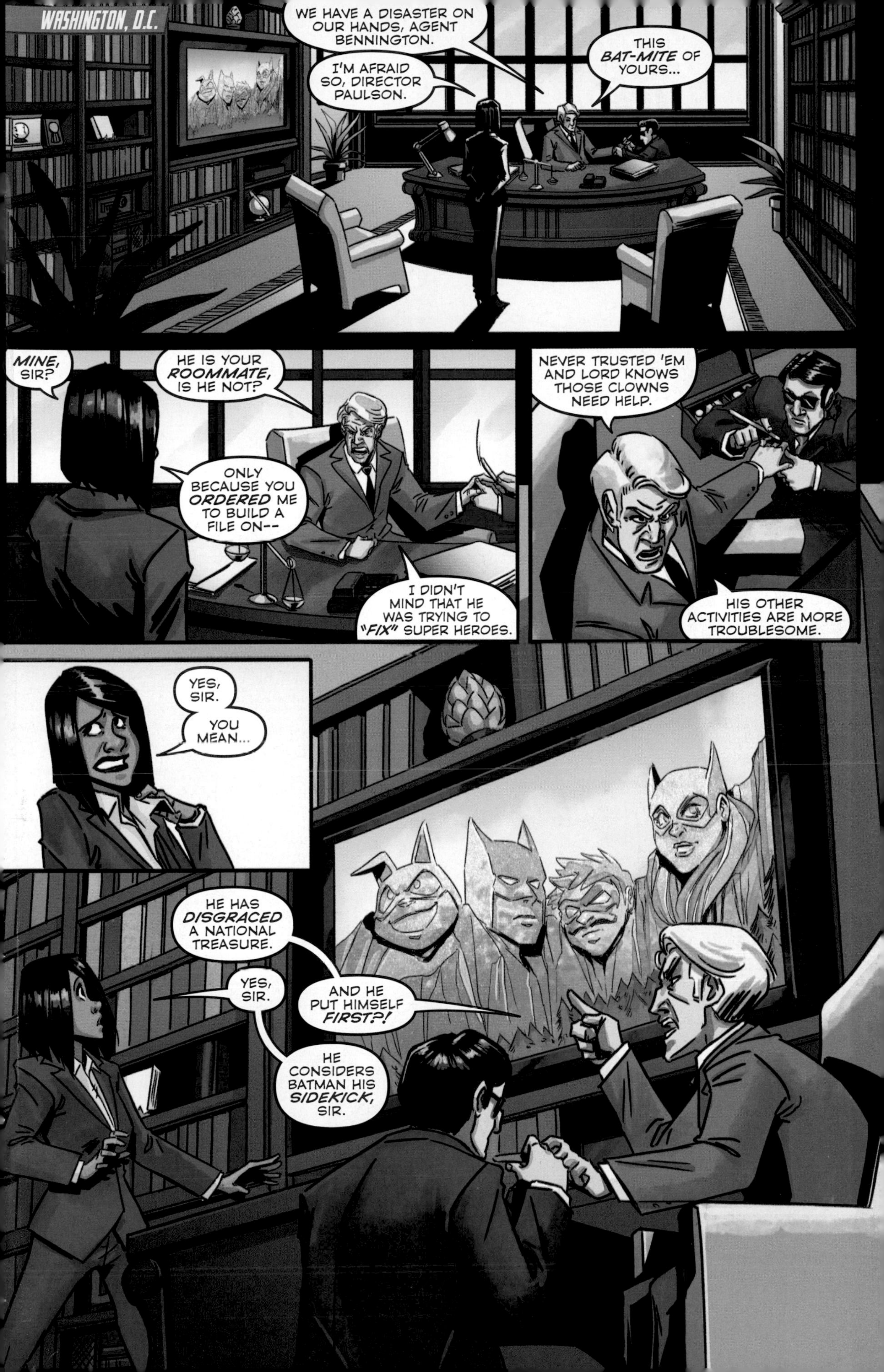
WASHINGTON, D.C.
WE HAVE A DISASTER ON OUR HANDS, AGENT BENNINGTON.
I'M AFRAID SO, DIRECTOR PAULSON.
THIS BAT-MITE OF YOURS...
MINE, SIR?
HE IS YOUR ROOMMATE, IS HE NOT?
ONLY BECAUSE YOU ORDERED ME TO BUILD A FILE ON--
I DIDN'T MIND THAT HE WAS TRYING TO "FIX" SUPER HEROES.
NEVER TRUSTED 'EM AND LORD KNOWS THOSE CLOWNS NEED HELP.
HIS OTHER ACTIVITIES ARE MORE TROUBLESOME.
YES, SIR.
YOU MEAN...
HE HAS DISGRACED A NATIONAL TREASURE.
YES, SIR.
AND HE PUT HIMSELF FIRST?!
HE CONSIDERS BATMAN HIS SIDEKICK, SIR.

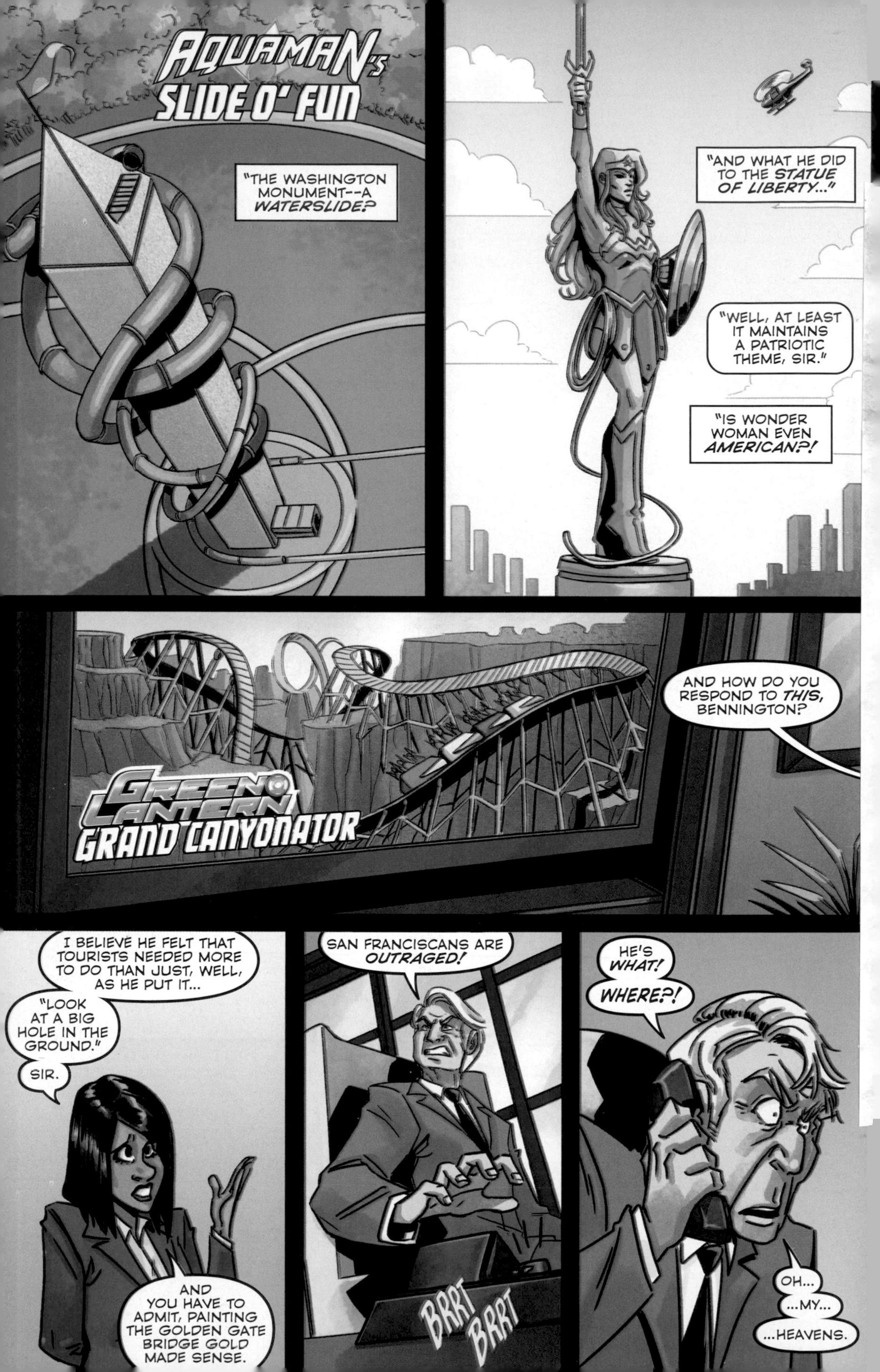
AQUAMAN'S SLIDE O' FUN
"THE WASHINGTON MONUMENT--A WATERSLIDE?
"AND WHAT HE DID TO THE STATUE OF LIBERTY..."
"WELL, AT LEAST IT MAINTAINS A PATRIOTIC THEME, SIR."
"IS WONDER WOMAN EVEN AMERICAN?!
GREEN LANTERN GRAND CANYONATOR
AND HOW DO YOU RESPOND TO THIS, BENNINGTON?
I BELIEVE HE FELT THAT TOURISTS NEEDED MORE TO DO THAN JUST, WELL, AS HE PUT IT...
"LOOK AT A BIG HOLE IN THE GROUND."
SIR.
AND YOU HAVE TO ADMIT, PAINTING THE GOLDEN GATE BRIDGE GOLD MADE SENSE.
SAN FRANCISCANS ARE OUTRAGED!
BRRT BRRT
HE'S WHAT!
WHERE?!
OH...
...MY...
...HEAVENS.

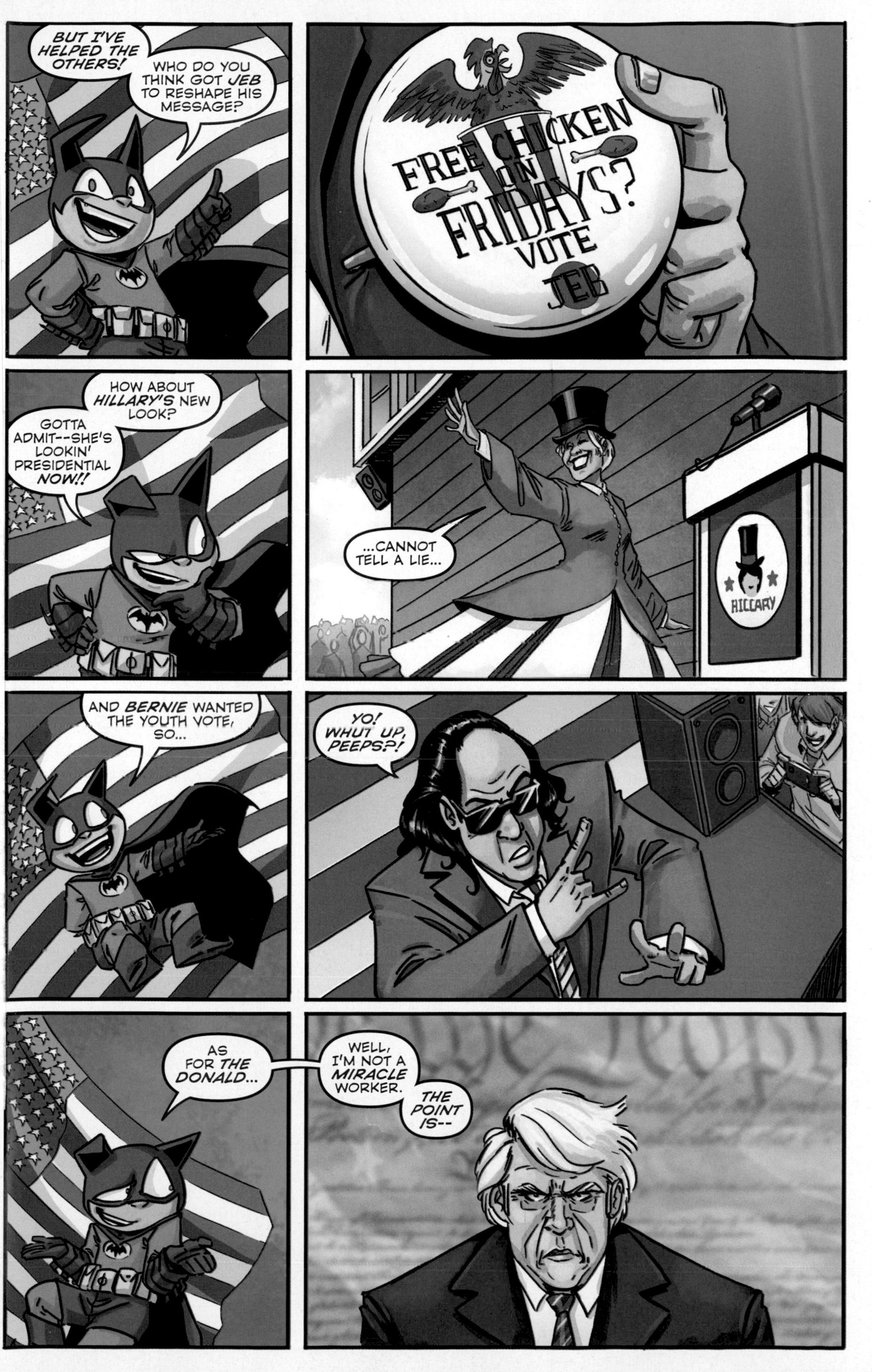
BUT I'VE HELPED THE OTHERS!
WHO DO YOU THINK GOT JEB TO RESHAPE HIS MESSAGE?
FREE CHICKEN ON FRIDAYS? VOTE JEB
HOW ABOUT HILLARY'S NEW LOOK?
GOTTA ADMIT--SHE'S LOOKIN' PRESIDENTIAL NOW!!
...CANNOT TELL A LIE...
HILLARY
AND BERNIE WANTED THE YOUTH VOTE, SO...
YO! WHUT UP, PEEPS?!
AS FOR THE DONALD...
WELL, I'M NOT A MIRACLE WORKER.
THE POINT IS--

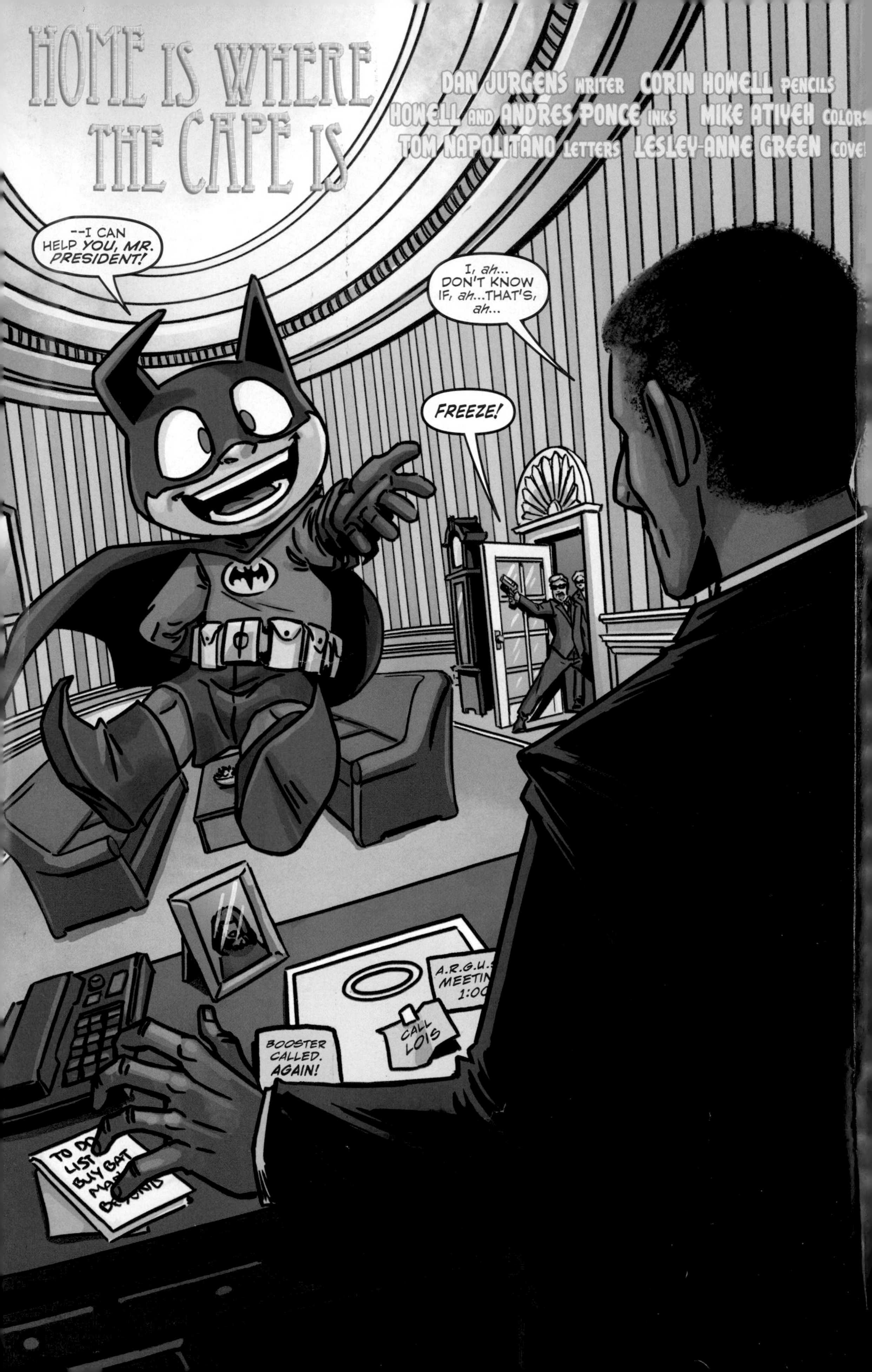
HOME IS WHERE THE CAPE IS
DAN JURGENS WRITER CORIN HOWELL PENCILS
HOWELL AND ANDRES PONCE INKS MIKE ATIYEH COLOR
TOM NAPOLITANO LETTERS LESLEY-ANNE GREEN COVE
--I CAN HELP YOU, MR. PRESIDENT!
I, ah... DON'T KNOW IF, ah...THAT'S, ah...
FREEZE!
CALL LOIS
BOOSTER CALLED. AGAIN!
TO DO LIST

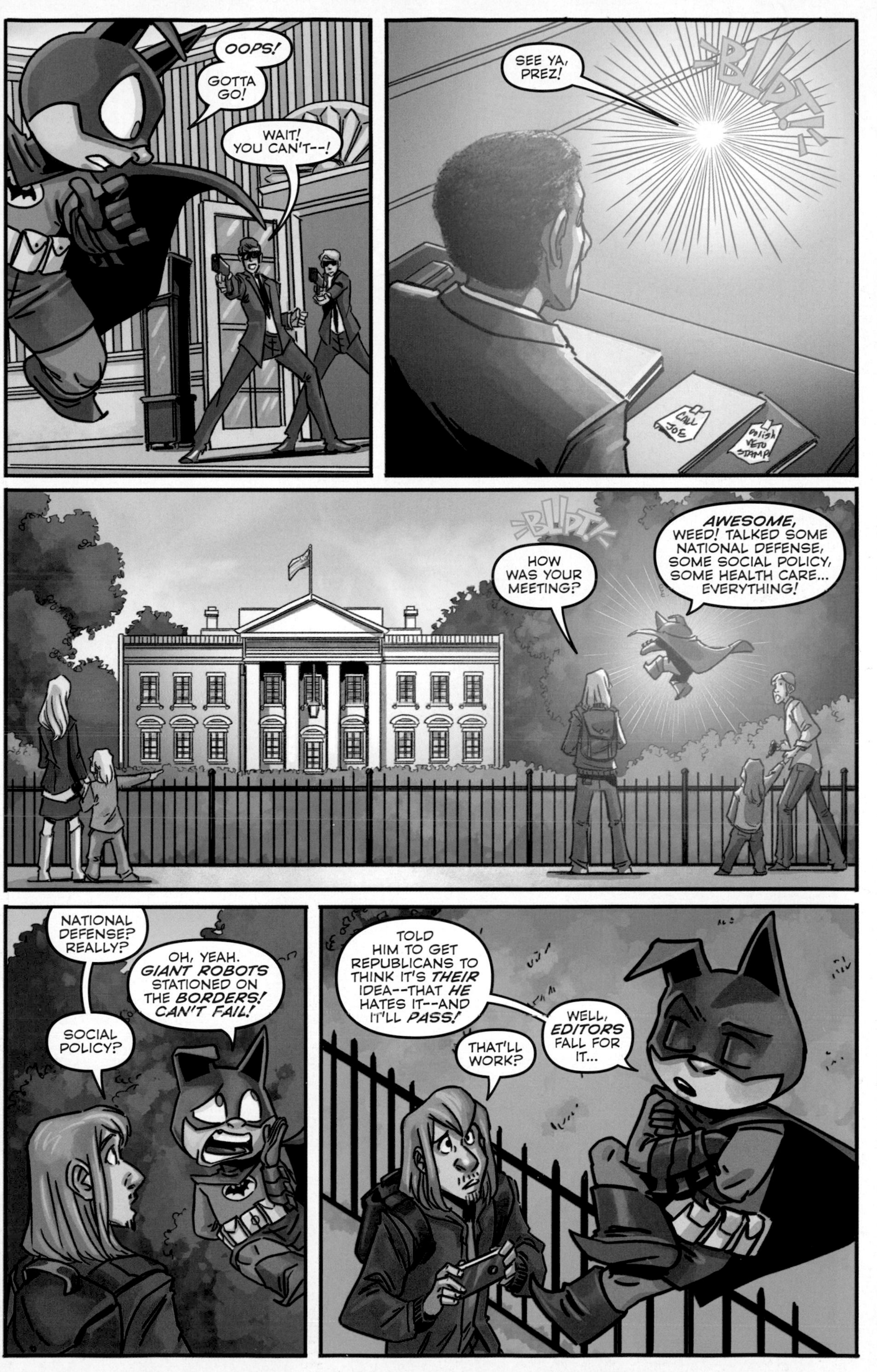
OOPS!
GOTTA GO!
WAIT! YOU CAN'T--!
SEE YA, PREZ!
-BLIPT!!-
CALL JOE
POLISH VETO STAMP!
-BLIPT!-
HOW WAS YOUR MEETING?
AWESOME, WEED! TALKED SOME NATIONAL DEFENSE, SOME SOCIAL POLICY, SOME HEALTH CARE... EVERYTHING!
NATIONAL DEFENSE? REALLY?
OH, YEAH. GIANT ROBOTS STATIONED ON THE BORDERS! CAN'T FAIL!
SOCIAL POLICY?
TOLD HIM TO GET REPUBLICANS TO THINK IT'S THEIR IDEA--THAT HE HATES IT--AND IT'LL PASS!
THAT'LL WORK?
WELL, EDITORS FALL FOR IT...

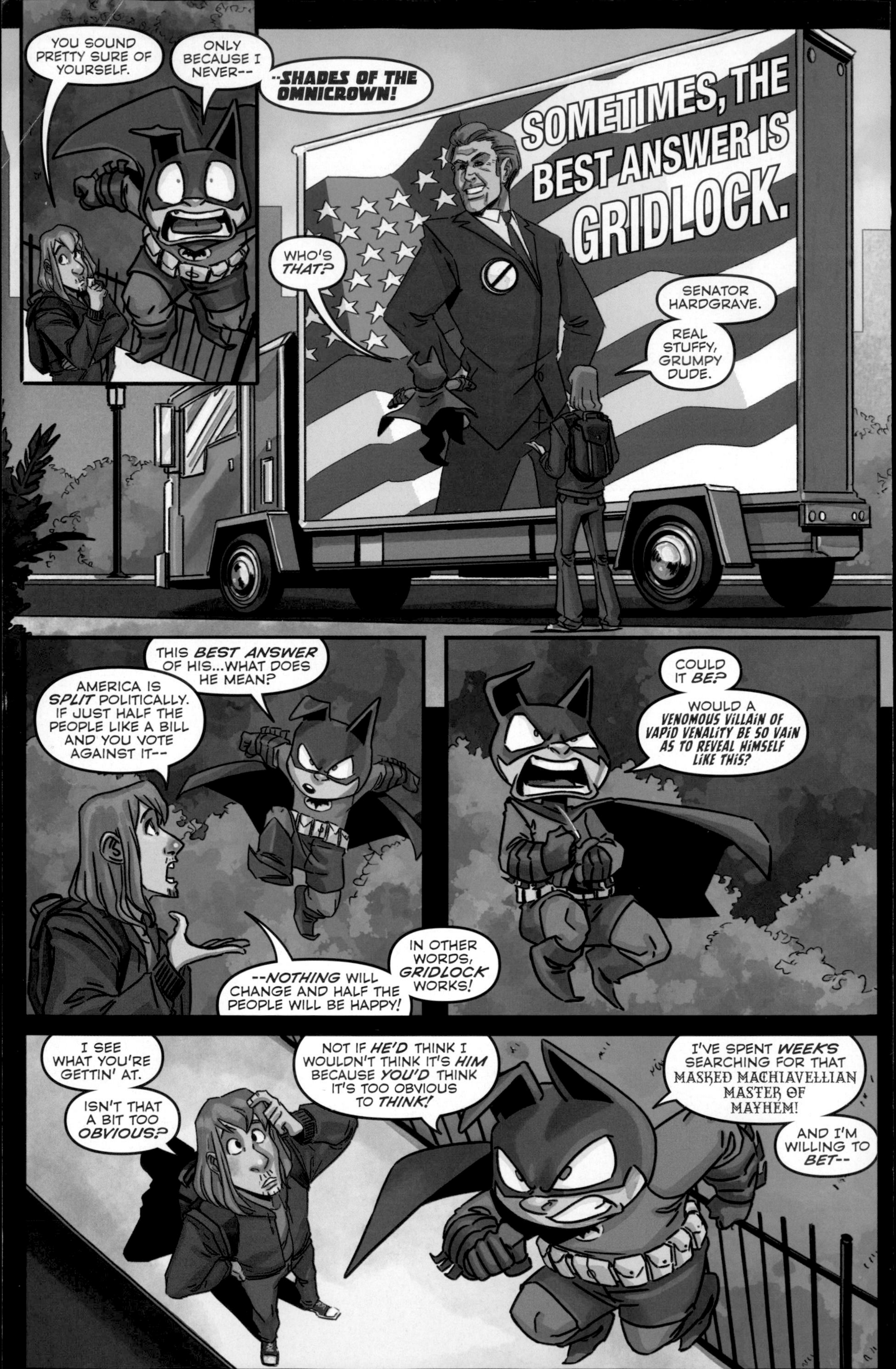
YOU SOUND PRETTY SURE OF YOURSELF.
ONLY BECAUSE I NEVER--
--SHADES OF THE OMNICROWN!
SOMETIMES, THE BEST ANSWER IS GRIDLOCK.
WHO'S THAT?
SENATOR HARDGRAVE.
REAL STUFFY, GRUMPY DUDE.
THIS BEST ANSWER OF HIS...WHAT DOES HE MEAN?
AMERICA IS SPLIT POLITICALLY. IF JUST HALF THE PEOPLE LIKE A BILL AND YOU VOTE AGAINST IT--
--NOTHING WILL CHANGE AND HALF THE PEOPLE WILL BE HAPPY!
IN OTHER WORDS, GRIDLOCK WORKS!
COULD IT BE?
WOULD A VENOMOUS VILLAIN OF VAPID VENALITY BE SO VAIN AS TO REVEAL HIMSELF LIKE THIS?
I SEE WHAT YOU'RE GETTIN' AT.
ISN'T THAT A BIT TOO OBVIOUS?
NOT IF HE'D THINK I WOULDN'T THINK IT'S HIM BECAUSE YOU'D THINK IT'S TOO OBVIOUS TO THINK!
I'VE SPENT WEEKS SEARCHING FOR THAT MASKED MACHIAVELLIAN MASTER OF MAYHEM!
AND I'M WILLING TO BET--

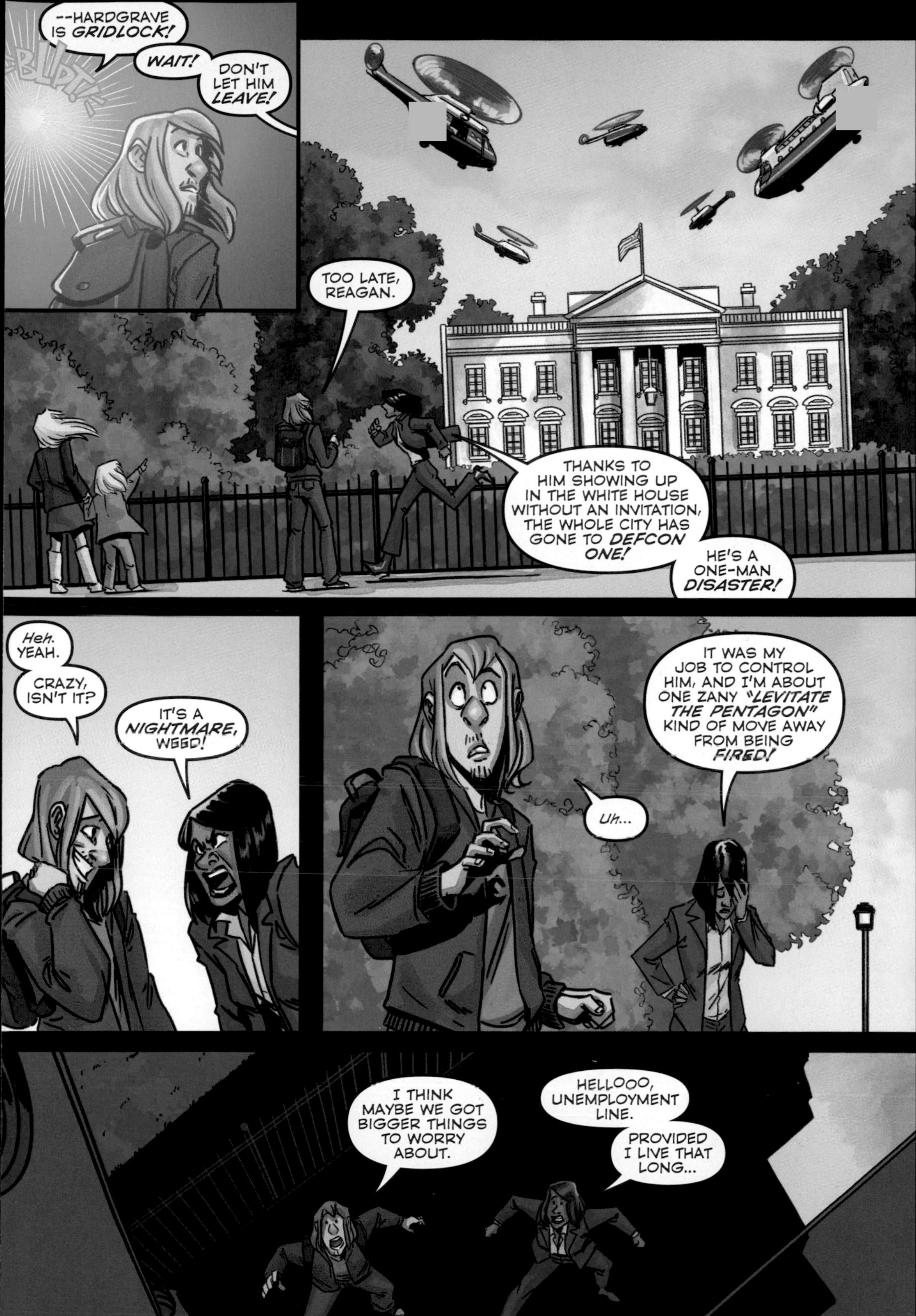
--HARDGRAVE IS GRIDLOCK!
BLIP!
WAIT!
DON'T LET HIM LEAVE!
TOO LATE, REAGAN.
THANKS TO HIM SHOWING UP IN THE WHITE HOUSE WITHOUT AN INVITATION, THE WHOLE CITY HAS GONE TO DEFCON ONE!
HE'S A ONE-MAN DISASTER!
Heh. YEAH.
CRAZY, ISN'T IT?
IT'S A NIGHTMARE, WEED!
IT WAS MY JOB TO CONTROL HIM, AND I'M ABOUT ONE ZANY "LEVITATE THE PENTAGON" KIND OF MOVE AWAY FROM BEING FIRED!
Uh...
HELLOOO, UNEMPLOYMENT LINE.
PROVIDED I LIVE THAT LONG...
I THINK MAYBE WE GOT BIGGER THINGS TO WORRY ABOUT.

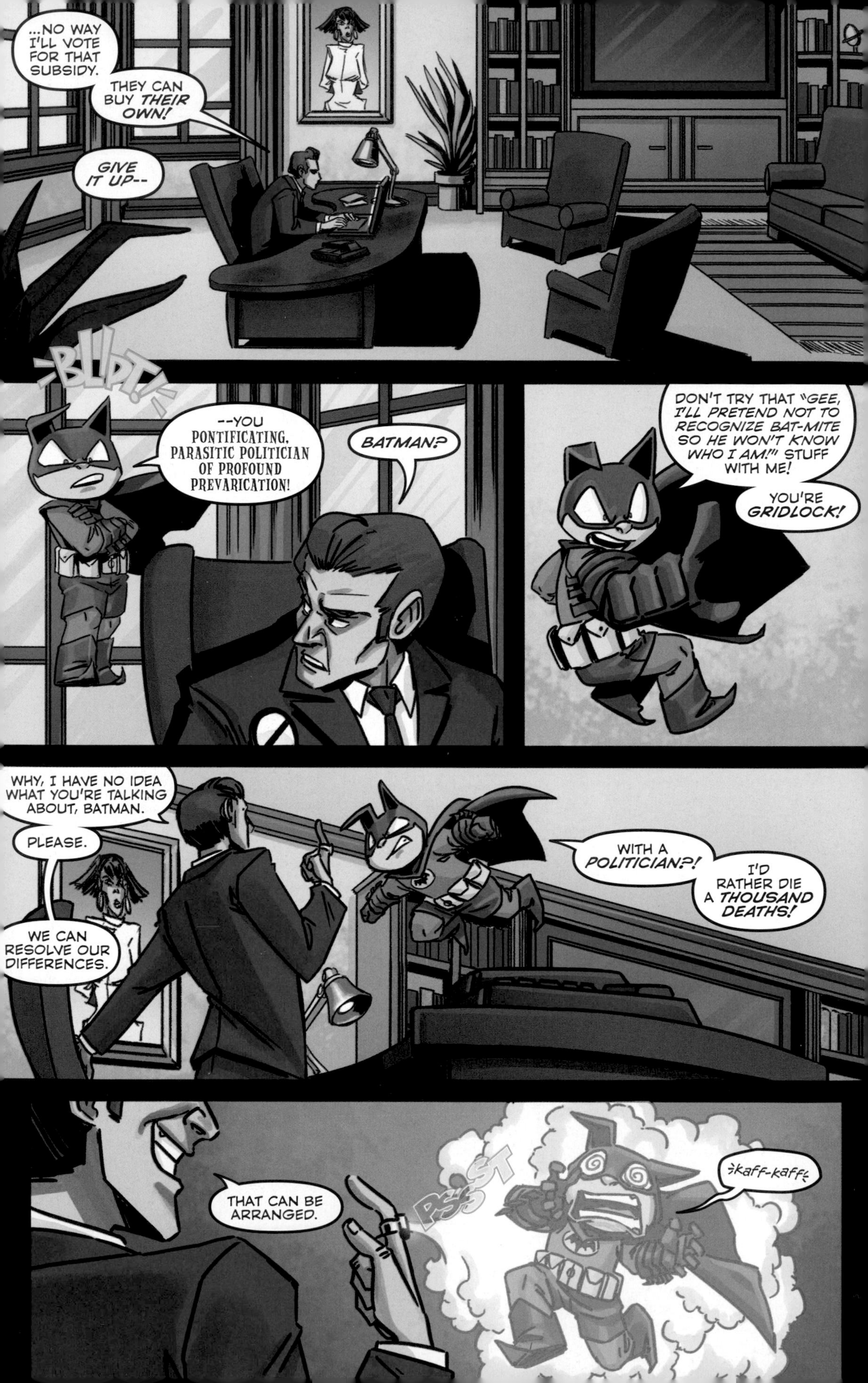
...NO WAY I'LL VOTE FOR THAT SUBSIDY.
THEY CAN BUY THEIR OWN!
GIVE IT UP--
BLIPT!
--YOU PONTIFICATING, PARASITIC POLITICIAN OF PROFOUND PREVARICATION!
BATMAN?
DON'T TRY THAT "GEE, I'LL PRETEND NOT TO RECOGNIZE BAT-MITE SO HE WON'T KNOW WHO I AM!" STUFF WITH ME!
YOU'RE GRIDLOCK!
WHY, I HAVE NO IDEA WHAT YOU'RE TALKING ABOUT, BATMAN.
PLEASE.
WE CAN RESOLVE OUR DIFFERENCES.
WITH A POLITICIAN?!
I'D RATHER DIE A THOUSAND DEATHS!
THAT CAN BE ARRANGED.
PSSST
kaff-kaff

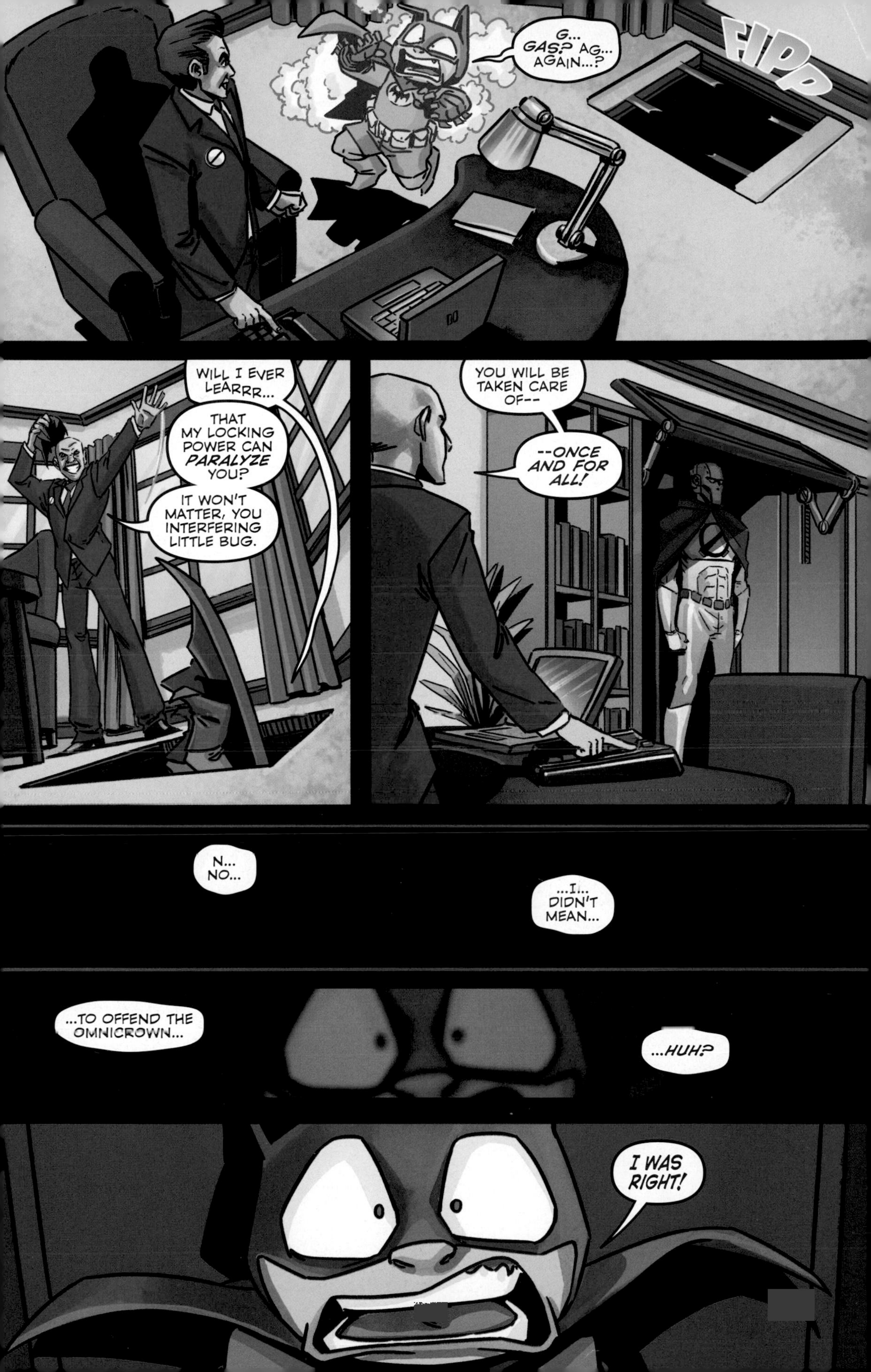
G... GAS? AG... AGAIN...?
FIPP
WILL I EVER LEARRR...
THAT MY LOCKING POWER CAN *PARALYZE* YOU?
IT WON'T MATTER, YOU INTERFERING LITTLE BUG.
YOU WILL BE TAKEN CARE OF--
--ONCE AND FOR ALL!
N... NO...
...I... DIDN'T MEAN...
...TO OFFEND THE OMNICROWN...
...*HUH?*
I WAS RIGHT!

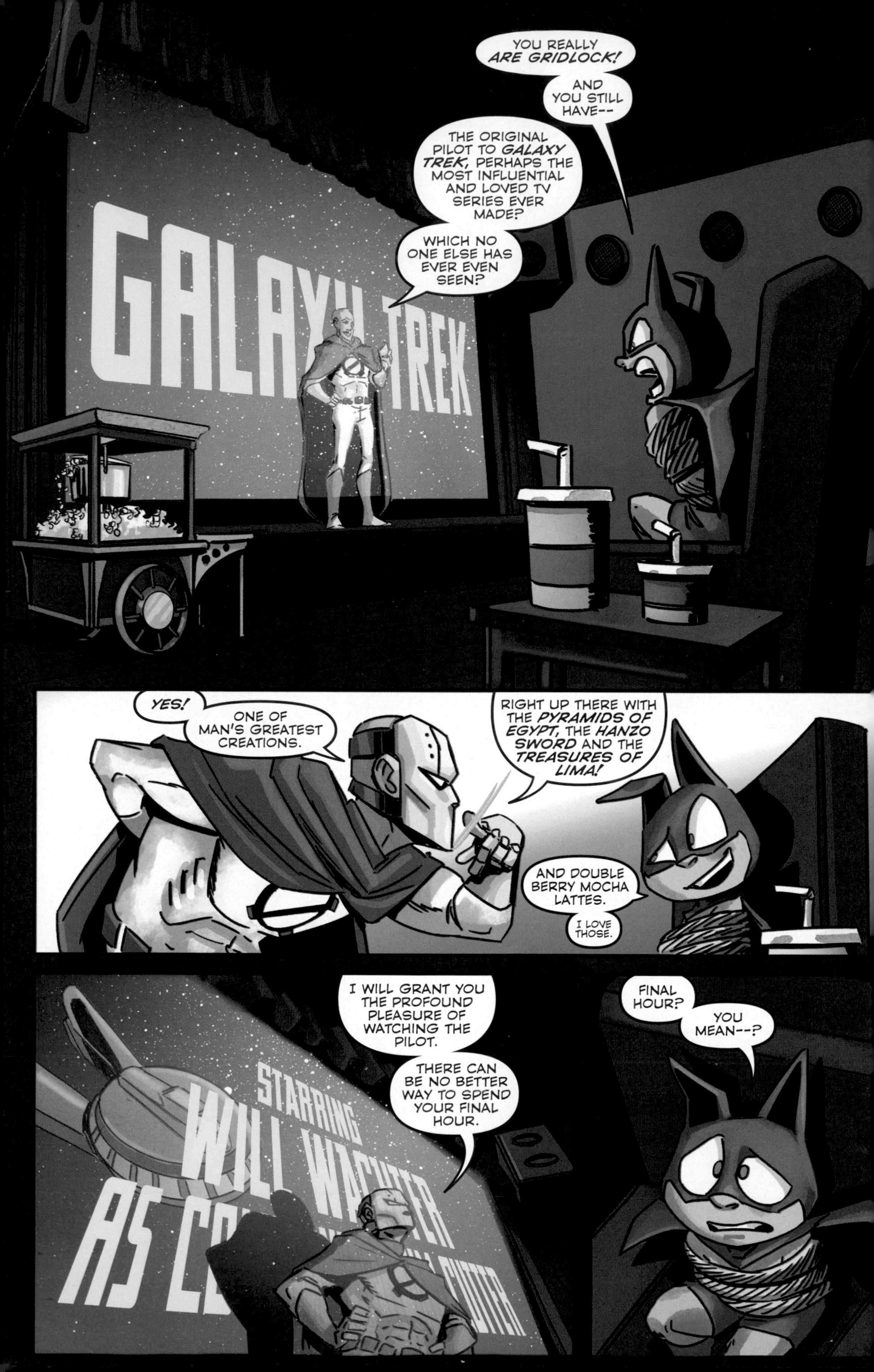
YOU REALLY ARE GRIDLOCK!
AND YOU STILL HAVE--
THE ORIGINAL PILOT TO GALAXY TREK, PERHAPS THE MOST INFLUENTIAL AND LOVED TV SERIES EVER MADE?
WHICH NO ONE ELSE HAS EVER EVEN SEEN?
GALAXY TREK
YES!
ONE OF MAN'S GREATEST CREATIONS.
RIGHT UP THERE WITH THE PYRAMIDS OF EGYPT, THE HANZO SWORD AND THE TREASURES OF LIMA!
AND DOUBLE BERRY MOCHA LATTES.
I LOVE THOSE.
I WILL GRANT YOU THE PROFOUND PLEASURE OF WATCHING THE PILOT.
THERE CAN BE NO BETTER WAY TO SPEND YOUR FINAL HOUR.
STARRING
FINAL HOUR?
YOU MEAN--?

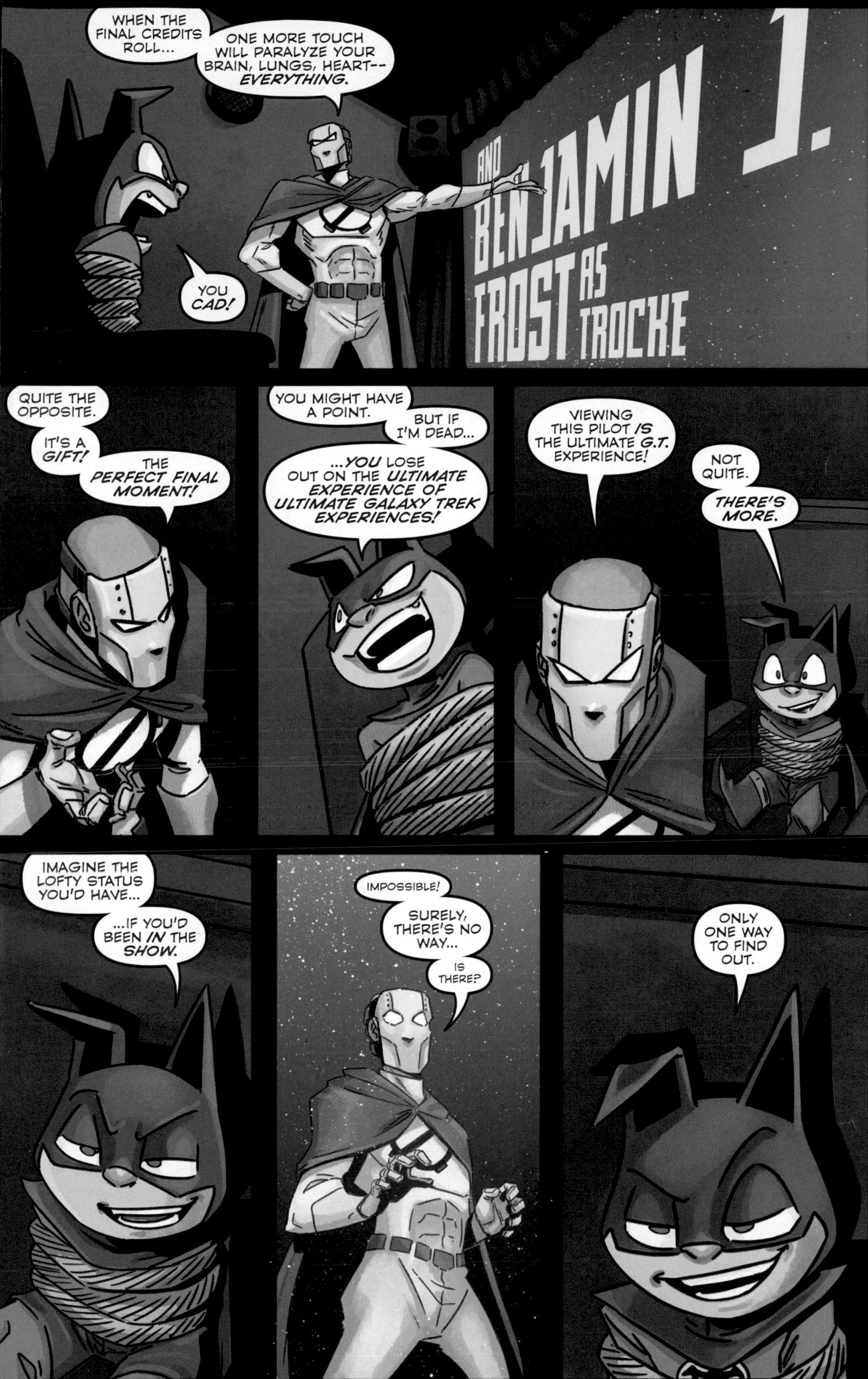
WHEN THE FINAL CREDITS ROLL...
ONE MORE TOUCH WILL PARALYZE YOUR BRAIN, LUNGS, HEART-- EVERYTHING.
AND BENJAMIN J. FROST AS TROCKE
YOU CAD!
QUITE THE OPPOSITE.
IT'S A GIFT!
THE PERFECT FINAL MOMENT!
YOU MIGHT HAVE A POINT.
BUT IF I'M DEAD...
...YOU LOSE OUT ON THE ULTIMATE EXPERIENCE OF ULTIMATE GALAXY TREK EXPERIENCES!
VIEWING THIS PILOT IS THE ULTIMATE G.T. EXPERIENCE!
NOT QUITE.
THERE'S MORE.
IMAGINE THE LOFTY STATUS YOU'D HAVE...
...IF YOU'D BEEN IN THE SHOW.
IMPOSSIBLE!
SURELY, THERE'S NO WAY...
IS THERE?
ONLY ONE WAY TO FIND OUT.

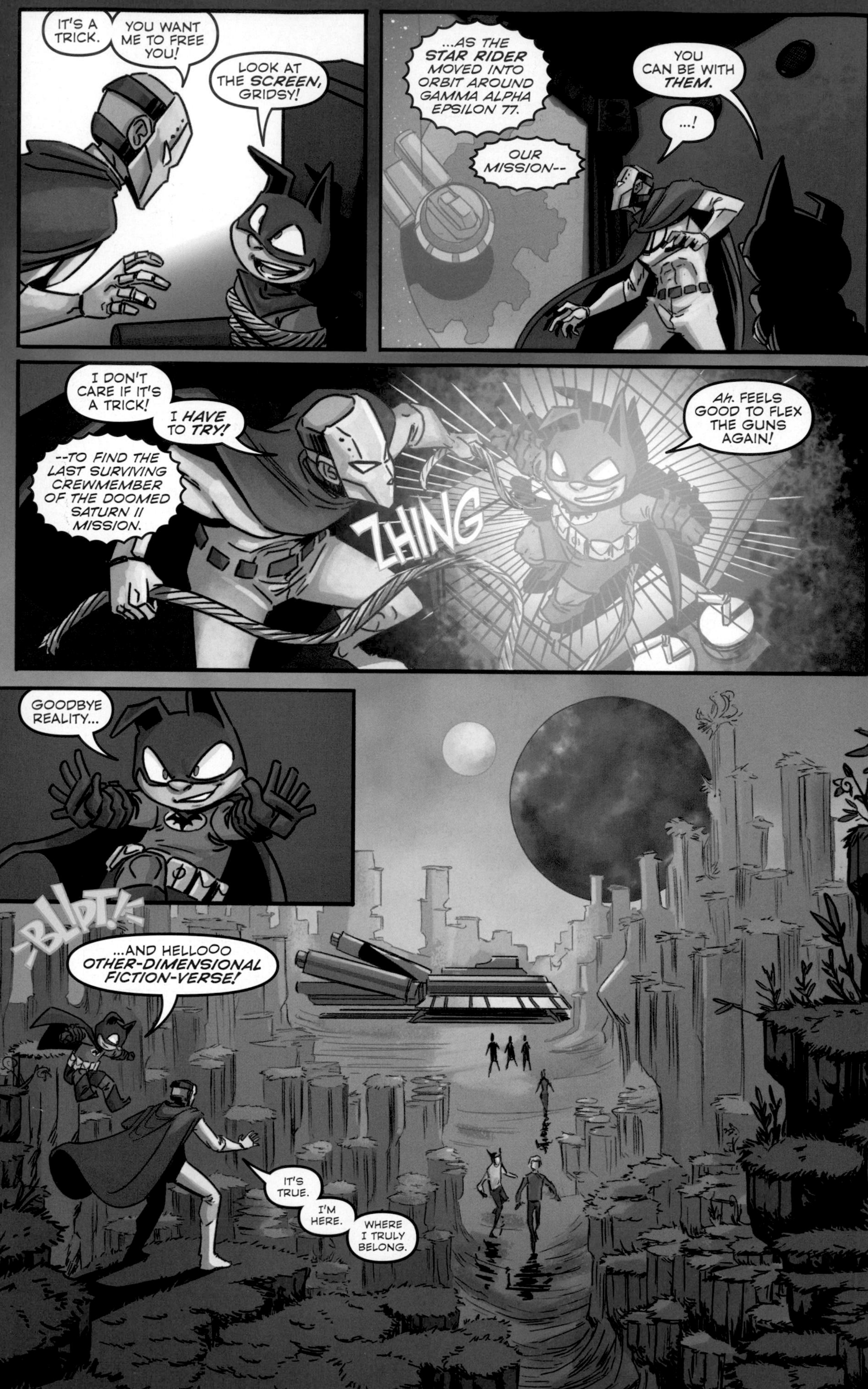
IT'S A TRICK.
YOU WANT ME TO FREE YOU!
LOOK AT THE SCREEN, GRIDSY!
...AS THE STAR RIDER MOVED INTO ORBIT AROUND GAMMA ALPHA EPSILON 77.
OUR MISSION--
YOU CAN BE WITH THEM.
...!
I DON'T CARE IF IT'S A TRICK!
I HAVE TO TRY!
--TO FIND THE LAST SURVIVING CREWMEMBER OF THE DOOMED SATURN II MISSION.
ZHING
Ah. FEELS GOOD TO FLEX THE GUNS AGAIN!
GOODBYE REALITY...
BLIPT!
...AND HELLOOO OTHER-DIMENSIONAL FICTION-VERSE!
IT'S TRUE.
I'M HERE.
WHERE I TRULY BELONG.

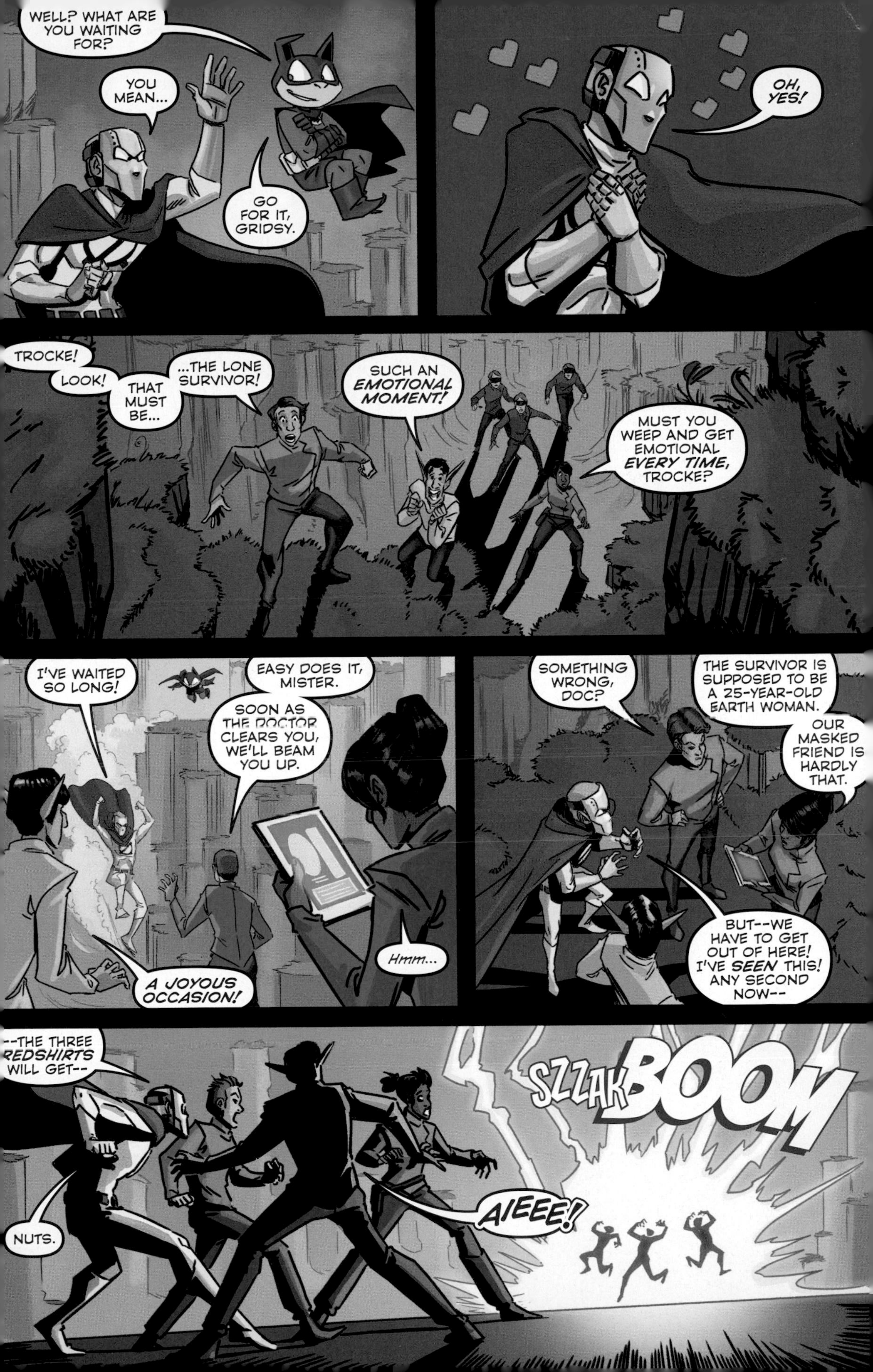
WELL? WHAT ARE YOU WAITING FOR?
YOU MEAN...
GO FOR IT, GRIDSY.
OH, YES!
TROCKE!
LOOK!
THAT MUST BE...
...THE LONE SURVIVOR!
SUCH AN EMOTIONAL MOMENT!
MUST YOU WEEP AND GET EMOTIONAL EVERY TIME, TROCKE?
I'VE WAITED SO LONG!
EASY DOES IT, MISTER.
SOON AS THE DOCTOR CLEARS YOU, WE'LL BEAM YOU UP.
A JOYOUS OCCASION!
Hmm...
SOMETHING WRONG, DOC?
THE SURVIVOR IS SUPPOSED TO BE A 25-YEAR-OLD EARTH WOMAN.
OUR MASKED FRIEND IS HARDLY THAT.
BUT--WE HAVE TO GET OUT OF HERE! I'VE SEEN THIS! ANY SECOND NOW--
--THE THREE REDSHIRTS WILL GET--
SZZAKBOOM
AIEEE!
NUTS.

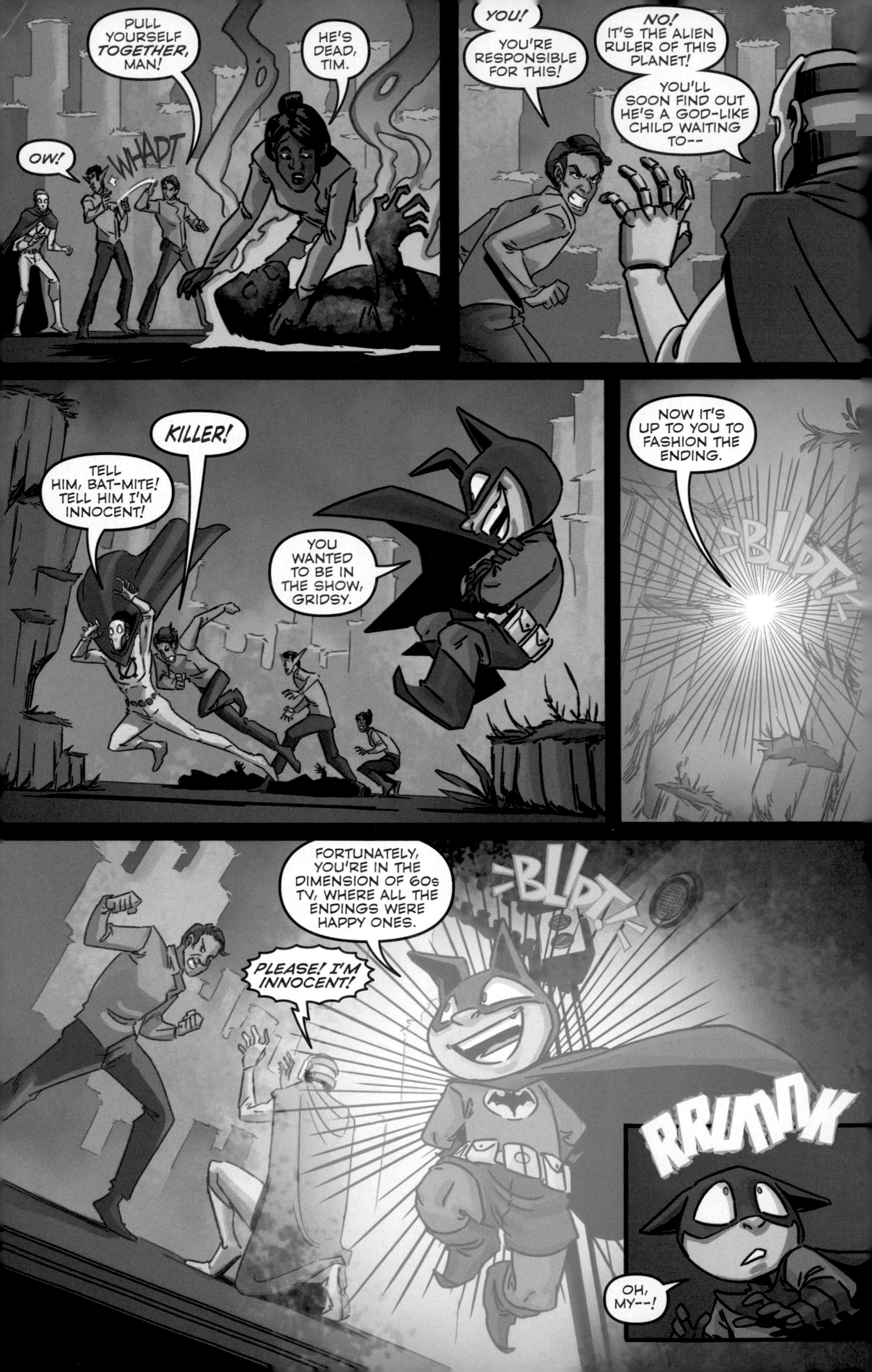
PULL YOURSELF TOGETHER, MAN!
HE'S DEAD, TIM.
OW!
WHAPT
YOU!
YOU'RE RESPONSIBLE FOR THIS!
NO! IT'S THE ALIEN RULER OF THIS PLANET!
YOU'LL SOON FIND OUT HE'S A GOD-LIKE CHILD WAITING TO--
KILLER!
TELL HIM, BAT-MITE! TELL HIM I'M INNOCENT!
YOU WANTED TO BE IN THE SHOW, GRIDSY.
NOW IT'S UP TO YOU TO FASHION THE ENDING.
BLIPT!
FORTUNATELY, YOU'RE IN THE DIMENSION OF 60s TV, WHERE ALL THE ENDINGS WERE HAPPY ONES.
BLIPT!
PLEASE! I'M INNOCENT!
RRUMK
OH, MY--!

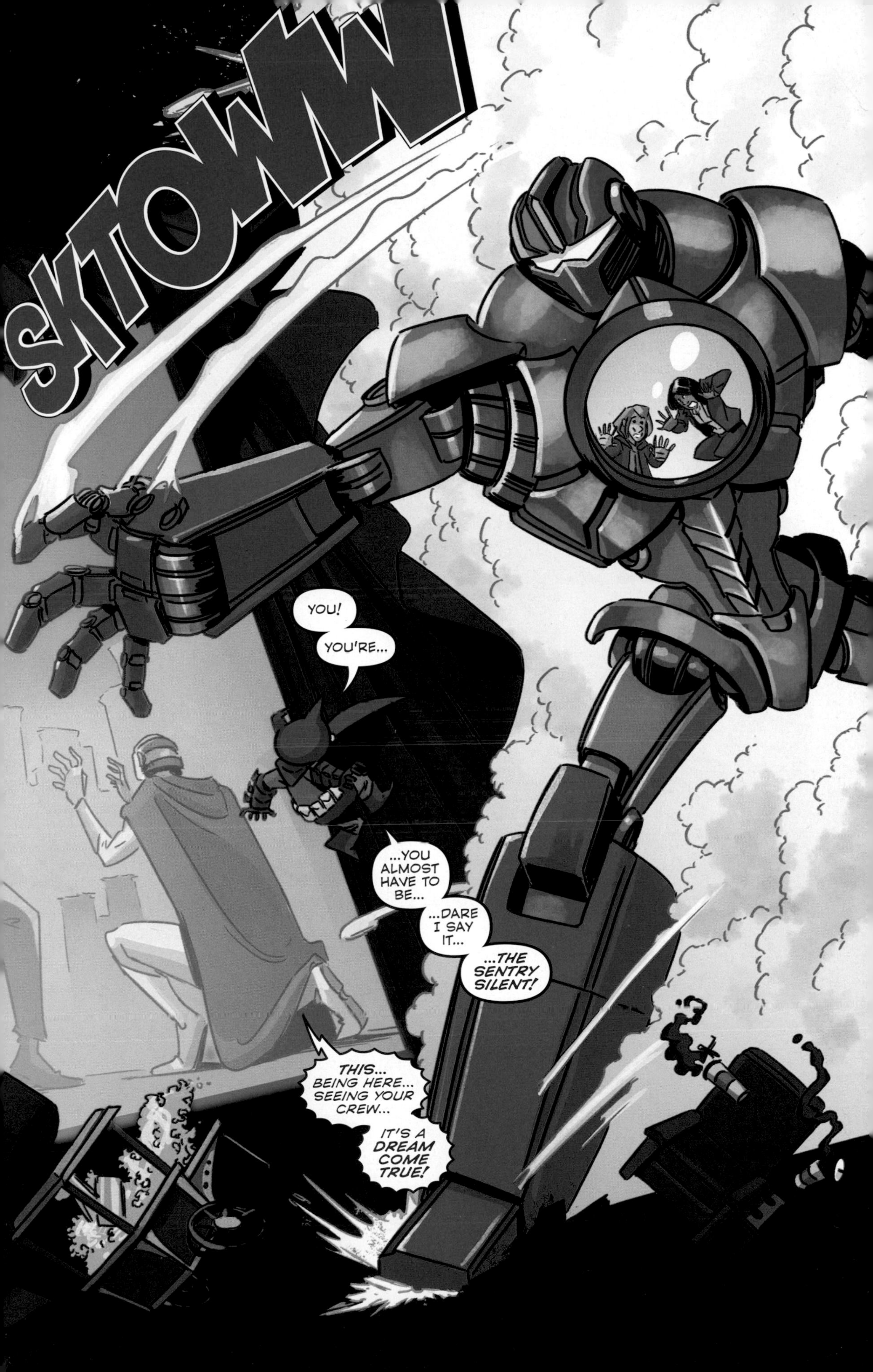
SKTOWW
YOU!
YOU'RE...
...YOU ALMOST HAVE TO BE...
...DARE I SAY IT...
...THE SENTRY SILENT!
THIS... BEING HERE... SEEING YOUR CREW...
IT'S A DREAM COME TRUE!

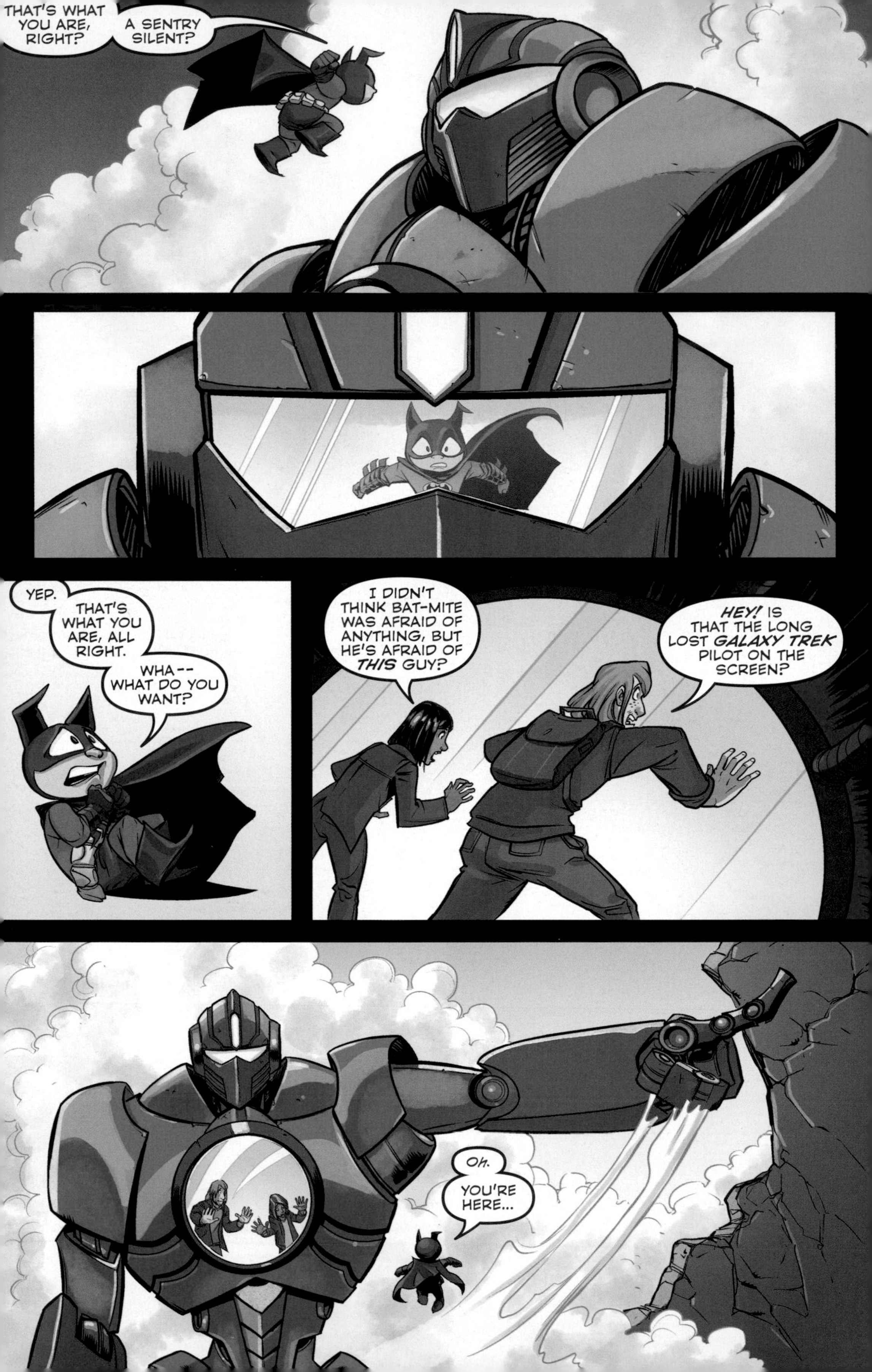
THAT'S WHAT YOU ARE, RIGHT?
A SENTRY SILENT?
YEP.
THAT'S WHAT YOU ARE, ALL RIGHT.
WHA-- WHAT DO YOU WANT?
I DIDN'T THINK BAT-MITE WAS AFRAID OF ANYTHING, BUT HE'S AFRAID OF *THIS* GUY?
HEY! IS THAT THE LONG LOST *GALAXY TREK* PILOT ON THE SCREEN?
Oh.
YOU'RE HERE...

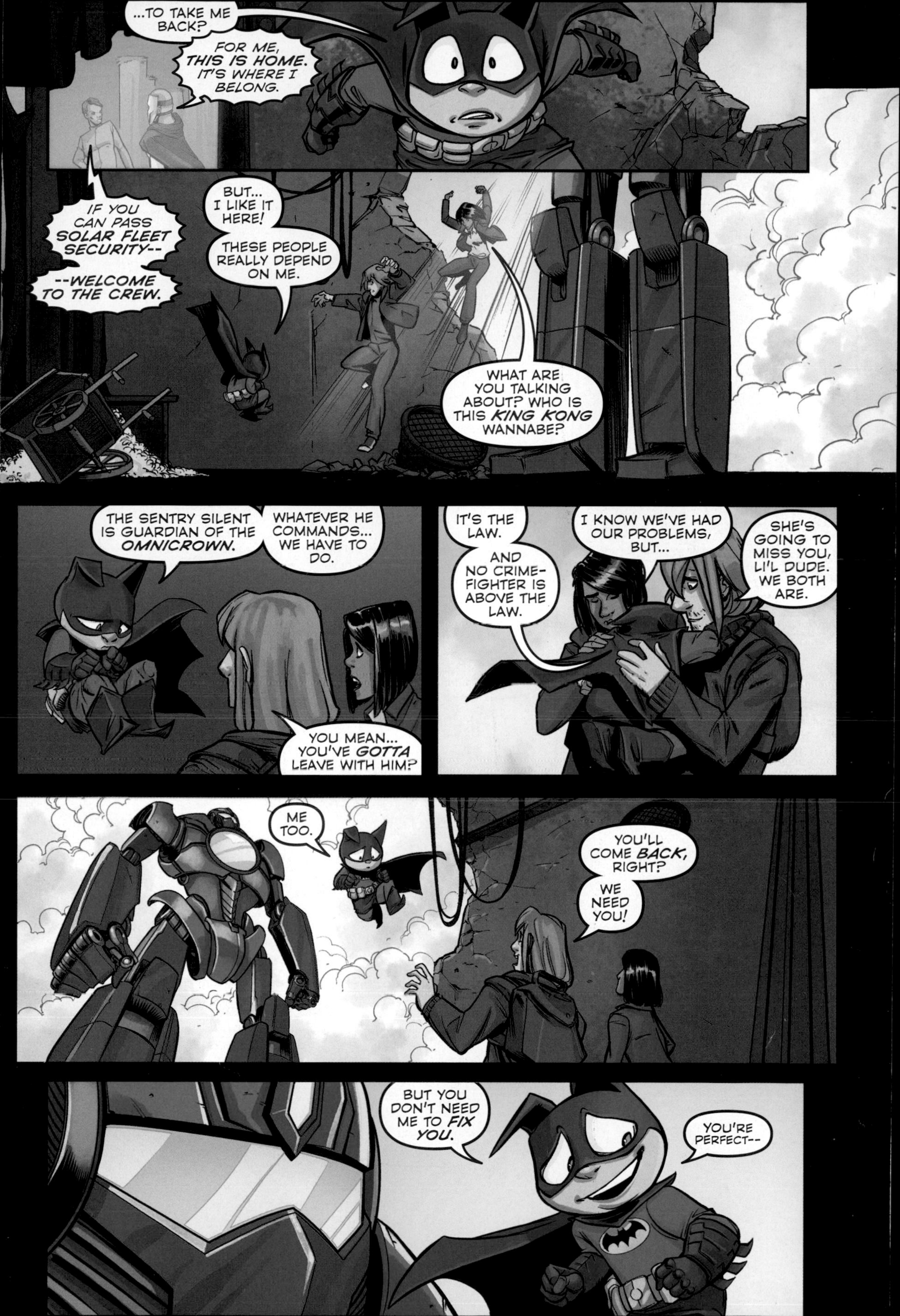

...TO TAKE ME BACK?
FOR ME, THIS IS HOME. IT'S WHERE I BELONG.
IF YOU CAN PASS SOLAR FLEET SECURITY--
--WELCOME TO THE CREW.
BUT... I LIKE IT HERE!
THESE PEOPLE REALLY DEPEND ON ME.
WHAT ARE YOU TALKING ABOUT? WHO IS THIS KING KONG WANNABE?
THE SENTRY SILENT IS GUARDIAN OF THE OMNICROWN.
WHATEVER HE COMMANDS... WE HAVE TO DO.
YOU MEAN... YOU'VE GOTTA LEAVE WITH HIM?
IT'S THE LAW.
AND NO CRIME-FIGHTER IS ABOVE THE LAW.
I KNOW WE'VE HAD OUR PROBLEMS, BUT...
SHE'S GOING TO MISS YOU, LI'L DUDE. WE BOTH ARE.
ME TOO.
YOU'LL COME BACK, RIGHT?
WE NEED YOU!
BUT YOU DON'T NEED ME TO FIX YOU.
YOU'RE PERFECT--

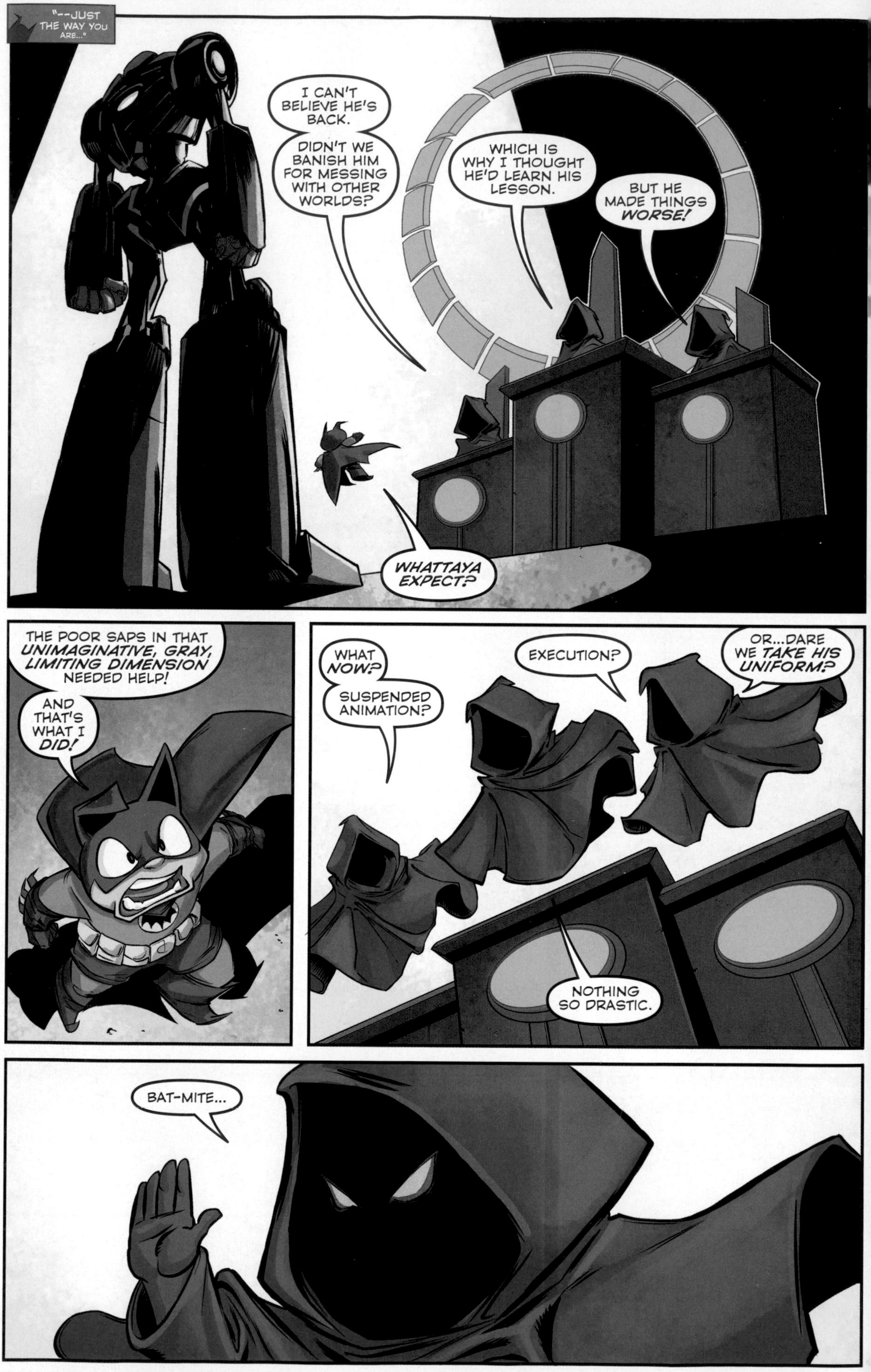
"--JUST THE WAY YOU ARE..."
I CAN'T BELIEVE HE'S BACK.
DIDN'T WE BANISH HIM FOR MESSING WITH OTHER WORLDS?
WHICH IS WHY I THOUGHT HE'D LEARN HIS LESSON.
BUT HE MADE THINGS *WORSE!*
WHATTAYA EXPECT?
THE POOR SAPS IN THAT *UNIMAGINATIVE, GRAY, LIMITING DIMENSION* NEEDED HELP!
AND THAT'S WHAT I *DID!*
WHAT *NOW?*
SUSPENDED ANIMATION?
EXECUTION?
OR...DARE WE *TAKE HIS UNIFORM?*
NOTHING SO DRASTIC.
BAT-MITE...

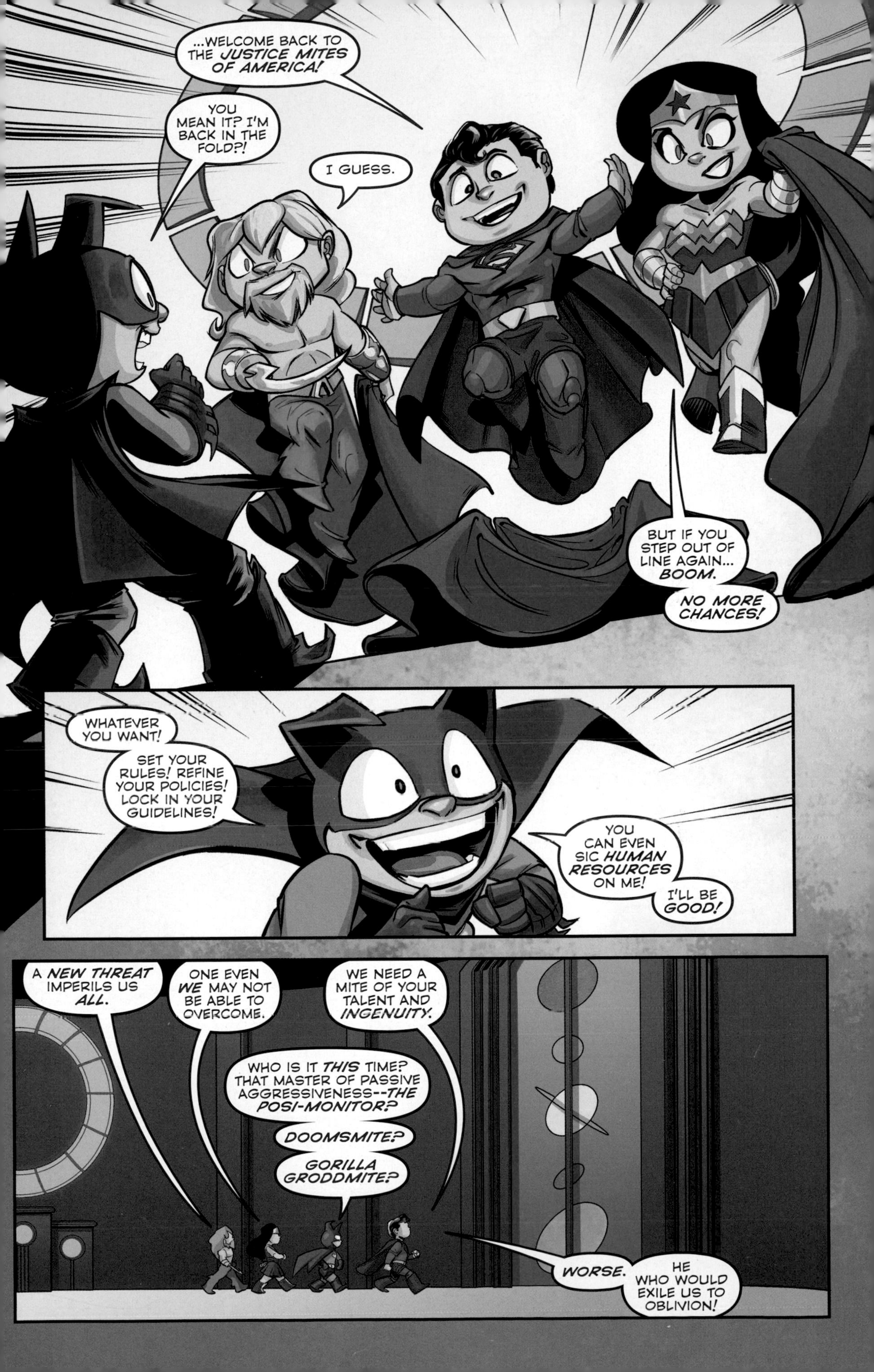
...WELCOME BACK TO THE *JUSTICE MITES OF AMERICA!*
YOU MEAN IT? I'M BACK IN THE FOLD?!
I GUESS.
BUT IF YOU STEP OUT OF LINE AGAIN... *BOOM.*
NO MORE CHANCES!
WHATEVER YOU WANT!
SET YOUR RULES! REFINE YOUR POLICIES! LOCK IN YOUR GUIDELINES!
YOU CAN EVEN SIC *HUMAN RESOURCES* ON ME!
I'LL BE *GOOD!*
A *NEW THREAT* IMPERILS US *ALL.*
ONE EVEN *WE* MAY NOT BE ABLE TO OVERCOME.
WE NEED A MITE OF YOUR TALENT AND *INGENUITY.*
WHO IS IT *THIS* TIME? THAT MASTER OF PASSIVE AGGRESSIVENESS--*THE POSI-MONITOR?*
DOOMSMITE?
GORILLA GRODDMITE?
WORSE.
HE WHO WOULD EXILE US TO OBLIVION!

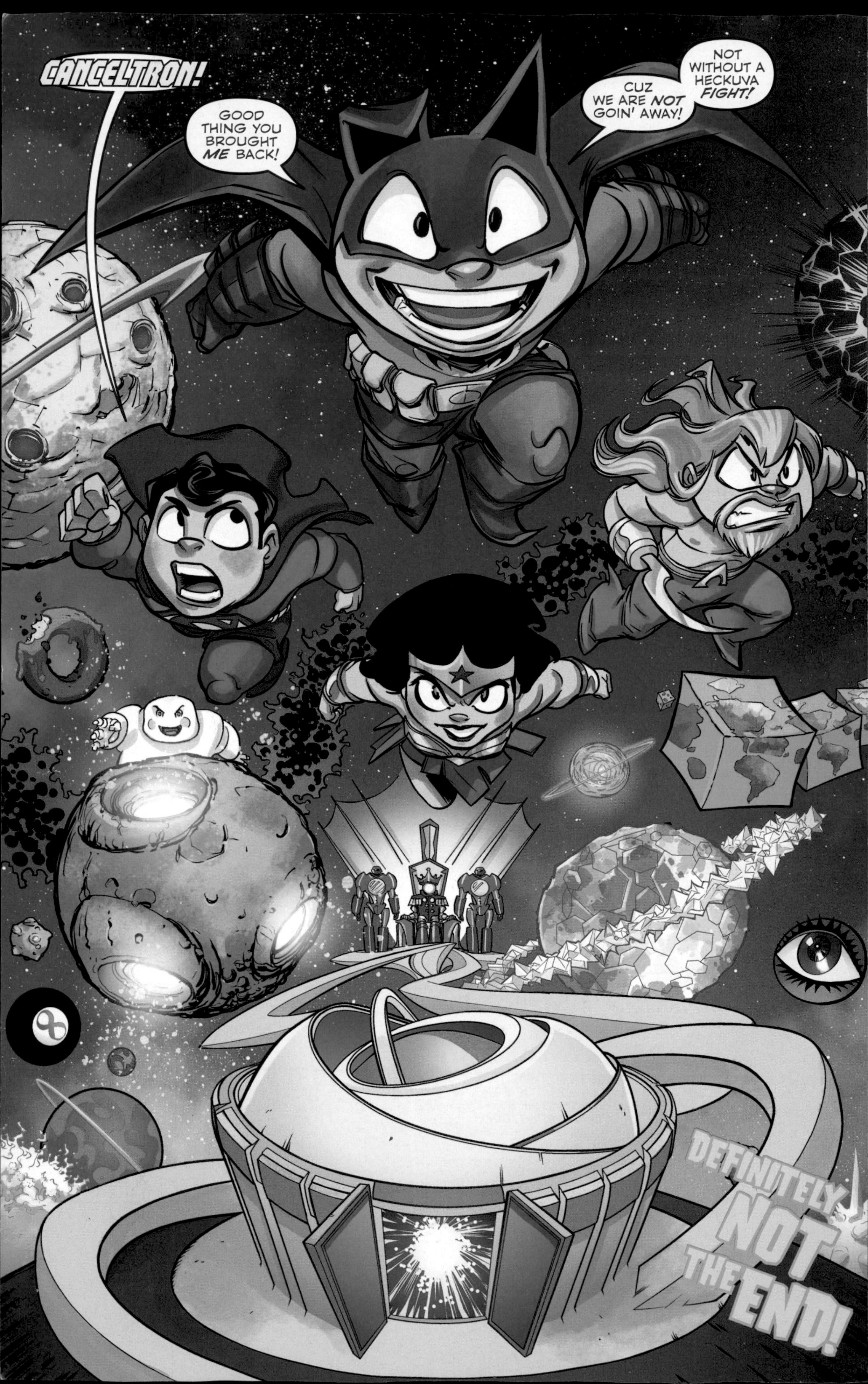
CANCELTRON!
GOOD THING YOU BROUGHT ME BACK!
CUZ WE ARE NOT GOIN' AWAY!
NOT WITHOUT A HECKUVA FIGHT!
DEFINITELY NOT THE END!

BAT-MITE #1 variant cover by
Corin Howell with Mike Atiyeh

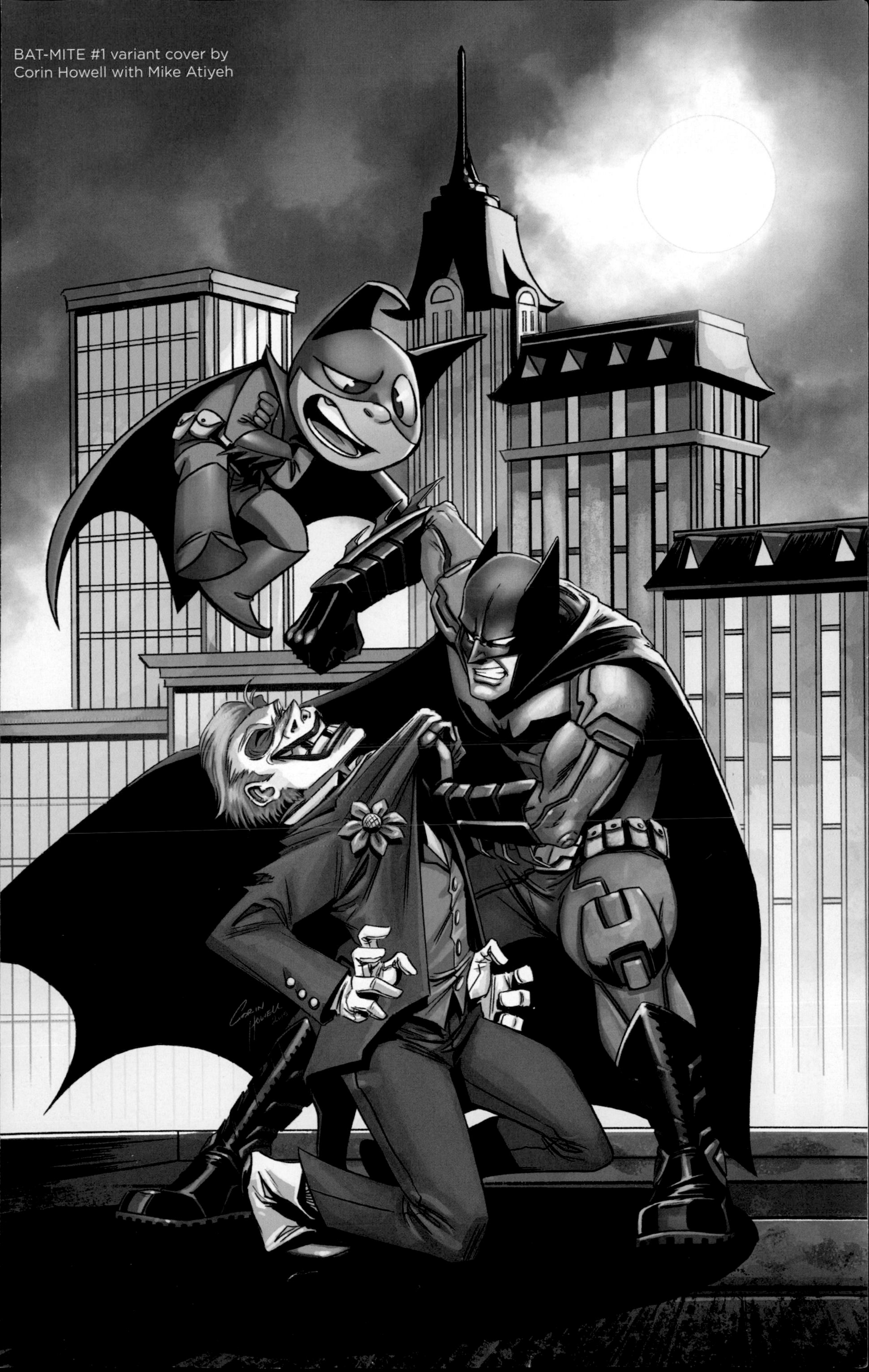

CHARACTER SKETCHES BY
CORIN HOWELL

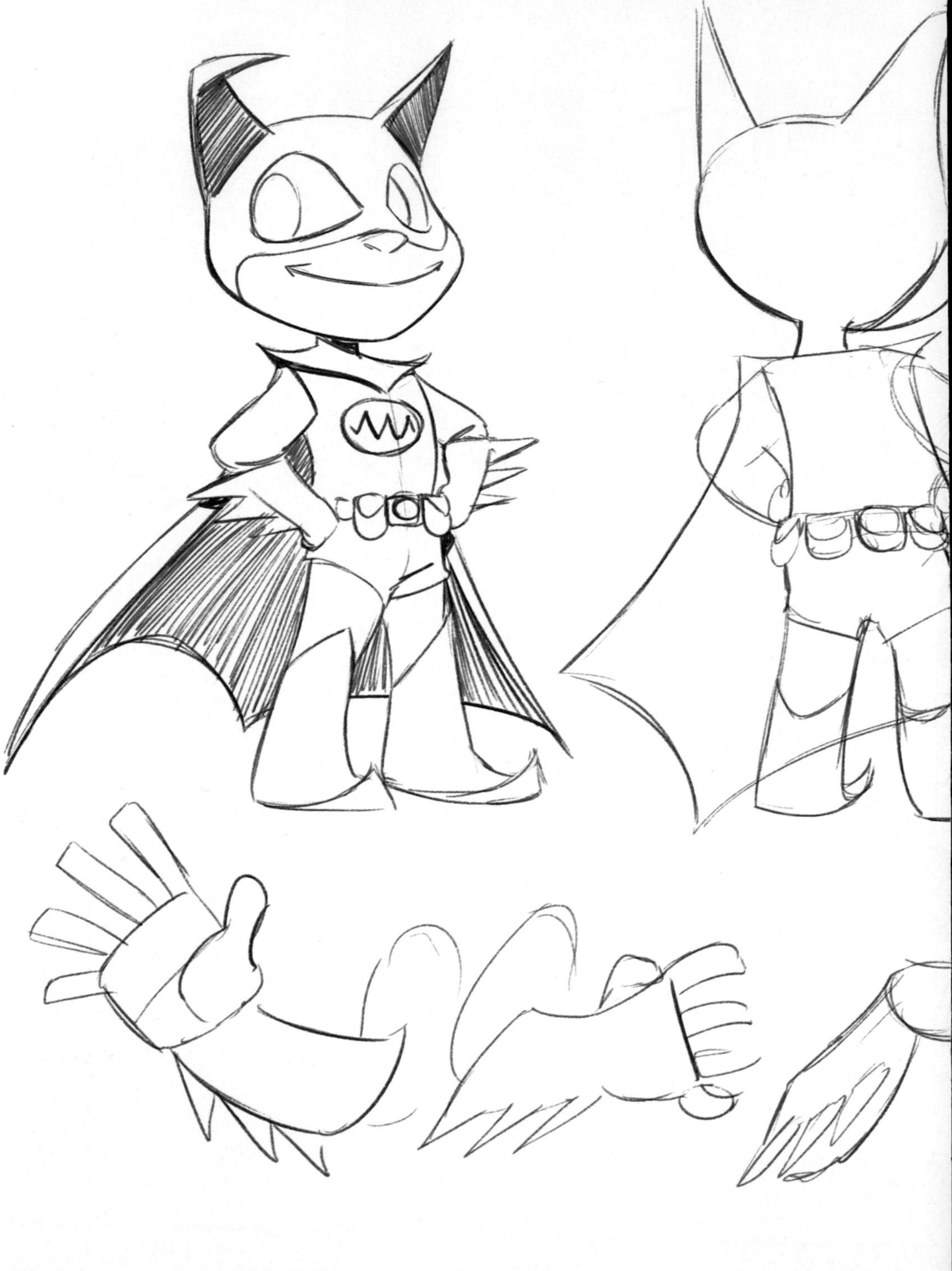

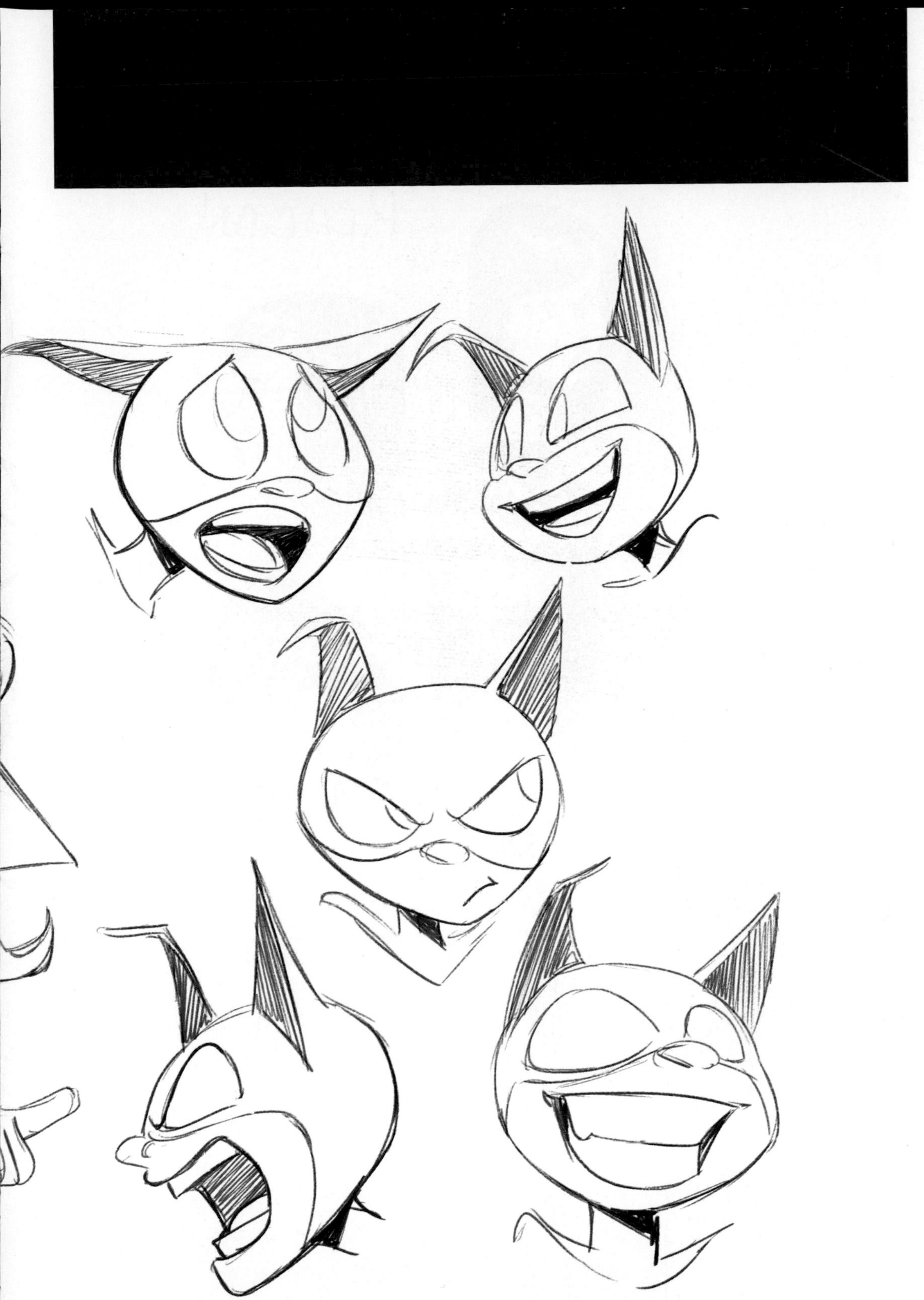

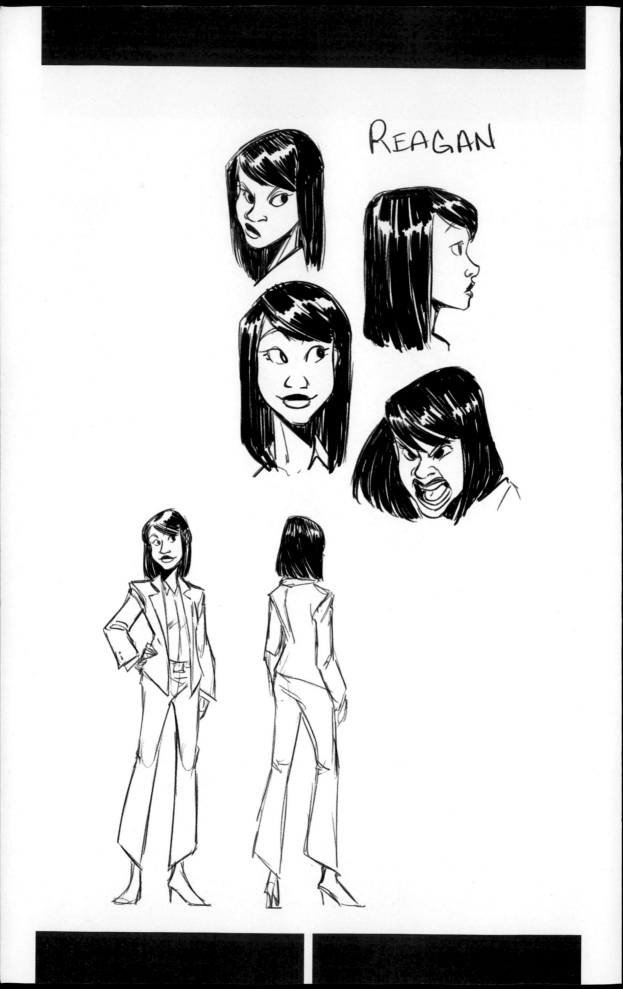

REAGAN

WEED

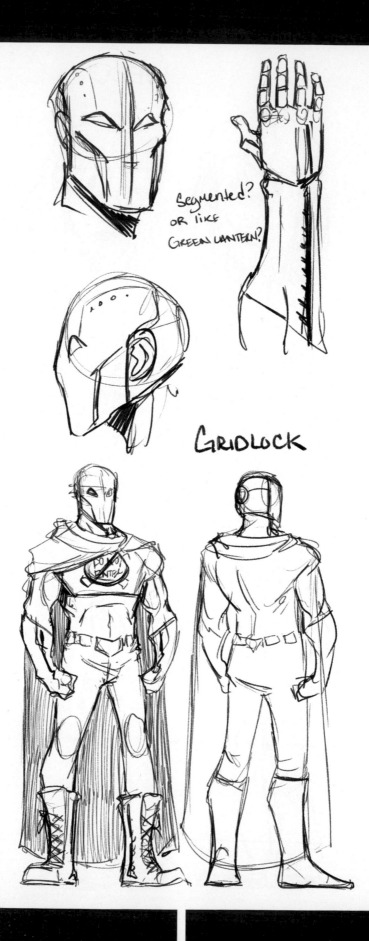

Segmented?
or like
GREEN LANTERN?

GRIDLOCK

STRAIGHT
OR
CURLY
HAIR?

Hawkman the Savage

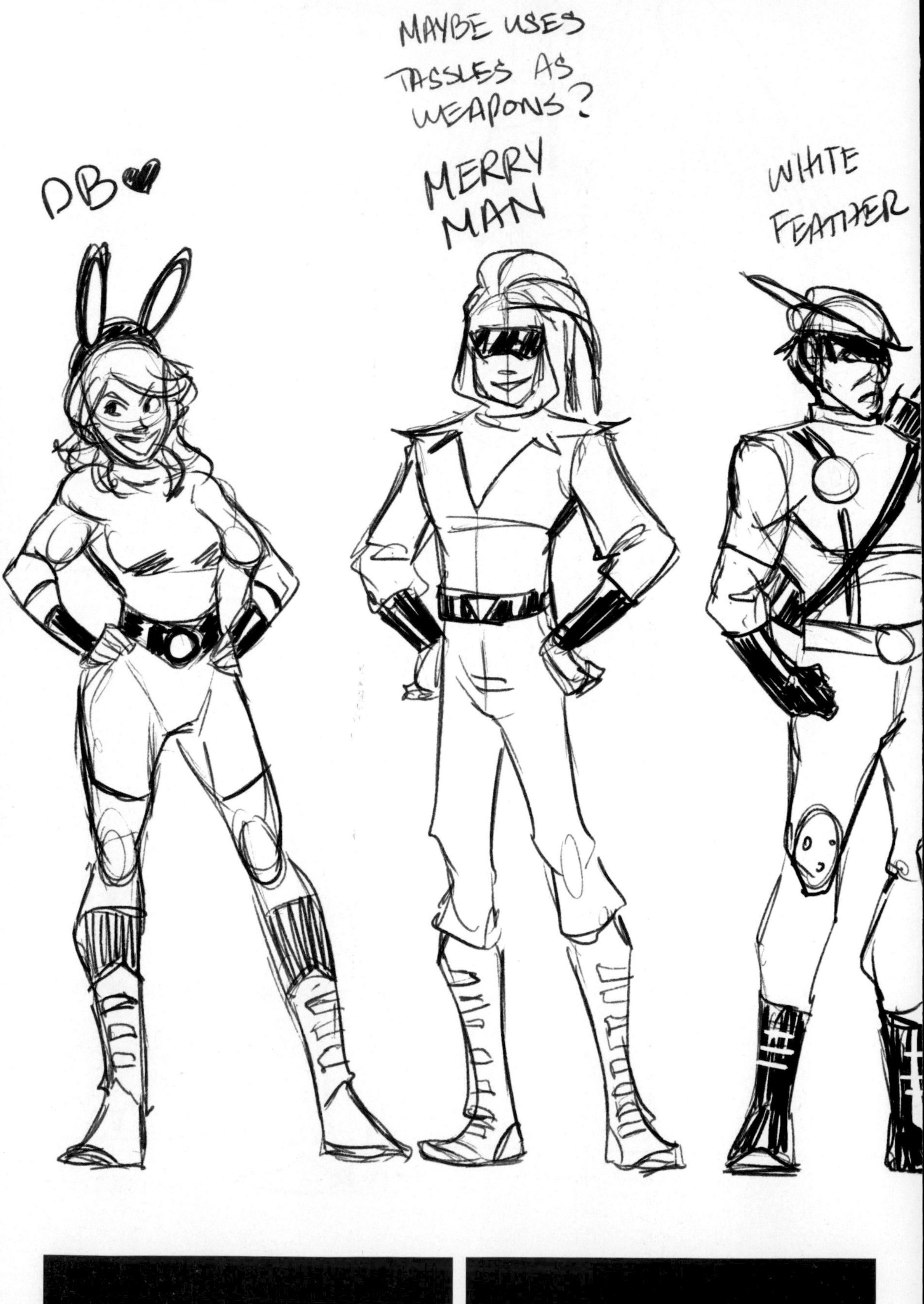
MAYBE USES TASSLES AS WEAPONS?
DB
MERRY MAN
WHITE FEATHER

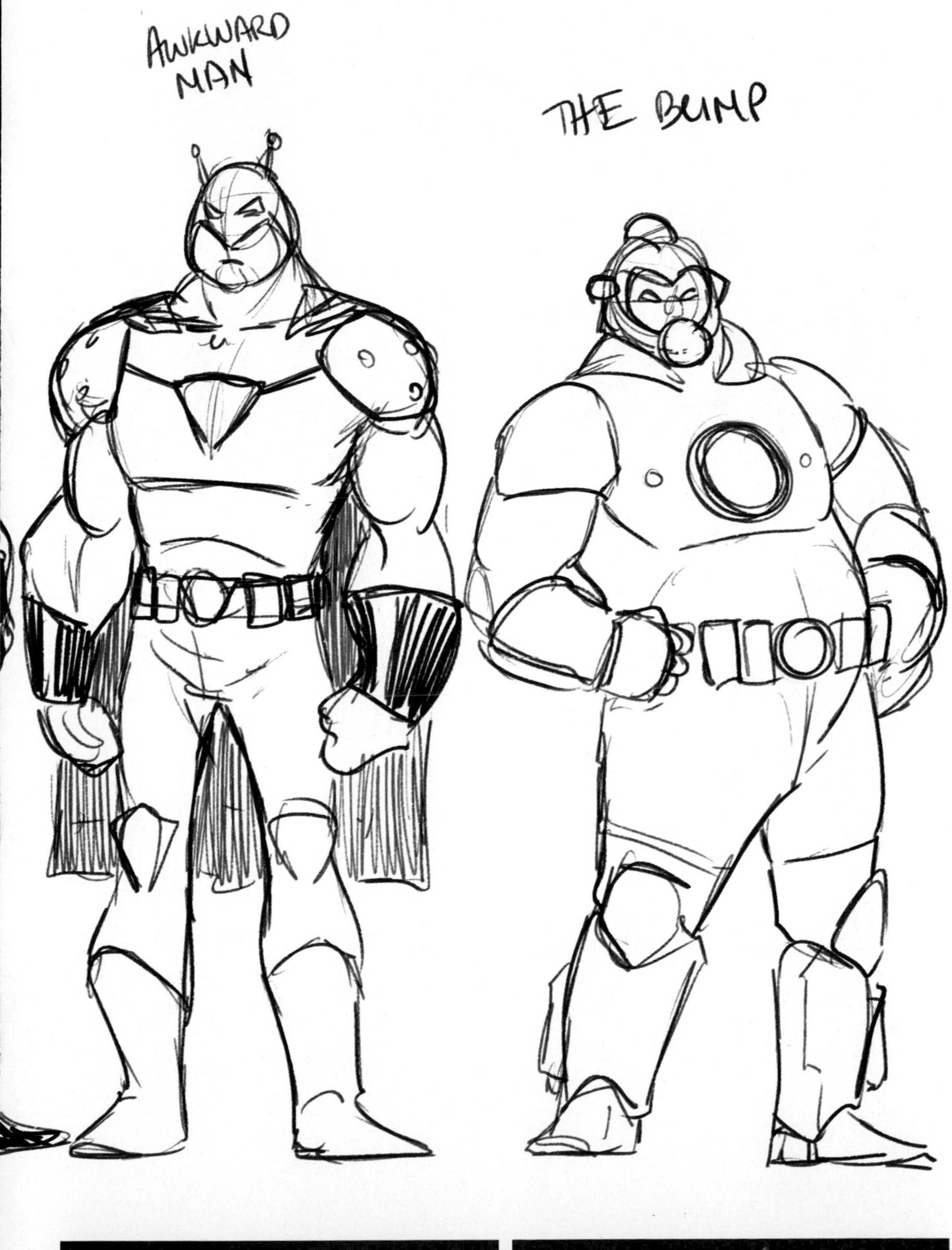
AWKWARD MAN
THE BUMP

Silent
Sentry

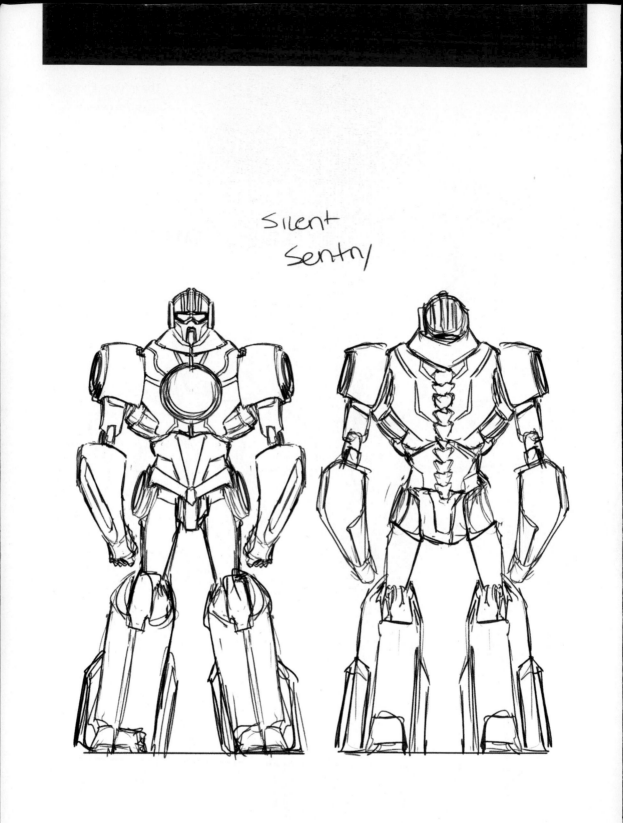

Gus Cutter   TROCHE

Judith

"Red Shirt"

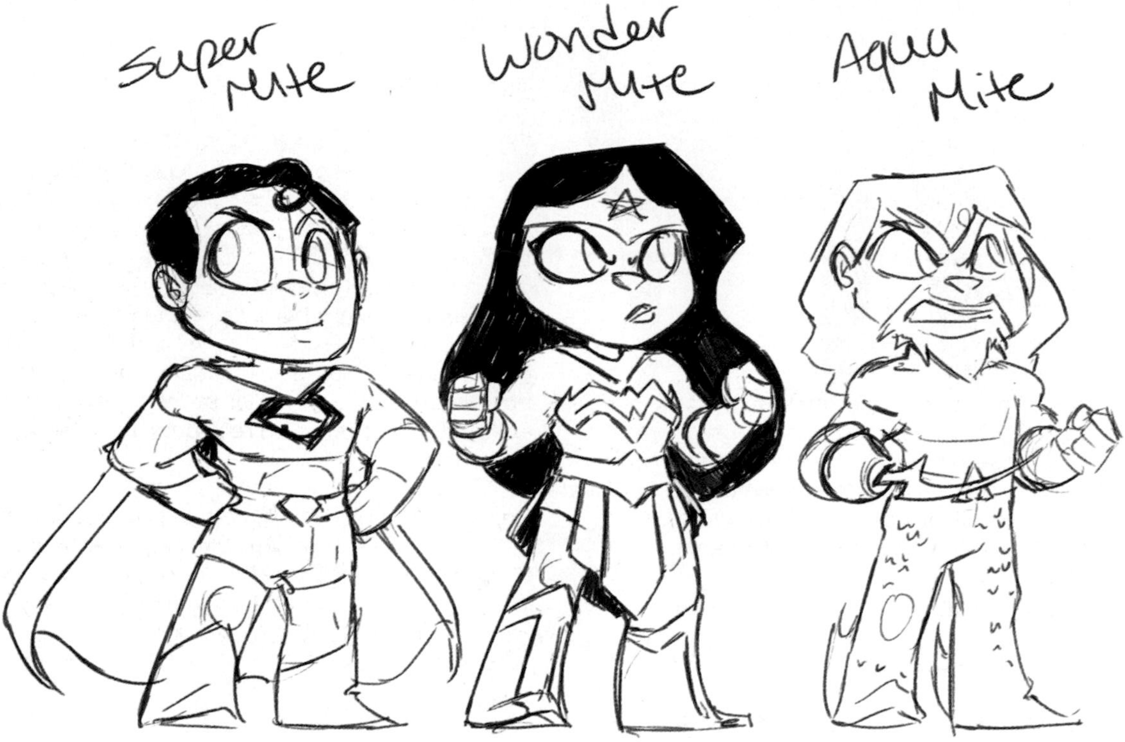
Super Mite
Wonder Mite
Aqua Mite

BAT-MITE ESSENTIALS
DAN JURGENS
MARCH 20, 2015

IDENTITY:

Who knows?

His true name is something we probably couldn't pronounce.

POWERS AND ABILITIES:

Bat-Mite is able to transport himself from one location to another by instantaneously moving through a dimensional wormhole of sorts.

His utility belt also has some kind of extra-dimensional quality. Despite the small size of the pockets, he is able to store almost absurdly large items. It's not impossible for him to pull a bazooka larger than himself out of his utility belt.

MOTIVATION:

Another mystery.

Identifies with superheroes, most notably, Batman. The reason for this is unknown.
Is dedicated to improving the others. "Fixing" them. Life coach to the super-heroes whether they want it or not. If he does enough good, might be allowed to return home.

HIS WORLD:

Where is he from?

Again, who knows? When asked, he'll frequently give a different answer. Another dimension, bitten by a radioactive bat, molded out of clay... any of those and more are possible.

Wherever he's from, however, it seems he can't return. The implication is that Bat-Mite is exiled here.

BAT-MITE'S NATURE:

Irascible. Testy. Quick and hot tempered.
A jokester. Quick with a quip.

To show depth, however, we'll need to see a softer side of his character emerge through loss. Likely the loss of not being able to return home.

CAST:

Reagan Bennington

Parents were wealthy industrialists from the pharmaceutical industry. She was named after their favorite president. Politically conservative. Now working as a young agent with the FSB. (Federal Security Bureau.) Assigned to Bat-Mite, though he won't know it until a little later down the road. He's considered so inexplicable that he must surely be a threat.

Dylan Weeden

"Weed" to his friends. During the 60's, his parents were hippies in the Haight-Ashbury District of San Francisco. They were wildly outrageous in their experimentation with drugs, all of which continued while Weed's mother was pregnant. He is their leftist, hippy-esque son who stopped aging around the age of 20. He has never aged beyond that. There is some indication that he has powers of some kind, most noticeably the ability to disappear and reappear. In actuality, he shrinks.

Reagan and Dylan will start out as prisoners of Dr. Trauma's and become allied with Bat-Mite after he frees them, mostly because he has nowhere to live. Dylan also floats around without a home so they both end up living with Reagan.

VILLAINS:

Booty and Bling-Bling

Social media icons. Take off on the Justin Beiber/Kardashian phenomenon. Become so intoxicated with themselves that they believe they're entitled to anything they want and don't have to pay for it. Both female.

Gridlock

Arch conservative. Right wing nut. Feels that society progresses best if everything is stopped. No development. If neither side wins, no one loses. Preferable to letting the other guy win.

Grood's illegitimate love child

Because, who doesn't love a gorilla?

Hawkman

Issues 1 and 2

Robin (Damian)

Issue 3

Booster Gold

Issue 4

Inferior Five

Issue 5 (Naturally.) So hopeless that he gives up.

Hawk and Dove

Ends with him sad because he still can't return home. Steals the Batmobile again. Full circle. Rides off into the sunset.

After that...

We should do a one-shot Bizarro/Bat-Mite special. "World's Finest". Seriously.